CRITICAL ENCOUNTERS

Critical Encounters:
Between Philosophy and Politics

FRED R. DALLMAYR

University of Notre Dame Press
Notre Dame, Indiana

The author is grateful to the MIT Press
for permission to reprint "Life World and
Communicative Action" from his *Polis and Praxis*
(MIT Press, 1984) and, in greatly revised form,
material from his Introduction to Theunissen's
The Other (MIT Press, 1984).

Library of Congress Cataloging-in-Publication Data

Dallmayr, Fred R. (Fred Reinhard), 1928–
    Critical encounters.

    Bibliography: p.
    Includes index.
    1. Political science—History—20th century.
2. Philosophy—History—20th century. I. Title.
JA83.D35 1987   320'.09   86-40240
ISBN 0-268-00760-8

Manufactured in the United States of America

FOR TOM AND KATHY

*Omni tempore diligit amicus
et frater in angustiis . . .*

Contents

Preface

THE ESSAYS COLLECTED in this volume were written during the last five or six years, mostly as corollaries of other types of inquiries. This was the time when I was trying to chart a course leading from critical phenomenology (or critical hermeneutics) in the direction of what I came to call "practical ontology." In moving along this path I was always closely surrounded or confronted by numerous companions or mentors either encouraging or cautioning or seeking to dissuade me from pursuing the adopted course—which prompted me to set out in essay-form my reasons for heeding or bypassing the offered advice. Apart from its broader theoretical relevance (which I leave to the reader to judge), I might mention some biographical as well as bibliographical motivations for assembling the present volume.

As regards my own development, the successive essays provided a valuable opportunity for intellectual catharsis and self-clarification. This aspect of self-discovery and self-clarification, I should point out, was initially not among my prominent concerns. In fact, commentators in the past frequently have singled out a certain talent for empathy in my writings—an empathy virtually submerging me in interpreted texts and thus purchased by the lack of a clearly defined "standpoint." Wedded to a post-egological or post-individualist perspective, I was at first not greatly troubled by this complaint; on the whole, I have never suffered from what Harold Bloom has labeled the "anxiety of influence." On the other hand, post-individualism never meant for me an indiscriminate merger of views. The present volume deliberately seeks to counter this misunderstanding by more clearly profiling and accentuating differences. Yet, even at this point, the primary focus of the volume is not an individual "standpoint." Together with Erhart Kästner I still believe that we are basically creatures of "complementarity," able to achieve whatever fragile identity we possess only through complementation by others. Thus, even when setting myself off against critical theory, transcendental hermeneutics or neo-pragmatism, I still consider these perspectives crucial ingredients in my context—in fact, constitutive ingredients in shaping and modulating my own voice.

In the past, it is true, empathetic interpretation on my part had sometimes yielded the tendency to bracket differences in favor of a celebration of affinities, a tendency I now would like to correct or at least modify. A case in point is my reading of Hannah Arendt's work —where I have preferred to stress neo-Aristotelian and phenomenological strands while deemphasizing the legacy of Kantian "faculties" and of Jaspers' transcendental existentialism. Partly instructed by Gadamer's critique of the "aesthetics of taste," I today find implausible the attempt to derive a viable political philosophy from Kant's notion of reflective-aesthetic judgment. Another case in point is Gadamerian hermeneutics—where I have tended to underscore the ontological dimension deriving from Heidegger while glossing over lingering Kantian themes (regarding the condition of possibility of understanding). More recently, the confrontation between interpretation and deconstruction has prompted me to sort out the various ingredients in philosophical hermeneutics. Concerning Habermas, my earlier inclination to amalgamate or reconcile his perspective with existential phenomenology has slowly given way—with the unfolding of his work—to a recognition of the rationalist and systematic bent of his arguments, a bent I cannot fully endorse.

In bibliographical terms, the present volume might be justified by its focus on a number of leading texts and authors. Without subscribing strictly to a "great books" orientation, I do believe that there are prominent texts and authors whose arguments capture and pinpoint the salient issues of our age in an exemplary fashion. To be sure, my selection of books and authors is contestable, but I think I can give good reasons for my choice. In my view, the intellectual agonies of our time are unintelligible without attention to phenomenology, hermeneutics, linguistics, critical theory, deconstruction, and various forms of pragmatism—that is, without attention to the subtle rifts between "modernity" or modern metaphysics (epitomized by Descartes and Kant) and incipient "postmodern" modes of thinking and acting. This means: whoever wishes to find his way in the thicket of contemporary debates must somehow come to terms with these perspectives and cannot remain ensconced in conventionally defined disciplines. In terms of authors, a required reading list today would have to include some works by Nietzsche, some works by Heidegger (chiefly *Being and Time*), by Wittgenstein (chiefly *Philosophical Investigations*), by Adorno (chiefly *Negative Dialectics*), by Habermas (chiefly *The Theory of Communicative Action*), by Apel (chiefly *Transformation of Philosophy*), by Gadamer (chiefly *Truth and Method*), as well as by Merleau-Ponty, Derrida, and Foucault. Among American neopragmatists and "practical" philosophers reference needs to be made to some of the writings by Rorty, Bernstein, and MacIntyre. The present volume contains discussions or commentaries on most of the works enumerated in the preceding list. I have commented elsewhere, sometimes at length, on the writings of Merleau-Ponty and Foucault (and I confess to the continuing fascination their works hold for me). I have added some further items to the reading list: especially Theunissen's *The Other* (because of his important contribution to the topic of otherness and encounter), and a few representative figures in contemporary social-political theory: Giddens as spokesman of genealogical "structuration" and Luhmann as advocate of functional "systems theory."

Apart from the authors discussed in this volume, I have benfitted over the years from exchanges and "encounters" with a number of colleagues and friends. Without trying to be exhaustive, I want to acknowledge my indebtedness to William Connolly, Calvin Schrag, William McBride, John O'Neill, Hwa Yol Jung, James Glass, and Thomas McCarthy. Together with these individuals (and especially with Connolly's conclusions in *Appearance and Reality in Politics*) I share a broad vision of political life as combining human freedom with social justice or a genuine concern for the "common good"—a vision which, in my view, must be articulated today less on a proprietary or deontological basis than in ontological (and post-structuralist) terms.

On a personal level, of course, my indebtedness extends beyond the range of academic colleagues. The present volume would not have been completed without the constant support and encouragement of my wife, nor without the patience of our children, Dominique and Philip, who—during the writing of these essays—managed the difficult transition from teenage life to early adulthood. The essays were typed with usual promptness and efficiency by Patricia Flanigan. The book is dedicated to two young friends who, in our age of the virtual "*trahison de tous par tous*," gave me a hint of what Marcel may have meant by "*fidélité créatrice*."

South Bend
December 1986

Introduction

Who's turned us round like this, so that we
always, do what we may, retain the attitude of
someone who's departing? (Rilke)

THE NOTION OF EXPERIENCE as a journey, or of man as *homo viator*, is no longer much in vogue today—having been replaced by the sturdier conceptions of man as fabricator or else as creative assembler and disassembler of symbolic designs. In invoking or reclaiming the eclipsed notion of a "journey" I wish to dissociate myself, however, from a number of accretions clouding the term. First of all, I do not identify the term with a deliberate venture or "project" (in a Sartrean or broadly existentialist sense)—irrespective of the deliberative or reflective posture of participants. Shunning the planned delights of organized tourism, I prefer to associate the term with unanticipated incidents or adventures which one does not so much charter as undergo. Moreover, journeying in my sense does not basically mean traveling along a well demarcated route in the direction of a carefully chosen and clearly specified goal. Rather, being properly underway or "abroad" denotes to me also frequenting byways, detours, and uncharted trails —sometimes exploring dead ends, cul-de-sacs, or *"chemins qui ne mènent nulle part."*[1]

Another, still more important point where I depart from existentialist accounts is in disavowing experience as "my" project in a proprietary sense. In my voyages or excursions, I have frequently felt myself being carried along by the voices of mentors or companions —voices whose inflections sometimes (at least temporarily) seemed deceptively like my own. On other occasions, I was confronted by, or attracted to, unfamiliar idioms on entering new terrains or after an abrupt bend of the road—situations which entailed the options of bland imitation, critical rejection, or attempts at negotiating the difference. Sometimes sorting out these options led to sustained discussions or at least to episodes of fragmentary conversation. The essays collected in the present volume are records or partial transcripts of such episodes. As used in the title of the volume, "encounter" does

1

not denote a purely external collision after the model of a stimulus-response mechanism—although some element of collision is hardly absent from the transcripts. Nor, on the other hand, is the term meant to suggest a particular state of intimacy, a meeting between "mind and mind" on a purely inner or internal plane. Least of all does "encounter" obey the *telos* of consensus or complete mutual understanding, and this not because of individual ineptitude or lack of empathy, but rather because none of the protagonists (myself included) is entirely "of one mind" or self-transparent—and because reciprocity always involves somehow a bodily dimension. Against this background the title carries overtones of a non-violent struggle, or "agon," of a risky, perhaps ontological, mutual engagement—that is, of an engagement of "character" where reason and passion are peculiarly linked. The recorded encounters are "critical," I might add, not only by virtue of formulating criticisms, but—more saliently—because they typically proceeded from a lived discrepancy or a crisis of self-understanding.

The collected discussions or reviews are episodes or subplots in a longer journey whose itinerary I have roughly sketched elsewhere. A crucial issue for me has been for some time the so-called "decentering" of the subject (or the *cogito*) and its repercussions in contemporary social and political thought. What would happen, I have asked myself for over a decade, if the traditional subject—with its attributes of identity, autonomy, and self-determination—were removed as linchpin of theoretical inquiry as well as practical interaction (a question predicated on the simultaneous unacceptability of collectivism)? Thus, taking its bearings from critical-phenomenological arguments, *Twilight of Subjectivity* explored the possibility of a "post-individualist" theory of politics, focusing on the implications of post-individualism in the domains of intersubjectivity, man-nature relations, social development, and ethics. Turning to more conventionally "political" themes, *Polis and Praxis* subsequently probed the relevance of the question in a number of correlated arenas: including the theory of political "action" (or *praxis*), the analysis of political "power" and political "freedom," and the theoretical construal of political speech and "conversation."[2] On both occasions I mentioned as a rough guidepost for my endeavors the notion of a "practical ontology" or "ontological praxis," surrounding the notion immediately with a number of caveats or provisos. The intervening years have not caused me to abandon either the phrase or the stipulated provisos; thus, "practical ontology" can still be seen as *leitmotiv* animating the present collection, within certain limits. By "ontology" I mean a substantive (but non-positivist) mode of thinking and acting, a mode exceeding the confines of a purely formal analysis; the adjective "practical" is added to accentuate the aspect of lived engagement. Basically, the phrase stands opposed to a traditional or strictly theoretical ontology focused on the contemplation of ultimate substances, primal causes, or foundational structures. In abandoning the spectatorial stance, the phrase reflects the contemporary concerns with practice and pragmatics—but without endorsing the stress on intentionality and subject-centered agency.

Neither the *leitmotiv* nor the question of decentering, I want to underscore, have been for me purely intellectual formulas or quandaries removed from "real-life" preoccupations. Differently phrased: I have not tried to formulate purely "philosophical questions" in the hope of finding for them "philosophical solutions." To this extent I do not accept the verdict pronounced by John Gunnell on most versions of contemporary social and political theory: that is, that such theory indulges in abstract-academic speculations radically divorced or "alienated" from concrete political issues. The verdict is expressed most eloquently in Gunnell's recent book entitled *Between Philosophy and Politics* (whose title I have deliberately borrowed for my subtitle). A main reason why I do not accept the charge is that I cannot concur with the argumentative strategy undergirding and buttressing the general indictment: a strategy which is predicated in large measure on the neat segregation between philosophy and politics, or between "political practice" (seen as "first-order" activity) and theorizing or philosophizing (as a "metatheoretical" or "second-order" enterprise).[3] Although useful for polemical purposes, this segregation seems to me highly dubious, and in fact untenable, in the context of post-Enlightenment politics. In an age when nearly one-half of mankind are wedded, at least rhetorically, to the establishment of a "classless society," the time of philosophical innocence seems irremediably lost. Nor can "liberal" politics afford to cling to habitual routines: in a century ravaged by two world wars and haunted by nuclear catastrophe, everyday politics can hardly remain aloof from the problems and dilemmas of "modernity." The essays collected in this volume inhabit the curious demi-monde "between philosophy and politics"—a region devoid of clear boundary lines. In my own view, politics and philosophy are surely not identical, but neither can they be opposed to each other (along a scale of authenticity). The theory-practice relation, to use a time-honored expression, can neither be collapsed into one term nor be styled into an antithesis—mainly because the boundary is philosophically and politically contestable (and not a fixed presupposition).

Another reason why I do not follow Gunnell's strategy is that I find his categories too elusive for purposes of a lived engagement or critical encounter. Above all, the charge of "alienation" strikes me as too sweeping and summary to permit sustained dialogue and interaction (for what might a response to the charge be, except bland acceptance or vigorous denial?). Approached from the angle of the philosophy-politics bifurcation, most contemporary thinkers quickly exhibit the stain of academic estrangement. Thus, speaking of Rawls and Habermas, Gunnell presents their work as "a species of academic dinosaur," and Habermas's writings in particular as the place where "the various myths of alienated political theory have been woven together in an epic manner" to the point of epitomizing "the alienated state of political theory." Similarly, Richard Bernstein's publications are portrayed as "the last whimper of metatheory and its enslavement to philosophical faddism in search of the transcendental foundations of social and political judgment."[4] One central problem with formulations of this kind resides in the invoked critical standpoint: for clearly, the charge of alienation or estrangement presupposes the critic's having access to, or being in command of, a basically unalienated, authentic, or genuine mode of political discourse. In Gunnell's case, this genuine mode finally is identified with the conception of politics as a species of "conventional objects"—where the meaning of both "conventional" and "objects" is doubtful and certainly exceeds the confines of conventional or non-philosophical language. As for myself, I remain suspicious of all claims to unmediated authenticity, inside or outside of academic treatises. This suspicion is motivated by both philosophical and political grounds. Perhaps in an age of large-scale dislocations, expatriations, and homelessness, there is even virtue in alienated discourse. In any event, non-alienation can only be the expression of a distant, counterfactually invoked hope, a verbal token or reminder of far-off possibilities.

The present volume opens with a tribute to a leading exile from modern conventions: Friedrich Nietzsche. Perhaps to people safely ensconced in traditional ways of life, Nietzsche has little or nothing to say; but such people are today a small minority. More than anyone of his contemporaries, Nietzsche was exposed to the subterranean tremors of his age, to the widening rift between past and future—and more than anyone he allowed these tremors to affect his language and his life. In his deepest urgings, I believe, he was bent on unsettling or overturning traditional "tablets": the tablets of Western metaphysical categories and the ways of thinking and acting associated with these categories. To this extent, his opus was a continuous-discontinuous journey, an exodus pitched on the perilous crest of *Übergang* and *Untergang*—of overcoming and undergoing. A crucial issue faced by the present-day reader is the coherence or uniformity of Nietzsche's opus, and particularly the degree to which his "deconstructive" élan was ultimately successful; the opening essay, called "Farewell to Metaphysics," addresses this issue by focusing on two related but conflicting interpretations: those advanced by Martin Heidegger and Jacques Derrida. While in Derrida's reading Nietzsche was basically able to smash the tablets inaugurating a stance of postmodern playfulness, Heidegger—at least in one of the lecture courses devoted to the topic—detected in Nietzsche a strong and particularly virulent strand of modern metaphysics: a strand epitomized by the "will to power." My argument is going to be that both interpretations are plausible and supportable by evidence: not for the spurious reason that the "truth" resides somehow in the middle, but because no exit from tradition can ever be complete (without being self-defeating). As it seems to me, Nietzsche's work does indeed project glimpses of postmodern lifeforms, but it does so by frequently using Cartesian-metaphysical vocabulary, especially the vocabulary of will. To this extent, his opus is profoundly ambivalent, making room both for the turbulent struggle for power and the Apollonian yearning for peace; speaking in the guise of Zarathustra, Nietzsche gives voice both to Promethean rebellion and to the quiet search for the "blessed isles," the visionary pursuit of his "children's land."

The second chapter is concerned more directly with Heidegger's work—this time in confrontation not with Derridean deconstruction but with Adorno's version of critical theory. As the reader will quickly detect, Heideggerian themes are replete throughout the present volume, even in contexts where his arguments are not directly invoked. This is proper and unsurprising, given that I consider myself strongly indebted to these arguments—although not without qualifications or critical reservations. Since points of affinity are likely to surface on their own accord, some reservations might usefully be mentioned. One possible dissonance has to do with the general status of Heidegger's philosophy—with my disaffection growing in proportion with the degree to which this philosophy is identified with the simple contemplation of "being" and its "destiny." In my view, this approach shortchanges and emasculates the radical-innovative thrust of Heidegger's thought—assimilating it instead to traditional metaphysics or modes of "theoretical ontology" (in the sense outlined above). Another point of possible divergence has to do with nostalgia: with suggestions contained in some Heideggerian passages (or interpretations of these passages) intimating a return to unmediated authenticity.[5] On these and related issues I have for some time found it preferable to read Heidegger "against the grain"— an enterprise for which Adorno's writings offer ideal assistance. What attracts me to Adorno on this score is his taste for concreteness and relentless opposition to metaphysical "solutions"; more centrally attractive still is his attempt to escape the prison of modern subjectivity and rationality, that is, his struggle to open thought to "non-identity," without courting regression or mystification. It is precisely with respect to non-identity, however, that qualms arise. Adorno's position, I want to claim, remains aporetic or mired in paradox: either otherness is treated as radically external to thought, in which case it loses its molding or transforming capacity (thus reinforcing solipsism); or else the antithesis is relaxed, in which case Adorno is pushed closer to a Hegelian mediation or at least a Heideggerian correlation of "ownness" and "otherness." As the chapter seeks to show, Adorno's central objection to Heidegger revolved around the issue of "ontology"—which he misconstrued as a lapse into objectivism; once this misconception is removed, the two perspectives appear more readily compatible and even complementary.[6]

My sympathies for critical theory do not extend with equal force to some of the more recent formulations of the Frankfurt program, especially Habermas's theory of communicative rationality. Actually, after initially having been quite close to Habermasian vistas, a slow disenchantment occurred in my case over the years — a process which intensified in the precise measure in which these vistas were progressively formalized and systematized.[7] My continuing agreement with Habermas concerns his preoccupation with intersubjective communication and recognition; my doubts pertain to the formalism of his argumentative design (and his general insensitivity to ontology). The third chapter offers a critical review of his *magnum opus, The Theory of Communicative Action,* focused on the key concepts of "life-world" and "communicative action." As I try to indicate, my reservations in the latter case have to do with the meaning of both "communication" and "action," and their mutual correlation. If, as Habermas argues, action per se is intrinsically strategic or "teleological" in character, communicative consensus becomes a purely formal, counterfactually postulated achievement—a result which, in turn, transforms language into an external "mechanism" of action coordination (robbing it of its disclosive potency). Regarding the concept of the "life-world," Habermas —in my reading—oscillates precariously between a "strong" and a "weak" version of the term, opting ultimately for the weak alternative which permits the life-world to be streamlined into an arena of sociological analysis and a pliant backdrop for processes of modernization and rationalization. Moving beyond the confines of limited conceptual issues, the chapter finally points to broader dilemmas besetting Habermas's approach: especially his continued indebtedness to the "philosophy of consciousness" (or subjectivity) and more generally to the legacy of metaphysics with its polar antinomies (of subject/object, man/nature, and the like). I also alert to the inchoate state of the theory of intersubjectivity and, more importantly, to the evanescence of politics and political *praxis*—a domain alien to the twin features of Habermasian society ("system" and "life-world").

Concerns of a more strictly philosophical (and less sociological) nature occupy center-stage in the fourth chapter, devoted to the "transcendental hermeneutics" articulated by Karl-Otto Apel. Despite critical objections raised in the chapter, I consider Apel's work highly significant for the ongoing intellectual "conversation" in our time—not only because of its impact on Habermas's critical theory, but (more importantly) because of its resolute effort to offer an "ultimate justification" or grounding of philosophical arguments, an effort seeking to match Kantian transcendentalism on the plane inaugurated by the "linguistic turn" in our century. Friends and critics alike are liable to benefit from Apel's rigorous analysis, especially his attempt to pit a "transformed" transcendental perspective against fashionable prognoses of an imminent demise of philosophical reflection. My critical queries in the chapter concentrate on the status of language and communication in Apel's approach. To the extent that it is meant to function as substitute for the (Kantian) synthesis of perception, I contend, language is bound to shrink into a transcendental "limit" of the world, relegating all modes of substantive experience to the level of *a posteriori* objects. These queries also affect the plausibility of a "transcendental hermeneutics" (where the latter term means a mediation of universals and particulars). On repeated occasions Apel opposes what he calls the "philosophical *logos*" to the "hermeneutical *logos*," ascribing to the former a higher degree of reflexivity and foundational solidity—thereby cancelling again the concrete mediations achieved by hermeneutics and the hermeneutical circle. The same scale of preferences or priorities pervades Apel's juxtaposition of "experience of meaning" and "reflection on validity," or of a "bodily *a priori*" and an "*a priori* of consciousness." These and similar expressions, I believe, are manifestations of a refurbished foundationalism which mesh uneasily (if at all) with Apel's professed ambition to anchor his arguments not in subjectivity but in the context of ordinary language and communication. The incongruence is accentuated by his extensive

comments on the writings of Heidegger, Wittgenstein, and Gadamer
— comments whose internal coherence or consistency I probe in the
same chapter.

Hermeneutics — its meaning, range, and limitations — forms the
topic of the following essay. In order to heighten the contours of the
hermeneutical enterprise, the chapter elaborates on a dialogue or exchange — partly real, partly imaginary — between Hans-Georg Gadamer,
spokesman of a "philosophical hermeneutics," and Derrida, advocate
of linguistic "difference" and deconstruction. From Gadamer's perspective, hermeneutical understanding is universal in scope and involves
ideally a "fusion of horizons" between interpreter and text (or between
two speakers). Although greatly attracted to his erudition and sensitivity for experiential nuances, I find Gadamer's position marred by
exegetic optimism and also by traces of the "philosophy of consciousness": traces evident in his conception of "effective-historical consciousness" and his faith in the continuity and coherence of cultural
traditions. The confidence in universal understanding is severely challenged by Derrida's stress on rupture, discontinuity, and misunderstanding; the fusion of horizons, from his deconstructive angle, appears as a delayed echo of the Hegelian "world spirit." My departure
from Derrida occurs at the point where mutual intelligibility is nearly
exorcised and dialogical exchange virtually cancelled. This aspect
brings into view more general reservations or apprehensions regarding deconstruction, mainly two. First of all, I detect in Derrida an occasional privileging of absence over presence, non-being over being,
abyss over ground — a privileging which to me appears dubious or for-
tuitous. (This point, I want to add, has nothing to do with his presumed
"nihilism" — a charge against which, on the contrary, I would want to
defend him in the most vigorous terms.) Secondly and more importantly, I find in his writings a tendency to celebrate "otherness" as such
or as a general principle; while captivating as a radical gesture, this
tendency has the effect of bracketing those concrete modes of difference or unfamiliarity which are the occasion of lived engagement or
critical encounter.[8]

The chapter on Ricoeur addresses possible political implications
of hermeneutics — although Ricoeur's approach clearly captures only
a limited slice of these implications (owing mainly to the antinomial
character of his arguments). The following essay deals with an intellectual trend closely akin to Continental hermeneutics: the rise of
"neo-pragmatism" in American philosophy, as exemplified by the work
of Richard Bernstein. I shall not recapitulate here in detail my comments on Bernstein's ambitious project of charting a course "beyond

objectivism and relativism"; instead I offer a few observations on pragmatism in general. Given my own "practical-ontological" inclinations, some facets of the pragmatist tradition are to me clearly appealing: including the motto of keeping theory closely attuned to practice, philosophical reflection to ongoing experience. Nevertheless, despite these assets, I am apprehensive about other features of the same legacy. There is, first of all, a disturbing undertow of instrumentalism evident in much of the relevant literature: an aspect captured in the popular adage that truth is measured by the "cash value" of a given doctrine or proposition. Closely allied with this aspect is an incipient "subjectivism" or anthropocentrism (deriving from the philosophy of consciousness): a proclivity to treat action or practice as an intentional project—although agency is often associated less with individual than with group or collective designs. Finally, I am chagrined by the elusive and nearly amorphous character of pragmatism and neo-pragmatism: its readiness to serve as umbrella for the most disparate enterprises. I have difficulty in grasping the substance of a label when its application extends from the ontological ruminations of Peirce over the Humean skepticism of Rorty and the semi-rationalist criticism of Bernstein to the non- and antirational bias of "down-to-earth" advocates of common sense. Although appreciative of the deeper resonances of common sense, I am appalled by the anti-intellectualism of some current versions of pragmatic realism or realist pragmatism.[9]

In a mitigated form, some of my apprehensions regarding pragmatism carry over to MacIntyre's defense of communitarian virtue. I basically concur with MacIntyre's judgment concerning the defects of recent and contemporary liberalism: especially its erosion of shared traditions and its replacement of normative bonds by a self-seeking and atomistic brand of "emotivism." I am also at one with his critique of both utilitarianism and deontological ethics for their failure to perceive the importance, and contribute to the task, of character formation—a task which can only be achieved through lived engagement in a communal setting. I am less fully in accord with the concrete implementation of MacIntyre's neo-Aristotelian vision. Regarding the notion of ethics as a communal "practice," I detect in *After Virtue* the same kind of "neo-teleological" or intentionalist slant which pervades contemporary neo-pragmatism. My doubts extend to the conception of "tradition" seen as a historical context or narrative framework sustaining particular moral practices. In MacIntyre's usage, tradition carries strongly Gadamerian overtones and suggests a steady transmission of shared cultural meanings, a transmission whose continuity is insured by the intelligibility of the overall story. What this conception neglects or shortchanges is the troublesome relation between history and nature, between meaning and non-meaning, and between continuity and rupture. Most importantly what is lacking in *After Virtue* is an "ontological" reformulation of such issues like "freedom" and "community," a reformulation which would salvage some of the legitimate aspirations implicit in modern (or Enlightenment) treatments of human autonomy and emancipation. This consideration carries over into the central dichotomy—between Aristotle and Nietzsche—erected in the study, where the former appears as spokesman of traditionalism and the latter as prototype (in fact as caricature) of an anti-social emotivism. Once these blinders are dropped, anti-liberalism and post-liberalism can be more readily distinguished. As it seems to me, civic virtue cannot be the outgrowth of a self-enclosed particularism, but only of the interplay of the leading forces of our time: the interplay between center and periphery, between proximity and distance, village and cosmopolis.[10]

The interchange of ego and *alter*, of selfhood and otherness, is the central theme of the ninth chapter, devoted to one of the leading works in this field: Michael Theunissen's *The Other*. In his study Theunissen distinguishes between two prominent approaches to the issue of intersubjectivity: transcendental phenomenology (anchored in the philosophy of consciousness) and "dialogism" or "philosophy of dialogical encounter" (associated chiefly with the work of Martin Buber). While, starting from the premise of subjectivity, the first approach seeks access to interpersonal relations by construing the Other basically as an "other I" or *alter ego*, the second approach treats the ego or self as a derivative achievement arising from an original encounter with a "Thou." Another conceptual distinction which permeates the entire study—and elevates it far above existentialist slogans—is the differentiation between alienation seen as reification or external repression and a more subtle kind of estrangement or "alteration" (*Veranderung*) which, far from entailing loss of authenticity, may be a precondition on the road to self-discovery. In juxtaposing and evaluating the two approaches, Theunissen's sympathies are quite clearly on the side of dialogism—but not in an uncritical or unqualified manner. As it happens, my own sympathies and preferences point in a similar direction, as do my critical reservations. As it seems to me, despite its rejection of a subject-centered metaphysics, dialogism is prone to cultivate a "higher" (or multiple) subjectivism by focusing on direct encounter. For one thing, Buber's distinction between "I-It" and "I-Thou" relations seems itself the outgrowth of subjective intentionality. More importantly, when segregated from worldly "I-It" relations, the immediacy of interpersonal contact lends to the latter an air of idealist transparency. A further criticism has been eloquently formulated by Theunissen himself in the second edition of his study. As he noted at the time, both transcendental and dialogical approaches are marred by their "elimination of a social (or sociological) theory from whose vantage point anonymous modes of interaction as well as interpersonal contacts could have been perceived as historically situated." Instead of adopting apriori formulas, he added, "one would have to examine to which extent we are still capable of being an I for a Thou," and to which degree the "objective requisites" for intersubjectivity can presently be found.[11]

The concluding chapters move into the terrain of sociological and social-political theory, in an effort to explore some of the concrete parameters invoked by Theunissen. Among sociological theorists today, Anthony Giddens occupies a place of deserved preeminence —deserved because of his vast productivity, his blending of AngloAmerican and Continental perspectives, and his innovative mode of analysis. My discussion of his work concentrates on two related concepts or themes: agency and structuration. Regarding the former, I find congenial his "practical-ontological" treatment of the topic: his insistence that action or agency must be seen as part of social practices inserted in a concrete time-space continuum of conduct—and even embedded in broader ontological contexts epitomized by the correlation of "being and action." Regarding structuration, one must note Giddens' sharp differentiation between "system" and "structure"—where the first designates a concrete temporal and spatial setting and the second a "virtual order of differences," that is, an "absent set" of elements temporally "present only in their instantiation." Structuration, against this background, denotes the genealogical emergence of various systemic possibilities, including the arrangement of nature-culture and subject-object polarities. My critical response centers on a certain vacillation in Giddens' approach or a bent toward "domestication": a bent manifest in the tendency to reduce action to intentional "doing" and structure to an empirical (not a virtual) set of differences. The convergence of structure and system is the hallmark of functionalist "systems theory," whose chief representative today is the German sociologist Niklas Luhmann. The concluding chapter focuses on the meaning and status of the "state" in social-political theory, with Luhmann defining the state as "self-description of the political system"— as a "self-simplifying device" designed to reduce systemic complexity —while, relying to some extent on Hegel and (more directly) on Heidegger, I seek to vindicate the connection between politics and "substantive reason" or "*Sittlichkeit.*" Going beyond the historical confines of the modern state, Heidegger in 1942 portrayed the "*polis*" as an ontological place, as a temporal and spatial setting in which everything that matters to human beings, and also everything that is "questionable and undomesticated" in life, happens and converges in a decisive way.[12]

1

Farewell to Metaphysics:
Nietzsche

CONTEMPORARY PHILOSOPHY, including political philosophy, is marked by a sense of ferment or adventure, a sense highlighted by such labels as "anti-foundationalism" and "end of metaphysics." Basically, what these labels pinpoint is the departure (or attempted departure) from the paradigmatic premises or "foundations" of modern Western philosophy—premises inaugurated and first elaborated in a coherent fashion by Descartes. To this extent, contemporary thought can in large measure be described as a "farewell to Descartes"—although a farewell mixed with strands of nostalgia and apprehension about future perils. Actually, on closer inspection, this farewell is not entirely of recent origin: critical forays against Cartesianism or Cartesian premises can already be found in various nineteenth-century intellectual movements, including life-philosophy and pragmatism. A pivotal role in this paradigmatic change is commonly assigned to Nietzsche — whose precise position, however, defies easy summary. For several decades now, Nietzsche has in fact been the focus of intense controversy in Continental (particularly in German and French) literature, a controversy fueled by radically divergent interpretations or assessments. Does Nietzsche's work, as some claim, represent essentially the culmination or completion of Western metaphysics—a completion transforming Descartes' *cogito* into subjective will-power or "will to power"? Or, by contrast, does Zarathustra (and the notion of "eternal recurrence") herald the definitive eclipse of the "last man"—and thereby also of the Cartesian *ego cogitans?*

In this chapter my endeavor is not so much to resolve or settle this controversy as rather to explore its multiple dimensions and implications. For the sake of brevity, I intend to concentrate chiefly on two opposing readings or construals: those advanced by Heidegger and by Derrida. In the case of Heidegger, my emphasis will be mainly on his lecture course of 1940 published under the summary title of "European Nihilism"; in Derrida's case, the accent will be placed on

13

Margins of Philosophy, Spurs (Éperons), and related shorter writings.
After reviewing or summarizing the two readings, I shall briefly comment on their respective merits and disadvantages, though without
any intention of awarding debating points. My own (very tentative)
argument shall be that Nietzsche heralds indeed a radically innovative, post-metaphysical posture—but that he does so by using often
a distinctly metaphysical-Cartesian idiom. Pinpointing this internal
tension, it seems to me, does not so much diminish the stature of
Nietzsche's work as rather enhance its continuing significance: riv-
eted between conflicting paradigms or modes of discourse, his post-
Cartesian Cartesianism can help illuminate our own intellectual me-
andering between past and future.

I

  As is well known, Nietzsche's teachings loom large in Heidegger's thought, especially during the period following the publication
of *Being and Time* (up until the end of the war). In the wake of his
ill-fated service as rector, Heidegger presented a number of lecture
courses at Freiburg University dealing with facets of Nietzsche's work,
including courses on Nietzsche's aesthetics ("the will to power as art")
and on the "eternal recurrence of the same." The reader familiar with
the published version of these lectures is bound to be struck by the
much more somber and critical mood pervading the course of 1940
titled "European Nihilism." While earlier lectures in large measure
tended to celebrate Nietzschean insights—vindicating them against
narrow political or ideological adaptations—the new course gives
evidence of a profound estrangement or distantiation between the two
thinkers, a distantiation deriving from the (presumed) "metaphysical"
character of Nietzsche's work.[1] As presented by Heidegger in 1940,
the central category of this work emerges as the universal "will to
power," a category ultimately wedded or paying tribute to the modern
legacy of anthropocentrism or metaphysical "subjectivity" initiated
by Descartes.
  The critical mood surfaces already in the opening sections of
the lecture course, devoted to a discussion of the meaning of "nihilism." Commenting on Nietzsche's statement "What does nihilism
mean? That the uppermost values devaluate themselves," Heidegger
complains about the shallowness or restrictiveness of this view on
an ontological plane. Judged on Nietzsche's terms, he notes, nihilism
signifies simply a process of devaluation and revaluation, that is, a

movement of shrinkage and reenlargement of values—a process, moreover, which is entirely dependent on human valuation as an act of meaning-bestowal or withdrawal; what is neglected or bypassed in this view is the radical ontological status of *nihil* or nothing as "non-being" (and as related to "being"). "What if," Heidegger asks, "nothing indeed were not a being but also were not simply null and void? And . . . finally, what if the *default* of a developed question about the essence of nothing were the *grounds* for the fact that Western metaphysics had to fall prey to nihilism?" Against this background, nihilism as seen by Nietzsche is characterized by "the essential non-thinking of the essence of nothing(ness)." "Here," Heidegger adds, "is perhaps the reason why Nietzsche himself was forced to adopt what from his perspective was 'complete' nihilism. Although recognizing nihilism as a movement of modern Western history but being unable to think or inquire about the essence of nothing, Nietzsche had to become a 'classical' nihilist who simply expressed the history that is now happening"; his own concept of nihilism thus turns out to be "itself nihilistic." What prevented a more adequate, trans-nihilistic grasp of the problem was Nietzsche's exclusive reliance on valuation or valuative thought with its subjective-metaphysical underpinnings: "Consequently, in spite of all his insights, he was unable to comprehend the hidden essence of nihilism because, right from the outset and *solely* on the basis of valuative thought, he conceived nihilism as a process of the devaluation of the uppermost values."[2]

Turning to valuation or valuative thought, Heidegger does not deny the innovative thrust of Nietzsche's work, his attempt to reformulate all categories on a new basis; being tied to meaning-bestowal, however, this thrust is viewed not as an exit from, but as an intensification or radicalization of Western metaphysical premises. In Nietzsche's terminology, "values" or ideals are basically the outgrowth of acts of estimation which, in turn, are rooted in human will-power or "will to power"; the latter phrase, however, is meant to designate the nature or essential being of all things—and thus functions as code-word for Nietzsche's general metaphysics. In traditional Western thought, it is true, ideals or uppermost values are granted a certain independence from human valuation and will-power—but this was due mainly to naiveté or an unwillingness to probe basic metaphysical beliefs. In the words of the lecture course: "Man remains naive to the extent that he posits values as an 'essence of things' happening to him, without realizing that it is *he* who posits them and that this positing manifests a will to power. . . . To be sure, as in every valuation, will to power governs even in naive valuation; but here this will

still remains an impotence to power." Nietzsche's radicalization consists basically in brushing aside this traditional naiveté: "No longer
should man be borrower or lender, nor submit himself to his own gift
as to an alien force"; instead, "man ought to claim everything for himself as his own—what he can only do if, first of all, he ceases to regard
himself as a wretch and slave before the universe, but prepares and
establishes himself for absolute dominion." In contrast to traditional
transcendental standards, Nietzsche's overman "no longer needs anything 'above' or 'beyond' because he alone wills man himself—and not
just in some particular aspect, but as possessor of absolute mastery
with the fully developed power resources of the earth." Seen in this
light, Nietzsche's innovation resides not simply in the replacement
of old values by new values, but in the construal of all beings and
categories as products of valuation and will to power: "Properly interpreted, the revaluation effected by Nietzsche does not consist in the
fact that he posits new values in place of the highest values of the
past, but that he conceives 'being', 'purpose', and 'truth' as *values* and
only as values. His revaluation thus is at bottom a rethinking of all
categories of being in terms of values."[3]

By treating all categories as products of valuation and will to
power, Nietzsche extricated and accentuated an important strand in
Western metaphysics—though a strand which traditionally was latent or buried under naively held assumptions.[4] According to Heidegger, all metaphysics is in some form anthropocentric or anthropomor-
phic, but Nietzsche sharpened this trait into the dominant feature
of thought: "Metaphysics is anthropomorphism—the formation and
perception of the world according to man's image. As construed by
Nietzsche and as postulated above all as future philosophy, metaphysics revolves decisively around man's relation to being as whole;
. . . such metaphysics, to which the doctrine of the overman belongs,
thrusts man (like no previous perspective) into the role of the absolute and unique measure of all things." A crucial stepping stone on
the road to Nietzsche's work, in Heidegger's reading, was the onset
of modernity as represented by Renaissance and Baroque thinkers; no
longer muffled by cosmological or theological doctrines, anthropomorphism at that time began to emerge into full view. "The newness
of the modern period as opposed to the medieval, Christian age," he
writes, "consists in the fact that—independently and by his own
effort—man contrives to become certain and sure of his human status in the midst of beings as a whole. The essential Christian notion
of the certitude of salvation is adopted, but 'salvation' means no longer
eternal, other-worldly bliss, and the way to it is not self-negation; rather,

the hale and wholesome is sought exclusively in the free emancipation of all creative powers of man." The way to find certainty or philosophical assurance in the modern age is said to reside in the search for a proven and secure "method" in contrast to dogmatic beliefs of the past: "The question of 'method', that is, the question about 'finding the way' and about attaining and grounding a certainty secured by man himself, moves to centerstage. 'Method' here is not to be understood 'methodologically' as a mode of inquiry or research, but metaphysically as the way to a definition of truth, a definition buttressed exclusively through human efforts." Viewed in this sense, method begins to occupy the traditional place of *prima philosophia* or first philosophy: "In the context of man's liberation from revelation and church doctrine, the question of first philosophy becomes 'How does man, on his own terms and for himself, arrive at a primary, unshakable truth, and what is that primary truth?' Descartes was the first to ask the question in a clear and decisive way; his answer was *ego cogito, ergo sum.*"[5]

At this juncture of the lecture course, Descartes emerges as key figure in Heidegger's argument: namely, as ancestor and pacesetter of Nietzschean thought. Underscoring and elaborating on this key role the course states: "At the beginning of modern philosophy stands Descartes' phrase: *ego cogito, ergo sum*, 'I think, therefore I am'. All awareness of things and of beings as a whole is referred back to the self-consciousness of the human subject as the unshakable ground of all certainty. In the wake of this phrase, the reality of the real is defined as 'objectivity'—as something that is conceived *by* and *for* the subject as jutting out or standing over against him. This means: reality is representedness *through* and *for* the representing subject." Couched in abstract-logical terms, Descartes' phrase adumbrates and underwrites a new prominence or predominance of the human ego and thus a new status of man in the universe: "Man does not simply accept a doctrine on faith; nor does he procure knowledge by following a random course. Something else comes to the fore: man knows himself absolutely and unconditionally as that being whose being is most certain; he comes to be the self-posited ground and measure for all certitude and truth." Read superficially, Descartes' phrase seems to resemble the teaching of the sophist Protagoras to the effect that "man is the measure of all things." In a careful comparison of the two statements, however, Heidegger explodes this surface similarity by pointing to hidden ontological dimensions of the sophist's world view. Contrary to the modern focus on self-certainty, the Greek notion of "man as measure" was still embedded in a broader cosmic context which simultaneously provided the measure for man. In the Greek case, we read, "the self of man becomes an 'I' or ego through its *restriction* to the surrounding context of disclosure; this limiting belonging to an ontological context helps to constitute the being of man. By means of this restriction man becomes an ego—not through a breakdown of limits elevating the self-representing ego to the midpoint and measure of the representable universe."[6]

In terms of the lecture course, this removal of limits was precisely inaugurated by modern, particularly Cartesian, philosophy. While in previous thought any kind of being could still function as "*subiectum,*" that is, as something (ontologically) pregiven or "underlying," Cartesianism treats the human ego as the crucial and ultimately as the only secure and indubitable subject. As Heidegger affirms: "Since Descartes and through Descartes, man—the human ego —becomes in a preeminent way the metaphysical 'subject.'" As a result, the traditional query "What is being?" is transformed into the question "about the *fundamentum absolutum inconcussum veritatis,* the absolute, unshakable ground of truth. This transformation *is* the beginning of a new thinking which is also the beginning of a new order ushering in modernity." Together with the stress on subjectivity, modern thought also relies centrally on human freedom—where freedom signifies no longer participation in a cosmic plan but rather independence from external bonds and autonomous authorship of all plans and initiatives. "To be free now means," we read, "that, in place of the certitude of salvation and its standard of truth, man posits the kind of certitude by virtue of which he becomes certain of himself as the being that grounds itself on itself. . . . If we pointedly say that the new freedom consists in man's legislating and choosing what is binding for himself, then we speak in Kantian language—and yet we hit upon what is crucial for the advent of modernity whose metaphysics distills itself historically into a position for which freedom is peculiarly essential." Pursuit of freedom and self-determination, however, requires power and the resources of power—and ultimately human control over nature and the universe: "Because freedom in the end implies human mastery over the definition of human nature, and because such mastery presupposes power in a central and explicit sense, the 'empowering' or unleashing of power as fundamental reality becomes possible only in and *as* the history of the modern age." In all those respects and dimensions, Descartes is said to have been the decisive architect; for, it was "his task to secure *the metaphysical ground of man's liberation in the new freedom of assured self-legislation.*"[7]

Focusing on Descartes' well-known "foundational" phrase—*ego cogito, ergo sum* — Heidegger seeks to sharpen its contours by extricating it from a number of misunderstandings impeding adequate comprehension. As he points out, *cogito* in the Cartesian sense does not simply denote a vague, indefinite "thinking," but rather a mode of "re-presenting," that is, of rendering objects present to a perceiving mind with the goal of pinpointing them as secure targets of knowledge. "*Cogitare*," he writes, "means presenting to oneself what is representable. In such presentation lies a yardstick, namely, the requirement that the re-presented is not merely generally pregiven but is presented to us as (securely) available." To assure availability, representative cognition along Cartesian lines involves doubt — but a doubt which seeks to terminate skeptical vacillation by reaching cognitive certainty: "That *cogitare* denotes essentially *dubitare* means basically that representation is tied to the goal of certainty. Thinking in the sense of calculation accepts nothing as secure and certain (that is, as true) which does not show itself ultimately to be *in*dubitable — whereupon thinking as doubting can come to an end, so to speak, and close the account." More importantly, representation is always simultaneously self-representation, and awareness a mode of self-consciousness — in accordance with the Cartesian formula *cogito me cogitare*. As a result, the knowing subject is not merely an external, accidental adjunct of cognition but a necessary premise or precondition: "For representation as described, the human self or ego is essentially the 'underlying' ground, that is, the *sub-iectum* of cognition." As a further consequence, the nexus between *cogito* and *sum* does not have the character of a logical deduction, but rather of mutual implication and elucidation: knowledge or cognition basically reflects a knowing subject, just as human existence is construed as cognitive-metaphysical subjectivity. In Heidegger's words: "*Cogito sum* does not merely say that I think, nor merely that I am, nor that my existence or being follows from my act of thinking or knowing. . . . Rather, the phrase says: representation conceived as self-representation posits being as cognitive representedness and truth as certitude. That to which everything is referred back as to an unshakable ground is the *essence of representation* itself, insofar as the latter determines being and truth as well as the nature of man as cognitive subject and yardstick of cognition."[8]

Commenting on its broader significance, Heidegger finds Descartes' phrase pregnant with implications for modern life and philosophy. In his assessment, the stress on subjectivity and the subordination of being to calculative cognition furnish a warrant for human mastery — and ultimately for technological dominion over the earth.

"Because man has essentially become the *subiectum* and being become equivalent to representedness (or truth to certitude)," he asserts, "man now has at his disposal the entire range of beings in a basic sense, since he provides the measure or yardstick for every individual being." In contrast to the contextual limitation of selfhood in antiquity, the modern self or ego tends to be essentially unlimited or unbounded in its reach: "The subject is 'subjective' in the sense that the definition of being and also of human nature is no longer constrained by boundaries, but rather de-limited in every respect. His relationship to beings involves a domineering advance in the direction of the conquest and domination of the world; man assigns their measure to beings by determining independently and with reference to himself what ought to pass as 'being.'" Distilled into this basic message, Cartesianism, according to Heidegger, functions as necessary prelude or stepping-stone to Nietzsche's overman—despite the latter's misgivings or reservations about Descartes deriving from his partial medievalism. "The period we call modernity and toward whose completion Western history is moving," we read, "is defined by the fact that man becomes the measure and center of beings. . . . No matter how sharply Nietzsche pits himself time and again against Descartes, that founder of modern metaphysics, he turns against him only because he still does not posit man *completely and decisively enough* as *subiectum*. Descartes' conception of the *subiectum* as ego, and thus his 'egoistic' construal of the subject, is for Nietzsche not subjectivistic enough. Only in the doctrine of the overman—the doctrine of man's absolute preeminence among beings—modern metaphysics reaches its complete and final culmination; here Descartes celebrates his supreme triumph."[9]

    In Heidegger's presentation, Nietzsche's critique or rejection of Descartes is based in large measure on misunderstanding of the Cartesian position—which does not affect their deeper affinity. An important misunderstanding concerns the character of the "foundational" phrase. Construing the phrase as a deductive syllogism Nietzsche discovers a vicious circle in Descartes' statement: instead of yielding a deduction of crucial categories—like being, existence, or subjectivity—such categories are actually presupposed by the statement itself. As Heidegger observes, however, this charge means pressing against open doors. In his words: "Descartes' phrase is of the kind that it expresses and determines the inner nexus of being, certitude, and thinking simultaneously and at once; in this lies its essence as an 'axiom'." Nietzsche's complaint of circularity is thus untenable in a dual sense: first, because the statement is no syllogism relying on prior premises, and secondly, because the statement itself "provides the pre-supposing which Nietzsche misses." Closely connected with this criticism is another complaint also involving logical derivation: the charge that Descartes deduces the nature of thought from his concepts of ego and subjectivity rather than proceeding in the reverse direction (as suggested by modern skeptical philosophy). Again, however, this attack means essentially pleading Descartes' own case. "What Nietzsche believes to advance against Descartes as a supposedly new perspective, namely, that categories derive from thinking," the lecture course states, "is actually the decisive principle for Descartes himself. Of course, Descartes was still striving for a uniform metaphysical grounding of thinking as *cogito me cogitare*, while Nietzsche—misguided by British empiricism—lapses into a 'psychological explanation'." Since Nietzsche himself, however, tried to explain categories on the basis of "thinking" (however ill-construed), he basically "agreed with Descartes on the very point on which he considered it necessary to oppose him."[10]

More crucial and potentially damaging are a number of other charges directed at Descartes' basic philosophical position. Attacking the Cartesian claim of the immediate self-evidence and certitude of the foundational phrase, Nietzsche presents the search for certitude as a disguised mode of the "will to truth"—which, in turn, only conceals an underlying "will to power." "Nietzsche," Heidegger comments, "refers the *ego cogito* back to an *ego volo* and interprets *velle* as willing in the sense of *will to power*, which he treats as the basic character of beings as a whole. But what if the positing of this basic character became possible only on the basis of Descartes' fundamental metaphysical position? In this case, Nietzsche's critique would reflect a misunderstanding of the nature of metaphysics"—a misunderstanding concealing the disguised operation of Cartesian premises in his own thought. Nietzsche attacks and misconstrues certitude, Heidegger adds, because he himself "takes the perspective of modern metaphysics as absolutely certain and stakes everything on the priority of man as subject—a subject now conceived as will to power." To be sure, the shift to willing entails a change in the conception of thought or cognition in the sense that cognitive truth claims are now regarded simply as means for the enhancement of power. Contrary to Descartes' emphasis on cognitive certitude and transparency, "truth" is now presented as a "kind of error" useful for purposes of survival. According to the lecture course, however, the change is more apparent than real: even the "reversal" of truth preserves traditional cognitive standards: "It would be rash to conclude from Nietzsche's critique

that he has in the least abandoned or overcome Descartes' interpretation of being as representedness, his definition of truth as certitude,
and his construal of man as 'subject'. In fact, . . . the continuity goes
so far that, without inquiry about justifications, Nietzsche equates
being with representedness and the latter with truth." A similar continuity prevails with regard to the ego or "subjectivity"—which Nietzsche transformed from a purely rational-cognitive faculty into an
"embodied" agency motivated by the will to power: "The critique of
subjectivity in the sense of the ego-structure of consciousness accords
nonetheless with Nietzsche's absolute acceptance of subjectivity in
the (unrecognized) metaphysical sense of *subiectum*. For Nietzsche,
the underlying is not the 'I' but the 'body'"; however, this still remains
"Descartes' fundamental position"—though more coarsely stated—
provided "we still have eyes to see, that is, to think metaphysically."[11]

Drawing the consequences from the preceding considerations,
Heidegger presents Nietzsche's work as the culmination of Cartesianism and, more specifically, as the completion and "end" of metaphysics. "In order to grasp Nietzsche's thought as metaphysics and to
pinpoint his place in the history of metaphysics," he writes, "it is not
enough to explain some of his basic concepts metaphysically; rather,
we must grasp his philosophy *as the metaphysics of subjectivity.*" Yet,
the latter characterization is still too vague and indefinite since it applies with equal right to Descartes as well as Hegel. Thus, Nietzsche's
position and the essence of "classical nihilism" must be "more clearly
delineated as the metaphysics of the *absolute subjectivity of the will
to power.*" The former designation was insufficient because it "also
applies to Hegel's metaphysics insofar as it is the metaphysics of the
absolute subjectivity of self-knowing will, that is, of 'spirit'." In contrast to the idealist stress on reason and spirit, subjectivity for Nietzsche becomes "absolute as subjectivity of the body, that is, of drives
and affects and thus of the will to power." The traditional formula of
man as *animal rationale* thus is differently weighted in nineteenth-
century thought: "While Hegel treats *rationalitas*—construed in a
speculative-dialectical manner—as the core of subjectivity, Nietzsche
takes *animalitas* as his guide. Seen in their historical connection, both
place *rationalitas* and *animalitas* respectively at centerstage." In a bitter and somber passage, Heidegger finally attacks the stress on *animalitas*. In Nietzsche's work, he observes, "the essence of subjectivity necessarily unfolds as the *brutalitas* of *bestialitas*; at the end of
metaphysics stands the motto *Homo est brutum bestiale*. Nietzsche's
phrase about the 'blond beast' is not a casual exaggeration, but the
sign and password for a context in which he consciously stood, with-

out being able to comprehend its historical connections." Against this background, the notion of an "end of metaphysics" signifies the exhaustion of its earlier potential, and its reversal and levelling into a worldview of condensed domination.[12]

II

Some two decades after Heidegger's lecture course on nihilism, Nietzsche's influence began to assert itself widely in French thought. Accompanying the eclipse of a subjectivist existentialism, this resurgence was heralded not as a strengthening of, but a challenge and antidote to Cartesianism and the legacy of modern (subjectivist) metaphysics. Given his partial implication in the existentialist movement, Heidegger's reading quickly became the target of critical scrutiny: according to many "neo-Nietzscheans," this reading was evidence of lingering metaphysical commitments in Heidegger's own thought, while the "overman" was said to inaugurate an "end of metaphysics" in the radical sense of termination or transgression rather than completion.[13] One of the first and most astute philosophers to voice this criticism was Jacques Derrida—who has articulated this theme on numerous successive occasions. "Far from remaining simply—with Hegel and as Heidegger wished—*within* metaphysics," Derrida asserted in 1967 (in *Of Grammatology*), "Nietzsche contributed a great deal to the liberation of the signifier from its dependence or derivation with respect to the 'logos' and the related concept of 'truth' or the primary signified (in whatever sense that is understood). . . . To save Nietzsche from a reading of the Heideggerian type, it seems that we must above all refuse to restore or explicate a less naive 'ontology' composed of profound ontological intuitions according to some originary truth, an entire fundamentality hidden under the guise of an empiricist or metaphysical text: the virulence of Nietzschean thought could not be more completely misunderstood." In lieu of incorporating Nietzsche into a philosophical legacy, it was necessary—in Derrida's view—to recognize the radicalism of a "breakthrough" which attempts to "step outside of metaphysics" and to criticize it thoroughly while still "utilizing it in a certain way"; only in this manner could his text regain its "absolute strangeness": Nietzsche "has written that writing—and first of all his own—is not originarily subordinate to the 'logos' and to truth; and that this subordination has developed during a period whose meaning we must deconstruct."[14]

A year later, in an essay titled "The Ends of Man," Derrida again

addressed this topic—this time even more pointedly and with specific reference to French thought. Differentiating between two modes
or strategies of moving beyond metaphysics—an immanent and a
radical-rupturing mode—the essay affirmed that "the style of the first
deconstruction is mostly that of the Heideggerian questions, and the
other is mostly the one which dominates France today." The latter
domination was ascribed chiefly to the "increasingly insistent and increasingly rigorous recourse to Nietzsche in France"—whose "overman"
was seen as rupturing radically the ties with the humanism and subjectivism of traditional (or "last") man. In Derrida's words, the overman "burns his text and erases the traces of his steps. His laughter
then will burst out, directed toward a return which no longer will
have the form of a metaphysical repetition of humanism, nor—at the
'other side' of metaphysics—the form of a memorial or guardianship
of the meaning of being, the form of the house and of the truth of being." Taking the offensive in this contest of readings, the essay placed
Nietzsche's work resolutely beyond the pale of Cartesianism and,
more generally, of Western metaphysics in the Heideggerian sense:
"No doubt that Nietzsche called for an active forgetting of being: it
would not have the metaphysical form imputed to it by Heidegger.
Must one read Nietzsche, with Heidegger, as the last of the great
metaphysicians? Or, on the contrary, are we to take the question of
the truth of being as the last sleeping shudder of the superior man?
Are we to understand the eve as the guard mounted around the house
—or as the awakening to the day that is coming and at whose eve
we are?"[15]

   That this string of questions was mostly rhetorical is evident
from Derrida's subsequent publications, especially his writings specifically devoted to the interpretation of Nietzsche. His *Spurs*, subtitled *Nietzsche's Styles* (1978), is over long stretches a direct confrontation with Heidegger's exegesis. As he admits in that monograph,
in talking about Nietzsche or the basic "meaning" of Nietzsche's work
"there is still the Heideggerian reading of Nietzsche which must be
accounted for. Whatever the allowances that have been made for it
and whatever the efforts that have been exerted (for recognizable reasons) in France to conceal, evade or delay its falling due, this account
still remains unsettled." In trying to square this account, Derrida initially acknowledges a number of important insights or merits present
in Heidegger's "great study" (*grand livre*), and particularly three warn-
ings or admonitions. First of all, Heidegger warns "against an aestheticizing confusionism which, as blind to art as it is to philosophy,
would—in a precipitate interpretation of such of Nietzsche's proposi-

tions as the coming age of the philosopher-artist—have us conclude that conceptual rigor is becoming less intractable and that henceforth it will be admissible to say anything in militating for the cause of irrelevance." In the final analysis, he concedes, such confusionism is nothing more than "the reassurance and corroboration of the very order it pretends to oppose and which itself remains intact." Secondly, Heidegger cautions "against mistaking an 'heroic-boastful' style for the 'grand style'"—the former being characteristic, in Nietzsche's view, of "the 'cultivated' class, that is, the vulgar crowd of Wagnerian philistines." And finally, Heidegger emphasizes the necessity "of reading Nietzsche in an unremitting interrogation of Western civilization"; for, "to neglect such an interrogation, and in particular now that one claims to have done with secular illusions, is merely to ruminate on accepted ideas."[16]

After applauding these and related insights, *Spurs* draws attention to three Heideggerian claims or propositions which Derrida considers problematic, or as opening wedges to the problematic character of Heidegger's reading. The first claim is the assertion that, in his epistemology as well as aesthetic theory, Nietzsche basically seeks to replace a passive-receptive by an active-productive perspective, that is, a feminine by a masculine aesthetics (in the following I shall bypass this issue or rather welter of issues). The second point—and here philosophical alternatives become more clearly profiled—is Heidegger's view that, properly construed, Nietzsche's thought on art "emerges as 'metaphysical in its most intimate intention' and this because art, for him, is the 'essential way in which a being creates itself as being'." Thirdly and most importantly, there is the claim that, in dealing with metaphysics and with Platonism or the Platonic tradition, Nietzsche "proceeds most frequently by simple 'inversion' (*Umdrehung*) which consists 'in turning the Platonic propositions upside down, in standing them on their head.'" Questioning and seeking to unsettle the last two claims (and especially the final one), Derrida shifts the focus to the famous story of "How the 'True World' Finally Became a Fable" (contained in Nietzsche's *Twilight of Idols*). Commenting on the phrase "With the true world we have also abolished the apparent one," he notes that—far from implying a simple "inversion" or the replacement of one hierarchy by another—the story adumbrates something more basic, namely, "a transformation of the hierarchical structure itself." Although elaborating astutely on Nietzsche's fable Heidegger, in Derrida's view, ultimately shrinks from probing its radical implications, preferring instead to subordinate Nietzsche's thought to the traditional yardsticks of "logos" and truth: "Heidegger indeed pursues

the Nietzschean operation into the very reaches where it exceeds
metaphysics and Platonism; but at the same time, it seems that what
he is after is in fact a type of question indigenous to hermeneutics
and to the kind of philosophy which Nietzsche's operation should
otherwise have *put out of order.*"[17]

Discarding Heidegger's scruples, Derrida ventures boldly into
"post-metaphysical" terrain. In his assessment, the crucial phrase in
Nietzsche's fable aims to unhinge the contrast between truth and appearance, truth and falsity, keeping the opposites at best in playful
suspense. As expressed in the fable, we read, Nietzsche's thought "suspends the decidable opposition of true and untrue and inaugurates
the epochal regime of question marks for all concepts belonging to
the system of philosophical decidability. As a result, the hermeneutical project postulating a true sense of the text is disqualified, while
reading is freed from the horizon of the meaning or truth of being,
liberated from the values of the product's production or the present's
presence." What emerges in lieu of traditional categories, like truth
or being, is the effect of a general potency or "will to power"—evident
in Nietzsche's (presumed) preference for "style" or stylistic accent over
substantive content or cognitive claims. "What is unleashed at this
point," Derrida observes, "is the question of style as a question of
writing—the question of a spurring-operation more powerful than any
content, thesis or meaning. The stylite spur (*éperon stylé*) rips through
the veil." Linking potency or empowerment with Heidegger's own notion of "propriation" or "propriating event" (*Ereignis*), *Spurs* asserts the
primacy and extrinsic status of this event over traditional ontological
categories. "The process of propriation," we read, "escapes any dialectics and any ontological decidability. Consequently, one can no longer
ask the question 'what *is* property, propriation, expropriation, mastery, servitude, and the like'. . . . Because it is finally undecidable, propriation is more powerful than the question '*ti esti*', more powerful
than the veil of truth or the meaning of being." In the end, the entire
history of truth or being, in Heidegger's own sense, must be seen as
a process of propriation or empowerment—a process not derivable from
ontology or hermeneutics for the simple reason that these perspectives are themselves "inscribed" in that process.[18]

In light of these considerations, the limits of Heidegger's exegesis of Nietzsche become obvious (though without vitiating its major
insights). "Throughout the near totality of its trajectory," Derrida states,
"Heidegger's reading subsists in the hermeneutic space of the question of the truth (of being). While presuming to penetrate to the most
intimate reaches of Nietzsche's thinking will, he concludes that this

will—though aiming to complete or culminate it—still *belonged* to the history of metaphysics. This might be granted *provided* some single meaning could still be attached to *belonging"* or property—which is clearly not the case given the mentioned process of empowerment. Once this process—the event of propriation—is fully taken into account, Heidegger's reading, we are told, is "opened up to a certain dehiscence" and forced to make room "to another reading which refuses to be contained therein." Although insisting on Nietzsche's metaphysical status and clinging to metaphysical categories in his exegesis, Heidegger's own ontological thinking tends to erode these categories and their foundational role. In Derrida's words: "The order of Heidegger's thought is regularly disoriented by an oblique movement which inscribes the truth of being in the process of propriation. Although magnetized (as it were) by valuation or an ineradicable preference for the 'own' or proper, this process nonetheless leads to proper-ty's abyssal structure; for in such a structure—which is nonfoundational, superficial though bottomless, and always 'flat'—proper-ty is literally sunk . . . passing into otherness." In the presentation of *Spurs*, this post-metaphysical abyss finally engulfs and swallows everything up in its vortex of nihilation: "In the end, the question of the *event* (which is one meaning of *Ereignis*) having been uprooted from ontology, property or propriation is named exactly as that which is proper to nothing and no one; it no longer decides the appropriation of the truth of being, but rather casts into its bottomless abyss truth as well as non-truth, concealment and unconcealment, enlightenment and dissimulation. As a result, the history of being becomes a history in which no being, nothing, happens except the unfathomable process of *Ereignis*—the property of the abyss which is necessarily the abyss of property, the violence of an event which befalls without being."[19]

More recently, following up an exchange with Gadamer (1981), Derrida has again returned to Heidegger's interpretation, shifting the accent this time from the process of propriation to what is uniquely "proper" to Nietzsche, namely, his signatures or proper names. Emphasizing the biographical singularity of Nietzsche's life and work, Derrida challenges the subsumption of this work under general metaphysical categories and abstractions. In Heidegger's reading, he notes, "there is a unity of Nietzsche's thought, although it may not be the unity of a system in the classical sense." Far from being attributable to biographical or historical contingencies, this unified coherence derives "from the unity of Western metaphysics which gathers itself here in its zenith or culmination, a zenith which also resembles the simple line of a geological divide. As a result, the biographical or auto-

biographical — the arena or potency of proper name(s) and signatures —
all this is relegated once again to that subordinate or marginal status
which it has always occupied in the history of metaphysics." From
a metaphysical perspective, Nietzsche's name appears not as that of
an individual or concrete signatory, but rather as "the name of a thinking or thought structure whose unity bestows meaning and reference
on the proper name: 'Nietzsche' is nothing but the name of this
thought." What is at issue here, Derrida concedes, is not a simple vindication of biological or psychological reductionisms — pitfalls which
Heidegger legitimately seeks to avoid: "Justifiably suspicious of
biographism, psychologism, and psychoanalysis" his exegesis attacks
reductive mechanisms which efface or "conceal the effort of thought."
However, in doing so "with the best of reasons," Derrida asks, "does
he not thereby return to a gesture of classical metaphysics, and this
at the very moment when he seeks to transgress metaphysics and present Nietzsche as its culmination? This classical gesture amounts to
the separation of life (biography) and proper name from the core of
thought."[20]

The separation of life and thought — or rather the subsumption
of the former under the latter — persists even in Heidegger's interpretation of *Ecce Homo* which he treats not as autobiography but again
as a zenith, namely, as culmination of the "history of modernity seen
as the eclipse of the West." This treatment concurs with his overall
strategy and interpretive thesis, to the effect that Nietzsche's thought
"has not truly transgressed the completion of metaphysics" and that,
"insofar as it inaugurates a transgression, it does so by inches and
only to remain perched on the precipice of the limit, that is, in complete ambiguity." In Derrida's view, this approach suffers from several
weaknesses, primarily an unwitting relapse into metaphysics. "If, instead of reformulating it," he writes, "Heidegger accepts the customary notion of autobiography, opposing it only to a Western destiny
represented by Nietzsche, one is entitled to ask: does he himself escape a fairly traditional dichotomy between biographical (psycho-
biological) empiricism, on the one hand, and on the other, an 'essential thought' at the height of historical decisions?" More importantly,
the subsumption of biography under metaphysics presupposes a certain stability or identifiability of the particular (as well as the general)
— which is more than doubtful in Nietzsche's case. If Nietzsche is to
be defined or determined by the unity of his thought, Derrida queries,
"is it at all clear that this thought is unitary as Heidegger claims; that
Nietzsche thus carries only one name? . . . But who has decided that
one carries only one name? Certainly not Nietzsche. And who has

likewise established that there is something like a Western metaphysics, something which can be gathered uniquely under that name?"
What needs to be questioned in Heidegger's exegesis, therefore, is
less its concrete content or specific propositions than a certain metaphysical presupposition or "logocentric" structure animating that exegesis: "Perhaps what animates it is the axiomatic structure of metaphysics itself, insofar as metaphysics as such longs for or fancies its
own unity."[21]

In the end, the confrontation of life (biography) and thought calls
into question the status and plausibility of traditional categories like
truth and being, as well as the "unity" or "totality" of beings. In Heidegger's reading, both the "will to power" and the notion of "eternal
recurrence" function as basic metaphysical titles or as unifying cate
gories permeating beings as a whole. More specifically, the will to
power is presented as "the principle of cognition of the eternal recurrence of the same: it is the constitution of being (its *quid, quidditas*
or *essentia*) while eternal recurrence denotes the modality (the
quomodo) of beings as a whole." Thus, the two titles respond in fact
to "two questions which are a pair in metaphysics (being as *quidditas*
or *essentia*, and being as mode of existence); . . . in both questions the
issue of the totality of being(s) remains dominant." According to Derrida, however, Nietzsche was deeply suspicious of wholeness or totalizing principles. In fact, he notes, his work "militates against everything characterizing a conception or simple anticipation of totality,
including the species-genus relationship. What prevails rather is a
singular inclusion of the 'whole' in the 'part' and this without any
possible totalization." If this is so, however—Derrida concludes—then
it may be "premature to treat Nietzsche as a metaphysician, even if
only as the last one." Perhaps, Nietzsche "is no longer a thinker of
being, provided there is an essential nexus between totality and being
as a whole."[22]

III

The preceding review should provide a brief glimpse of opposing arguments and interpretations (a glimpse particularly condensed
in Heidegger's case, given his extensive writings in this field). Yet,
while accentuating and profiling competing approaches, the topic of
discussion still remains elusive: behind the strong pleas of Heidegger
and Derrida, Nietzsche's own voice sometimes seems muffled or at
a distance. Heidegger, at least in 1940, argues against Nietzsche's will

to power; but actually, his argument aims through or via Nietzsche at a larger target: namely, Western metaphysics seen as pacemaker of modern anthropocentrism, will-power, and technological domination — a target to which Nietzsche is in some ways incidental. In turn, Derrida argues for Nietzsche; but the actual brunt of his critique aims — through or via Nietzsche — at Heidegger or (what he considers) Heidegger's own lingering attachment to metaphysics. Many of his more pointed objections, one feels, could be raised or articulated quite independently of Nietzsche's variegated texts. Thus, while challenging the equation of Nietzsche with a thought or thought structure, Derrida's own portrayal sometimes tends to equate him with a counter-thought: namely, with a radical post-metaphysics of which Nietzsche would be only an examplar or illustration. None of these comments, to be sure, can impair or weaken the cogency of the proposed interpretive schemes — at least in the absence of closer inspection.

In Heidegger's case, the relation to Nietzsche is obviously very complex — more complex than the analyzed text (and Derrida's rejoinder) suggests. In his writings and lectures before 1940, he also presented Nietzsche as a metaphysician — but he did so mainly to rescue him from unphilosophical (positivist, psychological) construals. By the time of the lecture course on nihilism, Western metaphysics itself had become suspect to Heidegger because he discovered in it the source of anthropocentric arrogance and destructiveness; Nietzsche's work came to be overshadowed by this assessment. Commenting on Heidegger's ambivalent attitude toward Nietzsche, Derrida observes that this ambivalence "remains constant: in rescuing Nietzsche he condemns him; he seeks to rescue and condemn him at the same time. While affirming the uniqueness of his thought, he simultaneously tries to demonstrate that it repeats the most powerful (and most general) scheme of metaphysics."[23] However, one should also note the ambivalent character of this "condemnation" — of Nietzsche and of metaphysics. In Heidegger's view, there cannot be a simple exit or straightforward departure from metaphysics, since such a move would only be another subjective-metaphysical strategem. Together with its premises and "logocentric" categories metaphysics can never be simply discarded like an old costume, but only be worn out or lived and suffered through (verwinden). As a result, the critical treatment of Nietzsche has the character less of a final verdict than of a farewell or a parting of the ways — a parting with a friend whose journey one can no longer completely share or comprehend.

Still, when all this is taken into account, Heidegger's lecture course — one has to recognize — is often less than friendly or sympathetic. Compared with his ingenuous and astute interpretations of other philosophers (from Aristotle to Kant and Husserl), his treatment of Nietzsche in 1940 strikes the reader frequently as downright "unfair" (if fairness is at all relevant to exegesis). To portray the "progress" of Western metaphysics as a movement from *rationalitas* to *animalitas*, and Nietzsche's own brand of metaphysics as culmination of the *brutalitas* of *bestialitas* is hardly a soft-spoken or mild-mannered kind of criticism. In fact, the passage (and related comments) reveals a bitterness and polemical intensity which otherwise is rare in Heidegger's writings. At this point, the historical context of the lecture course surely has to be taken into account. In 1940, the German war machine was overrunning Europe in a frenzy of destructiveness and brutal domination; and Nazi ideologues repeatedly invoked Nietzsche as inspiration of their "grand politics." As it seems to me (and as is manifest in a number of "political" statements strewn throughout its pages), Heidegger's lecture course was an act of inner emigration and peaceful resistance against the regime—although Nietzsche was at most obliquely involved in its policies. Yet, while surely not to blame for these policies, Nietzsche also was not entirely or unequivocally blameless. As Derrida writes at one point, in a judicious passage: "There is nothing purely contingent in the fact that the only kind of politics which used him as supreme and official emblem was that of the Nazi regime. With this I do not mean to say that this type of 'Nietzschean' politics is the only possible one, nor that it reflects the best adaptation of his heritage, nor even that those who refused to invoke him have understood him better. No, the future of Nietzsche's text is not yet finished."[24]

To some extent, the political animosity carries over into philosophical issues (which is likewise a rare occurrence). In interpreting Nietzsche's work, Heidegger frequently refuses to grant the possibility of ambivalence or multiple readings—a possibility he stresses and celebrates on other occasions. A case in point is Nietzsche's fragment dealing with the "Decline of Cosmological Values"—which looms large in Heidegger's exegesis and which, among other things, contains these phrases: "As a psychological state nihilism arises . . . when one has posited a *totality*, a *systematization*, indeed an *organization* in and beneath all occurrences—with the result that a soul craving for admiration and reverence can wallow in the idea of some supreme form of domination and governance. . . . The feeling of *valuelessness* was reached with the realization that the overall character of existence may not be interpreted by means of the concepts of 'purpose', 'unity', or 'truth'. Nothing is accomplished by it; any comprehensive unity in the plurality of events is lacking." While acknowledging the subtlety of the argument and the differentiation of three types of nihilism, Heidegger stubbornly insists on construing the fragment as manifestation of a metaphysical will to power, a will rooted, moreover, in a Cartesian subjectivity—as if his own writings did not constantly nourish our suspicions of logical-metaphysical "totalities" and of efforts to "systematize," "organize," or streamline the diversity of beings and events! Bypassing such nuances or "post-metaphysical" hints, Heidegger concludes somewhat stiffly: "What is involved is a 'psychological' reckoning and calculation of values, a reckoning in which we ourselves, of course, are included. But then to think 'psychologically' means to think everything as a configuration of the will to power . . . to appraise everything on the basis of its value and to calculate value on the basis of the fundamental value, the will to power."[25]

A similar stiffness or inflexibility prevails also in the exegesis of other Nietzschean statements, for example, of the following fragment: "Thinking is for us a means or instrument not of 'knowing' but of describing an event, cataloguing it, making it available for our use: that is what we think today about thinking—tomorrow perhaps something else." Although, on closer inspection, the statement literally bristles with nuances—opening up the possibility that "our" instrumental-utilitarian mode of thinking may not be necessary or perennial—Heidegger again bypasses multivocity in favor of a straightforward modern-metaphysical reading: "Thinking is meant here purely 'economically', in the sense of a 'machine economy'. *What* we think is, as something thought, 'true' only insofar as it serves the preservation of the will to power; but even *how* we think about thinking is measured solely by this standard." As it seems to me, even Nietzsche's key "category" of the will to power does not simply or unequivocally denote a subjective-metaphysical will-power, but conceivably a more subtle kind of empowerment (as Derrida suggests)—an empowerment adumbrated in Heidegger's own comments both on "being" and "propriation." Likewise, Nietzsche's abandonment of the Cartesian *cogito* in favor of the "body" or embodiment does not necessarily vindicate "biologism" or *animalitas*—as shown in (French) phenomenological literature where "embodiment" typically carries a post- or anti-Cartesian edge. Heidegger's assessment is sharp and dismissive: "To place the body first means that we must think more clearly and more concretely still than Descartes, but do so wholly and purely in his sense. The method is decisive: That Nietzsche posits the body in place of the soul and consciousness alters nothing in the basic metaphysical position defined by Descartes; Nietzsche merely coarsens it and brings it to the edge—or even into the realm—of complete senselessness."[26]

In these and similar respects, Derrida's critical rejoinders are frequently telling and persuasive—and perhaps more faithful to Heidegger's own perspective. Derrida is surely correct when he notes in *Spurs* (as cited above) that Heidegger "pursues the Nietzschean operation into the very reaches where it exceeds metaphysics and Platonism" while, at the same time, trying to contain this operation within the framework of "hermeneutics and (traditional) philosophy." This containment or ambivalence is particularly evident in the case of Nietzsche's fable regarding the transformation of the "true world"—which Heidegger in the main interprets in the sense of an "inversion" (*Umdrehung*). However, while stressing the reversal of Platonism—Derrida observes—"Heidegger does not restrict himself (as is often supposed) to this scheme. . . . Thus, he remarks that, although Nietzsche might seem or perhaps ought to employ the method of *Umdrehung*, it is nonetheless apparent that he 'is seeking something else' (*etwas anderes sucht*)." Metaphysical containment is also at work in the application of traditional "categories" like totality, unity, or system to Nietzsche's work, especially in reference to notions like the "will to power" or "eternal recurrence." As Derrida comments pointedly, and plausibly, in 1981: "Let us not forget that Heidegger defines metaphysics as thinking of beings as a whole to the exclusion of the question of the being of beings; and it is on the basis of this definition that he treats Nietzsche often as last metaphysician. Without entering into the complexities of this problematic," he adds, one can note that "Nietzsche distrusts every type of totalizing thought. Who says that 'although life may be little in comparison with the whole, everything was at some time alive, *ad infinitum*' expresses a view of life-and-death which obeys in no way a univocal conception of wholeness or of the relation of whole and part. The idea of eternal recurrence, which animates this phrase, is no idea of totality."[27]

Equally telling, and deserving of attention, are Derrida's observations on "body" and embodiment and on the relation between life and thought. Focusing on the role of life and biography in Nietzsche's work he asserts—echoing to some extent Heideggerian motifs: "Although life has a 'beyond' or transcendence, it cannot for this reason be rendered secondary. As itself and in itself life engenders even the movement of truth or cognition—in itself and beyond itself." Once this conception is taken into account, a reading of Nietzsche becomes possible which eludes metaphysics. Such a reading, he writes, "would surely escape every type of biologism—but mainly because it would dislodge every 'logism'. And a different style of autobiography would emerge bent on exploding the unity of the name and the signature (in every sense of the term *faire sauter*), bent on confounding biologism together with its critique to the extent that the latter relies, with Heidegger, on 'essential thought'." Elaborating on this point and its broader philosophical implications, Derrida states in another context: "Neither the 'immanent' readings of philosophical systems nor their external empirical-genetic reconstructions have ever penetrated to the question of the *dynamis* of the margin between 'work' and 'life', between system and author of system. This margin or chasm—I call it *dynamis* because of its force, its power, its virtual and moving potency—is neither active nor passive, neither inside nor outside. Above all, it is not a small line, an invisible or indivisible demarcation between philosophical propositions, on the one hand, and on the other, the life of an author identifiable already by his name. This divisible margin rather crosses through these two domains, the corpus and the body—according to laws which we are only beginning to suspect."[28]

While pregnant with insights and intimations, Derrida's arguments tend to be marred by a certain willfulness or brisk "leaping" gesture, suggesting an exit from metaphysics and traditional philosophical conventions. When asserting a radical "breakthrough" in Nietzsche's work which manages to "step outside of metaphysics" while still "utilizing it in a certain way," he insinuates an exodus which is not feasible (as indicated above) except in a purposive-metaphysical sense. For example, in his comments on biography, how can he invoke the term *dynamis* without conjuring up and coming to terms with the entire legacy of philosophical speculation (from Aristotle to Heidegger) devoted to *energeia, dynamis,* and potency? Willfulness or at least impatience is particularly evident in the treatment of philosophical categories like "truth" or "being." Occasionally, in *Spurs*, one finds lines like the following: "Indeed there is no such thing as a truth as such, but only a surfeit of it" (or about "woman": "There is no such thing as the truth of woman, but this is because of that abyssal divergence of the truth, because that untruth is 'truth'"). However, strictly construed, do such statements not amount to a simple metaphysical inversion—where untruth is equated or put in the place of truth—an inversion Derrida otherwise seeks to avoid (and which Heidegger likewise tried to bypass by reformulating the "essence of truth")? Equally problematic, in my view, are Derrida's comments on "being" and on the relationship between being and "will to power" seen as empowerment. Repeatedly, his writings not only juxtapose but oppose the two notions to each other in a dichotomous fashion—as if "will to power"

did not also say something about being and vice versa. And as if
Derrida himself had not been one of the first to alert us to the subtle
correlation between Heidegger's notion of "being" and the dimension of potency or empowerment (in an essay entitled "Violence and
Metaphysics").[29]

An important facet—probably the central facet—of the nexus between ontology and power concerns the relationship between "being"
and "propriation" (*Ereignis*)—terms which Derrida again treats as
strictly antithetical. As indicated, *Spurs* presents propriation as radically primary and outside the range of metaphysical or ontological
categories. However, placed beyond being and truth, propriation turns
itself into an empty metaphysical abstraction. For, if *"Ereignis"* means
an empowering or "giving" potency (in the sense of *"es gibt"*), what
else does it "give" but being? The intimate linkage between being and
propriation is repeatedly stressed by Heidegger, for example in this
passage from "Time and Being" (which Derrida cites but without drawing its implications): "Being belongs to the movement of *Ereignis*; thus
being would be a kind of *Ereignis*, not *Ereignis* a kind of being. But
the flight which seeks refuge in such a reversal is too easily come by.
. . . Inasmuch as it is in the quest of being itself that we think and
pursue what is proper to it, it proves itself the gift of the mission
(*Geschick*) of presence, a gift accorded through the reach of time." In
divorcing propriation from being, Derrida not surprisingly is led to
privilege nothingness or propriation's "abyssal structure": "The question of the *event* (*Ereignis*) having been uprooted from ontology, property or propriation is named exactly as that which is proper to nothing or no one; it . . . casts into its bottomless abyss truth as well as
non-truth, concealment and unconcealment, enlightenment and dissimulation. As a result, the history of being becomes a history in
which no being, nothing, happens. . . ." However, in privileging non-
being over being, *Abgrund* (abyss) over *Grund*, does he not again slip
into the kind of "inversion" he castigates in the case of "anarchy," saying: "What must occur then is not merely a suppression of all hierarchy, for an-archy only consolidates just as surely the established order
of a metaphysical hierarchy"?[30]

Moreover, while exempting Nietzsche from metaphysics, Derrida's own argument promotes occasionally a metaphysical reading—
specifically along Cartesian lines (as outlined by Heidegger). Although
seeking to bypass the subject-object polarity, the stress on biography
and proper name(s) sometimes carries overtones of anthropocentrism
as well as a particularist subjectivism. "Next to Kierkegaard," the essay
of 1981 states, "was not Nietzsche one of the few who multiplied his

names and toyed with his signatures, identities, and masks?"—a phrase which seems to make Nietzsche (or Nietzsche's ego) the source of his own plurality or dispersal. Referring to a passage in *Ecce Homo* Derrida notes elsewhere: "He forces himself to say who he is—which runs counter to his natural habitus which propels him toward dissimulation behind masks. The value of dissimulation, as you know, is constantly affirmed: life is dissimulation. When saying 'I am such and such' he seems to go against his instinct of dissimulation. . . . But *on the other hand*, this self-presentation might very well be a ruse of dissimulation"—statements which again seem to portray Nietzsche (his subjectivity) as the sovereign architect of his multiple appearances. Apart from this lingering Cartesianism or egocentrism, one also wonders whether Derrida always manages to escape a shallow kind of "life-philosophy"—the same life-philosophy which Heidegger (as he recognizes) castigated in *Being and Time*.[31]

At this juncture it may be appropriate—at last and by way of conclusion—to turn briefly to the target of these interpretations. As it seems to me, there can be little doubt that Nietzsche's work at many points reflects a pronounced Cartesianism or modern-metaphysical stance (in Heidegger's sense)—although this stance is riddled everywhere with deep ambiguity. Someone who writes about "the disparity between the greatness of my task and the *smallness* of my contemporaries" or who claims "I am not a man, I am dynamite" can hardly be said to nourish a low estimate of his ego or individual significance. And how else can the following passage be read but as expression of an emphatic anthropocentrism: "All the beauty and sublimeness which we have bestowed on real or imaginary objects I want to reclaim as the property and product of man: as his fairest apology. Man as poet, as thinker, as god, love, and power: O, with what regal generosity he has lavished gifts upon things, only to *impoverish* and feel miserable *himself!* This was hitherto his greatest unselfishness that he adored and worshipped—while concealing from himself that it is *he* who created everything that he adored." A similar man- or subject-centered focus can hardly be denied in this statement: "Whoever cannot posit *himself* as 'aim' or 'purpose' or who generally cannot posit aims on his own, pays tribute to the ethics of self-denial (*Entselbstung*)—instinctively. . . . And faith too is a self-denial." In my view, even Nietzsche's style(s)—including his rhetorical flourishes and exclamation points—sometimes exudes the mood of *fin de siècle* with its late Romantic (even Wagnerian) pathos—a mood which today is difficult to reenact or to appreciate.[32]

Yet, although not negligible, bursts of self-assertion or self-centeredness are regularly counterbalanced or crossed out in Nietzsche's work by an opposing mood. Thus, in a note of 1875 Nietzsche asserts pointedly: "To make the individual *uncomfortable,* that is my task." Three years later, in *Human, All-Too-Human,* he attacks a shallow kind of anthropocentrism: "All philosophers share this common error: they proceed from contemporary man and think they can reach their goal through an analysis of this man. Automatically they think of 'man' as an eternal verity, as something abiding in the whirlpool, as a sure measure of things." The same collection contains this admirable statement about education: "In the case of the individual the task of education is this: to put him on his path so firmly and surely that, on the whole, he can never again be diverted. Then, however, the educator must wound him, or utilize the wounds destiny inflicts upon him; and when pain and need have thus developed, something new and noble can then be inoculated in the wounded spots. His whole nature will absorb this and later, in its fruits, show the ennoblement." Sentiments of this kind are not limited to Nietzsche's "early" writings. In the first part of *Thus Spoke Zarathustra* (1881), the teacher makes this comment on valuation (which Heidegger neglects to mention): "Change of values—that is a change of creators. . . . First, people were creators, and only in later times, individuals"— adding shortly afterwards: "This is your thirst: to become sacrifices and gifts yourselves; and that is why you thirst to pile up all the riches in your soul. Insatiably your soul strives for treasures and gems, because your virtue is insatiable in wanting to give. . . . Upward goes our way, from genus to overgenus. But we shudder at the degenerate sense which says 'Everything for me'." Still later we find this fragment: "'Everything is subjective', you say, but even this is interpretation. The 'subject' is not something given, it is something added and invented and projected behind what there is."[33]

As it appears from these passages, Nietzsche speaks at least with two voices or in two idioms: a Cartesian and a post-Cartesian one (probably in more). This is not surprising in someone who was perched so perilously on the precipice or "geological divide" (Derrida's term) between ages or between paradigms of thought and discourse. That Nietzsche perceived himself as stretched between evening and dawn, between decline and a new beginning, is evident from *Ecce Homo* where he writes: "This twofold origin, as it were from the highest and the lowest rung of the ladder of life, at once *decadent* and *beginning*— this if anything explains that neutrality, that freedom from party in relation to the total problem of life which perhaps distinguishes me. I have a subtler sense for signs of ascent and decline than any man has ever had. I am the teacher *par excellence* in this matter—I know both, I am both." Being stretched between descent and ascent also means being torn between conflicting modes of language and speech. As Zarathustra exclaims at the opening of the second part: "New ways I go, a new speech comes to me; weary I grow, like all creators, of the old tongues. My spirit no longer wants to walk on worn soles." The transition from one tongue to the other, however, is uncharted, abrupt, and full of thunderbolts and spasms of intense self-assertion: "Like a cry and a shout of joy I want to sweep over wide seas, till I find the blessed isles where my friends are dwelling." Yet, cries and shouts are not the language Nietzsche ultimately seeks. "Would that my lioness, wisdom, might learn how to roar tenderly," Zarathustra continues. "Now she runs foolishly through the harsh desert and seeks and seeks gentle turf—my old wild wisdom. Upon your hearts' gentle turf, my friends, upon your love she would bed her most dearly beloved."[34]

Seen in this light, as a tension and a bridge, Nietzsche's work can still serve as a signpost for us today who, knowingly or unknowingly, are likewise stretched out between evening and dawn—a signpost both in an intellectual and a political sense. Read in the latter perspective his writings, I believe, can be a beacon illuminating our political past and present as well as possible aspects or dimensions of the future. As a political thinker, Nietzsche is frequently treated as the herald of an age of unprecedented conflict, global warfare, and immense destruction—experiences with which our century is saturated. But there is also a gentler theme in his work, or the anticipation of a different future. "From all mountains I look out for fatherlands and motherlands; but home I found nowhere," Zarathustra states. "Strange and a mockery to me are the men of today to whom my heart recently drew me; and I am driven out of fatherlands and motherlands. Thus I now love only my *children's land*, yet undiscovered, in the farthest sea: for this I bid my sails search and search."[35]

2
Phenomenology and Critique:
Adorno

Sunt lacrumae rerum (Virgil)

To the unsuspecting observer, the theme of this inquiry—the relation of phenomenology and critique—may appear bland and unproblematic. Judging by the statements of some phenomenologists, the two terms seem intimately linked, perhaps even synonymous. Richard Zaner, author of a well-written and popular introduction to the "way of phenomenology," used as subtitle for his study "Criticism as a Philosophical Discipline" and asserted in the opening pages that "phenomenological philosophy is most accurately conceived as criticism now firmly established on its own sound foundation."[1] Statements with a similar tenor could easily be culled from phenomenological literature. Yet, intellectual self-portrayals can hardly be given the last word; at a closer look, the proclaimed liaison of phenomenology and criticism seems excessively idyllic—like a paper truce which is disavowed by actual combat. The drama of the theme emerges as soon as the focus is shifted from internal self-assessments to external confrontations: especially to the program of "critical theory" sponsored by the Frankfurt Institute of Social Research. As is well known, the relationship between Freiburg and Frankfurt—or between the movement initiated by Husserl and the Institute shaped by Horkheimer and Adorno—has not been marked by indifference. Despite occasional episodes of fraternization, contacts have tended to be fraught with tension, punctuated periodically by spirited clashes.

Refocused as a comparison of phenomenology and "critical theory," the proposed inquiry is bound to be a hazardous enterprise: an atmosphere charged with suspicion and mutual recrimination is not particularly conducive to the calm arbitration of claims and the formulation of a balanced judgment. Moreover, the undertaking is complicated by the malleability of both camps and the shifting terrain of encounters. A synoptic overview of contacts reveals a broad panorama. Phenomenology, from this vantage point, extends from Husserl's transcendental perspective over Scheler's ontology and Heidegger's analysis of *Dasein* to formulations of a historical and cultural hermeneutics; critical theory, on the other hand, ranges from programmatic statements of the Institute's founders to the writings of contemporary Frankfurt theorists. The hazards of the comparative inquiry are offset, however, by the possibility of reciprocal clarification, especially through the exposure of underlying premises. To a considerable extent, for example, phenomenology presents itself as a philosophy of foundations, origins, or first beginnings, that is, as a revival in modern guise of *prima philosophia*.[2] Unless great care is taken, this posture may encourage — and has occasionally encouraged — intellectual rigidity, by sanctioning attachment to fixed apriori principles or unquestioned "ontic" structures. In its turn, critical theory may on occasion be too disdainful of substantive premises and linkages; since abandoning hope in proletarian spontaneity and in the inevitability of historical progress, the Frankfurt program sometimes seems in danger of courting intellectual self-sufficiency.[3]

The following pages do not propose to recount the entire story of encounters. For present purposes, I shall concentrate on one of the founders and leading representatives of the Frankfurt School: Theodor Adorno. The choice of Adorno as key figure is not arbitrary or unmotivated: more than anyone else his thought provides the crucial link between Frankfurt and Freiburg. While leaders of the phenomenological movement as well as other Frankfurt theorists have tended to pay at best intermittent attention to developments in the opposite camp, Adorno's life-work revolved to a substantial degree around the study and critical scrutiny of phenomenological and hermeneutical writings. This scrutiny, one should add, was never a mere outsider's gloss, but evidence of his serious (sometimes passionate) endeavor to grasp the basic thrust of philosophical conceptions — including their submerged premises and predicaments. To this extent, his commentary captured and highlighted some of the crucial junctures of contemporary philosophy. In his analysis of transcendental phenomenology, Husserl emerged as one of the last great spokesmen of Western rationalism and individualism — more precisely, of the modern "philosophy of consciousness" inaugurated by Descartes. By casting doubt on the foundational role of consciousness and by exposing the ambivalence of reason, Adorno was progressively catapulted beyond the confines of the Cartesian tradition; leaving behind the domain of "subjectivity" (and shunning a simple return to Hegelian dialectics), his thinking was bound to come into direct contact with Heidegger's arguments — a confrontation which overshadowed and consumed the later years of his life. The following presentation shall retrace briefly the main steps in this development: starting from some of Adorno's early writings the account shall delineate his major forays against Husserl and Heidegger, in order to cast a glance at the end at his own thoughts for a metaphysics "after Auschwitz."

I
(From Idealism to Dialectical Materialism)

Adorno's preoccupation with phenomenology dates back to his student days at the University of Frankfurt during the early years of the Weimar Republic. Under the guiding direction of Hans Cornelius —a neo-Kantian philosopher committed to a radical version of transcendental idealism—he submitted to that university in 1924 a doctoral dissertation with the title "The Transcendent Status of Thing and Noema in Husserl's Phenomenology" ("Die Transzendenz des Dinglichen und Noematischen in Husserls Phänomenologie"). The dissertation was not a very original piece of work; on the whole, its arguments reflected faithfully the teachings of Cornelius—including the latter's contention that mind was completely able to engulf or absorb reality, to the point that Kant's apriori categories of reason functioned simultaneously as principles of empirical psychology. Nevertheless, the central topic of the thesis, the relationship between consciousness and the external world, struck a theme which became one of Adorno's life-long concerns; despite the idealist recipe offered in its pages (a recipe he later vehemently disavowed), the focus of the study provided an avenue for probing important, unresolved issues in Husserl's thought. Briefly formulated, the dissertation tried to demonstrate that Husserl was insufficiently wedded to idealism— more precisely: that Husserl's attempt to trace all experience back to the "primordial evidence" of consciousness was basically inconsistent, since it was flawed by a continued endorsement of the Cartesian mind-body dualism or of the Kantian bifurcation of mind and "thing-in-itself."[4]

In developing this argument, the dissertation relied chiefly on Husserl's *Ideas for a Pure Phenomenology and Phenomenological Philosophy* of 1913 (and subsidiarily on his *Logical Investigations*). As Adorno noted, Husserl's *Ideas* were predicated on the proposition that consciousness signifies a "sphere of absolute origins," an endowment (in Husserl's words) capable "of forming judgments about reality, of raising questions, suppositions and doubts about it, and also

of resolving doubts and thus performing the 'jurisdiction of reason'."
All knowledge or cognition in this view was grounded in the immediate experience or evidence of consciousness, in "primordial giving
intuition"; the basic task of the phenomenological reduction or *epoché*
was to "bracket" conceptions about external reality and to reveal "pure
consciousness in its absolute autonomy." According to Adorno, however, notions of this kind were mingled with very different assertions
pointing in the direction of an ineradicable dualism. Objects, one reads
in *Ideas*, are "in principle transcendent" with regard to experience or
consciousness. This transcendence, Husserl affirmed, reveals "the basic
distinction between modes of being, a distinction more fundamental
than any other: that between *consciousness* and *reality*" or between
"*being as experience* and *being as object*." The dichotomy—between
whose poles, one is told at one point, "yawns a veritable abyss of meaning"—was bound to have profound repercussions on the search for "absolute origins." On the one hand, Husserl characterized consciousness
as an "immanent" and "absolute being" which "*nulla 're' indiget ad
existendum*"; on the other hand, cognition was defined in principle
as "consciousness *of* something"—where "something" could not reside
in consciousness if it was to be its object. "Consciousness," Adorno
summarized the dilemma, "whose evidence constitutes for Husserl
the sole source of knowledge, is juxtaposed from the beginning to a
transcendent world whose existence is not established by consciousness, although it derives its epistemological legitimacy only from its
reference to consciousness. . . . The assumption of a transcendent
world, however, is in conflict with the premise of consciousness as
a 'sphere of absolute origins'; it contradicts the basic principle of transcendental idealism."[5]

Exploring the background and ramifications of the dilemma,
Adorno traced Husserl's dualism to his disregard of submerged synthetic functions of consciousness. In Husserl's view, all knowledge
required vindication through direct experience; since the structural
or "primary" qualities of objects were immune from such experience,
recourse was taken to an extramental or "transcendent" status. According to Adorno, however, such recourse was spurious and unneces-
sary. The structural solidity of objects, he suggested, was due not to
a supposed transcendence but to their inherence in the apriori categories of mind—categories which were not accessible to direct experience. In his words: "Objects are not experiences but relationships
between experiences—laws or rules for their occurrence; as such they
are strictly and completely immanent in the framework of consciousness." Once the status of objects or things was clarified in this man-

ner, Husserl's concept of "noema" was placed in jeopardy. Differentiated from the "unreduced" world of reality and simultaneously from
the "noetic" acts of consciousness, the noema (or "intentional object")
in Adorno's judgment was a "hybrid" of mental and naturalistic ingredients: "neither immanent nor transcendent, suspended so-to-speak
in mid-air." If, however, the distinction between "reduced" and "unreduced" objects proved to be spurious, the entire phenomenological
method of reduction or *epoché* emerged as redundant and illegitimate.
Bracketing, Adorno urged, could not simply be used as a heuristic
method of inquiry, since any attempt to talk sensibly about the world
(including the world of the "natural attitude") required reliance on the
framework of consciousness. By way of conclusion, the thesis reviewed
Husserl's endeavor to link transcendence and consciousness "in the
long run," by submitting questions of "reality" and "unreality" to the
"jurisdiction of reason." In order to satisfy the postulate of immediate
evidence, Husserl was forced to the conclusion that the "idea" of a
transcendent object was directly evident in consciousness, although
its substantive content remained the goal of indefinite approximation.
This outcome, the thesis commented, was avoidable once the (paradoxical) idea of transcendence was replaced by the notion of the object as an "ideal rule" of appearances.[6]

The perspective of transcendental idealism—inspired partly by
Kant but actually fashioned by Cornelius—continued to dominate
Adorno's thinking for several more years, although reality, especially
social reality, began to impinge increasingly on transcendental formulas. Cornelius's influence was still evident in Adorno's first (subsequently discarded) *Habilitationsschrift* of 1927 which bore the title
"The Concept of the Unconscious in Transcendental Psychology" ("Der
Begriff des Unbewussten in der transzendentalen Seelenlehre"). The
central aim of the study was the elucidation of the meaning of "unconsciousness," a notion which had gained wide currency owing not
only to depth psychology but also to various anti-rationalist currents
of the time. Basically, the same approach which had been used to assess the status of "object" and "noema" in Husserl's thought was now
applied to the analysis of the new topic. Countering allegations that
the unconscious denoted an extra-mental realm of nature or a transcendent "thing-in-itself," Adorno insisted that all the qualities and
traits normally associated with the concept could be traced back to
the framework or reservoir of consciousness. As presented in the study,
the unconscious was a complex domain comprising chiefly a quasi-
experiential and an objective-categorial layer. While the former referred
to concrete experiences which had been forgotten or expunged from

memory, the second layer denoted a framework of lawful relationships or categorial rules which, though not accessible to direct experience, was the condition of the possibility of awareness. As tools for the recovery of these layers, the study recommended not only transcendental reflection but also Freudian psychoanalysis, chiefly because of Freud's simultaneous focus on conscious meaning and on hidden but rationally ascertainable psychic laws.[7]

Despite its somewhat academic or scholastic flavor, Adorno's study (in my view) still deserves attention for several reasons. First of all, the exploration of unconsciousness signaled Adorno's initial encounter with Freudian depth psychology, laying the ground for a life-long fascination. More directly important for present purposes is the study's frontal attack against (what one may call) "ontological objectivism" or "naturalism"—specifically against the doctrine that the unconscious was somehow a realm beyond consciousness and therefore immune from critical rational scrutiny. This polemical thrust, it seems to me, can be characterized as a core ingredient of Adorno's intellectual posture, an ingredient which survived his philosophical transformations virtually untouched. Subsequently—in fact soon after writing the study—Adorno came to question and finally to abandon idealism; this abandonment, however, never produced a sympathy for objectivism or a naturalistic ontology. To be sure, the simultaneous rejection of idealism and objectivism necessitated a move beyond traditional school doctrines and a recourse to complex philosophical arguments—what accounts at least in part for the "difficulty" of Adorno's later writings. Matters were relatively simple in the treatise of 1927. At that time what was at issue was the more or less straightforward confrontation between idealism and naturalism, between reason and unreason. As Adorno himself indicated, the analysis of the unconscious was bound to contribute to the "demystification" of supposedly irrational psychic forces. In this sense, the study was committed to the goal of rational "enlightenment"—the term taken in the dual sense of conceptual clarification and of the broader emancipation from dogma or spurious natural constraints.[8]

In contrast to the earlier dissertation, incidentally, the study of 1927 was not silent on the social and political ramifications of its topic. The scrutiny of the unconscious, Adorno affirmed, was prompted not merely by theoretical or speculative motives. In denouncing vitalistic and organismic ontologies and their attempt to convert depth psychology into a weapon against "rationalism," the study meant to challenge broad currents of the *Zeitgeist* which played a "clearly specified and dangerous role" in the social situation of the time. Briefly put,

this role was to provide an alibi and ideological camouflage for prevailing social and economic practices. Precisely because a developed
industrial and capitalistic society was far removed from any "natural"
or "organismic" order, the domain of the unconscious could serve as
a welcome supplement or counterpoise—a supplement granting individuals a temporary, albeit imaginary, refuge from the harsh features of economic competition. More importantly, the conception of
hidden and uncontrollable psychic constraints pointed to the dark
underside of the capitalistic system: its proclivity toward domestic
and foreign exploitation and its tendency periodically to be convulsed
by economic crisis. "Not only limitless egotism," the study noted, "but
also the most sinister machinations of imperialism find their ideological justification in the natural eruptions of unconscious psychic
impulses." On this level, irrational dogmatism and economic domination were inextricable allies: "In order to escape rational criticism
once and for all, imperialistic trends—most directly the ideology of
fascism—rely on ontological, extra-mental, transcendent and somehow sacred forces which present the destructive and self-destructive
effects of the economy as divinely ordained and necessary."[9]

The cited passages were evidence of emerging concerns and directions in Adorno's thought—concerns which could only with difficulty
be reconciled with his academic background and training. In conjunction with new intellectual attachments and loyalties, the darkening
political horizon in Europe steadily eroded his idealist moorings, while
strengthening his distaste for capitalism and bourgeois practices.[10]
When, in 1931, Adorno delivered his inaugural lecture as a teacher
at Frankfurt University, the tone and substance of his arguments had
profoundly changed. Entitled "The Role of Philosophy Today," the lecture contained no reference to Cornelius but several to Walter Benjamin, the Marxist aesthetician and literary critic, to whom it was
intended as a tribute. The opening sentences of the lecture were programmatic in character. "Whoever chooses philosophy as a profession
today," Adorno stated, "must from the very start renounce an illusion
which animated philosophical projects in the past: the illusion that
thought is able to grasp reality as a whole. No rational jurisdiction
can hold sway over a universe whose very structure repels the demands
of reason; a polemical ploy when treated as a whole, reality sustains
only in ruins and dispersed traces the hope of developing into a rational and decent world." Down to recent ontological conceptions,
Adorno added, much of traditional philosophy had been predicated
on the sovereign power of reason: more particularly on the premise
that thinking was somehow an adequate match for reality and even

for "being" itself (conceived as "idea" or essence of the universe). However, "the commensurability between thought and reality as a whole has disintegrated," with the result that "the idea of being has become philosophically impotent." The disintegration was a particularly rude blow to idealism—a perspective wedded more than any other to the absorption of reality by consciousness: "The crisis of idealism equals a crisis of the philosophical demand for total understanding."[11]

To illustrate the predicaments of philosophical reasoning, the lecture provided a brief survey of major contemporary trends or schools, including variants of neo-Kantianism and life-philosophy. Special attention was given in this context to the phenomenological movement. In a striking departure from the earlier dissertation, Husserl's approach was no longer chided for being insufficiently idealist, but rather for remaining a prisoner of the past. In general terms, phenomenology was defined as a "post-idealist" version of idealism, as "an effort to reach objectively valid conclusions after the collapse of idealism but with the very instrument of idealism": autonomous reason or subjective consciousness. In Husserl's case, the endeavor to reach objective reality was manifest in his reliance on "primordial evidence" and in his development of a rigorous method of phenomenological description; nevertheless, every evidence and every description were in the end rooted in the absolute jurisdiction of reason and transcendental consciousness. What lent Husserl's approach its special (not unattractive) flavor was his intellectual modesty and sobriety: his willingness to confine thought to the description and intentional replication of the world—whose real structure and movement remained beyond consciousness and rational control. This modesty was abandoned by his successors, with no solid gain compensating for the loss. According to Adorno, Scheler's writings were dedicated to the reconciliation of consciousness and objective or substantive reality and thus to the formulation of a "material phenomenology"; however, after experimenting with a number of dogmatic worldviews, he ultimately settled for a Manichean juxtaposition of material and ideal forces, of vitalism and rationalism. In Heidegger's case, the attempt to escape the bounds of consciousness took the paradoxical form of a direct assignment of substantive features to subjectivity—producing a "subjective ontology" in which concrete personal and historical experience acquired immediate ontological dignity. With this turn, phenomenology lapsed into its opposite: "Ontology honors only those categories whose dominion phenomenology sought to challenge: mere (mundane) subjectivity and historicity."[12]

Turning to the possible role of philosophical reflection in our

time, Adorno credited science and scientific rationality for debunk-
ing the excessive pretensions of speculative thought; however, he was
by no means ready to accept an "underlaborer" conception reducing
reflection to the handmaiden of science. Precisely when rigorously
pursued, empirical science could not claim self-sufficiency, since the
term "empiricism" itself presupposed thought. Even in a scientific
age, Adorno argued, science and philosophy were differentiated (though
not segregated) by diverse tasks: the tasks respectively of empirical
research and of interpretation, the former committed to relatively secure findings, the latter to permanent questioning. As the lecture
strongly insisted, however, "interpretation" did not and could not involve a probing of the inherent or underlying "meaning" of reality, since
reality was impervious to human purpose and subjective intentionality. The text which philosophy had to decipher was not a coherent
story but "incomplete, contradictory and fragile, in many passages perhaps the work of blind demons." Rather than delving into symbolism,
philosophical interpretation—faced with a non-intentional world—
had to resort to experimentation: to the arrangement of individual
parts or elements into new patterns or structural designs, in the hope
of finding the key which would unlock reality's riddle and thereby
break its spell.[13] In its reliance on experimentation, interpretation
—according to Adorno—was closely akin to dialectical materialism
whose aim likewise was to find the proper passkey to a basically non-
intentional and non-symbolic reality; actually, materialism's ability
to reach its goal was directly proportional to its success in "cleansing
its subject matter from any reference to 'meaning'." The affinity between interpretation and materialism extended to the effect of the
experimental method: the construction of a fitting design was not
merely a theoretical exercise, but meant to dislodge the strangle-hold
of social constraints. From a materialist perspective, this relationship
between theory and practical change was known under the label of
"dialectics."[14]

Adorno's inaugural lecture was an impressive and even provocative statement. Its review of intellectual currents was trenchant;
so was its critique of philosophical self-sufficiency, of the pretension
of reason to find within itself a reservoir of "absolute origins." Nevertheless, despite these qualities, portions of the arguments remained
uneven and subject to instant rejoinders. Thus, the juxtaposition of
interpretation and a non-intentional reality conjured up, albeit in a
new disguise, the Cartesian legacy of dualism which Adorno had castigated previously in Husserl's writings. Moreover, in stressing the experimental function of interpretation, the lecture seemed to equate

reflection with a purely "instrumental" type of rationality—or in any case with the construction of "heuristic" frameworks and models (familiar from positivist methodology as preambles to research).[15] In large measure, shortcomings of this kind were remedied or offset in a number of essays written by Adorno shortly before the collapse of the Weimar Republic. For present purposes, two major notions delineated in these essays deserve brief mention: those of "natural history" and of the "configurative" role of language. Reformulated and reassessed on subsequent occasions, both notions were destined to develop into central ingredients of Adorno's posture.

The first conception was sketched in a paper of 1932 entitled "The Idea of Natural History." The paper's point of departure was again the relationship between human design and unintentional world; however, the two domains were no longer presented as segregated and self-contained. As the opening paragraphs stated, the goal of the paper was to overcome the "customary antithesis" of the domains—now formulated as that between "nature and history"—and to push both to the point where their affinity and reciprocal impact emerged behind their difference. The term "nature" in this context was not (or not necessarily) meant to refer to the object of natural science, but rather to a realm of substantive, preordained or necessary reality in contrast to the dynamic, innovative features of historical life. As Adorno recognized, the phenomenological movement—especially in its post-Husserlian phase—had tried to overcome the antithesis. From its inception, he noted, phenomenology was characterized and permeated by the tension between nature and history; efforts of Husserl's successors to relieve the tension, however, were marred by the continued sway of idealist premises. Scheler's attempt to establish an ontological realm of objective and timeless meaning was vitiated by the arbitrary, subjective character of the chosen categories. The endeavor was intensified and radicalized by Heidegger who, instead of moving beyond appearance, coalesced and collapsed ontology and concrete historical existence; even in this case, however, idealism finally triumphed —as demonstrated in Heidegger's resort to tautological formulas submerging contingent experience in abstract concepts, and also in his stress on the notions of "totality" and human "project."[16]

In order to make headway beyond the phenomenological initiatives, Adorno argued, it was necessary not so much to indulge in conceptual synthesis as to hew as closely as possible to concrete contingency and to the actual interdependence of domains. What was at issue was not merely to establish a speculative correlation but to show how history in its very historicity was pervaded by nature just as nature in its presumed autonomy was a historical occurrence. The notion of "natural history" pointed in this direction. Two thinkers could claim parentage of the notion: Lukács and Benjamin. In his *Theory of the Novel*, Lukács had coined the term "second nature" to designate those layers of historical experience which had been emptied of meaning—which (to use his words) had been turned into "frozen, alien" complexes, into a "golgotha of decomposed internality." The notion was developed further by Benjamin, with less romanticism and more rigor. While Lukács' "second nature" was virtually cut off from history and only recoverable through an eschatological intervention, Benjamin presented history as an intrinsically "natural" process, due to its largely unintentional, inchoate and fragmentary character. At the same time, nature in his view bore a profoundly historical imprint —owing to the fact that it was transitory and perishable not only in its elements but in its core. The connecting link between nature and history, from this perspective, was provided by the aspect of finitude and mortality. Against the foil of nature, the story of human and social evolution revealed itself as a story of suffering or universal calvary "significant only at the points of decay." Under Benjamin's radical scrutiny—Adorno commented—"reality is transformed into a panorama of ruins and fragments, into a golgotha of experience where the key to the nexus of history and nature is buried."[17]

The notion of "configuration" was delineated first in an essay written at about the same time, entitled "Theses on the Language of Philosophers." The essay was directed chiefly against nominalist-instrumentalist as well as against idealist conceptions of language. Under the impact of modern subjectivism, Adorno noted, words or linguistic symbols have progressively been converted into vehicles of individual consciousness or intentionality; as a consequence, the intimate nexus of linguistic form and content has been sundered and been replaced by a contingent relationship amenable to arbitrary manipulation. To obviate this result, idealism sometimes presented language as adjunct of "objective" mind, as a self-contained reservoir of essential meanings; far from providing a corrective, however, this maneuver merely solidified the barrier between form and content. According to Adorno, a basic task of contemporary philosophy was to dismantle this barrier and to restore to language its openness to the world. The task, in his view, could not be accomplished by indulging in neologisms or linguistic idiosyncracy—in Heidegger's vein; instead of resorting to artifice, philosophy had to rely on ordinary language conceived not as an integrated fabric but as an array of fragmentary and partially decomposed concepts. The purpose of a "configurative" approach was to assemble words or symbols into nodal patterns or counterpoint arrangements which, bypassing subjective intentionality and conventional wisdom, would allow actual historical experience to "break into," and become manifest in, language. Given the linkage of form and content in this perspective, words or linguistic symbols were no longer mere utensils, but acquired intrinsic importance in the quest for truth: "The growing significance of a philosophical critique of language can be formulated as the beginning convergence of (literary) art and cognition."[18]

Shortly after the discussed essays were written, the Weimar Republic fell victim to the Nazi seizure of power—an event which disrupted and unhinged any unilinear teleology or purposive thrust which Western society, especially since the Enlightenment, may have followed. The event also completely disrupted Adorno's own life pattern, forcing him into emigration and prolonged exile. His odyssey took him first to England, more particularly to Oxford, and later to the United States. The move, in 1938, to America heralded Adorno's formal affiliation with the Institute of Social Research which, after a brief interlude in Geneva, had by that time been relocated at Columbia University. The invitation to join the Institute came from its director, Max Horkheimer, who had been a fellow-student under Cornelius in Frankfurt and who, like Adorno, had journeyed from idealism in the direction of a non-orthodox (and anti-positivist) dialectical materialism. The affiliation set the stage for a series of collaborative efforts and team investigations, many of which centered on circumscribed sociological and social-psychological topics. In the present context one collaborative venture in the area of broad philosophical exegesis deserves brief mention: *Dialectic of Enlightenment*, written by Adorno and Horkheimer during the war years and published for the first time in 1947.

In a sense, the study can be viewed as a capstone of Adorno's (and Horkheimer's) intellectual development during the preceding decades. The growing disenchantment with modern idealism and subjectivism, evident in earlier writings, led in the *Dialectic* to the recognition of a deep-seated crisis in Western life: the recognition that modern Enlightenment, with its stress on the emancipation of reason from nature, had progressively transformed the world into an assembly of objects for consciousness and ultimately into an arena of utensils for human manipulation and domination. The rise of instrumental rationality, however, was by no means synonymous with a growth in actual freedom. Due to the dialectical character of the master-slave relationship, man's mastery over nature coincided with his progressive enslavement by natural constraints, more precisely by the dictates of a naturalistic objectivism which governed not only man's contacts with nature but social or intersubjective relations as well. For Adorno and Horkheimer, the remedy for the sketched crisis resided not in an abdication of reason, and especially not in a surrender of thought to mystical visions or to a new "myth of the twentieth century." Despite its problematic effects, rationalism in their view was an experiential dilemma which had to be sustained in its ambivalence—until thought itself was able to break the spell of instrumental domination. Rather than signifying unilinear progress or regress, enlightenment was a sinew of "natural history." The basic critical thrust of the study, according to its authors, could be summarized in two theses: "that mythology points toward enlightenment, just as enlightenment tends to lapse into mythology."[19]

II
(The Metacritique of Phenomenology)

Adorno's association with the Institute, and especially with Horkheimer, occurred when he was approaching the mature height of his productive energies—not all of which could be absorbed in collaborative endeavors. The various notions and vistas which had been sketched in preceding publications were beginning to coalesce into an autonomous and complex version of "critical theory," a perspective which could compete with, and challenge the claims of, alternative philosophical currents of the time. To be sure, Adorno's outlook was not hospitable to a narrow polemicism; his diversified interests—including his prolific explorations in aesthetic and musical theory—shielded him from the temptation of formulating and defending a compact school doctrine. Yet, in comparison with other members of the Institute, Adorno was more acutely aware of the need to justify his arguments on strictly philosophical grounds; a large and important share of his mature writings were thus devoted to the task of philosophical criticism—a task for which he was eminently prepared by virtue of his philosophical training and his close familiarity with contemporary philosophical literature. Central among the targets of this criticism was a perspective or current which had occupied his attention since his student days: phenomenology or the "phenomenological movement," as represented chiefly by Husserl and Heidegger. His critical efforts in this domain culminated in several major studies which were published after his return to Frankfurt (in 1949):

especially *Towards a Metacritique of Epistemology* and *Negative Dialectics.*

Adorno's preoccupation with Husserl's brand of phenomenology had continued unabated since the time of his dissertation. As previously indicated, the philosophical underpinnings or premises of the study were abandoned within a few years after its completion; the implications of this change for the topic of inquiry, however, were unclear and surfaced only in sporadic comments during the Weimar period. After his emigration to England, Adorno returned in a sustained manner to the theme of his dissertation. While staying at Merton College in Oxford, he began to lay the groundwork for a comprehensive critical analysis of Husserl's thought and of phenomenology in general. Glimpses of Adorno's evolving views during the exile years can be gleaned from an essay which appeared in an American philosophy journal in 1940, under the title "Husserl and the Problem of Idealism." The essay reiterated and corroborated in greater detail some notions which had emerged in earlier contexts: especially the notion that Husserlian phenomenology was a perspective characterized by a tension or contradiction between idealism and realism — more specifically by the ambition to grasp a world of "things-in-themselves" on the basis of idealist premises (and also by the parallel ambition to overcome positivism through a positivist belief in absolute or objective "givenness"). As Adorno noted: "It appears to me that Husserl's philosophy was precisely an attempt to destroy idealism from within, an attempt with the means of consciousness to break through the wall of transcendental analysis, while at the same time trying to carry such an analysis as far as possible." The difficulties and paradoxes encountered in this quest, he added, were due chiefly to the circumstance that Husserl "never fully freed himself from the presuppositions of idealism."[20]

In order to illustrate this argument, the essay relied chiefly on the concepts of "intentionality" and "categorial intuition" (or *Wesensschau*) as outlined in *Logical Investigations* and *Ideas.* According to Adorno, the impact of Husserl's work on his generation derived mainly from its relentless "objectivist" thrust — that is, from its effort to rescue objective truth and meaning from the tentacles of a naive positivism and "relativistic psychologism." In this departure from positivism Adorno recognized one of its lasting achievements.[21] Simultaneously Husserl realized, however, that the postulate of objectivity was spurious and dogmatic in the absence of cognitive evidence and awareness. The notions of "intentionality" and "categorial intuition" were formulated to provide a bridge between thought and its objects; the

latter concept, in particular, was meant to establish the foundation
for the direct cognitive access to essentials or "ideal realities" (*ideale
Tatbestände*). Yet: how solid was this philosophical bridge and in
which sense were essences both ideal and real? Did the notion of "categorial intuition" not signify a return to "Platonic realism" and thus
a relapse into the dilemmas of a "doubled world"? More important:
how could "categorial intuition" be at the same time a cognitive and
judgmental act and a mere receptacle of pre-given, objective entities
—without shortchanging the mediated character of judgmental reflection, and also without shortchanging the concrete immediacy of intuitive experience? In the end, Adorno argued, Husserl's striving for
objectivity and realism had to resort to an apriori framework of mental categories—a framework even more transcendental and non-real
than in Kant's case. Husserl "wants to go to the *Sachen*," he wrote,
"not merely for avoiding the fallacies of arbitrary conceptual construction, but for getting hold of an absolutely secure, unshakable, unchal-
lengeable truth. This desire, however, to get hold of the absolute and,
in the last analysis, to deduce with an absolute stringency everything
from an absolute point, is an idealist desire, dwelling in the refuge
of an anti-idealist philosophy." Against this background the doctrine
of essences—regarded as Husserl's "main anti-idealist stroke"—revealed
itself "as the summit of idealism: the pure essence, the objectivity
of which seems to spurn any subjective constitution, is nothing but
subjectivity in its abstractness."[22]

Portions of the essay—together with other manuscripts or fragments written both before and after the war—were later incorporated
into the *Metacritique* which first appeared in 1956. As its subtitle
indicated, the chief aim of the study was to investigate and expose
the "phenomenological antinomies" evident in Husserl's thought. As
on previous occasions, but in a more rigorous and sustained fashion,
Adorno's attention was focused on the dilemmas of a post-idealist
idealism: on the effort to encompass reality by means of a purified
consciousness and, above all, on the overarching ambition to convert
subjectivity into a foundation if not a synonym for ontology. Regarding the search for foundational insights or an ontological framework,
the study occasionally went beyond the confines of Husserl's writings and extended its critical indictment to his successors and the
entire phenomenological movement, including Heidegger's existential analysis. For purposes of brevity, the present discussion will try
to limit itself as closely as possible to the narrower theme of transcendental phenomenology.

The basic thrust of Adorno's argument was sharply delineated in the opening statements of the study. Husserl's program, he wrote, "aims to uncover a 'sphere of absolute origins', immune from that 'organized spirit of contradiction'" which characterized Hegel's dialectical procedure. In the pursuit of this goal, Husserl was heir to a central and longstanding tradition in Western thought: the tradition of *prima philosophia,* of the search for "first principles" or "first beginnings." As one of the last outstanding examples of this legacy, his work also illustrated the contradictions or paradoxes inherent in traditional metaphysics: especially the contradictions arising from the attempt to found ontology on the bedrock of subjectivity. Husserl, one reads, "tries to reestablish *prima philosophia* by reflecting on a spirit or mind purged of any trace of ontic reality. The same metaphysical ambition which marked the beginning of the modern age reemerges at its end in a more sophisticated but also more emphatic and blunt manner: the ambition to develop an ontology (or doctrine of being) under nominalistic auspices, that is, on the basis of concepts derived from the thinking subject." According to Adorno, the paradox involved in this ambition was of the nature not of a dialectical tension, but of a simple antinomy: for it was contradictory to assume "that a doctrine of being—transcending subjectivity and its critical impulse—could be constructed, overtly or covertly, through recourse to the same subjective reflection by which the dogmatic character of ontology has successfully been unmasked."[23]

The linkage of objective foundations and subjectivity, in Adorno's view, had been the emblem of ontology since its inception. In every instance, ontology conceived as *prima philosophia* had tended to truncate the critical, mediating role of reflection by claiming to grant direct access to a "sphere of absolute origins" or to a realm of objective being "in-itself": "The first principles of philosophers involve a total claim: namely, that to be unmediated or immediate. In order to satisfy this claim, all mediations have to be removed as mere mental contraband, leaving behind the irreducible core of being-in-itself." However, the regress to foundations or first beginnings was deceptive and spurious. In Adorno's words: "There is no level of immediacy on which philosophy can hope to escape the mediating function of reflection; no factual reality is accessible to philosophy except through thought." Ultimately, the vice of *prima philosophia* consisted in the indiscriminate fusion of opposites—in the pretense of laying the groundwork for the merger or identity of subject and object, consciousness and reality: "Through the awakening of reflection (*noein*) a process is unleashed which necessarily destroys the pure identity or self-sufficiency of being (*einai*)." Transcendental phenomenology shared with traditional ontology the addiction to unmediated origins and ultimate identity. "The identity of spirit with itself or the 'synthetic unity of apperception,'" Adorno noted, "is projected onto the 'things themselves' by means of a methodological ploy (such as *epoché*) and the thoroughness of the projection corresponds directly to the rigor of methodology. This is the original sin of *prima philosophia*. The philosophy of first beginnings which initially generated the idea of truth is in its very beginnings a falsehood (*pseudos*)."[24]

In Adorno's presentation, the history of Western philosophy or metaphysics has been a story of growing falsehood or deception. The development of rational thought produced increasingly subtle and sophisticated attempts to camouflage the rift or contradiction embedded in the foundations of reason. "The progressive emancipation of rationality," Adorno observed, "requiring progressively complex mediations, led to more and more elaborate (though ultimately unsuccessful) devices to conceal the internal rift. In this manner the falsehood of first beginnings has been steadily intensified." In recent or contemporary ontological conceptions, the widening breach between thought and reality had given rise to drastic countermeasures, to efforts to resurrect first beginnings through intellectual fiat: "Subjectivism promulgates the law of objectivity." The notion of beginnings has tended to become in our time a synonym for primitivism and even for unreflected dogma: "Origins are purchased at the price of reflection." Husserl, to be sure, was not simply a doctrinaire ontologist. As Adorno acknowledged, Husserl's thought differed from competing perspectives by virtue of his stress on cognition and on the painstaking description of phenomena: *prima philosophia* in his case "took the rigorous-scientific form of epistemology." However, the attempt to erect consciousness or subjective reflection into a foundation of absolute knowledge was bound to fail due to a basic insufficiency of consciousness: "First beginnings cannot be identified with subjective reflection since subjectivity can never hope to absorb non-identical elements, and since reflection militates against the notion of immediately given beginnings. While *prima philosophia* aims at pure identity in a monistic fashion, subjectivity—supposedly the source of secure knowledge—cannot be leveled into monistic congruence."[25]

According to Adorno, Husserl's work provided itself testimony of the incongruence or insufficiency of subjective reflection. At crucial junctures, the postulated foundational structure generated intrinsic antinomies or polarities, especially the polarities between noesis and noema and between consciousness and external reality. As Adorno indicated, the antinomial character of Husserl's thought was reflected also in the juxtaposition of "apriorism," on the one hand, and naturalistic empiricism on the other. Husserl's theory of knowledge, he observed, derived its vindication from transcendental subjectivity or the notion of the *"eidos ego,"* while simultaneously claiming to grant access to an objective realm transcending subjective parameters. The term "phenomenology" expressed the inherently antinomial ambition to grasp "transsubjective 'things-in-themselves' as they appear to subjective consciousness." The very stress on transcendental reflection, in Adorno's view, had the result of transforming the world into external objects of consciousness, while relegating subjectivity to the status of an apriori premise devoid of concrete implications. In this respect, phenomenology was akin to early or still photography: "Just like the photographer of earlier days the phenomenologist covers himself with the black sheet of his 'epoché', entreats his objects not to move and finally snaps a family portrait in a passive manner without spontaneous involvement. . . . The same correlation which exists in photography between *camera obscura* and external object prevails in phenomenology with regard to immanent (or self-contained) consciousness and naive realism."[26]

The sketched epistemological dilemmas, Adorno added, were indicative of the social and political ramifications of Husserl's thought: phenomenological "reduction" and description corresponded closely to the situation of late-industrial society where the bourgeois individual—while still clinging to the doctrine of original freedom and contractual autonomy—was increasingly forced to retreat from public life into complete privacy and to adopt the role of passive recipient or consumer of goods and services. With the liberal individualism of an earlier age, today's consumer mentality was linked through the stress on the "possessive" character of man, on the individual's proclivity to treat the entire world (including cognitive insights) as personal property. Through its emphasis on absolute certainty and apriori evidence, Adorno wrote, Husserl's *prima philosophia* revealed itself as a theory of property: "Once the idealistic notion of transcendental subjectivity is accepted as central category, nothing remains that does not fall prey and in a strict sense belong to subjectivity." By comparison with past versions, contemporary individualism was marked by its bland and noncommittal character. From this perspective, Husserl's endeavor to move beyond Descartes toward pure reflection carried a price: that of progressive neutralization and privatization. While at the dawn of modernity, individualism was involved in public life as an agency transforming hierarchical feudalism, transcendental subjectivity was a synonym for passive consumption. In Adorno's words, Husserl's method was not so much an exercise of critical reason as an effort "to neutralize factual conditions whose dominance and legitimacy are no longer seriously questioned." With the advent of phenomenology "bourgeois thought in its final stages dissolves into isolated, fragmented categories and finds comfort in the mere reproduction of reality."[27]

As illustrated in its linkage with bourgeois society, phenomenology was intimately tied to the fortunes of modern Western individualism — and ultimately to the fate of Western metaphysics construed as a philosophy of consciousness. Erected on subjective reflection as pillar of *prima philosophia*, Western metaphysics was unable to break through its cognitive boundaries and thus condemned to persistent antinomies. The remedy to metaphysical quandaries could not be found in a further refinement of consciousness which merely accentuated its imprisonment. "The metacritique of epistemology," Adorno wrote, "requires the reflective reconstruction of its parameters as a nexus of guilt and punishment, of necessary mistake and unsuccessful correction." As he added, the basic illusion of metaphysics was the assumption that rational consistency was somehow a replica of reality and that thought was able to absorb the world; rather than extending the range of cognition, the task of "thinking the unthought" disrupted reason's claim to sovereignty. To be sure, awareness of the limits of reflection did not vindicate a leap into unreflected objectivism or immediacy (a leap practiced both by "contemporary ontologists" and the "intellectual functionaries of the East"). The defects of reason could be combated only by pushing reflection to its limits and by uncovering its mediating, dialectical role. By disclosing "non-identity" in the midst of sameness and "newness" at the heart of oldness or permanence, post-metaphysical thought was an exercise in "natural historiography": "Attentive to the suffering sedimented in concepts, such thought waits only for the moment of their disintegration. . . . What is needed today is not a first but a last philosophy."[28]

III
(Ontology and Negative Dialectics)

Although focusing chiefly on Husserl's writings, Adorno's arguments in the *Metacritique* were not narrowly confined to the topic of transcendental phenomenology. The indictment of *prima philosophia* was meant to apply with equal force to the entire phenomenological movement and especially to Heidegger's existential analysis or "fundamental ontology." Since the time of the Weimar Republic, Heidegger had repeatedly occupied Adorno's critical attention; some of the essays written prior to his emigration had sketched the contours of a philosophical rejoinder—contours which later were redrawn more carefully and with greater attention to detail. In the inaugural lecture of 1931, Heidegger's posture had been characterized as a precarious blend of subjectivism and ontological speculation, as an attempt to transcend the limits of consciousness through a leap into objectivism which insufficiently concealed its subjectivist motivations. In the paper on "natural history," *Being and Time* had been castigated for its indulgence in tautology and grandiloquence. Heidegger's notion of *Dasein* or existence, Adorno observed at the time, was merely an abstract and reified synonym for subjective experience, just as the term "historicity" was an ontological cloak designed to dress up contingent historical events.

On the whole, references to Heidegger in the *Metacritique* reiterated and fleshed out the critical arguments of earlier papers. As Adorno tried to show, Heidegger's perspective involved not so much a move beyond Husserl's antinomies, but the attempt to camouflage and suppress internal conflicts, especially the conflict between "timeless ontology and history." Both thinkers—the *Metacritique* noted—were engaged in the search for "first principles" or "first beginnings"; in Heidegger's case, however, subjectivity gave way to a foundational structure supposedly aloof of subjective reflection and endowed with objective-ontological significance: man's existential condition as rooted in being. Owing to the non-reflective and even anti-reflective character of this foundation, *prima philosophia* in Heidegger's version acquired an aura of compactness and archaic simplicity unequaled in Husserl's work: "Whatever is lasting and solid appears to philosophical speculation as basic and primordial. . . . On the assumption that the basis (*hypokeimenon*) is truer than the superstructure, truth and primitivism become synonymous. This is perhaps the most dangerous consequence of the doctrine of immediacy with its suppression of subjectivity and reflective mediations." Actually, Adorno added, the leap into immediacy yielded only a counterfeit objectivity: as in the case of traditional metaphysics, the postulate of objective ontological beginnings was ultimately an outgrowth of subjective fiat. Heidegger's insistence on the non-reflective and non-volitional status of existential categories merely accentuated the incongruence of *prima philosophia*, revealing "the arbitrary character of premises which supposedly are immune from arbitrary volition."[29]

Following the completion of the *Metacritique*, Heidegger's

thought steadily moved toward the center of Adorno's philosophical concerns. A first manifestation of this growing preoccupation was a study published in 1964, under the title *The Jargon of Authenticity*. The title of the study referred to certain linguistic habits or speech patterns which had become prominent in postwar Germany and whose chief trademark was the overburdening of language with philosophical meaning. According to Adorno, the jargon was basically a shortcut in the phenomenological (and neo-Romantic) quest of origins and first beginnings, in the sense that ontological profundity and archaic dignity were immediately bestowed on terms used in ordinary speech, while philosophical reflection was truncated. The outcome was a mixture of pseudo-objective concreteness and subjective idiosyncracy. Without direct appeal to revelation or a spiritual authority, Adorno noted, the adepts of the jargon simulate "the ascension of the word beyond the realm of the actual, conditioned, and contestable," giving the impression "as though a blessing from above were directly composed into that word"; as a result, hypocrisy "becomes foundational and everyday language is spoken here and now as if it were the sacred one." Socially and politically the jargon, in Adorno's view, was an expression of the withdrawal into privacy or subjective resentment on the part of a declining lower middle class incapable of shaping or altering its fate: "From its inability to cope practically or spiritually with social development, this class derives its claim to a special, elect status: that of primordial authenticity."[30]

Although superior in subtlety to popularized versions, Heidegger's philosophy was marked by an intrinsic proclivity to jargon. Like other central Heideggerian notions, Adorno observed, existence or *Dasein* was a deeply ambivalent term, suggesting a confluence of concrete experience and ontological foundation. Actually, the entire thrust of Heidegger's thought — his *"scène à faire"* — consisted in the effort not so much to overcome as to collapse traditional dichotomies, such as those between apriori and aposteriori, essence and fact, subject and object. "As is well known," the study indicated, "Heidegger supplants the traditional category of subjectivity by *Dasein* whose essence is said to be existence." This reformulation enabled him to take his point of departure from a concrete condition or givenness — an object of consciousness in terms of traditional epistemology — while at the same time treating this condition as "more than mere fact," as an "absolute primordial premise" or a "pure condition of being." Moving beyond Husserl, Heidegger preferred to interpret "subjectivity as a concept of indifference: essence and fact in one." According to *Being and Time*, the advantage of the notion of *Dasein* was twofold: on the one hand, it designated an ontic domain coextensive with concrete individual existence; on the other hand, it pointed to an ontological structure: "In this manner radically contradictory connotations are directly ascribed to subjectivity: it is treated as fact or reality and simultaneously—in line with traditional philosophy—it is viewed as consciousness and thus as basic condition of facticity, as its pure concept, its essence, and ultimately as Husserl's *eidos ego.*" Against this background, Adorno added, Heidegger's notion of *Dasein* emerged as a synonym for "a subjectivity without subject—a decapitated version of Fichte's absolute ego."[31]

As in the case of *Dasein*, Heidegger's "camouflaged idealism" or subjective objectivism was evident also in the concept of "authenticity." On the one hand, his use of the concept was indebted to Husserl's quest for objective reality or the realm of "things-in-themselves" —a quest which implied that the essence or authentic core of things was "not something arbitrarily fabricated by subjective thought, not a distilled synthesis of characteristics." As Adorno observed, Heidegger remained heir to Husserl's approach to the extent that it treated authenticity "directly as an aspect of things and thus as a special domain of reality"; from this legacy derived "the substantialization of authenticity, its elevation to an existential category and to a status of givenness" aloof from subjective reflection and amenable to a "purely descriptive account." Viewed from this perspective, Heidegger's use of the concept gave rise to reification and even naturalistic determinism: "Introduced initially as a descriptive category in response to the relatively innocuous question regarding the essential core of things, authenticity develops into a mythically imposed destiny; despite the antinaturalistic thrust of an ontology erected on transcendental foundations, the category operates as a naturalistic constraint." At the same time, however, Heidegger never succeeded in eradicating the subjectivist and idealist premises of the concept. According to Adorno, these premises were manifest in the treatment of authenticity as a personal (albeit purely internalized) property—as a final yardstick for the acquisition or loss of individual identity and selfhood. Once the concept was thus purged of external or empirical connotations, reification gave way to random choice: "Devoid of any objective content, authenticity falls prey to the arbitrary decisions of the individual determining his authentic selfhood."[32]

The confluence of subjectivism and reification, the study concluded, was ultimately the outgrowth of Heidegger's inability to resolve traditional antinomies—more specifically, of the tendency of such antinomies to rupture the bonds of a forced synthesis. Heidegger's basic strategy, in Adorno's view, was to reconcile and combine conflicts in a higher unity; since this unification, however, was a purely conceptual or theoretical undertaking (despite protestations to the contrary), his perspective involved in the last analysis a merger or identification of thought and reality, concealing their basic incongruence and the inevitably mediated character of their relationship. In the context of existential analysis, he commented, "mediation is transformed into an immediate identity of mediating reflection and mediated world; although neither element can subsist without the other, the two are by no means the same—as Heidegger's basic thesis alleges." The suppression of mediation entailed also the muffling of negativity and the mutilation of dialectics: "Heidegger manages to convert the dialectic between givenness and concept of subjectivity into a being of a higher order and thus to bring dialectics to a halt." In the end, Heidegger's synthesis was a merely synthetic and artificial *collage* in which conceptual categories were invested with spurious objectivity: "While claiming to penetrate behind the reflective concepts of subject and object into a realm of ultimate substance, he actually does nothing but reify the incongruence of these concepts—the impossibility of reducing one to the other—into a thing-in-itself. This is the philosophical underpinning of the sleight-of-hand which the jargon incessantly commits when—implicitly and without theological blessing—it propounds the essential as real and, by the same token, existing reality as essential, meaningful, and justified."[33]

As a postscript indicated, the *Jargon of Authenticity* was meant as a preparatory step or propaedeutic to a more comprehensive exploration of the philosophical situation of our time—an exploration which appeared under the title *Negative Dialectics* in 1966, three years before Adorno's death. Easily one of his most ambitious and demanding works, *Negative Dialectics* probed major problem areas in contemporary thought, including the notion of human freedom and its relevance to ethics, the issue of social and historical development (as seen from the perspective of "natural history"), and the domain of ultimate metaphysical questions. The central theme of the study, however, was the scrutiny and critical dissection of contemporary ontological doctrines, with special emphasis on Heidegger's conception of fundamental ontology. On the whole, the study was pervaded by a strong anti-subjectivist posture—but a posture which held no brief for ontological reification or for any type of a merely conceptual or imaginary synthesis. "Ever since he came to trust his own intellectual impulses," Adorno wrote in the Preface, "the author felt it to be his task to pierce the sham of constitutive subjectivity while relying on the

subject's capabilities; now he did not want to postpone this task any
longer. To move beyond the official segregation of pure philosophy and
substantive or formally scientific inquiry was one of the guiding motives in this undertaking." As he added, the attempt to transcend customary dichotomies did not involve a leap into harmony: "By means
of logically consistent arguments the study tries to substitute for the
principle of identity and the supremacy of synthetic concepts the notion of an experience which would be outside the sway of such unity."[34]

The simultaneous opposition to subjectivism and reification was
underscored in the introductory chapter of the study. As Adorno affirmed, traditional philosophy—especially in its idealist variety—was
marked by the ambition to absorb experience into mental categories
and ultimately to reduce reality to a set of concepts: "The appearance
of identity is an integral aspect of pure thought. To think means to
identify: self-contained and self-contented, the conceptual framework
obstructs access to the subject matter of thought." Idealism in particular was wedded to the doctrine "that the non-ego, the other and everything resembling nature is inferior—a ready prey to the voracity of
synthesizing and self-perpetuating thought." Despite the stress on objectification, even Hegel's philosophy was basically narcissistic "since
spirit extracts from objects only their spiritual or mental parameters."
The danger of narcissism, Adorno added, could not simply be remedied
by the abdication of reflection in favor of a naive realism or a spurious
immediacy of experience; only by pursuing its intrinsic antinomies
to their limits could thought hope to escape from its prison and to
reach its target: "The utopia of cognition would be the ability to unlock the nonconceptual domain with conceptual means—without reducing the one to the other." The basic strategy for breaking down
the prison walls of reflection was dialectics—but a dialectics which,
instead of clinging to a mental synthesis, pursued its aim in a strictly
negative manner, by realizing the insufficiency and incongruence of
its conceptual tools: "To change the thrust of conceptualization in the
direction of non-identity is the emblem of negative dialectics. Insight
into the constitutive character of the nonconceptual domain would
dissolve the constraint of identity which, in the absence of critical
scrutiny, characterizes conceptual frameworks. The seeming autarchy
of concepts as self-contained units of meaning is overcome by reflection on the purpose of knowledge."[35]

Turning to contemporary ontology, the study presented Heidegger's outlook as basically an outgrowth or continuation of traditional
philosophy—as a synthetic structure unable to disguise its internal
conflicts and antinomies, especially the antinomy of objectivism and

subjective volition. According to Adorno, one of Heidegger's chief motivations was the ambition to overcome Western metaphysics with its focus on subjective consciousness; however, in simply eradicating subjectivity and the mediating role of reflection, his thinking encouraged the leap into facticity or a primitive ontic immediacy. "While pretending to express a world-view antedating the lapse into a simultaneously subjectivist and objectivist metaphysics," the study noted, Heidegger's philosophy "congeals *contre coeur* into a thing-in-itself. The self-denial of subjectivity produces objectivism." Given its objectivist thrust, existential analysis also was a pacemaker of alienation and reification. To a large extent, ontological speculation could be viewed as the "metaphysics of reification," since the assumption of an immediately given facticity transformed reality into a set of reified data. The notion of *"Seinshörigkeit"* (openness and submissiveness to being)—in Adorno's view—was clear evidence of the alienating thrust of Heidegger's thought: its tendency to underwrite existing forms of social and political repression. "Although claiming attachment to the universe," he wrote, ontological submissiveness "supports without further ado every type of particularism or parochial arrangement which is able to demonstrate forcefully enough the subject's weakness." Under Heidegger's influence, ontology tended to be understood as "the willingness to endorse a heteronomous social order exempt from the need of rational legitimation."[36]

Ultimately, to be sure, the claim of unmediated objectivity was untenable since ontology—no matter how "fundamental" or foundational—was a reflective enterprise: Heidegger's attempt to escape from the prison of consciousness was nothing but "a leap into the mirror." By neglecting the mediated character of being, Adorno commented, Heidegger repressed and disguised the subject's contribution to ontology; in so doing, however, he merely erected subjectivity into a primordial and unexamined premise. The ontological elevation of subjectivity was particularly manifest in the notion of *Dasein* as used in *Being and Time*. Treated as a synonym of existential categories, subjectivity in this context was transformed into a "solid fortress," similar to Kant's transcendental consciousness; simultaneously, owing to the stress on concreteness and worldliness, *Dasein* acquired the connotation of contingent subjective experience, conjuring up the danger of relativism. Whatever the precise meaning of existence, the insistence on the internal character of authenticity deprived *Dasein* of objective standards and opened the door to arbitrary choice: "Removed from otherness and objectification, (authentic) existence—viewed as a yardstick of thought—implements its decrees in the same autocratic manner as in politics the dictator implements the ruling world-view. The reduction of reflection to the thinking subject brings to a halt the genesis and maturation of thought which alone would give sustenance to subjectivity."[37]

Regarding the alleged transcendence of the twin evils of subjectivism and objectivism, Adorno emphasized the imaginary character of the remedy. Heidegger—he argued—"proceeds dialectically to the extent that he treats neither subject nor object as immediate or ultimate data"; by turning toward being, however, "he ascends above dialectics and seeks to grasp an immediate origin beyond its antithetical terms." Given the constraints of rational argument, such an ascent was furtive and misleading: "Heidegger bypasses the central issue of dialectics by adopting a position transcending the difference between subject and object—a difference which merely manifests the incongruence of reason and world. This leap, however, cannot be accomplished through rational means: reason cannot vindicate a position which would eradicate the distinction between subject and object implanted in every notion and in thought itself." According to Adorno, the relationship between subject and object was a reflection of "nonidentity" and could neither be erected into a timeless conflict nor be collapsed into a ready-made synthesis: "If subject and object were treated as opposites, their conflict would become total and one-dimensional—akin to the repudiated principle of identity; absolute dualism would lapse into monism." At the same time, the dichotomy could not simply be removed "by the mere fiat of pure thought," since "every concept, even the concept of being, reproduces the difference between thought and subject matter." An outgrowth of a basic incongruence or ambivalence, the dualism involved a constant task—a task which could not be avoided by resorting either to segregation or conceptual fusion: "The subject is in truth never wholly subject, the object never wholly object; this does not mean, however, that the two terms are subsumed under a third and higher notion. . . . The distinction between subject and object must be critically maintained—in opposition to the claim to totality inherent in thought."[38]

What was true of the subject-object nexus applied with equal force to Heidegger's treatment of other traditional dichotomies, such as those between apriori and aposteriori, facticity and essence, ontic reality and ultimate being. In every instance, the proclaimed reconciliation remained an artificial maneuver. "Like Husserl," Adorno wrote, "Heidegger seeks to accommodate indiscriminately aspects which were found to be incompatible in the (too readily dismissed) history of metaphysics: the aspect of pure reflection or absolute validity aloof of all empirical connotations, and that of immediate, non-conceptual facticity." By proposing the notion of being as remedy for traditional antinomies, fundamental ontology moved into a "no man's land" of empty tautologies and abstract conceptual subterfuge, a terrain shielded from critical scrutiny: "The incompatibility of purity and concreteness makes it necessary to choose the locale of synthesis on such an indefinite plane that neither of the two constituent elements can be invoked to challenge the other: Heidegger's being therefore is neither ontic reality nor idea."[39] Even Heidegger's notion of "ontological difference"—referring to the difference between ontic "beings" and being—was ultimately a merely conceptual stratagem: despite the theoretical differentiation of the two domains, Heidegger's insistence on pure categories amounted to an "ontologization of ontic reality," just as his stress on concreteness ascribed to being ontic qualities. What was neglected in Heidegger's ontology and in the notion of "ontological difference," Adorno argued, was the actual distinction and incongruence of thought and reality: "Heidegger comes close to the dialectical insight into the non-identity of identity; however, instead of bringing the dilemma of ontology into the open, he suppresses it. Being—whatever its precise meaning—resists the identification of concept and substantive content; but Heidegger treats it as principle of identity, as pure self-contained essence untouched by otherness."[40]

Given the paradoxes of being viewed as conceptualization of ultimate reality, the only legitimate philosophy in Adorno's view was a philosophy of incongruence—one which took seriously the insufficiency of thought in pursuing its goal of absorbing reality: "What is proclaimed by ontology as manifestation of a positive entity, has its truth and legitimacy only in negativity." As Adorno added, the critique of Heidegger's thought was not meant to inaugurate a new ontology replacing being by facticity and non-identity; such attempts would be futile and self-contradictory by "conceptualizing the non-conceptual." Negation or negativity did not designate a spiritual haven or retreat but rather the scene of an incessant struggle or hand-to-hand combat between thought and reality—a struggle which ultimately was an outgrowth of man's involvement in nature and his concrete sufferings as an embodied creature. Wedded to the search for reality bypassing both reification and spiritual or ideological camouflages, negative thinking was a synonym for dialectical materialism, provided the latter was not erected into a metaphysical dogma. Countering Leninist epistemology, Adorno insisted that cognition could neither be leveled naively into objects nor be reduced to a reservoir of mental "images"

or "pictures." The notion of images in particular was an idealist ves-
tige: "The materialist aspiration to grasp reality aims at the opposite —
only.in the absence of images could objects be known. Such absence
concurs with the theological ban on images. Materialism secularized
this ban, preventing the positive portrayal of utopia: this is the core
of its negativity. . . . Its chief longing would be the resurrection of the
flesh — a notion completely alien to idealism and the realm of absolute spirit."[41]

IV
(Metaphysics after Auschwitz?)

By all standards *Negative Dialectics* constitutes a highpoint in
contemporary philosophical criticism; in terms of Adorno's intellectual development, the study culminated a life-long endeavor to come
to terms or settle accounts with dominant currents of our time, especially with the leading spokesmen of the phenomenological movement. At this point — having traced the main steps in this development as reflected in Adorno's key publications — it seems advisable
to pause briefly in order to assess the central claims or issues involved
in the controversy between "critical theory" and its adversaries. Regarding transcendental phenomenology, Adorno's arguments in my
view are trenchant and by and large persuasive. As it seems to me,
his studies on the topic correctly pinpointed the dilemmas and inherent antinomies of egological thought and of the traditional philosophy of consciousness in general; his *Metacritique* in particular
was successful in exposing the shortcomings and idealist premises
of a perspective which treats consciousness as gateway to a realm of
"absolute origins" and as cornerstone of a refurbished *prima philosophia*.[42] Concerning social and political implications, his writings revealed the bourgeois affinities of transcendental phenomenology —
by pointing to the linkage between the notion of "*eidos ego*" and the
legacy of "possessive individualism" and, more specifically, to the nexus
between phenomenological description and the consumer mentality
prevalent in late industrial society.

Despite such critical strictures and reservations, however, one
should note that Adorno's attitude was not one-sidedly hostile; numerous passages in his writings testify to his sympathy and respect
for some of Husserl's central endeavors. Thus, while complaining about
the inadequacy and counterproductive qualities of phenomenological methodology, Adorno applauded Husserl's ambition to cast off the

shackles of traditional dualisms and antinomies—including the bifurcation of idealism and objectivism. Moreover, in pursuing this aim and in formulating his phenomenological strategy, Husserl remained at least in one respect a model for Adorno: in his firm attachment to critical-rational inquiry and in his refusal to abandon reflection in favor of experiential immediacy or ontological intuition. From the vantage point of critical theory, the antinomial structure of traditional philosophy could not be overcome by intuitive shortcuts or by a leap into ready-made syntheses. As Adorno continually insisted, the remedy for past dualisms resided not in an indiscriminate merger or monistic identification of opposites, since identity was merely a synonym for idealist usurpation. Given the pitfalls of both segregation and fusion, the key to a post-Cartesian outlook could be found only in an open-ended (and non-idealist) dialectic—an approach which maintained at least provisionally the incongruence of subject and object, thought and reality, and in which the spark of insight was expected to emerge only from the strenuous encounter and interaction of opposing elements.

By comparison with the founder of the phenomenological movement, Heidegger's role in Adorno's thought is more complex and more difficult to disentangle. On the whole, Adorno's indictment of existential analysis tends to be severe and uncompromising; but overt statements in this case are not a fully reliable gauge of mutual relationships. Despite outward signs of antagonism, it is possible to detect a close kinship and even convergence of the two thinkers on a number of issues. Thus, Adorno's strictures against individualism and the philosophy of consciousness correspond closely to Heidegger's critique of "subjectivism" and of the tradition of Western metaphysics with its accent on subjective reflection. Likewise, Adorno's comments on the ambivalence of Enlightenment thought and modern rationalism find a parallel in the Heideggerian posture toward logical calculation and the conception of man as "rational animal"; in particular, the argument that the growing sway of "instrumental" rationality reflects ultimately man's "will to power"—the desire to subjugate and control nature—is reminiscent of Heidegger's treatment of modern technology as an anthropocentric stratagem (or rather as a *Gestell* transforming anthropocentrism into an ontological structure).[43] A further affinity—particularly revealing for the thrust of the "critical" program—can be found in the common stress of the two thinkers on historical exegesis and on the importance of "pre-understanding" or tradition for human cognition. The introductory chapter of *Negative Dialectics* contains an eloquent vindication of hermeneutical inquiry, a vindication furnishing a corrective not only to instrumental rationalism but also to the pretensions of a purely critical stance. The Enlightenment attack on prejudice and repressive authority, Adorno notes in that context, was by no means unprovoked or misguided—provided the attack is not viewed as a total destruction: "One easily forgets that tradition dwells at the heart of knowledge as the mediating element of the subject matter under scrutiny. . . . Even where form and content of cognition are segregated, knowledge takes part in tradition as a reservoir of unconscious recollections; no question can be articulated without somehow preserving and refocusing the legacy of the past."[44]

To be sure, similarities and linkages of this kind cannot entirely offset deep-seated rivalries and philosophical divergencies. Going over the details of Adorno's critique, it appears feasible to differentiate between charges which are relatively marginal or incidental and others of a more substantive character. In the first category, it seems to me, belong accusations regarding the linguistic peculiarity or "jargon-prone" style of Heidegger's writings, especially when "jargon" refers to an indulgence in neologisms and etymological contrivances. As Heidegger himself has insisted on numerous occasions—perhaps in an attempt to caution over-zealous imitators—etymological speculation, far from qualifying as a substitute, must always remain a handmaiden of philosophical argument.[45] More important—although basically misdirected or misguided in my view—is the charge regarding the alleged revival of *prima philosophia*. While lending itself to multiple interpretations, Heidegger's perspective, I believe, does not properly involve a return to "origins" or "first beginnings" in the sense of apriori principles; the reference to "being" or "ground of being" is not equivalent to foundationalism or the invocation of a set of premises from which further propositions could (deductively or inductively) be derived. Heidegger's doubts regarding *prima philosophia* are expressed in several of his later writings, including the essay on "The End of Philosophy and the Task of Thinking" where one reads: "What does ground and principle, and especially principle of all principles, mean? Can this ever be sufficiently determined—unless we experience truth (*aletheia*) in the Greek manner as unconcealment and then, above and beyond the Greek, as the opening of self-concealing?"[46]

Given the connection between Heidegger and Gadamer, some attention must also be given to the respective approaches to hermeneutics. Despite his appreciation of the role of tradition, Adorno is unwilling to restrict human cognition to historical exegesis or to the interpretation of cultural legacies. Human experience through the ages, in his view, does not simply reflect an intentional design or a continuous sedimentation of meaning which could be disentangled through a dialogue between participants and interpreters. While not devoid of meaningful patterns, history can also be seen as a sequence of unintelligible events or an array of "decomposed" clues and traces—in other words, as a "natural history." Access to this dimension is provided not so much through cultural exegesis as through complex decoding mechanisms, especially through structural "constellations" and linguistic "configurations" designed to unlock the riddle of reality. At this point, a major rift seems to emerge between Adorno and Heidegger—provided the latter is classified chiefly as spokesman of a philosophical hermeneutics. This assessment, however, may not be entirely adequate and be tailored too narrowly to Heidegger's early phase with its focus on "hermeneutical phenomenology." His later writings reveal a progressive disenchantment with intentionality and a growing preoccupation with the embeddedness of thought and action in a broader network of relationships. Thus, the essay entitled "The Thing" depicts things or objects not as targets of intentional consciousness nor as instruments "to-hand" for human purposes, but rather as nodal junctures of a "gathering" or "assembly" (*Versammlung*) of elements—a gathering which is also described as an "appropriating event" (*Ereignis*) since it permits the elements of the world to come into their own and to occupy their proper place.[47] Is there not a similarity, one may ask, between this portrayal and the constellations of "natural history" adumbrated by Adorno? Does "gathering" not denote a structural configuration—although not simply a cognitive or mental structure nor a reified set of empirical components?

Of central significance in the present comparison is the issue of ontology and its philosophical status. Clearly, as the preceding discussion has shown, Heidegger's ontological leanings are at the heart of Adorno's critical indictment. Briefly formulated, this indictment treats Heidegger's perspective as an adjunct of traditional metaphysics and the notion of "being" as a synthetic philosophical construct—a construct which camouflages rather than resolves traditional antinomies. Differently phrased, Heideggerian ontology is characterized as a philosophy of "identity" pretending to have captured in thought contingent experience and the domain of ultimate reality. Again, as in the case of hermeneutics, the adequacy of this account can seriously be questioned; to some extent, the account seems in fact to reflect quandaries endemic to Adorno's own approach. As I have indicated, a guiding motif of Adorno's work is the attempt to overcome the subject-object bifurcation—but without relinquishing their intrinsic opposition; *Negative Dialectics* in particular seeks to clear a path beyond the confines of "reason" seen as an instrument of domination and self-aggrandizement—while retaining the critical potency of human rationality and subjectivity. With steadily growing intensity, his writings betray the ambition to move beyond "identity" construed as indiscriminate merger of thought and reality—while simultaneously resisting the lure of a dualistic non-identity shielding mind from the world. Although immensely fertile and suggestive, Adorno's arguments frequently seem to end in paradox—or at least in aporetic formulations awaiting further philosophical elucidation and scrutiny. Against this background, is there not some plausibility to an "ontological" move seeking to provide a (non-foundational) grounding or warrant for the conception of a non-antithetical difference?

As it seems to me, Heidegger's philosophy offers at least helpful clues along these lines; many of his writings—especially those of his later phase—are replete with passages strongly denouncing identity and its connotations. Thus, one of his essays on Hölderlin affirms that genuine concord or harmony "is never synonymous with sameness nor with the empty uniformity of mere identity." While identity "tries to level everything into a uniform mold devoid of differentiation," concord signifies or is predicated upon "the togetherness or mutual belonging (*Zusammengehören*) of distinct elements as they are gathered in their difference."[48] The issue is dealt with at greater length, and with explicit reference to ontology, in the treatise on *Identity and Difference*. Commenting on an epigram by Parmenides linking thought and being, Heidegger completely rejects the interpretation of this linkage in terms of the traditional "principle of identity," suggesting instead that the relationship be viewed as a gathering or "mutual belonging" accomplished on the basis of a reciprocal "appropriation" (*Ereignis*). The latter perspective, he adds, can be reached only by breaking away from traditional metaphysics which tended to treat "being" either as explanatory ground of ontic reality or as absolute reflection or as a synthesis of the two. Arguing against Hegelian philosophy depicted as an "onto-theological" system submerging being in the knowledge of reality as a whole, *Identity and Difference* insists on the differentiation of being both from ontic reality and speculative thought—a differentiation which does not rule out their "mutual belonging." "Provisionally stated," Heidegger writes, "the proper task of thinking for us is to think the difference *as* difference." As he cautions, however, the accent on difference does not sanction a lapse into dualism or rigid metaphysical categories. Construed as a juxtaposition of separate notions or elements, he observes, difference or non-identity is "reduced to a conceptual distinction, to an artificial construct of reason." What renders differentiation and appropriation compatible, in Heidegger's view, is the realization that being is always the "being of concrete ontic reality" (*Sein des Seienden*) just as ontic reality is always the "reality of being" (*Seiendes des Seins*). In another context, this reciprocal nexus is portrayed as the "twofold unity" or differentiated concord of being and reality (*Zwiefalt*).[49]

Are considerations of this kind sufficient to quiet Adorno's complaints and perhaps even to effect a reconciliation of the two thinkers? This is probably an excessive hope. In my view, Heidegger's later writings have important implications for his overall position—implications which he did not always choose to explore. If being and world are indeed linked in the intimate manner suggested in these writings, then being is clearly not a topic which can be discussed abstractly or in a merely speculative mode (with the result that, in a sense, it must be "crossed out" as an idealist concept). Instead of vindicating a purely meditative retreat, the "being of beings" would appear to entail concrete worldly and even political concerns—without on this count endorsing a myopic positivism. In other words: the notions of "ontological difference" and "mutual belonging" seem at odds with a stance of social-political abstinence or indifference—a stance ascribed by some readers to Heidegger during his later life. Since, in terms of his own writings, ontology does not provide a refuge from the world, it is hard to see how the philosopher can remain aloof of worldly dilemmas, including the social-political agonies of the contemporary period. Against this background, the central merit of Adorno's critical queries may be this: to have reminded us (and Heideggerians in particular) that ontology in our time cannot simply signify the withdrawal into esoteric wisdom nor the return to a feigned innocence. Adorno's comments, from this vantage point, offer not merely an external gloss but an internal critique of ontological thought—or rather a platform enabling the reader at some junctures "to think with Heidegger against Heidegger."[50]

In order to illustrate this internal counterpoint, I want to allude briefly, by way of conclusion, to a few key terms in Heidegger's vocabulary. Notions like "homelessness" and "homecoming" seem to reveal Heidegger as an eminently "worldly" thinker concerned with a crucial predicament in our age; but their meaning is ambivalent. To start with the diagnostic term: Is "homelessness" nothing but a synonym for the rootlessness and restless mobility of a technological-industrial era—in contradistinction to the presumed safety and stability of earlier times? In this case, does the proposed remedy consist in a simple rejection of modernity? Does "homecoming" involve a purely regressive or restorative move—back into the haven of a rural lifestyle? Some passages in Heidegger's writings—passages accentuated by Adorno—seem to encourage such an interpretation and have in fact been construed by many readers as endorsement of a rustic parochialism opposed to the complexities of modern life.[51] Yet, Heidegger's views on the matter can hardly be compressed into a one-dimensional formula.

The possibility of non-parochial and non-archaic connotations of "homecoming" is intimated in one of his most famous postwar writings: the essay on "Serenity" (Gelassenheit). As the essay suggests, our time is indeed marked by a loss of rootedness or "autochthony" owing to the progressive sway of "planning and calculation"; but the dominant mood is not nostalgia. Even though the "old rootedness" has vanished in our era, Heidegger queries whether the basis for a "new autochthony" might be found "even in the atomic age"—proposing as guidepost the attitude of "serenity" involving a "simple and relaxed" posture in the midst of technological change. To be sure, this guidepost cannot in turn be used as an alibi or as a guise for Stoic indifference or apathy, as Heidegger would probably have agreed—which raises anew the question: What is the proper role of reflection or meditation in a disjointed world? The last chapter of Negative Dialectics, styled "Meditations on Metaphysics," opens with a section entitled "After Auschwitz." The section stands as a strong caveat against philosophical complacency. "Committed to the self-reflection of thought," Adorno writes, "negative dialectics implies concretely that, in order to be true (at least for today), thought must also be ready to think against itself. Unless willing to measure itself against those extreme situations which elude conceptual formulation, thought assumes from the outset the character of a mere accompaniment—similar to the background music with which SS officers liked to drown out the screams of their victims."[52]

3

Life-World and Communicative
Action: *Habermas*

Initium sapientiae . . .

AS IN THE CASE OF literature and philosophy, "classic" texts in social
theory are usually a matter of the past; only rarely does one witness
the emergence of such a text as a contemporary. Habermas's *Theorie
des kommunikativen Handelns* is one of the few exceptions to this
rule: both in terms of its range of coverage and its trenchant mode
of analysis the sprawling, two-volume study carries all the earmarks
of a sociological "classic."[1] Apart from its intrinsic merits, the classical quality attaches to the work also through a kind of osmosis: over
long stretches the study offers a detailed discussion of the founders
of modern sociology, notably Weber, Durkheim, Mead, and Parsons —
a discussion which, in my view, has no equal in recent literature. To
be sure, *Theorie des kommunikativen Handelns* differs from its fore-
bears by a number of innovative features: both by the incorporation
of recent, sophisticated methods of inquiry (like "reconstruction") and,
more importantly, by its attunement to pervasive intellectual changes
characterizing our age. On the latter plane, the most significant innovation is Habermas's departure from the traditional "philosophy of
consciousness" (or subjectivity) dating back to Descartes and Kant,
and his resolute turn toward language and intersubjective communication. Moving beyond initial steps made in this direction by Mead
and Durkheim, the study elevates speech and communication to primary categories of sociological theory. Given its central status, a chief
question raised by the study is whether, as formulated in its pages,
the "linguistic turn" constitutes an adequate response or remedy to
the dilemmas bequeathed by the philosophy of consciousness.

The wealth and complexity of issues covered in *Theory of Communicative Action* (to use the English title) militates against a comprehensive review in the confines of a short essay. For present purposes I intend to focus on two major topics or conceptual themes,
those of "communicative action" and of the so-called "life-world" —

although I shall also attempt to indicate the significance of these themes in Habermas's broader theoretical frame of reference. The choice of the two topics, I believe, is not the result of idiosyncratic preference. The importance of "communicative action" is already amply attested by the overall title of the work. In addition, Habermas underscores the weight of the themes by devoting to them two "theoretical interludes" (Zwischenbetrachtungen) which punctuate the argument of the two volumes: the first deals with social action and "communication," and the second with the relation between "system and life-world."[2] In the following I shall, first of all, recapitulate in some detail Habermas's own presentation of the two concepts in his study. Next, I shall point to some quandaries or unresolved issues besetting these concepts both singly and in their mutual relation. Finally, by way of conclusion, I endeavor to project these quandaries against the larger tapestry of the work—using them as a sort of fulcrum to detect more deep-seated fissures or antinomies—while simultaneously suggesting alternative pathways of thought conducive to a lessening of such tensions.

I

Communicative action, as any attentive reader will recognize, is not a novel feature in the Habermasian opus. One of his earliest publications, entitled Strukturwandel der Öffentlichkeit, deplored the progressive dismantling of public debate and communication in favor of technical-functional imperatives. His main epistemological work, Knowledge and Human Interests (1968), focused more directly on the notion, attributing to it a quasi-transcendental cognitive status. In discussing Peirce's theory of science the study observed: "The community of investigators, however, requires a use of language not confined to the limits of technical control over objectified natural processes—a use which arises from symbolically mediated interactions between social subjects who know and recognize each other as unique individuals. Such communicative action forms a system of reference that cannot be reduced to the framework of instrumental action."[3] The "postscript" to the same study (written some five years later) differentiated more carefully between experiential "interests" and knowledge claims or between the domains of "life-praxis" and "praxis of inquiry"—but without abandoning the distinction between empirical-instrumental and communicative endeavors. Communicative action or interaction was now assumed to occur both on the level of everyday experience and on that of reflectively refined, "discursive" inquiries. As Habermas elaborated, the "linkage between knowledge and interests had been developed in the study without sufficient attention to the critical threshold separating communications embedded in experiential and action contexts from 'discourses' permitting rationally grounded and thus properly cognitive knowledge."[4]

Following *Knowledge and Human Interests* the theme of communicative action surfaced repeatedly in Habermas's publications, including his writings on linguistic competence, universal pragmatics, and cognitive and moral development; for the sake of brevity, however, I shall omit citation of relevant passages.[5] In *Theory of Communicative Action* the theme is first introduced in an epistemological context, namely, during a discussion of modes of rationality and rationalization. Critiquing the Baconian focus on science as technical control—a focus strongly reverberating in Max Weber's perspective—the study comments: "By concentrating on the non-communicative use of propositional knowledge in purposive action we make a prior choice in favor of *cognitive-instrumental rationality*, a concept which, via empiricism, has strongly shaped the outlook of modernity and which carries with it connotations of successful self-preservation, rendered possible through informed control over, and intelligent adaptation to, the conditions of a contingent environment." By contrast, "when starting from the communicative use of propositional knowledge in speech acts, we opt in favor of a broader meaning of rationality linked with older notions of 'logos'. This latter concept of *communicative rationality* carries with it connotations which ultimately derive from the central experience of the quietly unifying, consensus-producing function of argumentative speech where participants overcome their initial subjective views and, through the bond of rationally grounded convictions, assure themselves both of the unity of the objective world and the intersubjectivity of their life context." The differential use of knowledge, according to the study, determines in the end the basic direction or objective of reason: "In the one case the intrinsic telos of rationality is *instrumental control*, in the other *communicative consensus* or agreement."[6]

Communication and communicative rationality, in the new work, are by no means limited to "propositional" knowledge or propositions about empirical phenomena (in the external or "objective world"). In line with arguments familiar from his "universal pragmatics," Habermas extends the range of rational speech from factual assertions to intersubjective norms and modes of self-reflection and self-expression (in his terms, to the dimensions of the "social" and the

"subjective world"). "Norm-regulated actions, expressive self-presenta-
tions and evaluative utterances," he writes, "complement and round
out constative-factual speech acts to form a broad communicative
praxis. Against the backdrop of a 'life-world' this praxis aims at the
attainment, preservation and renewal of consensus—more specifically
of a consensus resting on the intersubjective recognition of arguable
validity claims. The rationality inherent in this praxis manifests itself in the fact that a communicatively reached consensus must *ultimately* be grounded on reasons." Regarding the rational validation of
cognitive claims, some types of communication are said to be amenable to "discursive" scrutiny (especially the domains of factual propositions and intersubjective norms), while other types permit only more
limited versions of "critique" (such as the critical analyses operative
in individual therapy and aesthetics). "We can summarize our views
by saying," Habermas affirms, "that rationality is a disposition of speaking and acting subjects that manifests itself in forms of behavior
backed up by good reasons." Accordingly, "any explicit examination
of controversial validity claims requires an exacting mode of communication satisfying the conditions of argumentation."[7]

So far, the presentation has concentrated chiefly on the rational-
discursive aspect of communication, while relatively neglecting its
"active" or practical connotations. The latter topic is broached in a
subsequent section of the study dealing with "sociological concepts
of action" and their linkage with modes of rationality. Habermas at
this point differentiates communicative action from three competing
action types prominent (in his view) in recent sociological literature:
namely, "teleological (or purposive-rational) action," "norm-regulated
action," and "dramaturgical action." As the study emphasizes, the first
type has at least since Aristotle been the focus of theoretical attention. Acting teleologically, an actor seeks to implement his objective
or "telos" by choosing the means appropriate to his aims, that is, by
selecting a given course of action among available alternatives. Individual teleological choice is transformed and amplified into "strategic
action" whenever the decision of one actor is influenced by, or a response to, decisions by another agent (or agents). In its strategic guise,
the teleological model forms the bedrock of the theory of "economic
choice," as developed by the founders of classical economics, and also
of more recent formulations of "games of strategy." In terms of its
linkage with rationality the model, according to Habermas, is basically guided by the standard of rational "efficiency"—although this
standard cannot be entirely divorced from valid propositional knowledge. As he points out, teleological action necessarily involves a re-

lation between an actor and the external or "objective world," where "objective world" means the "totality of states of affairs which either exist or can be made to exist through purposive intervention." While, in principle, such a relation can support a purely cognitive or contemplative stance, action becomes teleological (or strategic) through the accent on intervention and efficiency.[8]

As portrayed in the study, other action types or models can be understood in terms of the progressive differentiation of actor-world relations. In contrast to the individualistic and "one-world" mentality operative in teleological endeavors, "norm-regulated action" refers to consensual activity among members of a social goup, that is, to activity in accordance with accepted cultural norms and values where the latter express "a prevailing consensus among group members." In Habermas's account, this action type was first introduced by Durkheim and subsequently fleshed out by Parsons and other spokesmen of sociological "role theory"; action from this vantage point always means compliance with socially prescribed behavior expectations. Regarding its rationality potential, the type is said to involve basically a "two-world" orientation, namely, orientation both to the objective and the "social world"—where "social world" means a given "normative context" specifying the "totality of legitimate interpersonal interactions" and where legitimacy is judged by the standard of (normative) "rightness." While role theory points to the normative-social dimensions of behavior, "dramaturgical action" uncovers the domain of subjectivity by concentrating on the self-disclosure of agents in front of each other or in front of an audience. In this case, Habermas writes, the actor "evokes in his audience a particular image or impression by means of a more or less deliberate revelation of his subjectivity." With this action type, he adds, a new "world" or dimension of behavior comes into view: namely, the agent's "subjective world" defined as the "totality of subjective experiences to which the actor has privileged access" and governed by (potentially rational) standards of truthfulness and authenticity. Despite its discovery of this new terrain, Habermas finds dramaturgical action still restricted to a "two-world" outlook: the correlation of inner and outer, subjective and objective worlds.[9]

In Habermas's presentation, communicative action is distinguished from the mentioned action types both by its range of coverage and its uniquely reflective-rational capacity: that is, both by its ability to encompass the "three worlds" simultaneously and by its rootedness in language seen as a reflective "medium" of interaction. In his words, the concept refers to the interactive "negotiation of definitions of situations amenable to consensus"; with this action type "the further premise of a *linguistic medium* comes to the fore in which the world-relations of actors are mirrored as such." First initiated by Mead, the category was subsequently developed—though insufficiently and sketchily—by interactionism, speech-act theory, and sociological hermeneutics. According to the study, the chief advantage of communicative action resides in its capability to correct the one-sidedness of alternative approaches, mainly through its reliance on language. While, in the teleological type, language serves merely as a subordinate means for utilitarian calculations, and while normative and dramaturgical actions thematize language only as a reservoir of cultural values or an instrument of self-display, the communicative model alone "presupposes language as a medium of unrestricted consensual interaction in which speakers and hearers make simultaneous reference to aspects of the objective, social, and subjective worlds, against the backdrop of their pre-interpreted life-world." As Habermas adds, this multi-dimensional use of language can be explicated more fully in a theory of "formal" or "universal pragmatics"—a theory which transcends narrow linguistic concerns with syntax. While conducive to mutual comprehensibility, adherence to syntactical rules alone does not yield access to the "pragmatic" dimensions of speech, that is, its embeddedness in world-contexts or "world-relations" which, in turn, can be reflectively scrutinized: "In the communicative model of action, language is relevant only from the pragmatic angle that speakers, by uttering statements in a communicative fashion, enter into distinct world-relations" and that they do so "in a reflexive manner." Against this background, communication functions "as a mechanism of coordination" in the sense that participants "reach agreement on the claimed *validity* of their utterances, and thus grant intersubjective recognition to reciprocally raised *validity claims*."[10]

In *Theory of Communicative Action*, the formal or "universal-pragmatic" underpinnings of communicative exchanges are elaborated in greater detail in the first "theoretical interlude" dealing with action theory and communication. Following a critical review of Weber's typology of actions, Habermas at this point introduces a broad distinction between "success-oriented" and "consensus-oriented" actions, where "success-orientation" is basically a new description of the teleological model (comprising both instrumental and strategic behavior), while "consensus-orientation" serves as trademark of communicative action or interaction: "I call *communicative* those actions in which the behavioral goals or plans of actors are coordinated not via egocentric calculations of success but through consensual exchanges." In Habermas's portrayal, consensus or consensual interaction (*Verständi-*

gung) does not merely denote a psychological convergence of feelings or dispositions nor a purely factual-prudential accord, but rather points to a rationally achieved and grounded agreement. Communicative processes, he writes, "aim at a consensus that satisfies the conditions of a rationally motivated assent to the content of an utterance"; thus, consensus rests on "common *convictions*" supported by "potential reasons." To buttress the mentioned dichotomy, the interlude takes recourse to contemporary linguistic analysis and speech-act theory, and especially to Austin's differentiation between "locutionary," "illocutionary," and "perlocutionary" speech acts (or rather components of speech acts). While locutionary utterances report on given states of affairs and while illocutionary acts signal the "pragmatic" sense of speech, perlocution in essence has to do with the impact of speech on listeners. Transplanting Austin's differentiation onto the plane of action theory, the study associates communicative action chiefly with locutionary and illocutionary utterances, while finding the central trait of success-orientation in its emphasis on perlocution. "The self-sufficiency of an illocutionary act," we read, "is to be understood in the sense that both the communicative intent of the speaker and his pursued illocutionary goal result from the manifest meaning of the utterance." By contrast, teleological behavior is guided by extrinsic and instrumental objectives: "Just as for illocutionary acts the *meaning of the utterance* is constitutive, so for teleological behavior it is the *intention* of the actor"—an intention directed at exerting influence or at the "performance of a *perlocutionary* act." As Habermas adds: "I thus label 'communicative' those linguistically mediated interactions in which all participants pursue with their utterances *exclusively* illocutionary aims; on the other hand, interactions in which at least one participant seeks to produce perlocutionary effects I regard as linguistically mediated strategic action."[11]

Having stressed the illocutionary character of communication, the study proceeds to delineate the pragmatic ingredients of consensus, that is, the conditions required for the consensual coordination of behavior. In a nutshell these conditions include: first of all, comprehension of the semantic meaning of an utterance; secondly, understanding and acceptance of the pragmatic motivations and implications of the utterance ("acceptability conditions"); and lastly, implementation of the obligations deriving from the utterance. Differently phrased, a hearer must be able to grasp the meaning of a statement as well as to take a stand toward it (by responding with "yes" or "no") and orient his actions accordingly. In Habermas's view, semantic meaning cannot be rigidly divorced from pragmatic connotations, since (to use an example) understanding a command implies knowing how and why to comply with the command. In the case of communicative interaction, understanding a statement typically implies knowing the conditions which would validate, justify, or argumentatively corroborate it. Habermas at this point returns to the theme of validation and validity claims familiar from his earlier writings. Narrowly construed, communicative interaction is said to include "only such speech acts in which the speaker advances validity claims amenable to critical scrutiny." As in previous publications, these claims assume mainly three forms, and include claims regarding the "truth" of propositions, the "rightness" of normative obligations, and the "truthfulness" of self-disclosure—a tripartition which again is linked with the actor's (or speaker's) "world-relations": his relation to the "objective," "social," and "subjective" worlds. "A communicatively achieved consensus," we read, "depends on precisely three reviewable validity claims because—in deliberating about something and articulating their views—actors cannot help but embed their speech acts in exactly three world-relations and claim validity for them in each of these dimensions." Habermas proceeds to define three types of speech acts ("constative," "regulative," and "expressive") corresponding to the three validity claims and all sharply distinguished from perlocutionary or strategic behavior.[12]

In its concluding paragraphs the interlude draws attention to the second major topic I wish to explore in this context: the concept of the "life-world." As Habermas notes, the focus on rationality or rational validation shortchanges the domain of everyday experience against which processes of rationalization are silhouetted. The concept of the "life-world"—defined as the arena of "implicit knowledge"—serves at this point as a supplement or corrective designed to remedy this defect and to provide rationality with concrete social or sociological moorings. In Habermas's words, the concept refers to the "background of implicit knowledge which enters into cooperative efforts of interpretation *a tergo;* communicative action always occurs within a lifeworld that remains in the back of communicative participants." In the same context the concept is also circumscribed as an "implicit knowledge not representable in a finite number of propositions"; as a "holistically structured knowledge"; and as a kind of knowledge "which is insofar not at our disposal as we are unable to render it conscious or subject it to doubt at our discretion."[13] Although elaborated at length for the first time in *Theory of Communicative Action,* the topic is not an entirely new ingredient in Habermas's vocabulary. As previously indicated, his earlier works on cognitive interests already made reference to a diffuse "life-praxis" seen as a foil or backdrop to the "praxis of inquiry" in which validity claims are scrutinized. In *Legitimation Crisis* the notion of the "life-world" was specifically introduced to counterbalance the category of "systemic" imperatives, that is, imperatives geared to the instrumental-rational efficiency of social systems. We speak of "life-world," the study noted, when focusing on patterns of institutions "in which speaking and acting subjects are socially integrated" or which are "symbolically structured." While, from the systemic angle, "we thematize a society's steering mechanisms and the extension of the scope of contingency," the life-world perspective accentuates "the normative structures (values and institutions) of a society."[14]

Only loosely sketched in such earlier passages, the life-world is a persistent theme running through the two volumes of *Theory of Communicative Action* and culminating finally in the second "theoretical interlude"; here only a few glimpses of this recurrent treatment must suffice. In the opening chapter, the notion surfaces first during a discussion of modes of rationality and particularly of Alfred Schutz's concept of "mundane reasoning." Appealing to the insights of phenomenological sociology, Habermas defines the life-world as an "intersubjectively shared" or "collective life-context" comprising the "totality of interpretations which are presupposed as background knowledge by members of society." The topic reemerges again in a section devoted to the differentiation between primitive-mythical and modern-rational "world-views." In every instance, the life-world is said to be a reservoir of implicit knowledge, that is, a collection of "more or less diffuse, always unproblematical background convictions" providing a "source of situation definitions." The difference between world-views, however, resides in the potential for rationalization. In Habermas's portrayal, primitive-mythical world-views exhibit relatively closed and unquestioned patterns of belief and behavior: "To the extent that the life-world of a social group is governed by a mythical world-view, individual members are relieved of the burden of interpretation and also of the chance to bring about a critically reviewable consensus. As long as it remains 'sociocentric' (in Piaget's sense) the world-view prevents the differentiation between the 'worlds' of existing states of affairs, of valid norms and of subjective experiences amenable to expressive display." Modernization or rationalization from this angle signifies chiefly the progressive differentiation between dimensions of the taken-for-granted life-praxis, and particularly the segregation of reviewable "worlds" from the matrix of the traditional "life-world"—what Habermas describes as the "decentering of world-views." "Only to the extent," he writes, "that the formal reference system of the three worlds is differentiated, is it possible to formulate a reflexive concept of 'world' and to gain access to this world through the medium of common efforts of interpretation understood as cooperative negotiation of situation definitions. . . . In performing their interpretation members of a (modern) communicative group delimit the objective world as well as the intersubjectively shared world against the subjective worlds of individuals and (other) collectives."[15]

The most elaborate treatment of the concept occurs in the second "theoretical interlude" (which forms the centerpiece of the second volume). Drawing on arguments borrowed from Mead and Durkheim, the interlude initially contrasts the concept as a purposive category to purely instrumental or functional criteria. On Mead's interactive premises, we read, "society is construed from the participant perspective of acting subjects as *life-world of a social group.*" On the other hand, "from the observer perspective of an outsider society appears simply as a *system of behavior* where behavior is more or less functionally related to system maintenance." Pursuing the insider's approach, Habermas in the following appeals again to the precedent of phenomenological sociology. Invoking Schutz's distinction between "situation" and "horizon" (or context) he writes: "A *situation* is a thematically focused, action-pertinent segment of patterns of relevance in the life-world which are concentrically ordered and whose anonymity and diffuseness increases with growing social and spatio-temporal distance." Situations, in this terminology, are always embedded in broader "horizons" which in turn are grounded in the life-world. For participants, we are told, the concrete situation is "always the center of their life-world; but it has a moving horizon because it points to the complexity of the life-world"—a life-world which is constantly "present" but only as "background of actual events." Noting certain subjectivist limitations of Schutzian phenomenology (deriving from the Cartesian legacy), Habermas seeks to correct this defect through recourse to hermeneutics and ordinary language theory. From a linguistic angle, he observes, "communicative actors always move *within* the horizon of their life-world"—a life-world which now can be defined as "a culturally transmitted and linguistically organized reservoir of meaning patterns." The fabric and structures of the life-world, from this perspective, can be said to "determine the forms of possible intersubjective communication and consensus."[16]

Despite this invocation of phenomenology and hermeneutics Habermas does not limit his discussion to the level of taken-for-granted convictions and implicit meanings. Reacting against a narrowly "culturalist" construal of the life-world—and also against a pre-cognitive focus inhibiting sociological analysis—the interlude translates background convictions into the concept of "everyday practice" (*Alltagspraxis*) by means of which distinct life-world spheres and their modes of reproduction can be scrutinized. The reformulation yields three "structural components," labeled respectively "culture," "society," and "personality"—where culture denotes a reservoir of shared knowledge and pre-interpretations, society a fabric of normative rules, and personality a set of faculties or "competences" enabling individuals to speak and to act. In terms of generative potential, the three components are said to undergird processes of cultural reproduction, of group and solidarity formation, and of individual socialization. "Under the functional aspect of consensual agreement," we read, "communicative interaction serves tradition and the renewal of cultural knowledge; under the aspect of action coordination it promotes social integration and the establishment of solidarity; under the aspect of socialization, finally, it supports the achievement of personal identity." In light of previous descriptions of communicative action, the three components can readily be grasped as life-world underpinnings of the "three worlds" characterizing rational argumentation (with culture being related at least in part to "objective" cognition, society to the "social" and personality to the "subjective world"). Underscoring the internal connection Habermas proceeds to depict modernization as the gradual replacement of implicit by explicit meaning patterns—a change involving the progressive "differentiation" of life-world components and the move from everyday exchanges to rational communication thematizing reviewable validity claims. In his words: "A directional transformation of life-world structures prevails to the extent that evolutionary changes can be analyzed in terms of a structural differentiation between culture, society, and personality. Distinct learning processes can be postulated for this structural differentiation if it can be shown that such differentiation signifies a growth in rationality."[17]

Modernization (one needs to add) does not entirely coincide, however, with the differentiation of communicative structures or components—an emphasis which would shortchange processes of material reproduction. Habermas at this point returns to the distinction between instrumental (or functional) and communicative rationality and also to the dichotomy between "system" and "life-world" familiar from *Legitimation Crisis*. As he affirms, long-range social development involves not only the internal diversification of life-world components but also the growing segregation of symbolic-communicative patterns from reproductive endeavors governed by standards of technical efficiency—a process which can be described as the "uncoupling" of system and life-world. "If we view the cohesion of society exclusively as 'social integration'," he writes, "we opt for a conceptual approach concentrating on communicative action and construing society as human life-world." If, on the other hand, we grasp the same phenomenon "from the angle of 'system integration', we adopt an approach which conceives society after the model of a self-regulating system." Seen jointly from the two angles, society as a whole emerges as "an entity which in the course of evolution is increasingly differentiated both as system and as life-world. Systemic evolution is measured by the growth of a society's steering capacity, while the segregation of culture, society, and personality indicates the evolutionary stage of a symbolically structured life-world." According to Habermas, the main social domains dedicated to the enhancement of "steering capacity" are the economy and the state; with the disintegration of mythical and traditional worldviews, the two domains are said to be steadily transformed into "subsystems" ruled by efficiency criteria and "uncoupled" from symbolic interaction: The "steering mechanisms of money and power" sanction an "instrumental concern with calculable quantities and thus permit a generalized strategic manipulation of the decisions of other agents bypassing modes of linguistic communication." Once instrumental subsystems are no longer merely coordinated with communicative patterns but begin to invade and subdue the latter, the uncoupling of system and life-world is converted into a direct "colonization of the life-world," that is, its subjugation to alien standards of technical control.[18]

II

Before entering into a critical review of Habermas's arguments, I want to stress again some of the obvious merits of *Theory of Communicative Action*. As suggested previously, these merits include the departure from narrowly individualistic premises and the turn to "language" and "intersubjectivity" (although the meaning of these terms is at this point still opaque). Another obvious achievement is the sheer size of the study and the vast range of coverage: a coverage extending from the exegesis of sociological "classics" over discussions of social development to the analysis of modes of rationality and rational argumentation. The very size of the study, however, may also be one source (although not the only source) of pervasive ambiguities and theoretical quandaries besetting Habermas's presentation: Looking over the two volumes the reader occasionally has the impression that the study is the work not so much of a single author but a collective of authors whose views are not always synchronized. Accents set in one section or chapter are sometimes strongly revised if not entirely revoked in another portion of the study; occasionally this imbalance occurs even in the same section or on the same page (as I intend to show). Because of their central role in the study's overall framework I want to concentrate at this point on the key concepts of "communicative action" and "life-world" in an effort to disentangle their meaning and mutual relationship.

Given the crucial weight placed on "communicative action" one might assume that its meaning is relatively clear and unproblematical; this, however, is not the case. One quandary concerns the status of communication (and implicitly of language). Despite recurrent references and attempts at clarification, the study oscillates precariously between a mode of action predicated on a prior, pre-subjective consensus and another view treating consensus as outcome of divergent individual designs. The oscillation can be restated as the query whether communication signifies a matrix underlying social interaction, or else a relatively extrinsic mechanism of social coordination. The quandary seems endemic to Habermas's entire opus. In his earlier publications, "communicative action" tended to denote usually (if not preponderantly) an action orientation proceeding on the basis of conventional or consensually accepted norms and meaning patterns. Thus, in the words of *Knowledge and Human Interests:* "In everyday life-contexts, ordinary-language communication is never isolated from habitual interactions and attendant or intermittent experiential expressions." The view was more poignantly stated in another essay of the same time. "By 'interaction'," Habermas affirmed there, "I understand *communicative action,* symbolic interaction. It is governed by binding *consensual norms* which define reciprocal expectations about behavior and must be understood and recognized by at least two acting subjects. Social norms in this case are enforced through sanctions and their meaning is anchored in ordinary-language communication." These comments did not prevent him from portraying communicative action in another passage (cited before) as a "system of reference" coordinating "interactions between social subjects who know and recognize each other as unique individuals."[19]

The quandary is not entirely resolved in *Theory of Communicative Action*—although the overall tendency is toward the latter meaning. Thus, a passage in the introductory chapter defines communicative action as the kind of "praxis" in which agents rely on "their

common life-context, the intersubjectively shared life-world." Similarly, a later section describes communicative action as a consensual
mode of interaction, a mode in which "participants pursue their plans
consensually on the basis of a common situation definition." Noting
the limitation of this formulation, however, Habermas adds in the
same paragraph: "If a common situation definition must first be negotiated, or if consensual efforts fail in the context of a common definition, then consensus—which normally is the condition for the pursuit of goals—is itself transformed into a goal or objective." In view
of the study's pervasive stress on rationality and rationalization, it
seems fair to construe consensual interaction more as an achievement
than a premise. This construal is buttressed by Habermas's own distinction between "communicative" and "norm-regulated" action—
where the first type denotes a particularly reflexive or rational-
discursive form of interaction while the second type involves behavior in accordance with conventional rules (akin to Weber's notion of
"traditional" action). The construal is further underscored by Habermas's comments on consensus or consensual interaction (*Verständigung*). As indicated, consensus in his view does not merely mean a
merger of feelings or dispositions nor even a factual convergence of
opinions, but rather a rationally grounded accord: Communicative processes "aim at a consensus that satisfies the conditions of a rationally motivated assent to the content of an utterance." The same focus
on achievement is also evident in the category of "communicative rationality" which serves as a *leitmotiv* throughout the entire study.
"The concept of *communicative rationality*," we read (in a passage
mentioned earlier), "carries with it connotations which ultimately
derive from the central experience of the quietly unifying, consensus-
producing function of argumentative speech where participants overcome their initial subjective views and, through the bond of rationally grounded convictions, assure themselves both of the unity of
the objective world and the intersubjectivity of their life-context."[20]

The ambiguities surrounding communication have a direct bearing on the status of language in Habermas's framework and on the
significance of his "linguistic turn." Appealing to the Humboldtian
legacy in ordinary language philosophy, Habermas at various points
portrays language as a concrete presupposition of human interaction
which is never fully at the disposal of participants. "Language and
culture," he affirms, "are neither identical with the formal world-
concepts by means of which participants jointly define their situation, nor are they generally something mundane or 'inner-worldly';
rather, they are constitutive for the life-world itself. They neither coin-

cide with one of the formal worlds to which participants ascribe components of their situation, nor are they part of the objective, social or subjective worlds." In a formulation reminiscent of Gadamer's hermeneutics (which in turn is inspired by Heidegger) the study notes that ordinary language always remains *"in the back"* of participants: "Communicative agents always move *within* the horizon of their life-world which they cannot surpass or transcend." Statements of this kind, however, do not prevent Habermas on other occasions—and sometimes in the same context—from depicting language as a usable instrument, that is, as a "means" of communication or a "mechanism" of action coordination. The same passage pointing to the *"vis a tergo"* character also speaks of language as a "medium" of consensual interaction. The discussion of action theory differentiates communicative action from other types by its reliance on the "linguistic medium in which the world-relations of actors as such are mirrored." Linguistic communication, Habermas adds, is "simply the mechanism of coordination through which the action plans and purposive goals of participants are interactively correlated." The same view is restated in the first theoretical interlude. "For a theory of communicative action," we read there, linguistic communication "seen as mechanism of action coordination becomes the focal point of interest." The stress on coordinating functions—intimately associated with rationalization processes—is bound to cast doubt on Habermas's linguistic turn, by revealing language either as a usable means or else as a property or "competence" of individual speakers (a construal not radically at odds with the traditional philosophy of consciousness).[21]

Another quandary—not unrelated to the status of communication—concerns the distinction between action types, especially between "teleological" and "communicative" action or between "success-orientation" and "consensus-orientation." The quandary seems again endemic to Habermas's approach. Regarding the dichotomy between "labor" and "interaction" (as used in his earlier works), the difficulty of effecting a neat separation has been noted by numerous critics, including Anthony Giddens who wrote: "All concrete processes of labor, as Habermas emphasizes in his discussion of Marx, and as Marx emphasized so forcibly himself, are social: or in Habermas's terms, involve interaction."[22] Rather than recapitulating Giddens' able critique I want to concentrate here on the special or intrinsic dilemmas of the new study. As it seems to me, not only is instrumental or teleological action regularly social or interactive in character, but communicative action (to the extent that is a mode of "action") is invariably animated by a "telos" and thus teleological; I shall emphasize the second aspect.

Theory of Communicative Action repeatedly chides "intentionalist semantics" for reducing communication or semantic understanding to speaker's intentions. This type of semantics, we read at one point, "does not come to grips with the coordination mechanism of linguistically mediated interactions because it construes communication after the model of teleological action." At the same time, however, Habermas is unable to isolate the communicative category from purposive intent. This is evident already in the adopted terminology: for example, in the opposition between "success-orientation" and "consensus-orientation"—where orientation seems readily interchangeable with intention (or at least closely allied with it). Similarly, the study persistently speaks of the "goal" or "aim" of both illocutionary and perlocutionary acts (and occasionally of the illocutionary "success" of communication). While the "illocutionary aim" of a speaker is said to result from the meaning of the utterance itself, the "perlocutionary aim" is manifest only in effects or consequences of speech. To recall a passage cited earlier: "I label 'communicative' those linguistically mediated interactions in which all participants pursue with their utterances *exclusively* illocutionary aims."[23]

The goal-aspect, moreover, is not only incidental to communicative action but a central ingredient whose status is steadily enhanced in the course of rationalization, that is, with the transition from ordinary exchanges to rational-discursive communication. As Habermas himself admits (and I again repeat his statement): "If a common situational definition must first be negotiated, or if consensual efforts fail in the context of a common definition, then consensus—which normally is the condition for the pursuit of goals—is itself transformed into a goal or objective." In another context, the study is even more forthright by acknowledging the necessary teleological structure of action, including its communicative mode. In an effort to differentiate communicative "action" from communication or rational consensus per se, Habermas observes: "Language is (simply) a medium of communication which serves the task of consensus whereas agents — in interacting with each other and seeking to coordinate their actions — pursue their own distinctive goals. To this extent, the teleological structure is fundamental to *all* types of action" — although these types differ in their specification of contextual conditions. Differently phrased: reciprocal understanding and communicative consensus represent merely a "mechanism of action-coordination"—which does not fully absorb or exhaust the active component of the communicative mode. Regardless of different accents and contextual conditions, action types are said to converge at least on this level: "In all cases the teleological structure of action is presupposed in the sense that actors are presumed to be endowed with the capability of goal-orientation and purposive action, and also with the interest in implementing their action plans."[24]

The prominence of teleology, one might add, casts doubt on the internal coherence of "communicative action" (at least in its rational-reflective mode), that is, on the compatibility between action and communication or between "telos" and consensus. Again, there is a history to this dilemma in Habermas's thought. His early publications, notably *Knowledge and Human Interests*, insisted on the close amalgamation of action and communication, presenting both as symbiotic elements of everyday experience. "In everyday life-contexts," he wrote at that time, "ordinary-language communication is never isolated from habitual interactions and attendant or intermittent experiential expressions. . . . Language and action in this case interpret each other reciprocally: this is spelled out in Wittgenstein's notion of 'language games'." As he added, further underscoring this view: "The 'grammar' of ordinary language determines not only internal linguistic relations, but regulates the communicative nexus of sentences, actions, and expressions as a whole, that is, a habitual social life-praxis." The "postscript" to the same study (mentioned earlier) introduced a sharp conceptual distinction between everyday exchanges and rational-discursive communication, a distinction centering on the respective role of action. The claim to "objectivity" associated with science, the essay stated, is based on the consistent "virtualization of the pressure of action and decision which renders possible the discursive testing of hypothetical validity claims and the accumulation of valid knowledge." Rephrasing the distinction in terms of the dichotomy between "discourses" (or "praxis of inquiry") and "life-praxis," the postscript elaborated: "In everyday life-praxis, we gain and exchange action-related experiences; statements made for the purpose of communicating experiences are themselves actions." By contrast, "given their communicative structure discourses are divorced from the constraints of action; nor do they provide room for processes of *generating* informations. Rather, discourses are immune from action and free from experience."[25]

The segregation of discourses from ordinary life-praxis has never been revoked in Habermas's subsequent writings. Given the stress on rationality in his recent work, the notion of "communicative action" thus appears fraught with profound tensions if not entirely paradoxical: in the course of social rationalization communication is bound to be progressively purged of its active components or concrete action contexts; in any event, the distance between consensus and active "telos" is liable to widen. In *Theory of Communicative Action* Habermas seeks to circumvent or at least to mollify this conclusion through recourse to speech-act theory and especially through reliance on the concept of a "formal" or "universal pragmatics" of speech. As indicated, the first interlude associates rational communication or consensus not only with a purely semantic understanding of utterances, but also with the pragmatic acceptance of validity claims and the practical implementation of the consequences of speech; in this manner, despite recognition of the gulf between communication and communicative "action," the interlude seeks to effect a reconciliation or partial reunion of reason and life-praxis. A closer inspection of the argument, however, cannot fail to reveal the imbalance of the merger: that is, the relative accentuation of cognitive understanding over practical implementation (or of theory over practice). The distinctive mark of a "formal-pragmatic" approach, Habermas asserts, resides in its focus on the question "what it *means* to *understand* a communicatively employed sentence or utterance." In addition to a narrowly semantic grasp of terms, such understanding in his view includes various other types of "knowledge": "We understand a speech act if we know what renders it acceptable. . . . A hearer understands the meaning of an utterance if—apart from its grammatical correctness and contextual premises—he knows the essential conditions through which he can be motivated by a speaker to take an affirmative stance." Yet, knowing clearly is not the same as doing; nor is cognitive understanding synonymous with will-formation or social action. As Agnes Heller observed pointedly (and correctly) in one context: "The assumption that consensus can be achieved in a process of enlightenment is in fact no answer: the *will* to achieve consensus is the problem in question." From Habermas's own perspective, communicative rationality, she added, seems to involve "a choice, a value-choice." While, seen as a cognitive endowment or competence, reason is simply a "rationality in-itself," "to transform it into a rationality for-itself we have to choose communicative rationality as a value."[26]

The quandaries besetting communicative action are matched if not exceeded by those surrounding the "life-world" concept. I shall bypass or downplay difficulties of a terminological kind—some of which have surfaced already in previous discussions. Thus, it is at least awkward or confusing to encounter "culture" as a synonym for language and background assumptions in general, and subsequently as label for one of the sub-components of the life-world. The same might be said about the term "society" which in some instances designates the fabric of social interactions as a whole, and in others a particular subdivision dealing with normative integration. More important are ambiguities affecting the status of the life-world itself. On repeated occasions the life-world is depicted as an arena of purposive meanings and symbols animating individual agents or speakers. As mentioned, *Legitimation Crisis* contrasted systemic steering mechanisms to the life-world seen as an institutional matrix "in which speaking and acting subjects are socially integrated." The formulation is picked up in the second interlude where the "life-world of a social group" is identified with society as "construed from the participant perspective of acting subjects." The same view also underlies the appeal to Schutzian phenomenology—especially the portrayal of "situations" as experiential patterns "concentrically ordered" around individual agents for whom a given circumstance is "always the center of their life-world." With a slight change of accent (but again with reference to Schutz), the study at another point associates the category with a "subject-writ-large," claiming that "members of a collectivity" typically rely on it "in the first person plural." Statements of this kind are clearly at odds with passages stressing preconscious and pre-subjective background conditions—unless subjective meanings are supposed to operate as "*vis a tergo*" behind social subjects (which is barely intelligible). The two opposing approaches can be termed respectively the "weak" and the "strong view" of the life-world—with the first drawing its inspiration chiefly from Schutzian (and Husserlian) phenomenology and the second tracing its roots to Gadamer (and Heidegger); while in the former the life-world appears as a network of potential or embryonic subjects, the latter breaks more resolutely with traditional subject-object (and ego-alter) polarities. By combining the two approaches, the study seeks to incorporate advantages intrinsic to both—but at the price of diminished coherence. The need to separate the two views has been recognized by numerous observers, including a philosopher as congenial to Habermas as Karl-Otto Apel. Assessing recent trends in philosophy, Apel in one instance differentiated "Heidegger's more radical 'analysis of Dasein'" from Husserl's "phenomenology of the life-world," noting the comparatively greater proximity of phenomenology to traditional problems of "transcendental constitution."[27]

In *Theory of Communicative Action*, the incoherence of the mixed perspective surfaces in numerous forms and contexts; one has to do with the availability of the life-world for sociological analysis. On repeated occasions the study insists on its strictly non-available or non-objectifiable character. Elaborating on the notion of background assumptions Habermas states that communicative agents cannot objectify or face frontally "the horizon of their own life-world": "As interpreters they are with their speech acts part of the life-world, but they cannot refer to 'something in the life-world' in the same manner in which we refer to facts, norms or experiences. . . . Differently put: participants cannot distantiate language and culture in a way akin to their treatment of the totality of facts, norms or experiences about which communication is possible." The concluding section of the study reiterates this ("strong") view of the life-world by presenting the latter as a kind of background pre-understanding "which is at no one's arbitrary disposal." Given these and several other statements to the same effect, the reader is bound to be surprised by the study's tendency toward progressive objectification, that is, the transformation of the life-world into a pliant target of sociological inquiry. This transformation occurs in several stages. The initial, relatively subtle shift involves the bracketing of the life-world concept in favor of the notion of everyday interaction or "everyday practice," a notion amenable to narrative description and especially to the portrayal of processes of social reproduction. In quick succession, this shift is then found to yield a whole host of sociological categories and distinctions no longer recalcitrant to empirical research: first, the differentiation between three "structural components" of the life-world (culture, society, and personality), and subsequently the segregation between symbolic and material modes of reproduction or between "system" and "life-world." Clearly, the introduction of these categories would serve little purpose if it were not possible to pinpoint their substantive content and respective boundaries. In the case of the three structural components, Habermas indicates their close affinity to existing sociological subdisciplines: namely, sociology of knowledge, institutional analysis, and social psychology. The second and more basic distinction is presented as the opposition between "inner" and "outer" dimensions, or else as the contrast between divergent "subsystems"—in the sense that, in the course of modernization, the life-world is "steadily reduced to one subsystem among others." At one point, the study even speaks of the "everyday practice of the life-world" as a "clearly demarcated object domain."[28]

The sketched transformation of the life-world is problematical not only because of its objectivist bent, but also in terms of its claimed sociological results. As previously mentioned, the "components" of the life-world in Habermas's account correspond to the three formal "world" concepts of rational discourse—concepts which in turn can be correlated with "subject-object" and "ego-alter" distinctions; treated as "inner" and "outer" domains even the system—life-world bifurcation can be traced back to the same set of categories. To the extent that this is the case, however, the life-world ceases to function as polar counterpoint to the formal "worlds," being reduced instead to their simple anticipation. As can readily be seen, the contrast between "weak" and "strong" views surfaces here again, with wide-ranging effects on the study's arguments. Basically, Habermas in this instance exploits the advantages implicit in the weak conception of the life-world—but at the cost of tautology or definitional circularity: culture, society, and personality can be presented as "structural components" because the life-world has been defined from the beginning as a matrix composed of embryonic subjects (and objects). The dilemmas besetting this approach are not only definitional, however, but carry over into other topical areas, including the theory of social development. Portrayed as "structural components," subject-object and ego-alter relations are treated as invariant features of social life—a perspective compressing social "change" into the teleological unfolding of a timeless potential.[29] More important at this point are the developmental implications for the life-world itself: Once modernization is seen as a progressive rationalization of background assumptions through discursive thematization, the life-world is bound to be not only weakened but steadily eclipsed and finally absorbed by world-concepts. Consistently pursued, this process would render nugatory a central pillar of the entire study, thus depriving communicative action of its social moorings. As it happens, however, other arguments of the study tend to cast doubt both on this outcome and the invariance of structural components.

The ambivalent status of the life-world, from a developmental perspective, emerges chiefly in Habermas's discussion of primitive or "archaic" societies. The case is instructive because of the exemplary character ascribed to these societies—the fact that (as the study says) they are "virtually synonymous with the life-world matrix." Given the theoretical prominence of structural distinctions one would expect them to operate at least incipiently in pre-civilized or "tribal" settings; this, however, is not the case. Pointing to the centrality of lineage and family relations and the prevalence of "mythical world-views," Habermas notes the amorphous blending of culture, personality, and social integration and the virtual absence of rational world-concepts: mythical orientations, he states, "obliterate the categorial distinctions between objective, social and subjective worlds." The same situation obtains regarding the opposition between symbolic and material reproduction. As Habermas observes, primitive world-views do not yet differentiate between society and its "natural environment"; nor do they support a strict dichotomy between instrumental-teleological and communicative action or between systemic imperatives and consensual agreement: "Systemic mechanisms are not yet divorced from institutions promoting social integration"—to the point that "social and systemic integration actually converge." If this is correct, however, how can the study subsequently segregate "system" from "life-world," reducing the latter to a mode of symbolic reproduction—given the absence of this distinction in archaic societies whose life-world is nonetheless presented as prototypical (and as "closest to furnishing an empirical warrant for the life-world concept as such")? Differently phrased: how can the life-world be depicted as an "inner" domain made up of symbolic subcomponents—given the relatively modern character of the inner-outer division and of the subcomponents themselves?[30] At a minimum, Habermas's account at this point conveys a sense of anachronism: the impression that, projected onto an amorphous canvas, recent sociological categories are surreptitiously endowed with structural invariance.

III

Having scrutinized the two key concepts of Habermas's study I want to allude briefly to some broader (and perhaps more worrisome) implications or corollaries. First, to stay with the life-world theme, it seems fair to underscore its generally precarious status in the confines of *Theory of Communicative Action*. In the concluding passages of the study, Habermas reiterates its cognitive unavailability—the fact that life-world patterns are "at no one's disposal." The "horizon knowledge" underlying everyday praxis, he observes, has the character of taken-for-granted assumptions; "but it does not satisfy the criterion of a *knowledge* which is intrinsically related to validity claims and thus can be critically assessed." Although not an isolated instance, this comment seems odd or out of place in a study whose centerpiece is discursive rationality and a theory of communication anchored in reviewable validity claims. In the same context, reflecting on general philosophical underpinnings, Habermas is content to claim for his overall approach at best a "felicitous coherence of different theoretical fragments" and even to regard coherence as "the only criterion of judgment" on this level—a view which is hardly congruent with the strong doctrine of discursive truth (and rightness) championed elsewhere in the study. At another point, Habermas exempts the "totality of a life-form" or life-world from the application of specific rationality standards, stating: "Life-forms and life stories are judged implicitly by criteria of normalcy which do not permit approximation to ideal yardsticks; perhaps we should speak instead only of a balance between mutually complimentary life-elements." This assertion—one should note, however—occurs at the end (as a kind of afterthought) in a section devoted to the differentiation between mythical and modern world-views where modernity is singled out precisely for its superior rationality. As it seems to me, life-world arguments cannot simply be juxtaposed to, or amalgamated with, the defense of rationalization —without incurring the risk of incoherence (which is not the same as fragmentary coherence). Differently put: rationality criteria cannot simultaneously be bracketed in favor of "normalcy" and extolled as pacemakers of processes in which earlier life-forms are "categorially devalued."[31] Far from effecting a judicious "balance," one might say, rationality in Habermas's overall presentation tends to jeopardize or erode the life-world (and vice versa).

The same presentation—and this may be more crucial still—places in jeopardy also the role of communicative action and thus the "normative foundations" of critical social theory. Habermas's vindication of rationalization and of modern rationality is predicated basically on the saving virtues of communicative consensus—virtues he seeks to guard jealously against the encroachment of systemic imperatives. At a closer look, however, this vindication is deeply problematical because, in Habermas's own account, rationalization and consensus are by no means readily compatible. In a previous context I pointed to the tension between the active and consensual components within the concept of "communicative action," indicating how, with growing rational reflexivity, the former are increasingly ejected or purged from the consensual ideal. Looking at things from the other side of the coin, a similar purge can be shown to affect consensus itself. According to *Theory of Communicative Action*, modernization involves the steady separation or "uncoupling" of system from life-world, that is, the growing autonomy of systemic social domains (chiefly the economy and the state) governed by success-orientation and standards of rational efficiency. Simultaneously, modernization is said to denote the increasing differentiation of the symbolic life-world itself, that is, the progressive division between its "structural components" and between the three dimensions of the objective, social, and subjective worlds. Translated into "subject-object" and "ego-alter" categories, social development in this sense signifies the growing segregation of the subject from the object world—and actually the relentless subjugation of "nature" by man—and also the segregation of

ego from alter or of personal "identity" from social "solidarity." Against
this background it is entirely unclear how and why ego (or individual
agents) should seek consensus rather than success in any and all areas
of behavior, or try to curb teleological-strategic impulses. Contrary
to Habermas's claims, the "colonization of the life-world" is not simply a deplorable but avoidable hazard, but a necessary consequence
of his own premises and conception of rationalization.

Repeatedly *Theory of Communicative Action* sounds a somber
note on the prospects of communicative consensus. Thus, at one point
the study speaks of the *"irresistible momentum"* of instrumental-
functional subsystems which is "simultaneously the cause of the colonization of the life-world and of the segmentation between science,
ethics, and art." As in the discussion of the life-world, however, these
and similar comments do not affect the general thrust of the argument; in fact, the same passage ascribes possible "pathological" consequences "neither to the secularization of world-views nor to the structural differentiation of society *per se.*" Pressed on the immunity of
the life-world from (irresistible) strategic imperatives, Habermas occasionally retreats to an "innatist" position: the thesis that symbolic
domains of the life-world are somehow "by nature" (*von Haus aus*) consensually constituted or pregnant with communicative "order." Despite
its time-honored status, however, the thesis seems anomalous in a
study which otherwise strongly opposes "foundational" or ontological presuppositions. Once instrumentalism is given free rein against
nature (as it is in these volumes), what "natural" barriers could
plausibly safeguard the integrity of human or social bonds? Actually,
faced with the progressive "anomie" in modern societies, Habermas
seems in principle reduced to the same kind of counterfactual plea
he ascribes at one point to Durkheim: namely, that there simply ought
to be some "oughts." Moreover, even assuming the presence of "oughts"
in rationalized settings, Habermas persistently emphasizes the purely
"formal" or procedural character of modern norms—a character compatible with any kind of substantive content including success-
orientation (or the manipulation of procedures for strategic ends). Occasionally, it is true, the instrumental implications of pure formalism
and legalism are acknowledged in the study—for instance, in the query
how social identity is supposed to be preserved once social bonds have
"evaporated into a merely procedural consensus on the basis of communicative ethics"—but again without noticeable effect on the rationalization model.[32]

The elusiveness of consensus can be traced at least in part (I
believe) to a curious gap in Habermas's presentation: his nonchalance

regarding intersubjectivity or its treatment largely as a non-issue. Given the sketched processes of rationalization and modernization, however, intersubjectivity or social "solidarity" can by no means be taken for granted. Due precisely to the growing differentiation of life-world components and formal world-concepts, the status of the "social world" (so-called) is bound to be precarious. Once ego, as Habermas postulates, is increasingly segregated from objects—to the point of even acquiring, through reflexivity, an "extramundane" position toward phenomena—how can one subject maintain a straightforward relation to another (extramundane) subject, without reducing the latter somehow to a mundane occurrence? Differently put: how can ego's steady internalization fail to produce the distantiation and externalization of alter? As is well known, the issue has been discussed at length in phenomenological literature—from Husserl's *Cartesian Meditations* to Sartre's analysis of "the Look" in *Being and Nothingness*. Without necessarily endorsing the cogency of the phenomenologists' arguments, one certainly cannot deny the seriousness of their endeavor to come to terms with the problem. Given the centrality of interaction in Habermas's framework, the topic would seem to have merited an equally serious or extensive treatment. At one point the study chides Husserl for not "resolving" the intersubjectivity issue, and Schutz for bypassing its significance—but without offering an alternative approach (beyond a problematic restatement of Mead's self-society correlation). Basically, Habermas seems to regard the issue as settled due to his turn to language; yet, in view of the dilemmas besetting this "turn"—the portrayal of language as a "mechanism" of action projects—the remedy is hardly adequate or persuasive.[33]

As it seems to me, the mentioned quandaries or weaknesses are ultimately linked with an important feature of Habermas's opus, a feature striking because of his guiding ambition: the persistent influence of the "philosophy of consciousness" (or subjectivity), and more generally of the legacy of metaphysics. The influence is evident in the pervasive emphasis on "basic dispositions" or "attitudes" (*Grundeinstellungen*)—which can only be dispositions of consciousness. Thus, the differentiation between formal world-concepts is associated by Habermas with a corresponding distinction between "attitudes towards worlds"—chiefly: the "objectifying" attitude toward facts, the ethical attitude toward social norms, and the reflective attitude toward self (and language)—all of which are said to depend on "changes in perspective or attitudes which we perform." The same emphasis recurs in the discussion of action types and of speech-act theory. While the contrast between success- and consensus-orientation is traced to the respective "attitude assumed by actors," the classification of speech acts is founded on the "basic attitudes" of individual speakers—with constative, regulative, and expressive speech acts being matched by objectifying, normative, and expressive attitudes or dispositions. Further repercussions of traditional philosophy surface in "inner-outer" dichotomies and in the crucial role assigned to "world-views." On various occasions, the "objective" and "social" domains are jointly juxtaposed to the "subjective" sphere under the labels of "outer" and "inner" worlds (or perspectives), while "world-views" are singled out for their contribution to "identity-formation" and their ability to "furnish individuals with a core of basic concepts and assumptions."[34] As it happens, of course, most of these notions or categories have come under serious attack in recent decades. Thus, speech-act theory has been denounced for its subjectivist leanings, just as "world-views" for their ideological overtones. On a broader scale, traditional subject-object (and ego-alter) polarities have been challenged by a host of phenomenological, structuralist, and "post-structuralist" writings— writings stressing the porousness of consciousness and the necessary interpenetration of subject and world. Habermas may not personally wish to venture in these directions, preferring instead the *terra firma* of time-honored maxims. But why should "critical theory" (of all outlooks) be hardened into a barrier against innovation and against a critical rethinking of the metaphysical tradition?[35]

There is a corollary to traditional categories (bound to be noticed by students of political theory): the disappearance of politics or political praxis in Habermas's recent work. His early publications, as is well known, were still strongly preoccupied with political praxis and its progressive disintegration under the impact of social-empirical and instrumental-technical imperatives. In an intriguing and challenging passage, *Theory and Practice* bemoaned the medieval substitution of the "social" domain for the Greek "polis" and the redefinition of man as "social" rather than "political animal"—changes which were viewed as harbingers of an impending erosion and decay. *Theory of Communicative Action* bears few if any traces of this original concern. Taking his bearings from Durkheim, Mead, and other sociological "classics," Habermas in the study reveals himself squarely as a "sociologist" (*cum* moralist) or a theorist of the social domain—while relegating politics to the status of a specialized subdiscipline or subsystem.[36] As indicated, in the course of modernization both the economy and the "polity" (or state) are claimed to be progressively transformed into functional-systemic structures governed by success-orientation and standards of technical efficiency, a trend submerging politics inexorably in bureaucrating controls. At the same time, politics has no clear place within the communicative life-world—an arena devoted to symbolic reproduction and differentiated into the subcomponents of culture, society (or social solidarity), and personality (or socialization). At this point the Habermasian dualism of "labor" and "interaction" (or of system and life-world) exacts its price: by exorcising political praxis seen as an activity which in neither external nor internal, neither purely instrumental-technical nor communicative-consensual in character. Wedged between the alternatives of material and symbolic processes or between "outer" and "inner" worlds, politics as a concrete-transformative enterprise thus appears doomed to insignificance if not extinction.

Politics, moreover, is not the only casualty of Habermasian categories and dichotomies. Coupled with the "inner-outer" distinction, the process of rationalization is liable to tarnish the emancipatory aspiration (that is, the core) of critical theory. In portraying the image of an "idealized" or fully rationalized life-world, Habermas projects a condition of life in which all "natural" limitations as well as limitations of "otherness" are finally extirpated. "Universal discourse," we read, "points to an idealized life-world" reproduced entirely through rational "mechanisms of consensus"; in this setting the "natural growth" (*Naturwüchsigkeit*) of social traditions is dissolved by reason in the same way as are religious traditions by "modern natural science, formalized jurisprudence, and autonomous art."[37] Joined with the study's endorsement of science and technology, this attack on nature reveals ultimately (as Adorno and Horkheimer insisted) an impulse of control and domination—an impulse starkly at odds with the proclaimed goal of freedom from domination. Simultaneously, in the domains of social integration and personality, modernization yields an increasing formalism and abstractness of social bonds and identity structures, a formalism purged entirely of historical or substantive content. Yet, removal of content also means the elimination of all forms of "otherness" and concrete human "difference." Against this background, "universal discourse" signifies basically a retreat to a formal level of identity on which all non-identical properties are erased and "others" can no longer really happen to ego. Differently put: communicative interaction in an idealized setting bears no longer any trace of a real human encounter involving love and hate, joy and pain. Contrary to the professed "decentering" of the *cogito*, *Theory of Communicative Action* thus conjures up the specter of solipsism.

In contradistinction to formalized discourses, the contours of a communicative-political praxis akin to human encounter have been

outlined by several writers, including Agnes Heller. Adopting a narrowly rationalist approach, she observes, Habermas is led to conclude
that "reflexive theory cannot be applied to strategic activities, that
force and discourse cannot be conceived together." Actually, however,
social or political struggle "cannot be described—at least not in all
its forms—as merely strategic activity and . . . the models of force and
of discourse could be interconnected." As Heller continues: "Human
beings do not accept social theories (philosophies) from the standpoint of their group-interests, but from the standpoint of their lives
as a whole, from their systems of needs. 'Readiness' for rational argumentation about values and theories presupposes the involvement of
the human being as a whole, as a needing, wanting, feeling being."
Moreover, "if we accept the plurality of ways of life, we have to accept the plurality of theories as well."[38] In a more philosophical vein,
the ontological dimensions of communication or communicative
praxis have been highlighted by Heidegger. Commenting on one of
Hölderlin's later poems, Heidegger distinguishes communication (Ge-
spräch) sharply from "language use" or the mere exchange of "performative utterances." Participants in communicative interaction, he
notes, do not properly initiate, conduct, or perform the communicative process; instead, they become partners in a reciprocal endeavor
only by virtue of language and its recollective and disclosing potency.
What genuine communication yields, Heidegger adds, is not simply
a uniform rational consensus, but rather a substantive mode of mutual recognition—including recognition of "difference" (which is not
synonymous with non-rational particularity): Communicative differentiation is "not separation, but a form of emancipation which
creates between speakers that open space in which uniqueness can
occur" as well as the "harmony" of differences.[39]

4
Apel's Transformation of Philosophy

THAT OURS IS AN AGE of profound ferment and transformation is nearly a commonplace observation. Philosophically, dissatisfaction with a narrow empiricism as well as with Descartes' rationalist *cogito* has engendered widespread disenchantment with "systems" of thought and a willingness to bid "farewell to metaphysics"—that is, to abandon constitutive premises of modernity in favor of (yet dimly perceived) contours of "post-modernism." In some quarters, attacks on philosophical "foundations" or transcendental moorings have been so exuberant and relentless as to conjure up the vision of an imminent "end of philosophy" or at least of the "sublation" (*Aufhebung*) of its traditional concerns—a vision greeted, for the wrong reasons, both by *blasé* intellectuals and by political activists seeking to shore up ideological fervor. Simultaneously, paralleling radically "deconstructive" initiatives, however, one cannot fail to notice intellectual trends pointing in the opposite direction, the direction of a reappropriation of the past; in the West German context, in particular, postwar thought is rife with efforts to revive and reassess classical-idealist, especially Kantian and Hegelian, teachings. Against this background, Karl-Otto Apel's philosophical writings emerge as a sensitive intellectual barometer of the times. His *Transformation der Philosophie*—first published in two volumes in 1973 and translated in a condensed format in 1980—seeks to move resolutely beyond Cartesian and Kantian modes of subjectivity, but without relinquishing the quest for ultimate foundations or a *fundamentum inconcussum veritatis*.[1]

Taken as a whole, Apel's study offers a far-flung and perceptive account of philosophical developments in our century—an account spanning both Continental and Anglo-American trends and in which subtlety of description is judiciously balanced with critical judgment and constructive innovation. The balance of description and innovation is reflected in the choice of the study's original title. As Apel observes in the Preface (to the English edition): "The German title was intended to be ambiguous in that it referred both to a hermeneutic reconstruction of the process of *transformation in recent philoso-*

101

phy and to an outline of the author's program of a *transformation of (transcendental) philosophy* along the lines of a *transcendental hermeneutics* or *transcendental pragmatics of language.*" In Apel's use of the phrase, "transformation of philosophy" is meant to differentiate his approach explicitly from bolder, deconstructive endeavors, and especially from claims of an impending "end" or "withering away" of philosophy. Countering such claims, the study tries to chart a precarious middle course between restoration and radical change—a course respectful of the "more or less successful institutionalization" of philosophy since the days of Socrates while distancing itself, at the same time, from the comprehensive world-views or systems of the "great thinkers" of the past. According to Apel, a genuine withering away of philosophy would presuppose the latter's full-fledged realization or implementation in the world—a condition from which we are as far removed as ever. "As little as the community of philosophers constitutes by itself a *realization* of philosophy," the (German) Introduction states, "as little can any political implementation of human solidarity claim to be the realization of *philosophy.*"[2]

As a collection of essays, *Transformation der Philosophie*—especially in its longer German version—does not present an entirely homogeneous or uniform argument. As Apel concedes, adding a further connotation to the study's title, the reader perusing the essays cannot help noticing "that the author's position has itself undergone a transformation." The change of perspective is evident already in the subtitles of the two original volumes—with the first focusing on "linguistic analysis, semiotics, hermeneutics" and the second on "the *a priori* of the community of communication." In terms of the (German) Preface, the first volume assembles essays and monographs "which are basically inspired by Heidegger"—even though their "heuristic-methodological impulse" derives from "the confrontation of ontological hermeneutics with the linguistic critique of meaning." By contrast, the second volume contains essays "which, in the author's view, are no longer marked primarily by fascination with the absolutely incalculable event of linguistic world-disclosure, but rather by the attempt of a normative orientation in the direction of a transcendental justification of knowledge claims in the broadest sense." Reinforcing the latter orientation, Apel voices his belief—or else his "operative illusion"—that only a "transcendental philosophy capable of answering the question regarding the conditions of the possibility and validity of *conventions* (or communicative agreements) is able to furnish something like a foundation (*Letztbegründung*) of theoretical and practical philosophy as well as of science."[3] In the following I shall first trace the author's intellectual journey by highlighting central features of the collected essays in their original sequence; against this background I shall then explore both the motives underlying the author's own development and, more importantly, the status and meaning of the proposed "transformation of philosophy."

I

Apel's rootedness in phenomenology and ontological hermeneutics (or onto-hermeneutics) is amply illustrated in the first volume of the study. Its opening essay on "The Two Phases of Phenomenology" reveals him as an attentive student of the development of phenomenological thought from Husserl to Heidegger and Gadamer. As the essay tries to show, phenomenology from its very inception segregated itself radically from positivism and from all "tendencies of ontic reduction" prevalent during the nineteenth century, tendencies which sought to collapse human experience in empirical processes (of a sociological, psychological or biological sort). Deviating from the lingering "psychologism" still present in Dilthey's writings, the thrust of phenomenology—as inaugurated by Brentano and Husserl—was encapsulated in the thesis that "being" or the "meaning of being" was not reducible to ontic occurrences, nor the relationship between man and environment to a causal or functional nexus. In its early, Husserlian phase this thesis of phenomenology gave rise to a strict dualism between invariant meaning-contents and psycho-physiological processes, between "eidetic essences" and empirical motivations of cognition. As a consequence of this "Platonizing" approach, meaning-contents and language itself were elevated to the status of "ideal-noematic objects"—a construal obviously predicated on the constitutive accomplishments of transcendental subjectivity or consciousness. Difficulties arising from the subject-object bifurcation as well as from the (Platonic) "doubling" of the world were chiefly responsible for the anti-idealist insurgency during the second phase of the movement, especially for the reformulation of "eidetic inspection" (*Wesensschau*) in terms of an inquiry into the "being" of the world. In Heidegger's *Being and Time*, the separation of consciousness and noematic objects is transformed into the dialectic of "being" and ontic "beings"—a dialectic sustained neither by logical deduction nor by empirical induction but by the open texture of the "hermeneutic circle." Meanings and symbolic expressions are seen no longer as cognitive objects or instruments, but as signposts to the ground of "being"; poetic language in particular is portrayed as an ontological "clearing" of meaning and as a "linguistic constitution of being."[4]

The constitutive role of language in the disclosure of meaning is further elaborated in a subsequent essay dealing with the correlation of "Language and Truth in Contemporary Philosophy." According to Apel, Western philosophy since antiquity has progressively tended to strip the notion of "truth" of linguistic substance, reducing it instead to an abstract correspondence between subject and object, between symbolic statements and empirical referents. In our own century, this tendency was evident in the program of "logical atomism"—with its aim of submerging referents in logical structures—as well as in "constructive semantics" animated by the goal of fashioning artificial symbol systems matching the empirical world. In all these instances, from Russell over the early Wittgenstein to Carnap—Apel notes—the integral relevance of language to truth claims was circumvented or ignored. An important corrective to the one-sidedness of syntax and semantics was provided by Charles Morris with his notion of a linguistic and semiotic "pragmatics"—a notion distantly linked with the humanist legacy of rhetoric and "topics." As the essay cautions, however, ordinary pragmatics is not entirely able to escape from positivism: especially when identified with observable behavior (a danger courted by Morris himself), linguistic performance is readily subsumed again under an empiricist semantics. From Apel's perspective, the peril is obviated only by a resolute turn to creative pragmatics and especially to poetic language, a turn adumbrated in Heidegger's thought. As portrayed by Heidegger, linguistic praxis aims at participation in the ongoing constitution of meaning, at human collaboration in the "project" of the clearing of being; closely connected with this constitutive conception of language is Heidegger's attempt to provide a poetic and ontological reformulation of the "essence of truth."[5]

Heidegger's language theory provides the chief inspiration also for another essay in the same volume which seeks to bridge the gulf between Continental and Anglo-Saxon philosophy, and especially between onto-hermeneutics and linguistic analysis. Entitled "Wittgenstein and Heidegger" the essay juxtaposes the hermeneutical "question regarding the meaning of being" and the analytical "suspicion of meaninglessness directed against all metaphysics." In Apel's presentation, the two thinkers emerge as "key figures in the philosophical constellation of our century," mainly because of their common move beyond traditional metaphysics—a move prompted in Wittgenstein's case by the claim of "meaninglessness" and in Heidegger's case by the charge of "oblivion of being" (*Seinsvergessenheit*). Despite this common initiative, however, the essay notes important differences between the two approaches. In the *Tractatus* of the early Wittgenstein, language functioned basically as the transcendental-logical structure of experience, a structure not open to reflective scrutiny: due to the coincidence of linguistic statements and empirical referents, "beings" or objects of experience were likewise not amenable to further interpretation. By contrast, Heidegger's *Being and Time* (1927) emphasized already the notion of an "ontic-ontological difference" whereby "beings" are embedded in a matrix of pre-predicative, ontological understanding and historical disclosure of meaning. While Wittgenstein treated the human subject as marginal "limit" of the world, Heidegger portrayed man as a "being-in-the-world" marked by "ek-static" openness — an openness enabling man to interpret beings and objects of experience "*as* something" in terms of a language framework. Turning away from logical semantics, the later Wittgenstein accorded center-stage to the "pragmatic" dimension of language — but without abandoning his antimetaphysical suspicion. The identification of language games with "forms of life" had the effect of inserting human experience into a shared linguistic frame of reference, just as the later Heidegger subordinated individual interpretation of meaning to the prior "interpretedness" (*Ausgelegtheit*) of the world. Yet, according to Apel, the later Wittgenstein stopped in mid-course: by assimilating language use to an instrumental nexus of behavior his *Philosophical Investigations* shortchanged linguistic pragmatics in favor of a relativistic-behavioral construal. Heidegger's writings, on the other hand, proceeded with passing years increasingly beyond the boundaries of instrumental "solicitude" in the direction of the "happening of truth" seen as a process of ontological concealment and unconcealment.[6]

The mentioned themes are further probed and elucidated in "Heidegger's Philosophical Radicalization of Hermeneutics," an essay trying to situate Heidegger's existential analysis vis-à-vis the competing traditions of hermeneutics, on the one hand, and linguistic analysis, on the other. Regarding the former perspective, the essay provides a detailed and instructive overview of the history of hermeneutics, ranging from Renaissance humanism and the Reformation over Schleiermacher to Dilthey. While Dilthey — Apel observes — was still basically concerned with the formulation of a methodology for the humanities (or *Geisteswissenschaften*), Heidegger transformed interpretive understanding into a constitutive category of human *Dasein*, a transformation entailing a far-reaching "radicalization" of the hermeneutical problematic. In a similarly detailed manner, the genealogy of linguistic analysis is traced from modern empiricist and rationalist philosophy back to medieval nominalism and finally to Aristotelian logic. As Apel tries to show, the question of meaning looms large both in existential and in linguistic analysis, although onto-hermeneutics is intent more on the discovery or disclosure and linguistic analysis on the critique of linguistic meaning. Both perspectives, Apel emphasizes, depart from the traditional metaphysics of substances, concentrating their attention instead on the preconditions of the linguistic access to "beings." As in the preceding article, the argument of the essay ends on a critical note. While Heidegger's turn to language tends to undergird his preoccupation with the meaning of "being," linguistic analysis tends to suppress interpretive understanding; in the case of the later Wittgenstein, this suppression results from the instrumental treatment of language use and from the bracketing of reflective mediation between language games.[7]

Elaborating on this last point, the first volume concludes with an essay entitled "Wittgenstein and the Problem of Hermeneutic Understanding," an essay offering a comprehensive overview of Wittgenstein's intellectual development seen from the perspective of onto-hermeneutics. In Apel's portrayal, a crucial isue in Wittgenstein's early writings was the status of so-called "belief-sentences." Countering traditional subjective construals, Wittgenstein's treatment basically amounted to the endeavor to replace intentional consciousness by a logical semantics uniting linguistic structure and empirical reference. Since, from this vantage point, the understanding of sentences was tied not to a speaker's intentions but purely to linguistic structures, the *Tractatus*—in Apel's view—championed a radical "transcendentalization of the logical form of language and simultaneously of the intentional subject" (the latter being reduced to a marginal "limit" of the world). In his later writings, Wittgenstein abandoned the notion of a privileged logical language in favor of a multitude of ordinary language games which, at the same time, encapsulated a multitude of diverse "life-forms." Yet, even at this point, his critical attitude toward intentional meaning remained intact—although its precise implications, especially for the construal of linguistic rules, were elusive and to some extent contradictory. According to Apel, Wittgenstein's conception of such rules oscillated between behaviorism and a quasi-existential pragmatism, without clearly pinpointing the contours of either alternative. To the extent that the rules of language games are the target of reductive-behavioral analysis, the persisting ambition of a critique of meaning becomes itself opaque (being in turn subject to reduction). On the other hand, insofar as rule-governed language use is possible only through participation in a given linguistic tradition, Wittgenstein's approach presupposes a pragmatic exegesis of meaning—an exegesis reflectively related to ordinary language and situated midway between everyday conventions and philosophy. "The confrontation between these apparently contradictory results indicates," Apel writes, "that the philosophical problem of hermeneutic understanding lies precisely between the two models at least intimated by Wittgenstein's conception of language games. . . . What is at issue is a procedure which is constrained to deal with the quasi-transcendental rule of a language game in a virtually 'objective' manner . . . and yet does this only in order to 'understand' the possible motivation of one's own or another's behavior in the light of this quasi-objective rule."[8]

As previously indicated, the second volume is separated from the first by a kind of intellectual sea-change: steadily the focus on onto-hermeneutics and on the ontological "disclosure" of meaning recedes into the background in favor of questions relating to the "transcendental justification" and validation of knowledge claims. Actually, an attentive reading of the first volume provides several glimpses of the impending mutation. Thus, the last-mentioned essay ends with a discussion of the relation between hermeneutics and reflective philosophy, a discussion culminating in an appeal to the "open issue of a critical renewal of the rationality of Hegelian dialectics." Somewhat earlier, the comparison of "Wittgenstein and Heidegger" chided both thinkers for their presumed "oblivion of logos" (Logosvergessenheit), a phrase coined explicitly as a rejoinder to the Heideggerian "oblivion of being." Still earlier in the same volume, two of the essays dealing with language theory conclude with a footnote underscoring the importance of rigorous, non-contextual reflection. Referring to critical arguments levelled at Heidegger's conception of truth—arguments which "Heidegger himself recognized as legitimate"—Apel notes in both instances that the ontological premises of valid statements (emphasized by Heidegger) "have to do not so much with truth as rather with disclosure of meaning seen as transcendental-hermeneutical precondition of truth."[9] Despite these and similar clues and marginal glosses, the reader is liable to be struck by the different, more coolly reflective temper pervading the second volume.

The change in intellectual climate is immediately noticeable in the opening essay of the volume dealing with "Reflection and Material Praxis" and subtitled "On the Cognitive-Anthropological Foundation of Dialectics in Hegel and Marx." Concentrating on the aftermath of

Hegelian philosophy, the essay focuses, on the one hand, on the perspective of "dialectical criticism" seeking to integrate dialectics into a renewed Kantian transcendentalism and, on the other hand, on Marxist "dialectical materialism" with its effort to anchor dialectics in concrete historical developments and especially in "material praxis." Although Hegel's continuing effectiveness (*Wirkungsgeschichte*) may not be exhausted by these positions, most post-Hegelian trends in Apel's view lean toward one or the other alternative. According to the essay, both perspectives are defective—although the second seems more irremediably flawed than the first. While encouraging universal reflection, dialectical criticism is said to conjure up the peril of an empty formalism; by contrast, offsetting its practical bent, Marxist dialectics has ruptured its ties with critical reflection and with the category of "consciousness as such" (or transcendental consciousness). Despite manifest political divergences, onto-hermeneutics—as represented by Heidegger and Gadamer—is claimed to share the flaws of dialectical materialism. Thus, while elucidating the substantive or "material" dimension of language and experience, Gadamer stands accused of truncating the range of philosophical reflection and of sundering the link between praxis and valid knowledge. "That Gadamer's hermeneutics ignores the critical dialectic of transcendental idealism," Apel writes, "is shown among other things by the fact that he leaves unanswered the question regarding the conditions of possibility of the universal validity claims of his own assertions—more sharply formulated: that (like Heidegger) he no longer recognizes the need to mediate an ontological, historical, contextual, and substantive mode of thought with the standard of *noological reflection* established by Descartes and later by Hegel." Consistently with this argument, the essay champions at this point the (at least partial) rehabilitation of Cartesian rationalism: "The underestimation of the Cartesian foundation of science by Gadamer (as previously by Heidegger) derives in my view from the effort—however legitimate—to distance oneself from the representational and control-oriented type of knowledge of modern natural science. But, as Hegel explicitly recognized, the genuine truth of Descartes' philosophy consists rather in the extreme sublimation (so to speak) of domineering knowledge, a sublimation in which thinking . . . assures itself reflectively of the universal validity of its standpoint."[10]

The vindication of Cartesian reflection reverberates throughout the volume, and especially through Apel's endeavor to formulate a comprehensive, transcendentally grounded epistemology in "Scientistics, Hermeneutics, and Critique of Ideology." Easily one of the best-known and most widely discussed writings of the author, the essay presents the "sketch" of a general theory of knowledge articulated from a "cognitive-anthropological" vantage point, a sketch differentiating between a limited number of cognitive orientations rooted in distinctive life-perspectives or "interests." The phrase "cognitive anthropology" is rendered intelligible by Apel's thesis that substantive knowledge always involves an interplay of "bodily *a priori*" and "reflective *a priori*," of "interest" and philosophical reflection. In the context of a positivist philosophy of science, Apel's essay is frontally opposed to the doctrine of a "unified science" with its attempt to level all forms of knowledge into causal explanation, and cognitive interests into psychological motivations. Taking his cues from the Weberian distinction between explanation and understanding, Apel assigns the exploration of intentional actions and meanings to the domain of hermeneutics and hermeneutical historiography. Yet, countering the Gadamerian claim regarding its universal scope, he clearly delimits or circumscribes hermeneutics at least in two directions: those of "noological" reflection and of the methodological distantiation of phenomena characteristic of empirical science. The juxtaposition of "scientistics" and hermeneutics does not exhaust the range of cognitive orientations. According to Apel, a distinctive symbiosis of explanation and understanding occurs in "critique of ideology" or critical social science—a type of inquiry seeking to uncover or emancipate authentic human aspirations buried under layers of social or natural constraints. In the case of all three orientations, cognitive interests are only genetically related to, but not identical with, specific knowledge claims—a relationship whose looseness testifies to the ineradicable tension between "bodily" and "reflective *a priori*" or between material praxis and reflection. As Apel writes (in a later context): "Despite the identity of reason and the interest in being rational, theoretical reflection and material-practical engagement do not coincide, but are differentiated on the highest level of philosophical speculation as antithetical elements within the emancipatory cognitive interest."[11]

Transformation der Philosophie reaches its culmination in the last section of the second volume broadly titled "Transformation of Transcendental Philosophy: The *A priori* of the Community of Communication" (most of the essays in the English translation are taken from this section). The opening essay, "From Kant to Peirce," immediately introduces the central issue: the thesis that modern "philosophy of consciousness" is in the process of being replaced by the philosophy of language and, more precisely, that the role of (Kantian) transcendental subjectivity is now fulfilled by the transcendental-pragmatic dimension of language. The turn toward a "transcendental pragmatics of language"—a turn deviating both from logical semantics and from empirical behaviorism—is said to inaugurate both a revival and a transgression of transcendental philosophy, in the sense that language now furnishes the "semiotic substitute" for Kant's "transcendental synthesis of apperception." "Just as Kant, as an analyst of consciousness," Apel notes, "had to postulate as a premise of epistemology that through cognition something like the *synthetic unity of consciousness* can be reached—in just the same way modern theorists of science, starting from a semiotic or linguistic basis of analysis, have to postulate that through semiotic exegesis something like an *intersubjective unity of world-interpretation* can be obtained." In Apel's presentation, Peirce was a leading pioneer in this turn from consciousness to linguistic pragmatics. Contrary to narrow empiricist construals, the essay underscores Peirce's "semiotic transformation of Kant" whereby reflection was anchored no longer in a solitary *cogito* but in the anticipated "unity of communication in an unlimited intersubjective consensus." Deviating from the Cartesian subject-object model, Peirce accomplished this change by relying on a "triadic" structure of knowledge, a structure differentiating between three modes of inference (induction, deduction, and abduction) as well as between "signifier," "signified," and the pragmatic interpretation of signs in the "community of investigators."[12]

The implications of the linguistic turn for epistemology are specified more concretely in subsequent chapters. Under the title "Scientism or Transcendental Hermeneutics?" the next essay invokes again the triadic structure of language, focusing this time on Charles Morris's distinction between syntactics, semantics, and pragmatics. Despite the seminal character of this distinction, Morris's later writings tended to equate language use and empirical behavior, thus collapsing pragmatics again into scientism. In Apel's view, by contrast, pragmatics has to be seen as a non-empiricist or "transcendental hermeneutics" in which the speaking subject is neither empirically objectified nor reduced to a mere "consciousness as such" (nor, with the early Wittgenstein, to a marginal "limit" of the world). Peirce was one of the first to undertake resolute steps in this direction—although his initiative was limited largely to experimental research or the domain of natural science. This limitation, Apel notes, needs to be corrected through the conception of a broader intersubjective or communicative pragmatics—a conception first intimated by Josiah Royce and later developed by Heidegger and Gadamer along the lines of onto-hermeneutics. As on previous occasions, however, Apel detects in onto-hermeneutics a contextual-historicist truncation of transcendental knowledge as well as a bracketing of the idea of cognitive "progress," features which conjure up the peril of positivism and scientism. "If, instead of an empirically limited community of experimenters, the historical community of interaction is seen as relevant semiotic subject," Apel writes, then "a regulative principle of potentially unlimited progress can be discovered: the principle in question, I believe, resides in the idea of the realization of an *unlimited community of interpretation* which everyone participating in argumentation (that is, every thinking being) implicitly presupposes as *ideal standard of control*."[13]

Epistemologically, intersubjective linguistic pragmatics is particularly crucial for social inquiry—a point underscored in the essay "The Community of Communication as Transcendental Premise of the Social Sciences." In Apel's portrayal, the modern preoccupation with the "egological evidence of consciousness"—a preoccupation still present in Husserl—needs to be replaced and expanded through focusing on the intersubjective "validity of meaning": "Specification of meaning in a *communicative synthesis of interpretation*—and not simply 'synthesis of apperception'—is what provides the basis for the 'highest point' (Kant) of a semiotically transformed transcendental philosophy. . . . In Kantian terminology one might say: in the 'synthesis of apperception', in which the self posits both its objects and itself as *cogito*, the self must simultaneously identify with the transcendental community of communication which alone can confirm the validity of meaning of its own knowledge of self and the world." As before, Peirce and the later Wittgenstein are singled out as pacemakers of a linguistic-communicative pragmatics; in Apel's view, both were intent on mediating the language use of concrete linguistic communities with the postulate (deriving from idealism) of transcendental communicative norms and rules—a mediation particularly significant for social inquiry: "The antagonism between normative-ideal and material factual elements in the transcendental matrix of a community of communication yields, I think, a dialectical feature in the philosophy of science which becomes particularly manifest at the point where this community, while forming the transcendental subject of science, turns at the same time into the object of inquiry: at the level of the social sciences in the broadest sense." Especially as developed and elaborated by Peter Winch, the Wittgensteinian theory of language games is said to furnish a viable model or paradigm for social research—despite the persisting need to guard against the dangers of behaviorism and contextual relativism present in the two writers.[14]

The normative-transcendental thrust of Apel's position is reinforced and solidified in the concluding chapters of the study, especially in "Language as Topic and Medium of Transcendental Reflection" and "The Transcendental-Hermeneutical Concept of Language." According to the first essay, language theory can assume the function of a (transformed) Kantian philosophy only if language is seen as the medium of a transcendental reflection involving the subjective conditions of possibility of cognition. Reviewing philosophical developments in our century, Apel finds very little inclination to undertake such reflection. Both the *Tractatus* and linguistic structuralism are said to bypass subjective pragmatics, while positivism and constructive semantics have tended to replace reflection by stipulating a hierarchy of "meta-languages." Even the theory of language games verges on reductive empiricism through its neglect of the role and status of philosophy; a similar peril of contextualism besets Continental onto-hermeneutics. Countering all these tendencies, Apel vindicates transcendental linguistic reflection—or the "always already presupposed *transcendental language game*"—as the highest mode of self-reflection and as "*basis of the validity* of the principle of reason." The second essay presents language theory as the appropriate contemporary version of "first philosophy" or *prima philosophia*—in contradistinction to classical ontology and modern "philosophy of consciousness." Surveying in broad outlines the history of Western philosophy, Apel notes the traditional philosophical distrust of language and its reduction to a means of information exchange. Modern philosophy in particular, in both its empiricist and rationalist variants, has sought to bypass or bracket language by emphasizing either direct sense perception or else abstract logical structures and principles—approaches which coalesced in logical empiricism. In contrast to this traditional neglect, recent and contemporary philosophy testifies to a broad-scale "linguistic turn." According to Apel, the chief task today is to reconstruct the Kantian legacy "in light of the transcendental-hermeneutical concept of language," in a manner which replaces the unity of consciousness by the "regulative principle of a critical formation of consensus in an ideal speech community, a community which still needs to be implemented in real-life communities." The final essay of the volume builds on this tension between real and ideal communities in an effort to pinpoint the "Foundations of Ethics" and to uncover the ideal norms of behavior implicitly present or presupposed in actual social contexts.[15]

II

Before pondering the character of the proposed "transformation of philosophy," it may be appropriate to consider briefly the author's own intellectual metamorphosis and its underlying reasons or motivations. Given the absence of an explicit treatment of the issue, this exploration has to rely at least in part on dispersed clues and intimations. One motivation is relatively clear and straightforward: Apel's progressive dissatisfaction with existential analysis and onto-hermeneutics and his steadily growing conviction that "world disclosure" and constitution of meaning are unable to do justice to the integrity of reflection and the validation of knowledge claims. The repeated references to Heidegger's presumed "self-correction" (regarding the theory of truth) obviously seek to mollify the harshness of the rupture and to legitimate the latter somehow as a continuation of onto-hermeneutics. A further motivation, closely linked with the first, derives from a certain shift in geographical focus. Despite a persistent concern with Wittgenstein, Apel's earlier writings (especially those assembled in the first volume) are marked by a predominantly Continental outlook, while his later phase gives broader room to issues endemic to analytical philosophy and more generally to Anglo-American intellectual trends. In this respect, his study is impressive evidence of the growing reception of Anglo-American thought in Europe during recent decades. Whatever else the intended "transformation of philosophy" may mean, one feature is clearly the broadening of horizons and the vindication of a trans-Atlantic (and, in the long run, universal) "community of communication." An important effect of this broadening of horizons is the distantiation of distinctly Continental traditions — including the legacy of onto-hermeneutics — and the erosion of ethnocentric leanings or overtones.

The aspect of distantiation is explicitly invoked by Apel as counterpoise to philosophical self-enclosure or self-sufficiency, a counterpoise particularly significant in view of the ongoing "globalization" of cultural relations or the emergence of a universal civilization. As he notes, the rise of this universalism constitutes a profound challenge to an existentially anchored onto-hermeneutics and its focus on "effective-historical" (*wirkungsgeschichtlich*) continuity. What is involved in this process, he writes, "is not the eclipse of history as the mediation of tradition as such, but rather the eclipse — itself historically induced — of certain concrete 'traditions' of the pre-industrial or pre-scientific age. In this epochal crisis — a crisis much more unsettling for non-European cultures in the twentieth century than for

Europe in the nineteenth century—lies the actual core problem of (ni-hilistic) historicism." Despite the persisting importance of historical continuity for individual and social life—Apel adds—the exegesis of tradition today must take on a completely new form: the immediacy of understanding "as it functioned in Europe until the Enlightenment period and in non-European cultures until the present time cannot be restored." Forced to adopt from the West the "technological-industrial form of life and its scientific underpinnings," Third World cultures are constrained "to undergo a much more radical distantiation and estrangement from their own traditions than we ever were; they can-not even dream of compensating the existing rupture with their past solely through hermeneutical reflection." Instead, such cultures are from the beginning confronted with "the necessity to supplement hermeneutical understanding of their own and alien traditions through the construction of a quasi-objective, historical frame of reference—a framework enabling them to situate their own position in the world-historical and global context fashioned (without their collaboration) by European and American civilization."[16]

   Observations of this kind clearly reveal Apel as a socially con-cerned philosopher closely attuned to pressing historical dilemmas —notwithstanding his stress on distantiation and questions of valida-tion. Against the sketched historical background, *Transformation der Philosophie* emerges itself as a document of philosophical reflection in a time of ferment and transition, a time in which Western civiliza-tion generates increasingly global repercussions while being in turn tested and challenged by these repercussions. Yet, in our age as in pre-vious periods, historical trends are hardly unambiguous or unidirec-tional; globalization is a case in point. In Apel's presentation, this pro-cess is invoked chiefly as evidence of the limitation or insufficiency of hermeneutical reflection; simultaneously, however, his study rec-ognizes (at least intermittently) that "hermeneutical understanding cannot simply exit from the context of historical tradition" and that without such a context "man could never really exist"—a concession at odds with the general tenor of his argument. As it seems to me, our time is in fact marked by a dual development: globalization is matched by parallel efforts to revive or preserve local ethnic or cul-tural legacies (as in the case of "négritude"). Both movements are in-timately correlated and intermeshed: while local traditions are increas-ingly permeated by global-scientific perspectives, universalism in turn has to rely on particularistic resources to provide the soil for a global culture. Without this nourishing soil, global order would remain an abstract and meaningless formula, and the members of the "unlimited community of speech" would have nothing concretely to communicate about. In the absence of particular traditions, moreover, universalism would seem to be hostile to identity formation: distantiation would coincide simply with alienation and "anomie." To the extent that self-discovery or self-understanding is possible only through concrete interpersonal encounters, human identity in a global age must be anchored not only in abstract-universal principles but in viable local and regional modes of life.[17]

The preceding considerations are significant also for the juxtaposition or confrontation of Continental and Anglo-American philosophical perspectives. As indicated, Apel's growing preoccupation with discursive validity is paralleled by an intensified immersion in Anglo-American "analytical" literature. Yet, the assessment of this literature remains ambivalent throughout the study. On the one hand, "analytical" rigor is championed as an antidote to, and a means of distantiation from, the vagaries of onto-hermeneutics; on the other hand, Apel persistently criticizes the Western or Anglo-American predilection — evident in recent philosophical trends — for scientism, instrumentalism, and the objectification of experience. Logical positivism in particular is chided for its fusion of empiricist semantics and abstract logic, two ingredients which singly or in combination undermine reflection and the hermeneutical scrutiny of meaning. What is defective in "logical atomism" as well as in semantic constructivism, in Apel's view, is the neglect of the "pragmatic" dimension and thus of the rootedness of cognitive endeavors in communication and in a viable, historically grown social life-world. Against this background, analytical philosophy cannot unequivocally qualify as corrective to hermeneutical intuition — at least so long as distantiation is not treated as a synonym for alienation and reification.

This ambivalence regarding linguistic analysis is matched by the ambivalent treatment of Continental thought, and especially of onto-hermeneutics and its leading representatives. Among all the discussed philosophical positions, no portrayal is more oscillating and elusive than that of Heidegger. Prior to focusing critically on this aspect, however, the fact of this portrayal itself deserves applause — given the widespread silence on the topic in the philosophical profession. In his "Introduction" to *Transformation der Philosophie*, Apel refers to Heidegger as to a philosopher "who at this time is no longer fashionable among us." Depicting the existential structure (or "pre-structure") of understanding as the "basic thesis" of Heideggerian philosophy, he writes: "Precisely in view of the presently pervasive tendency to bypass Heidegger and to appeal, for extra-philosophical motives, to Husserl's phenomenology of the 'life-world' (even when Heidegger's more radical 'existential analytic' is actually intended), it needs to be acknowledged that the possibility to reflect on the quasi-transcendental status of basic human structures (like embodiment, labor, and language) . . . was essentially provided or introduced by Heidegger." As Apel adds, Heidegger's emphasis on human "being-in-the-world" seen as a "future perfect" of experience was basically responsible for "inaugurating a new style of transcendental reflection; and this style no longer permits the explication of the Husserlian problem of 'constitution' of meaning in terms of the subjective 'accomplishments' of a 'pure consciousness'."[18]

Yet this appreciation of Heidegger's contribution to the "transformation" of contemporary philosophy is only one facet of a broader and more complex assessment. In fact, Apel's evolving attitude toward Heidegger offers important clues for understanding his own metamorphosis and the change of perspective evident in the study. The first volume relies strongly on Heidegger's notions of ontological constitution and hermeneutical disclosure of meaning; although the discussion refers mainly to *Being and Time,* no effort is made to differentiate rigorously between existential analysis and Heidegger's writings after the so-called *Kehre.* Apel's interpretation in the first volume, however, carries a distinct accent: an emphasis on the subjective or anthropological components of Heidegger's teachings and (occasionally) on the uniqueness of individual experience in different historical contexts. "The relational structure of language," we read at one point, "presupposes (even synchronically viewed) the special qualitative contents which only the individual can experience: There are as many linguistic structures as there are distinctive contents available to experience—although structures always transcend content in the direction of universality, just as contents transcend structure in the direction of the mystical uniqueness and ineffability of human experience." In view of this correlation of structure and content it is not surprising that Apel's "substantive" notion of truth and of meaning-disclosure at this point hovers precariously at the brink of relativism. "There are for us as many different facts 'in the world'," he writes in one context, "as there are horizons of the original understanding of 'something as something'; and without the 'truth' of those linguistically constituted horizons there would be no understanding of pure 'facticity' and thus no 'facts' as such."[19]

The "existentialist" focus on subjective uniqueness—it seems fair to surmise—has something to do with Apel's own progressive turn toward intersubjective discourse and the discursive redemption of validity claims. The second volume of *Transformation* and also the (subsequently written) "Introduction" limit Heidegger's significance entirely to the dimension of meaning-constitution and meaning-disclosure, while the domain of validation is placed beyond the range of his competence. Meaning-constitution, in this context, is presented basically as a reformulation and radicalization of the transcendental-categorial structuring of cognition envisaged by Kant; at this point, the difference between the "early" and the "later" Heidegger tends to be thematized in terms of the respective proximity to, or distance from, transcendental arguments. As indicated, the Introduction applauds Heidegger's *Being and Time* for inaugurating a "new style of transcendental reflection." The same essay portrays ontological understanding as revolving around the "transcendental constitution" of meaning, and hermeneutics as concerned with the "clarification of the *categorial pre-understanding* of experience." Although conceding Heidegger's effort to "problematize the abstract dualism of apriorism and empiricism," the Introduction speaks broadly of various apriori structures of existence (like "apriori of understanding," "bodily apriori," and "linguistic apriori"), while defining the "hermeneutical circle" as the nexus of "apriori anticipation and empirically induced correction of understanding." More generally, Apel credits *Being and Time* and its existential analysis with "not yet having ruptured completely the ties to a transcendental philosophy of 'subjectivity' in the Kantian sense." By contrast, the later Heidegger is chided for his abandonment of subjectivity and for having drawn "from the apriori fact of the 'disclosed character of *Dasein*' the consequence of a far-flung '*Kehre*'— a reversal leading from the still quasi-transcendental analysis of *Dasein* to a thinking attentive to the 'history of being' but divorced from all normative and methodological moorings." By distancing itself from normative-transcendental standards, this thinking is said to court the peril of an empirical or historical descriptivism.[20]

In my view, this portrayal of Heidegger is highly problematical, both as it pertains to the early and to the later phases of his thought. First of all, I find dubious the charge of descriptivism levelled at the writings after the *Kehre*. Absorbed by questions of "destruction" or "deconstruction," Heidegger admittedly may not always have explicated sufficiently the normative or methodological implications of his work. Notwithstanding this fact, the charge appears to me implausible because it runs counter to the "ontic-ontological difference" and thus to the fundamental thrust of Heideggerian philosophy. If it really were satisfied with an empirical description of ontological events, his later opus would be guilty of a gross inconsistency or incongruence: namely, the tendency to reduce "being" (and its history) to ontic "beings" and their temporal succession. Conversely, I find unconvincing the attempt to force existential analysis into the Procrustean scheme of transcendental philosophy. Once the "pre-structures" of meaning-disclosure are seen as pure "conditions of possibility" of understanding, the concrete substantive content of experience necessarily assumes the character of an empirical or aposteriori correlate of cognition. In this case, however, Heidegger's "transformation" of traditional philosophy would simply be a matter of detail or modest reformulation; likewise, the transition from the early to the later phase of his thought could not possibly involve a *Kehre*, but at most a shift of accent from apriori structures to the description of aposteriori processes (within a transcendental or metaphysical framework).[21]

The problematic status of this approach affects also the crucial distinction between meaning-constitution and validation or "reflection on validity" (*Geltungsreflexion*). While acknowledging the unquestionable contribution to the "transcendental-hermeneutical problem of *meaning-constitution*," Apel's Introduction advances the thesis that Heidegger "on the other hand has failed—according to his own admission—to address the question of *truth* (and thus of the *validity* of statements for us)." Due to this failure, Heidegger's thought is said to entail the "separation" of the two domains and consequently to "divorce completely the issue of constitution from the issue of validation or justification in the Kantian sense." At this point, it seems necessary to cast at least a brief glance at Heidegger's presumed "admission" or self-critique. Both in the Introduction and in later contexts, Apel refers primarily to this passage in *Zur Sache des Denkens*: "The question of *aletheia* or of unconcealment as such is not identical with the question of truth. Therefore, it was inappropriate and thus misleading to designate *aletheia* in the sense of 'clearing' as truth." Yet, read in context, the passage points not merely to a mistake or terminological confusion but rather to a complicated nexus of *aletheia* and truth which requires further inquiry and reflection (*fragwürdig*). "Late, perhaps belatedly, the question arises," Heidegger writes: "Why is *aletheia* no longer translated by the customary label of 'truth'? The answer must be: As long as truth is taken in the traditional sense of correspondence between knowledge and reality (corroborated by ontic beings)—but also if truth is identified with certitude of cognition—*aletheia* or unconcealment in the sense of 'clearing' cannot be equated with truth. Rather, *aletheia* or unconcealment grants first of all the possibility of truth." Elaborating on this relationship Heidegger adds: "Against this background is *aletheia* less than truth? Or is it more—

since it is *aletheia* which grants truth understood as *adaequatio* and *certitudo*, and since presence and being present cannot happen outside the range of unconcealment or clearing? This question remains a task for thought. Such thinking must ponder whether it can even adequately pose the question as long as it proceeds philosophically or within the bounds of metaphysics which interrogates being only in regard to its presence."[22]

Once this broader argument is taken into account, Apel's charge of a "separation" of domains appears highly questionable; actually, Apel's own approach seems much more prone than Heidegger's to encourage a divorce of experiential meaning from truth or validity. By presenting meaning-disclosure strictly as a preamble to validation, Apel's study in effect begins to approximate the positivist or logical-empiricist construal of understanding—a construal rigorously segregating pre-scientific insight or "serendipity" from intersubjective verification. The proximity is particularly evident in a passage which —linking meaning-constitution with the epistemological notion of "context of discovery"—insists that the focus on validation is not meant to deny or shortchange the role of "constitutive meaning-events in all processes labelled 'creative' in traditional philosophy (and also in modern scientific theory)." At a later point in his Introduction, it is true, Apel seeks to extricate himself from this proximity. "In terms of meaning-constitution," he observes, "all knowledge originates in practical cognitive interests just as it terminates, in terms of possible application, in a mediated life-praxis. Thus, it may be possible to differentiate epistemologically the 'context of discovery' from the 'context of justification'; but one should not try to answer the question of validity independently from the question of the relevant and presupposed *meaning-constitution*." What remains unclear at this juncture is the character of the respective dependence (or lack of "independence") of the two domains. The issue can hardly be resolved through a simple juxtaposition or external accommodation—for example, through an arrangement supplementing pre-predicative meaning-disclosure with the coordinates of a Kantian or quasi-Kantian "reflection on validity."[23]

The unevenness of Apel's interpretation of Heidegger carries over to his interpretation of other spokesmen of onto-hermeneutics, most notably to his assessment of Gadamer's *Truth and Method*. To put it simply, unevenness in this case involves the tension between idealism and naturalism. On the one hand, Gadamer is depicted as representative of a "philosophical hermeneutics" and even as champion of the "universality" of hermeneutics—with the latter being defined as a mode of cognition in which "the *symmetry* of interpersonal dialogue is in principle presupposed." Given such interpersonal symmetry, reciprocal understanding of meaning results — in a quasi-idealistic vein — from face-to-face communication and from the transparency of ego to alter (or of one consciousness to another). On the other hand, Gadamer also appears in the study as an opponent of transparent communication and of genuine philosophical reflection. Thus, the essay on "Reflection and Material Praxis" portrays him as a thinker who, adverse to a truly "dialectical criticism," neglects or shortchanges the "dialectics of transcendental idealism" and the "reflective preconditions of dialectics." In the subsequent "Sketch of an Epistemology," Gadamer's reliance on life-praxis and practical application is said to be hostile to the "method of (philosophical) abstraction." According to the Introduction, his work exemplifies the tendency of the later Heidegger and his disciples to replace transcendental reflection with the description of ontological events — which, in this manner, begin to resemble material processes. To the extent that Gadamer's perspective is really "normatively and methodologically" neutral, Apel notes, "the talk about a 'happening' of being or a 'happening' of truth involves a 'naturalistic fallacy', and does not in any way provide an answer to a transcendental inquiry."[24]

As in Heidegger's case, the charges directed against Gadamer are hard to sustain and, in good measure, are indicative of Apel's own approach. In his presentation, hermeneutics appears indeed largely as a synonym for face-to-face communication or "direct" understanding. At the same time, he concedes that Gadamer's position in its basic thrust aims to transgress the transparency of ego to *alter*. "Once it is seriously recognized," the study observes, "that philosophical hermeneutics involves not merely the direct grasp of objectified spiritual meaning-contents, but the insertion of man as such into the immemorial happening of the mediation of tradition . . . it becomes clear that the fundamental project of a pure *'Geisteswissenschaft'* or a 'philosophy of spirit' is at this point left behind." For his own part, Apel is not unaware that direct communication is in fact a rare occurrence (if it is possible at all) — an insight which prompts him in the end to postulate mutual transparency as a normative standard or regulative principle on the level of the "ideal speech community." As counterpoise to an "idealistic" simplification of understanding, Apel himself recommends recourse to the systematic procedure and explanatory method of empirical science. Yet, is it not precisely this recourse which conjures up the peril of naturalism — given that science basically objectifies its targets of inquiry (including history and society) into an external "nature"? Moreover, does scientific method not in turn presuppose a neutral spectator or "transcendental subject"—a subject who can utilize laws of nature for his or her benefit and thus transform explanation into a means of control or domination?[25]

In my view, what distinguishes Gadamer's hermeneutics from both idealism and naturalism is his abandonment of monologue — differently phrased: his awareness of the difference or non-identity of consciousness and world (and of ego and *alter*). This awareness is particularly evident in a thesis which Apel criticizes at length: the thesis of the basic or at least normal "superiority of the *interpretandum*." In Apel's assessment, the conception harbors the danger of a "conservative dogmatism." Yet, disregarding certain extreme formulations in *Truth and Method*, the thesis seems to encapsulate no more than the (plausible) demand that interpreters submit themselves first of all to the inherent claims or unique "otherness" of texts and events. Countering the thesis, Apel invokes the basic "insight of German idealism" to the effect that "understanding means self-understanding of spirit or recognition of self in the other"; to the extent that an interpreter really wishes to understand—he insists—he must have self-confidence that he can "understand an author better than the latter understood himself." As long as the interpreter, he adds, "does not claim for himself the right of a critical assessment of the *interpretandum* and thus of a genuine access to truth, he does not yet occupy the standpoint of a *philosophical* hermeneutics."[26] What Apel overlooks at this point (I believe) is an important complication of self-understanding: the fact that "recognition of self in the other" involves a transformation of the original "self." To this extent, the interpreter cannot simply or unequivocally claim to "understand better"—since the one who finally understands (and perhaps understands better) is not entirely identical with the one who initially embarked on understanding. Seen in this light, Gadamer's thesis is important not only for textual interpretation but also for interpersonal contacts and for the relation between man and the "happening of being." In *Truth and Method*, history appears not so much as an intentional project but rather as a "story of suffering" (*Leidensgeschichte*)—where suffering denotes not merely a detour or distortion to be critically unmasked but a necessary ingredient in human maturation and self-understanding.

To be sure, Apel is not entirely unfamiliar with the issue of "otherness." His Introduction points to the "dialectical" consideration that "the synthesis of understanding seen as temporal mediation presupposes always both *identity and otherness*," and to the circumstance that such dialectics "cannot be grounded in spirit or thought alone."

Thought, we read, "bears the mark of temporality not on its own, but due to its mediation (unsurpassable by consciousness) with nature as its otherness." Unfortunately, comments of this kind do not seem to affect Apel's general argument; despite the author's own metamorphosis (between the two volumes), the study construes cognition or cognitive progress largely as a linear advance in transparency or as "self-escalation (*Selbstaufstufung*) of spirit." The sketched theory of knowledge leaves the subject of cognition in large measure undisturbed; in none of the diverse cognitive pursuits does the inquirer seem impelled to risk himself and thus to jeopardize the framework of monologue. In the domain of "scientistics," the researcher appears entirely untouched by the targets of his investigations, while the "community of investigators" resembles a transcendentally pre-stabilized soliloquy. As regards hermeneutics, the symmetry of dialogue allows the subject only to encounter a transparent *alter* and thus a modification of himself. In critique of ideology, objectification and self-knowledge are precariously linked: as neutral observer the analyst treats the "patient" or ideologue initially as an object of causal explanation—up to the point when the latter recognizes himself as a subject and emancipates himself from all alien constraints. What surfaces from this review of cognitive modes is at a minimum this lesson: that the turn to language and communication does not necessarily signify an end of monologue. How, indeed, should the subject escape from this prison as long as cognition confronts him either with a mirror of himself or else an objectified and externalized nature?[27]

III

This query can serve as an entry into the broader question raised in the study: the "transformation" or rejuvenation of philosophy. What is to be transformed, in Apel's view, is modern transcendental philosophy or "philosophy of reflection" as it had been formulated chiefly by Kant; the aim of the transformation is the expansion and "normative-semiotic" reinterpretation of transcendental premises in the direction of a "transcendental language game" or of the "a priori" of an unlimited speech community. In Apel's words: "What is at stake is the hermeneutical 'pre-structure' of a transcendental philosophy which—deviating from Kant's transcendental idealism—relies no longer on the postulate of a 'subject' or 'consciousness as such' as warrant of the intersubjective validity of knowledge, but rather on the premise that we are all a priori participants in intersubjective communication — in line with Wittgenstein's maxim that 'one person alone and only once' cannot follow a rule (of language)." Implying as it does a "consensus theory of linguistic communication and of possible truth" this conception, he adds, decisively overcomes "the lure of 'methodological solipsism' which—from Occam and Descartes to Husserl and Russell—has tended to lead philosophical epistemology astray." The second volume of the study presents transformation as the turn to "linguistic pragmatics" or to the pragmatic dimension of semiotics — a pragmatics in which (ideal) speech fulfills the function of Kant's "transcendental synthesis." "What is crucial for a consistent reconstruction of transcendental philosophy in terms of the transcendental-hermeneutical notion of language," we read, "is the replacement of the 'highest point' of Kantian epistemology—that is, the 'transcendental synthesis of apperception' as unity of object-consciousness— . . . by the *transcendental synthesis of linguistic interpretation* seen as unity of communication in a speech community."[28]

What remains elusive in this formulation is the status of language and communication in the context of the "transformed" philosophy. In large measure, Apel's portrayal suggests that language simply steps into the vacant place of "consciousness as such"—a switch tending to reduce the proposed transformation to a terminological matter. As Apel repeatedly affirms, language philosophy and transcendental pragmatics today provide the "conditions of possibility" of cognition, thus assuming the role of traditional epistemology. Language, he states at one point, constitutes a "transcendental category in the Kantian sense"—more precisely: it denotes "a condition of the possibility and validity of communication and self-knowledge, and thus also of conceptual thought, of self-cognition and meaningful action." As subject of cognition the study postulates mankind or at least the "ideal" and unlimited community of speech—a construal which projects the apriori qualities of "consciousness as such" onto a global scale. Most importantly, the focus on the linguistic premises of thought encourages, in Apel's view, the continuation or revival of "foundationalism" or of *prima philosophia* in the form of transcendental-hermeneutical reflection. "Through the a priori of communication," the Introduction observes, "the human species viewed as quasi-transcendental subject of truth recaptures its autonomous sense of joint responsibility vis-à-vis the meaning-events of history (no matter how uncontrollable they may be as events)—a responsibility it seemed to lose in Heideggerian philosophy. In this manner, transcendental reflection on the conditions of the possibility and validity of understanding yields something like a Cartesian point of *ultimate justification* (*Letztbegründung*) of philosophy."[29]

A chief difficulty with this approach, in my judgment, resides in the fact that—treated as a formal "condition" of possible knowledge—language tends to assume the place of a transcendental "limit of the world," while substantive experiences are reduced to mundane objects of signification. This is precisely the danger which Apel himself criticizes both in Kantian philosophy and in the "logical atomism" of the early Wittgenstein. Kant's model of transcendental philosophy, he writes at one point, basically recognizes only two alternatives: "The subject of knowledge must either be subsumed, as empirical agent, under the categories of scientific objectification (especially the category of causality) or else it cannot be empirically thematized; in other words: already for Kant the subject of knowledge constitutes the 'limit of the world.'" In a similar vein, the study comments on the early Wittgenstein as follows: "Behind the appearance of ordinary language and its apparent subjects there exists for him in reality only one universal form of world-picturing language and one subject of this language constituting the limit of this world. According to Wittgenstein, sense and nonsense of statements is determined not by the opinion of concrete subjects but by the opinion—manifest in the logical form of sentences—of the quasi-transcendental subject of (ideal) language as such." As Apel emphasizes, the Wittgensteinian notion of a transcendental subject as limit of the world is unable by itself to overcome the legacy of solipsism; in fact, intersubjective communication appears against this background as a meaningless undertaking: "The concrete-hermeneutical issue of understanding is finally carried *ad absurdum* by this undialectical kind of transcendental philosophy; for, assuming a pure language of a transcendental subject picturing the factual contents of the world, all actual human subjects would already be consensually unified on a formal level."[30]

These and related quandaries are not entirely absent from Apel's own position or approach; occasionally they lead him into the proximity of a pragmatic or "dialectical" hermeneutics no longer compatible with a rigid apriori-aposteriori scheme of cognition. "Compared with the limit-status of the subject of pure language in the *Tractatus*," the essay on "Scientism and Transcendental Hermeneutics" observes, pragmatic semiotics is "distinguished by the fact that the subject of interpretation cannot shrink into an 'extensionless point', leaving only a 'reality coordinated with this point'; rather the subjects of the pragmatic dimension of semiotics must be recognized in a distinctive, anthropologically, historically and sociologically concrete sense as condition of the possibility of the perspectival interpretation of reality 'as something'." According to Apel, even the *Philosophical Investigations* of the later Wittgenstein is still marred by traces of the earlier bifurcation or antinomy. "The dualistic scheme of the difference between logical form and mundane content governing the *Tractatus*," he affirms, "is not so much transcended in the notion of 'language games' but only differentiated. Therefore, on the basis of his model, Wittgenstein cannot really grasp but at best concede the genuine historicity of understanding, the mediation of decaying and emerging language games . . . across time, the revival and appropriation of the past in the life-form of the present." As corrective to Wittgenstein's position Apel invokes the concrete-dialectical notion of the "hermeneutical circle," a notion first sketched by Dilthey and philosophically elaborated by Heidegger and Gadamer. Precisely at this point, he comments, where "the historical mediation between language games is at issue—and thus also the mediation between form (apriori rule) and content (objectified meaning) of a human life-form —Dilthey reaches the greatest rationality of his thinking: in the concept of the 'hermeneutical circle'." What is involved in Dilthey's and especially in Heidegger's hermeneutics, is not the subsumption of substantive data under fixed, apriori rules but rather the concrete "installation of new possibilities of life and understanding," that is, the inauguration of "a genuine perception (*Wahrnehmung*) of things, of persons and their behavior." Thus, the traditional apriori-aposteriori scheme is replaced in their writings by "the 'hermeneutic circle' of formal and substantive conditions of understanding, a circle trying to understand the historical constitution of human life-forms."[31]

Notwithstanding this recognition of the form-content nexus, however, *Transformation der Philosophie* seeks to vindicate—with growing insistence—the right of transcendental reflection even vis-à-vis a dialectical hermeneutics mediating apriori and substantive elements. The basic insight of the hermeneutic circle, we read, must not be allowed "to erase the persisting *polarity of form and content*, of perspectival experience and universal order, of practical-bodily engagement and eccentric reflection." In Apel's portrayal, the embeddedness of thought in ordinary language does not alter the fact that "language —transcending the dogmatism of particular standpoints—is simultaneously rooted in the absolutely universal 'logos' as such, a rootedness which alone makes possible interpersonal communication, translation from one language into another, and finally a comparative and substantive linguistics." In the essay on "Wittgenstein and Heidegger," the "philosophical logos" is pitted in the end against the "hermeneutical logos" and credited with representing a "higher level of reflection." Facilitating through "a renewed reflection on the hermeneutical logos the 'formal use' of such concepts as 'individuality', 'historicity' and the like," the essay states, the philosophical logos "overreaches the hermeneutical logos in the same basic manner as the latter overreaches the objectivist logos of 'object-languages' (as, for instance, natural science)." Compared with Hegel's postulate of "absolute knowledge," it is true that the study concedes the substantive "poverty" and emptiness of pure reflection, noting that in philosophical discourse "all meaning-content, even the material content of categories and existential structures, is derived from the hermeneutical logos through which 'being-in-the-world' articulates effectively its historical and ontological understanding." Still, the same essay concludes by celebrating the transcendental vista of idealism which, in Apel's words, demarcates "the point at which philosophy and the universal validity of science are ultimately anchored in the formal anticipation of any possible *telos* of history. It is at this point that any discussion can ground the rational sense of possible arguments and thus bring into play the critical power of reason vis-à-vis an historical 'disclosure of truth', a disclosure which in its dogmatic-one-sided character always implies also the untruth of the concealment of possible truth."[32]

There can be little doubt, in my view, that the tension between thought and experience, between universal reflection and substantive hermeneutics, constitutes a central problem of contemporary philosophy and a challenge to any attempt at transformation. One can also readily concede the "transcendental" element in human maturation, the fact that thought and experience always must "transcend" existing horizons or boundaries in the direction of new horizons. What is really at issue is the character of this active transcendence — more precisely: whether it is at all intelligible as long as this act does not simultaneously affect thinking or the subject of thought itself. Apel's formulations in this respect are at least ambiguous. Thus, it is not clear how philosophical reflection can "overreach" or transcend the hermeneutical logos — without at the same time cancelling the dialectical mediation of transcendence and immanence operative in hermeneutics, and without reducing substantive experience to empirical objects of cognition. Apel queries in one passage whether, in reflecting on linguistic and experiential life-forms, the philosopher must not have established with them "the unity of a dialogue." And he responds: "This is no doubt correct in the sense that the philosopher cannot comment on the structure of human language games as if he were like a behaviorist from another galaxy"; nevertheless, he adds, "on a higher level of intentionality, the philosopher can articulate the precondition of historical dialogue for hermeneutical understanding as a formal requirement." In the Introduction, philosophy is presented as a "unique language game" functioning within the categorial "pre-structure" of understanding; in other contexts, however, language is portrayed as a "bodily experience" of meaning-intentions, and the "bodily a priori" is explicitly contrasted to the "a priori of reflection" or consciousness. What remains particularly obscure in these and similar instances is the status of language and its relation to thought. To the extent that this relation is defined in terms of the "basic dependence" of reflection on the "*irreducible* but *reconstructable* matrix of ordinary language," the meaning of "dependence" and "reconstruction" demands further elucidation.[33]

As it seems to me, quandaries of this kind can be traced ultimately to a certain unevenness in the proposed "transformation of philosophy": While paying tribute, in the domain of meaning-constitution, to the initiatives and teachings of Heidegger and Wittgenstein, Apel's arguments in the field of reflective validation frequently convey the impression of an (at least partial) restoration of Cartesian and Kantian legacies. To be sure, Apel himself is not unfamiliar with this unevenness and the philosophical issues arising from it; despite his fascination with validation he is far removed from endorsing an orthodox transcendentalism. As mentioned before, several passages in his study point in the direction of a dialectical hermeneutics not readily compatible with a transcendental framework; these examples could easily be multiplied. Thus, the essay on "Language and Order" opposes the segregation of pure reflection from the pre-reflective matrix of ordinary language, arguing that "a pure, impartial reason—if we accept for the moment this fiction—could not detect any significance in the world." Contrary to Schlick and logical positivism, Apel adds, ordinary language "cannot be grasped in its cognitive function by relying on the abstract bifurcation between what we merely 'experience' and 'encounter' and what we 'know about' it by means of a sign system; instead, such grasp can only derive from the hermeneutic circle of cognitive or linguistic 'form'—a form always already prejudiced by a concretely experienced subject matter—and a substantive content which already in the act of experience is captured under general categories 'as something' and thus anticipates public formulation." Similarly, exploring the "cognitive-anthropological relation between reflection and praxis in the basic elaboration of a situational dialectics," a subsequent essay reaches the conclusion that language involves not only the "emerging *consciousness* of man's practical encounter of the world," but also and simultaneously, "even on the highest and most sublimated level, a *mediation* of consciousness through the bodily engagement of man in the world."[34]

In his writings since *Transformation der Philosophie*, Apel has tended to strengthen the correlation of reflection and praxis or form and content by invoking the Wittgensteinian notion of "interdependence" or "interpenetration" (*Verwobenheit*). Thus, an essay published a year later observes that the concept of language games necessarily entails the conclusion that "by virtue of language reflective acts are apriori interdependent or interlaced (*verwoben*) with concrete bodily action."[35] Rigorously pursued, however, this conception is liable to jeopardize crucial dichotomies favored by Apel, especially his tendency —evident in the second volume and later—to jettison Heideggerian themes in favor of a pure "reflection on validity." Clearly, if reflection always has to rely on and be nourished by pre-reflective experience, the domains of meaning-constitution and validation cannot be as strictly differentiated as Apel frequently suggests. More importantly, dialectical interdependence casts doubt on the proposed rejuvenation and transformation of transcendental philosophy. Is it still feasible to talk about "transcendental" (or transcendental-hermeneutical) reflection on the "apriori conditions of possibility" of knowledge, once these conditions are acknowledged to include the existence of a concrete "life-world" and of bodily engagement together with all the other ingredients of pre-reflective experience? These considerations also affect the implicit ethical dimension of Apel's argument, especially his confrontation of a concrete or real society and an "ideal" speech community. Occasionally, his writings portray the actual life-world simply as "bad reality"— in the sense of a naturalistic, morally defective mode of life to be overcome or corrected by an ideal model. But, in this case, does the latter not acquire the status of a mere fiction or fictive utopia, by being entirely divorced from reality (*Wirklichkeit*)? To avoid this consequence, must the actual life-world not at least contain the nucleus of the "good life"—not as its antithesis but as its inner sense?

As a discerning and circumspect philosopher, Apel does not pretend to have definitively "resolved" these and related issues. His writings repeatedly and eloquently point to the vast area of persisting challenges and dilemmas. "A philosophy which would establish itself solely on the highest level of noological reflection," *Transformation der Philosophie* notes, "would purchase its lack of engagement with substantive emptiness and irrelevance. On the other hand, a philosophy solely relying on historical engagement surrenders man to historical fate, thereby relinquishing the level of human emancipation from fate achieved under the auspices of philosophical enlightenment. We still lack a philosophy, I believe, which would be able to mediate adequately the profound insights of the last hundred years into the ontological embeddedness of consciousness — from the social philosophy of Karl Marx to the works of Wittgenstein and Heidegger — with the ec-centric claim to universal validity inherent in the intersubjective logos of reflection." In another passage, Apel describes his own explorations simply as a cipher "for the open problem of a critical renewal of the rationality of Hegel's dialectics."[36] One can leave aside here the question whether Hegel's dialectics (rooted in the modern metaphysics of subjectivity) can be a sufficient guidepost for present day quandaries. There can be little doubt, however, that Apel's study has admirably pinpointed, and established standards for, the crucial task of contemporary philosophy: the task of probing the complex relations between reflection and pre-reflective experience, meaning-constitution and validation, and — more generally — between reason and non-reason, concealment and unconcealment.

5

Hermeneutics and Deconstruction:
Gadamer and Derrida in Dialogue

ISSUES OF INTERPRETATION are presently at the forefront in the humanities and also in the social sciences. Eclipsed by post-empiricist and Continental philosophical arguments, positivist modes of social inquiry have given way to—or at least made room for—novel approaches stressing intersubjective understanding (*Verstehen*), textual analysis, and cultural exegesis. A common denominator in these approaches is frequently said to be the focus on "meaning" or significance—a meaning generated by actions or events and recovered or decoded through hermeneutical efforts. Yet, contrary to initial expectations, the recent hermeneutical "turn" has not produced a paradigmatic consolidation. On closer inspection or in actual practice, interpretation emerged as a far from straightforward or unilinear enterprise; once the correlation and mutual implication of interpreter and texts (including social events) was fully taken into account, the status of significance quickly appeared dubious. What surfaced at this point was not so much an external boundary of hermeneutics as rather an internal ambivalence or rift. For, does the notion of meaning not inevitably presuppose a dimension of non-meaning—just as intentional acts intimate a non-intentional foil? Over two-hundred years ago, Vico's *New Science* alluded to this dilemma in these terms: "Just as rational metaphysics teaches that man becomes all things by understanding them (*homo intelligendo fit omnia*), imaginative metaphysics shows that man becomes all things by *not* understanding them (*homo non intelligendo fit omnia*); and perhaps the latter proposition is truer than the former, for when man understands he extends his mind and takes in the things, but when he does not understand he makes the things out of himself and becomes them by transforming himself into them."[1]

In the contemporary setting, the fissures of interpretation or of interpretive perspectives were for some time kept in abeyance (partly due to a shared anti-positivist stance). To the extent that dilemmas were articulated, the emphasis was placed on external limits or boundaries of hermeneutics supposedly erected by empirical science or the structures of power.[2] More recently, however, attention has begun to shift to more intrinsic dilemmas or conflicts. The main conflict in this area is highlighted by the labels of "hermeneutics" and "deconstruction" or by the opposition (to speak loosely) between the German and the French schools of interpretation—the former represented chiefly by Gadamer and the latter by Jacques Derrida. In large measure, it is true, "opposition" has tended to amount to little more than coexistence without contact or mutual engagement. In April 1981, an important event took place in Paris: namely, a tentative exchange of views between the leading spokesmen of the two camps—an exchange whose German version was recently published under the title *Text und Interpretation*.[3] Even in this case, one must admit, the exchange took the form more of an alternation of statements than of a genuine dialogue. Over long stretches, the linking ingredient in the opposing statements was Heidegger or Heidegger's mode of exegesis, a fact not entirely surprising given the Heideggerian affinities of both spokesmen —affinities, to be sure, pointing in radically different directions. While Gadamer's *Truth and Method* may be said to integrate the tradition of *Geisteswissenschaften* with existential analysis (as outlined in *Being and Time*), Derrida pursues themes in Heidegger's later work where notions like "meaning" or "being" are already problematical (though hardly abandoned).

The conflict of interpretations is not simply an academic debate. Behind seemingly esoteric questions of textual reading and exegesis, broader issues of a practical-political sort can be seen to surface. As it appears to me and as I intend to argue, one of the central issues raised by the Gadamer-Derrida exchange concerns the political communication and interaction appropriate to our "global city" or to the emerging cosmopolis. This implication, I acknowledge, is not immediately evident and requires some careful preparation. In the following pages I shall approach this goal in several successive steps. The initial section shall review the main themes of the Gadamer-Derrida exchange of 1981, leaving intact the somewhat disjointed and non-dialogical character of the exchange. The second section shall reconstruct and flesh out the same encounter in the direction of a more cohesive dialogue or confrontation, by relying on additional texts published by the two spokesmen. The aim of the third section, finally, is to explore the broader implications, including the practical-political dimension, of the exchange—an endeavor placing its accent in large measure on the relationship between hermeneutical "good will" and deconstructive "will to power" or, more generally, between political education (*Bildung*) and aesthetics.

I

Judged by the yardstick of hermeneutical understanding, the exchange between Gadamer and Derrida was a curious mélange of comprehension and noncomprehension, of engagement and soliloquy. The standard of mutual comprehension was upheld unflinchingly by Gadamer in his opening statement (and its printed, expanded version). In his presentation, "understanding" was not merely a specialized endeavor restricted to the humanities but a basic presupposition of culture and communication—an argument familiar to readers of *Truth and Method*. "The capacity of understanding," he noted, "is a basic human endowment which sustains social life and functions through the medium of language and the community of dialogue; in this sense the universal claim of hermeneutics is unquestionable." The universality of hermeneutics was already recognized during the Romantic era and, in a more truncated form, in Dilthey's life-philosophy; however, its full significance was only articulated in *Being and Time:* "It was particularly Heidegger's deepening of the concept of understanding into an existential category, that is, into a categorial feature of human *Dasein*, which became crucial for my development; it was the impulse which prompted me to move critically beyond methodological discussions and to expand the hermeneutical issue beyond the domain of specialized sciences to encompass the experience of art and history." Again reminiscent of *Truth and Method*, Gadamer's statement credited Heidegger with a decisive reformulation of the "hermeneutical circle" in a manner radically at odds with traditional logic: "According to this concept of the hermeneutical circle, understanding does not involve the deduction of conclusions from premises; thus, the logical flaw of circularity is here not a defect of procedure but rather the appropriate description of the structure of understanding." In Heidegger's "existential" formulation, moreover, the hermeneutical circle designated not merely a literary device but rather "the structure of human being-in-the-world, that is, the distinctive movement beyond the subject-object division" animating the analysis of *Dasein*.[4]

Despite this endorsement of *Being and Time*, Gadamer's comments did not completely identify with Heideggerian philosophy—especially with Heidegger's later "reversal" or turning away from traditional metaphysics and the legacy of the humanities. "I am fully aware of the fact," Gadamer confessed, "that my own endeavors to 'render' or translate Heidegger are bound to reveal my limitations and above all the extent to which I remain rooted in the Romantic tradition of *Geisteswissenschaften* and its humanistic heritage." The comments even acknowledged the fact that, in his later writings, Heidegger "completely abandoned the concept of hermeneutics since he realized its inability to help him break through the parameters of transcendental reflection." In a candid disclosure unmatched in his other publications (including *Heideggers Wege*), Gadamer's statement alluded to a pervasive tension between the later Heidegger and himself, a tension centering chiefly on the issue of hermeneutical understanding: "I can see why the later Heidegger felt—and Derrida would presumably concur on this point—that I do not really transgress the sphere of phenomenological 'immanence' which was constitutive for Husserl and also animated my own early, neo-Kantian training. I can also understand why one believes to detect the same methodological immanence in my attachment to the hermeneutical circle." Seen from this angle, Gadamer added, his own interpretive efforts could not properly match the "radicalness" of Heidegger's description of "boundary experiences" nor the stringency of his "critique of Husserl's phenomenological neo-Kantianism," a critique which finally enabled him "to recognize Nietzsche as the extreme culmination" of Western metaphysics.[5]

Retreating from this radicalness—and seeking to vindicate this retreat—Gadamer insisted on the ineluctable task of understanding. Hermeneutical inquiry, in his argument, was not so much a closed or "immanent" domain as rather an open arena of interpretation. The notion of disrupting or escaping from the hermeneutical circle, he observed, "appears to me indeed as an impossible and truly nonsensical (or counter-sensical) demand. For—as shown in the work of Schleiermacher and his successor, Dilthey—hermeneutical immanence is nothing but a description of what understanding really is." In Gadamer's opinion, hermeneutics could not properly be subsumed under metaphysics or any closed philosophical system since even the transgression of "systems" required interpretive attentiveness and comprehension. "My own view of the matter," we read, "is that no conceptual language—not even what Heidegger called the language of metaphysics—constitutes an unbreachable barrier for thought, provided the thinker places his trust in language, which means: provided he enters into a dialogue with the thought of others and with different modes of thought." At this point, a central feature of Gadamer's opus emerged into prominence: his strong reliance on intersubjective encounter and especially his virtual identification of hermeneutics and dialogue:

"While fully recognizing Heidegger's critique of the concept of subjectivity (whose ontological background he demonstrated), it was my ambition to grasp dialogue as the original phenomenon of language. This meant simultaneously a hermeneutical reconstruction of 'dialectics', that is, an attempt to trace dialectics—construed by German idealism as a speculative methodology—back to the art of living dialogue." Through the medium of dialogue, philosophical hermeneutics was thus linked—via the tradition of *Geisteswissenschaften*—with Hegel's phenomenology and his dialectics of experience: "What Hegel calls the 'speculative element' in philosophy and what forms the premise of his observations on the history of philosophy, remains (I believe) a constant challenge for the endeavor of dialectical explication"—which can only be fulfilled through hermeneutical exegesis.[6]

In Gadamer's account, the invocation of Hegel and Schleiermacher did not signal a simple return to idealism or an idealist metaphysics. While shunning the "radicalness" of the later Heidegger, his own approach still shared (or at least claimed to share) some of the latter's post-idealist impulses. Notwithstanding the ineluctability of understanding, Gadamer affirmed, "I was for my part always careful not to forget the limits implicit in the hermeneutical experience of meaning. When I wrote that 'intelligible being is language' I meant to say that being can never be completely understood—since every linguistic medium always points beyond what is directly articulated." Untroubled by potential tensions or dilemmas inherent in his argument, Gadamer's statement proceeded to endorse *both* the notion of hermeneutical "limits" and the postulate of universal intelligibility and, more specifically, to portray dialogue as a kind of mid-point between the two. "In view of the broad scope of understanding," we are told, "the circularity obtaining between interpreter and *interpretandum* can claim for itself true universality; and this is precisely the point where I believe to have followed up Heidegger's critique of phenomenological immanence as it operates in Husserl's transcendental foundationalism. The dialogical character of language which I have tried to elaborate leaves behind the subjectivity of the subject, and also the intentional orientation of the speaker toward meaning." Viewed in an existential or existentialist vein, dialogue signifies not merely the linear pursuit of intentions but rather the willingness to test prevailing understandings, including the self-understanding of participants: "What is involved in talk is not a mere fixation of intended meaning but a constantly renewed attempt—or rather the renewed temptation—to become engaged with something or someone, that is: to expose or risk oneself." Countering a purely discursive-argumentative construal, Gadamer emphasized the quasi-ontological matrix of dialogue: "Dialogical experience is not restricted to the range of reasons and counterreasons whose exchange and settlement may be the goal of discourse; rather, we find in it something else: namely, a potential of difference (or otherness) which transcends uniform consensus."[7]

The discursive curtailment of dialogue is not of recent origin but endemic in the history of Western philosophy (or, in Heidegger's terms, in Western metaphysics). According to Gadamer, the curtailment could be traced back over Hegel to classical Greek philosophy. In the case of Hegel, the potential of otherness was precisely "the boundary which he did not transgress"; although recognizing and dramatically illustrating "the speculative principle inherent in 'logos'," Hegel ultimately remained captive to the "'logocentrism' of Greek ontology"—a logocentrism critically challenged already by Old Testament prophets and later by St. Paul, Luther, and their modern disciples. Even the classical Socratic model of dialogue—in *Truth and Method* still extolled as the prototype of hermeneutical understanding—was now presented as flawed by its inability "consciously to articulate and conceptualize" the dimension of difference. As portrayed in the opening statement, the "real depth" of the dialogical principle was perceived only "in the twilight of metaphysics, in the era of German Romanticism"; more recently it has been marshalled as "an antidote against the subjectivity-focus of idealism." Notwithstanding his avoidance of radicalism, Gadamer defined his own opus basically as a continuation of this "depth" perspective or post-metaphysical inquiry. In his words: "This is where I found my point of departure; and my question became how the unity of meaning established in dialogue and the impenetrability of otherness can be reconciled or mediated—that is, what language (*Sprachlichkeit*) ultimately signifies: bridge or barrier."[8]

Although not directly addressed or confronted by either spokesman, the last question—language: bridge or barrier?—actually formed the *leitmotiv* of the entire Gadamer-Derrida exchange. On Gadamer's side, the exchange basically involved a test of his allegiance to traditional hermeneutics—and also of his existentialist reading of Heideggerian philosophy. As he readily acknowledged, the encounter with "the French philosophical scene" constituted for him a "real challenge." Without lingering on marginal issues, Gadamer immediately turned to the central bone of contention: Heidegger's ontology. In assessing Heidegger's later opus, he noted, "Derrida has claimed that the latter did not really overcome the logocentrism of metaphysics. By inquiring into the essence of truth and the meaning of being, Heidegger is said still to speak the language of metaphysics which regards meaning as a more or less given or discoverable object." In Derrida's account, Nietzsche emerges as "more radical" on this score: "His concept of interpretation is said to denote not the discovery of an existing meaning, but rather the constitution or creation of meaning in the service of the 'will to power'; only in this manner can the logocentrism of metaphysics genuinely be transcended." In an effort to vindicate Heidegger's post-metaphysical (but still hermeneutically well-grounded) inclinations, Gadamer pointed to the nuances of Heidegger's interpretation of Nietzsche, nuances blunted by Derrida's deconstructive zeal (or his super-radicalism). "What I miss in the French Nietzsche-revival," he observed, "is an appreciation of the experimental or tentative character of Nietzsche's thought." Equally missing is an appreciation of the "deep ambivalence" of Heidegger's exegesis, an ambivalence evident in the fact that "he follows Nietzsche into the last consequences of his thought in order to detect precisely there the flaw of metaphysics — by showing that, in the midst of valuations and the transformation of all values, being itself degenerates into a value-concept in the service of the 'will to power'." Seen in this light, he added, "Heidegger's attempt to 'think being' advances far beyond such a reduction of metaphysics to valuation — or rather: it moves back behind metaphysics itself without, however, being satisfied with its radical-extreme dissolution like Nietzsche" (or we might add: like Derrida).[9]

Since the remainder of Gadamer's comments was only obliquely related to the issue at hand (and in part recapitulated views published elsewhere), I shall limit myself here to a few additional highlights. A central topic of the remaining comments was the status of textual exegesis and especially the relationship between text and interpretation. According to Gadamer, "text" had to be seen as a hermeneutical or semantic concept and by no means as the mere product of grammatical or syntactical rules and operations. Viewed hermeneutically, he argued (reiterating a position known from *Truth and Method*), a text is normally not a separate entity or a thing-in-itself, but rather a phase or a medium in the "process of communication and understanding." In reading a text we regularly "anticipate already the understanding of the text's meaning and only in this sense do we qualify the text as legible"; conversely, recourse to specific linguistic or syntactical features indicates a difficulty or breakdown of comprehension. In normal situations, texts thus tend to submerge in the communicative flow, and the role of the interpreter is to facilitate this submergence. To this extent, the relation between reader and author is akin to the relation of speakers in a dialogue in that, in both instances, successful communication yields a "fusion of horizons." Moreover, the two cases also share a common normative component: "Written communication relies basically on the same premise which underlies oral exchange: both presuppose the 'good will' of participants to achieve reciprocal understanding. In fact, good will is implied wherever communicative understanding is sought." In Gadamer's view, this hermeneutical yardstick was operative even in disguised modes of communication—what he called "pre-texts"—where manifest or overt meanings conceal hidden motives or interests. Particularly in the case of psychological blockages or distortions, the task of therapy was to remove the discrepancy (between pre-text and text) and thus to accomplish the interpretive goal through an analytical detour (which Ricoeur labeled the "hermeneutics of suspicion").[10]

In his initial intervention or response, Derrida concentrated chiefly on three issues or themes: namely, the issues of the ethical underpinnings of exegesis, of the relation between hermeneutics and psychoanalysis, and of the range and status of hermeneutical understanding itself. The first issue in particular became the target of deconstructive critique. Citing Gadamer's appeal to the "good will" (of speakers and readers), Derrida acknowledged the philosophical aura surrounding the phrase but attacked its metaphysical moorings. In Gadamer's formulation, he noted, good will is not simply a vague postulate but "the premise of any ethics governing a speech community, even in cases of controversy or misunderstanding." What he found troublesome in the phrase—and in traditional ethics in general—was the foundational role assigned to "will" or human "willing" (in a polemical word-play, his intervention was entitled "Good Will to Power," where goodness is simply a synonym for the will to power). In his words: "What is will if, as Kant claims, there is nothing genuinely good outside the good will? Does this definition not belong to the conception—rightly challenged by Heidegger—which identifies being with will or a willful subjectivity?" Regarding the second point, Derrida questioned the extension of hermeneutical yardsticks to psychological depth analysis, opposing to this view the necessity of an interpretive "rupture"—a rupture, to be sure, which had to be carried inside the domain of psychoanalysis itself and which, in any case, seemed to be "closer to the interpretive style of Nietzsche than to the hermeneutical tradition stretching from Schleiermacher to Gadamer." The notion of rupture also affected the status of communicative understanding or dialogue: "Regardless of whether one starts from understanding or misunderstanding, one always needs to ask whether communication—far from being a continuously unfolding process or medium (as Gadamer thinks)—is not rather a rupture of communion, rupture as medium so-to-speak, a suspension of all mediation?"[11]

In his rejoinder, Gadamer voiced chagrin at being misunderstood and, more importantly, at the tendency to privilege non-understanding. Regarding "good will," he objected to its heavy metaphysical treatment and especially to its construal as a Kantian maxim. "I have trouble grasping the questions posed to me," he observed. "But I make an effort—as does everybody who seeks to understand or be understood by another. I cannot at all see that this effort should have anything to do with the epoch of metaphysics or even with the Kantian concept of good will." In trying to bypass modern metaphysics, Gadamer appealed to the legacy of classical philosophy and especially to Plato's notion of *eumeneis elenchoi*. Seen in this light, good will signifies basically exegetic generosity: "One does not seek to score a point by exploiting the other's weaknesses; rather, one seeks to strengthen the other's argument as much as possible so as to render it plausible. Such an effort seems to me to be constitutive for any communication." According to Gadamer, Derrida himself was unable to escape this hermeneutical standard—as was evident in his engagement in a question-and-answer sequence: "Whoever opens his mouth would like to be understood; otherwise he would neither speak nor write. And finally I have on my side this convincing evidence: Derrida addresses questions to me and must thereby presuppose that I am willing (or have the good will) to understand them." Failure to accept this proposition was tantamount to self-contradiction—a consequence, it is true, which Derrida seemed ready to shoulder and even to legitimate by relying on the precedent of Nietzsche.[12]

Regarding the other two points, Gadamer made some concessions to exegetic limits imposed by "otherness"—but without abandoning his basic hermeneutical framework. A central issue in both instances was the notion of "rupture." Rejecting the alleged amalgamation of psychoanalysis and hermeneutics, Gadamer acknowledged the difference between the two approaches—with the one focusing on intended meanings, the other on distorted or repressed motivations—but ascribed the difference or "rupture" ultimately to a divergence in intention (or orientation toward meaning): "I deny by no means that utterances can be approached with a purpose diverging from a communicative intent; my question was only: when and for what reason does one embark on this break?" The issue loomed larger in Derrida's final question—especially given the latter's assumption "that this rupture or breach must *always* be performed since there is no undisrupted understanding of others." Relying on Heideggerian teachings, Gadamer seemed ready at this point to qualify or restrict linear exegesis, especially in the case of literary texts and "art-works": "In Heidegger's language, an art-work is experienced as a push or breach (Stoss) and by no means as confirmation of complacent meaning-expectations. On this point we should be able to concur." The experience could be generalized to literary and poetic texts: for, a reader's coming to terms with such texts does not imply self-confirmation; rather, "one relinquishes oneself in order to find" and "does not know beforehand how (or as what) one will be found." Arguments of this kind, however, did not herald a paradigmatic change. Notwithstanding his previous critique of Greek "logocentrism," Gadamer buttressed the universal claims of hermeneutical dialogue through recourse to Greek antecedents: "The exchange of speech and counterspeech, of question and answer, can produce genuine consensus. This is the method—constantly emphasized by Plato—for dissolving spurious agreements, misunderstandings, and misreadings which words per se may engender." Thus, he added, "I feel justified in starting from the process of an evolving and constantly renegotiated consensus in trying to give an account of language and the function of written texts"; without such a premise, "all human solidarity and the viability of society" would vanish.[13]

Derrida's second intervention did not so much reply to Gadamer's arguments as rather distend or "rupture" communication further: namely, by concentrating on Heidegger's interpretation of Nietzsche. What Derrida found particularly dubious in this interpretation was the emphasis on the coherent synthesis or "wholeness" of Nietzsche's ideas—a synthesis, moreover, construed as end point of a uniform metaphysical teleology. In his words: Heidegger's reading "aims at gathering the *unity* and *singularity* of Nietzsche's thought, a thought which in turn is perceived as function of a completed unity, namely, the completion of Western metaphysics." What this stress on wholeness bypasses is the concrete difference or biographical particularity of Nietzsche's life, including the role of his proper name(s) and signature(s); more importantly, it neglects the fragmentary, internally refracted character of his work, a character which makes it necessary to speak not of "Nietzsche" but of several "Nietzsches" (incommensurable with each other and unable to be assembled into a synthesis or an internal consensus). From Heidegger's perspective, Derrida noted, Nietzsche "is not the name of an individual or signatory; rather, it is the name of a thought whose unity bestows meaning and reference onto the name. Nietzsche thus is nothing but the name of this unity." This unified thought, moreover, is itself absorbed into the holistic story of metaphysics; for Heidegger, it is itself "grand metaphysics" and to the extent that it inaugurates a rupture, it does so "by inches and only in order to remain perched on the precipice of the limit, that is, in ambiguity." By treating him as a metaphysician, Heidegger is said to extol and criticize Nietzsche, and to do both simultaneously: "By salvaging Nietzsche Heidegger condemns him; he salvages and condemns him at the same time."[14]

Countering this unified vision, Derrida unleashed the full potential of deconstruction and dissemination. "Who," he queried, "has decided that one carries only one name? Surely not Nietzsche. And who in turn has determined that there is such a thing as Western metaphysics which could be gathered and unified under this name?" Next to Kierkegaard, "was Nietzsche not one of the few who multiplied his names and played with signatures, identities, and masks—who named himself several times and with different names? And what if this were the basic issue or 'cause' of his thinking"—rather than a presumed perpetuation of logocentrism?[15] Contrary to Heidegger's exegesis, Nietzsche's work—in Derrida's view—was not a unified or holistic opus; in fact, he was "suspicious of any notion of totality." In particular, the concept of "eternal recurrence"—which figures prominently in Heidegger's assessment—was not a "holistic thought," just as little as was the "will to power." Together with the abandonment of totality, Nietzsche's work also escaped the traditional polar correlations of whole and part, genus and species, particular and universal. If this is so, however—Derrida concluded—was it not "premature to treat Nietzsche as a metaphysician, even as the last one" (assuming that metaphysics tries to grasp being as a whole)? Perhaps Nietzsche "was not even a thinker of being—provided being and wholeness are essentially linked."[16]

II

The sketched exchange clearly touched on crucial questions regarding interpretation and intersubjective communication—but it did so in a somewhat oblique and elusive fashion. Frequently, the two spokesmen seemed more intent on reiterating firmly held positions than on exposing them to mutual testing and scrutiny. Occasionally, as in the case of "rupture," the issues underlying the exchange were nearly joined (or capable of being joined)—only to be abandoned or set aside in favor of more marginal concerns. To some extent, the joining of issues was complicated by a partial overlap or convergence of perspectives, an overlap due (as indicated) mainly to shared Heideggerian leanings. Among the two protagonists, Gadamer was certainly more ready and eager to engage in conversation or a genuine interplay of question and response; however, this willingness was counterbalanced by a certain oscillation of views, especially by the juxtaposition of intentional hermeneutics—inspired by the tradition of *Geisteswissenschaften*—and existential ontology. In the following I intend to flesh out the contours of the respective arguments by drawing on relevant additional sources—in an effort to approximate the exchange more closely to a dialogical interaction. In Gadamer's case, I shall rely chiefly on his magisterial *Truth and Method* (containing a kind of *summa* of his teachings); in the case of Derrida, the primary focus will be on his interpretations of Nietzsche (and Heidegger).

Although immensely impressive in both its scope and structure, Gadamer's *Truth and Method* manifests the same kind of ambivalence noted in the preceding review: while seeking to articulate a "philosophical" or "ontological" type of hermeneutics, the study gives ample room to such concepts as "hermeneutical consciousness" and intentional "meaning"—thus paying tribute to the traditional philosophy of reflection (that is, to the legacy of modern metaphysics). Gadamer's ontological ambitions emerge powerfully in the first part of the study, dedicated to the critique of modern aesthetics and especially of the linkage of art with subjective taste, a treatment inaugurated by Kant and continued by Romanticism. As presented by Kant, he observes, taste is a purely "subjective principle to which common sense is reduced; abstracting from the content of objects judged to be beautiful, taste merely claims that they are accompanied a priori by a feeling of pleasure in the subject." As employed and modified by Romanticism, the Kantian concept of taste was entirely divorced from ethical and ontological considerations and anchored in subjective feeling styled as "aesthetic consciousness." From the vantage point of this feeling, Gadamer continues, "the connection of the work of art with its world is no longer of any importance; on the contrary, aesthetic consciousness becomes itself the experiencing center from which everything termed art is assessed." Regarding criteria of aesthetic beauty, the Romantics and their epigones ascribed such standards at best to the special competence of the artist seen as creative "genius." In application to the multitude of readers or interpreters, on the other hand, aesthetic consciousness gave way to an anarchy of private whims and arbitrary preferences—to what Gadamer calls "an untenable hermeneutic nihilism." In terms of this outlook, he writes, "every encounter with a work of art has the rank and legitimacy of a new production. . . . If Valéry occasionally drew such conclusions for his work in order to avoid the myth of the unconscious productivity of genius, he actually (in my view) became only more deeply entangled in this myth: for now he transfers to reader and interpreter the power of absolute creation which he himself no longer desires to exert." In the end, "absolute discontinuity, that is, the disintegration of the unity of the aesthetic object into a multiplicity of experiences, is the necessary consequence of an aesthetics of feeling" and subjectivity.[17]

Against the subjectivism of modern aesthetics, *Truth and Method* marshals an ontological conception of art revolving around the pivotal notion of "play"—a notion, to be sure, purged of Romantic or subjectivist connotations. "What matters here," Gadamer asserts, "is the need to free this concept from the subjective meaning it has for Kant and Schiller and which dominates the whole of modern aesthetics and philosophical anthropology. If, in connection with the experience of art, we speak of 'play', this refers neither to the behavior nor to the feeling-state of the artist or the consumer of art, nor to the freedom of a subjectivity expressed in play, but rather to the mode of being of the art-work itself." In common parlance, play tends to be opposed to seriousness or the world of earnest behavior; however, the opposition is misleading since—in Gadamer's words—play can have "its own, even sacred, seriousness." Still, seriousness is not an external yardstick or purpose imposed on play—which, generally speaking, does not obey extrinsic intentions or instrumental objectives. Basically, play "fulfills its 'purpose' only if the player loses himself in the play. It is not an extrinsic relation to seriousness but only seriousness in playing that allows the play to be wholly playful." Contrary to the Romantic tradition, an ontological approach to art thus shifts the accent from feeling to the play or the art-work itself. What must be "maintained against the levelling effect of aesthetic consciousness," Gadamer states, in a passage clearly reminiscent of Heidegger's "art-work" lectures, "is that works of art are not objects standing over against an isolated subject; rather art-works have their true being in the fact that they generate a transformative experience. The 'subject' of the experience of art, that which remains and endures, is not the subjectivity of the experiencing individual, but the art-work itself. This is precisely the significance of the mode of being of play: for play has its own essence, independent of the consciousness of players."[18]

Truth and Method is emphatic in downgrading the role of subjects or intentional agents in the domains of art and play. "The subject of play," we read, "are not the players; instead, through players the play merely reaches presentation (*Darstellung*)." In a sense, the dynamics or movement of a play operates "without a substrate": what matters alone is "the game that is played, irrespective of whether there are subjects at play." In Gadamer's perspective, ordinary language provides support for this construal of "play" by using the term frequently in a "medial" or intransitive sense (as when we say that a film is "playing" at a theater): "As far as language is concerned, the actual subject of play is obviously not the subjectivity of an individual who among other activities also plays, but rather the play itself. But we are so used to relating a phenomenon like playing to subjectivity and its modes of behavior that we miss these clues supplied by language." An important corollary of the primacy of play is the risk involved for players or participants: by engaging in play their original identities are liable to be jeopardized. In participating in a play and its various possibilities or moves, Gadamer writes, "we may become so engrossed in them that they, as it were, outplay and prevail against us. The attraction that the game has for the player lies precisely in this risk." Actually, in his view, the hazard or "overplaying" element involved in play is so pronounced that activity begins to shade over into passivity, playing into being played: "From this vantage point we can indicate a general characteristic of the way in which the nature of play is reflected in playful behavior: *all playing is a being-played.* The attraction or fascination that a game exerts consists precisely in the fact that the play tends to master the players." Differently phrased, playing is a peculiarly purposeless or non-intentional kind of activity, an activity at rest (or carrying its purpose) within itself: The action or agency of a play is located not "in the player, but in the game itself; the game is what holds the player in its spell, draws him into play, and keeps him there."[19]

From the perspective of players, engagement in play involves a transformation or change of status—a change particularly evident in artistic plays amenable to performance or presentation: "I call this change in which human play finds its genuine completion as art, 'transformation into structured form or work' (*Gebilde*); only through this change does play acquire its ideality so that it can be intended and understood as play." According to *Truth and Method*, change in this sense does not mean an incremental, continuous development, but rather a complete reversal or rupture. In Gadamer's words, the implications for the definition of art "emerge when one takes the sense of transformation seriously: Transformation is not ordinary change, not even a change of particularly large proportions." Ordinary change denotes that what is changed "also remains the same and is held on to." By contrast, transformation means "that something turns suddenly and as a whole into something else; that this other transformed thing that it has become is its true being, in comparison with which its earlier mode is nothing." Thus, there cannot be a "transition of gradual change leading from one to the other" since the two modes imply a "mutual denial." The effects of transformative rupture are manifest on a number of levels, especially the level of intentional agents — including artists, performers, and interpreters. In relation to all of them, Gadamer affirms, art-work seen as play possesses "an absolute autonomy." What is put aside and counts no longer is "first of all the players, with the poet or composer being considered as one of the players." Properly construed, play is transformative to such an extent "that the identity of the players remains for no one the same." On another level, the rupture affects empirical reality or the world of everyday life: "What exists no longer is above all the world in which we live as our own. Transformation into structure is not simply transposition into another (ordinary) world"; rather, a new and transfigured world arises in the play. Finally and most importantly, art involves a kind of ontological "sea-change," a shift from contingent phenomena to true being or the truth of being: "Transformation at this point is transformation into truth. It is not enchantment in the sense of a bewitchment that waits for the redeeming word to return things to their previous state; rather, it is itself redemption and restoration to true being. In the presentation of play 'what is' comes to the fore."[20]

As sketched so far, Gadamer's outlook in *Truth and Method* carries a distinctly post-Cartesian and post-idealist (perhaps even post-metaphysical) cast; yet, references to rupture or reversal are offset or counterbalanced by repeated endorsements of a subjective-intentional hermeneutics. Pondering the transformative effects of art and aesthetic experience, Gadamer quickly retreats to the vantage point of finite individual existence. Even if aesthetics should erect limits to self-consciousness, he notes, "we do not have a standpoint which would allow us to see these limits and conditions in themselves, and us as limited or conditioned from the outside. Even what transcends our understanding is experienced by us as *our* limit and thus belongs to the continuity of self-understanding in which human existence moves." What play and playfulness, therefore, involve is not so much a transgression of understanding as rather a distinctive challenge: the challenge "of preserving — despite this discontinuity of aesthetics and aesthetic experience — the hermeneutic continuity which constitutes our being." In the end, art-works are explicitly integrated in, and subordinated to, a quasi-idealist hermeneutics of understanding and self-consciousness — notwithstanding the discussed "ontological" reformulation of aesthetics. "Actually," Gadamer affirms, "hermeneutics should be understood in so comprehensive a sense as to embrace the whole sphere of art and its range of questions. Like any other text a work of art, not only literature, needs to be understood — and this understanding must be nurtured and trained. With this, hermeneutical consciousness acquires a comprehensive scope that surpasses even aesthetic consciousness: *aesthetics must be absorbed into hermeneutics*." To facilitate this absorption, to be sure, hermeneutics itself needs to be reinterpreted in a manner which "does justice to the experience of art." Accordingly, understanding has to be seen as part of the "event or happening of meaning" (*Sinngeschehen*) in which "the significance of all statements — those of art and of tradition in general — is formed and completed."[21]

Read in conjunction with the Gadamer-Derrida exchange, the preceding comments are prone to highlight a profound antagonism: if there is a central focus or target of Derridean deconstruction it is the notion of an unfolding meaning or continuity of understanding. This target furnishes the critical impulse in all of Derrida's writings; it looms particularly large in his assessments of Nietzsche. His *Spurs*, subtitled *Nietzsche's Styles*, is a concerted attack on the search for continuous meaning or what Derrida calls (somewhat elliptically) "onto-hermeneutics." Over long stretches, the monograph offers a discussion of "woman" or womanhood — mainly because "woman" is seen as the basic confounder and antagonist of cumulative meaning and stable identity. Woman, Derrida writes, is "perhaps not a distinct thing, not the determinable identity of a figure or appearance. . . . Perhaps — as a non-identity, non-figure, a simulacrum — woman is the very *abyss* of distance, the distancing of distance, the thrust of spacing, distance itself or *as such* (if one could still say such a thing which is no longer possible)." Contrary to an essentialist ontology and to a hermeneutics wedded to stable meanings, there is for Derrida "no such thing as the essence of woman because woman differentiates, and differentiates herself from herself. Out of endless, bottomless depths she engulfs and distorts all vestiges of essentiality, of identity, and of propriety or property. And philosophical discourse, blinded, founders on these shoals and is hurled down these depthless depths to its ruin." Despite his occasional diatribes against women and his apparent "anti-feminism," Nietzsche himself is approximated in the study to this vertiginous quality of womanhood. By placing traditional essences or meaning-structures "between the tenterhooks of quotation marks," we read, "Nietzsche's writing is at best an 'inscription' of truth. And such an inscription, even if we do not venture to call it the feminine itself, is indeed the feminine 'operation'."[22]

Apart from contrasting essence with non-identity, *Spurs* also links "woman"—and Nietzsche—with artistry or aesthetics. In Derrida's.presentation, woman cannot be subsumed under the rubrics of linear-cognitive "truth," rubrics celebrated by traditional philosophy (or metaphysics). "There is no such thing as the truth about woman," he writes; "but this is so because that abyssal divergence of truth or that non-truth *is* 'truth': woman is but one name for that untruth of truth." At the same time, however, woman is not just the negation of truth or the identity of non-truth, for "she knows that such a reversal would only deprive her of her powers of simulation" and would "force her just as surely as ever into the same old apparatus." Instead, woman places truth in quotation marks or under "veils" of modesty, with which she toys playfully: not believing in truth she still "plays with it as she would with a new concept or doctrine, gleefully anticipating her laughter." According to *Spurs*, woman occupies basically three positions vis-à-vis truth or cognitive meaning. In the first, she is identified with untruth and denounced as a "potentate of falsehood —in the name of truth and dogmatic metaphysics"; in the second case, she is placed on a pedestal and idealized as truth or as a "potentate of truth," again by "credulous" philosophers. Only in the third case does woman escape this dichotomy and come into her own: "Beyond the double negation she is recognized and affirmed as an affirmative power, a dissimulatress, an artist, a dionysiac." Actually, woman is able to exert this playful potency in the first two instances as well: "Seen as a model for truth she can display the gifts of her seductive power, which rules over dogmatism and disorients and routs those credulous men, the philosophers. And to the extent that she does not believe in truth (but still finds it in her interest) she is again a model, only this time a good model—or rather a bad model, because she plays at dissimulation, at ornamentation, deceit, artifice, at an artist's philosophy, manifesting her affirmative power." The same playful delight or artistry—the study claims—can also be found in Nietzsche, as is shown in his (alleged) preference for "style" or multiple "styles" over stable meaning: "With its spur (or pointed thrust) style can also protect against the terrifying, blinding or mortal danger of whatever *presents* itself or is obstinately encountered: presence, content, the thing itself, meaning, or truth."[23]

In emphasizing playfulness and artistry, Derrida in a sense complements Gadamer's discussion of "play"—but with a radical difference: instead of integrating play into the understanding of meaning, or aesthetics into hermeneutics, *Spurs* presents art as the rock or riff (another sense of the French *éperon*) on which intentional hermeneutics founders. As portrayed in that text, woman—according to one passage—"describes a margin where the control over meaning or code is without recourse" and which "erects a limit to the relevance of hermeneutical or systematic inquiries." Assimilating—perhaps too abruptly—existential or ontological hermeneutics with the cognitive aspirations of traditional logic (or metaphysics), Derrida finds in woman the antidote to univocal meaning and intelligible continuity. "From the moment," he writes, "the question of woman suspends the decidable opposition between the true and non-true; from the moment it installs the epochal regime of quotation marks for all the concepts belonging to the system of philosophical decidability—from that moment the hermeneutical project postulating a true sense of the text is disqualified. Reading at this point is freed from the horizon of the meaning or truth of being, liberated from the values of the product's production or the present's presence. Whereupon the question of style is immediately unleashed as a question of writing." As he adds, the "spurring-operation" of this question of style—in Nietzsche's case the operation of the "grand style" manifest in the will to power—"is more powerful than any content, thesis or meaning."[24]

These strictures against the "hermeneutical project" are said to apply also to Heidegger's textual exegesis, especially to his attempt to find *a* meaning or *the* meaning of Nietzsche's writings—an endeavor which, in Derrida's words, "remains throughout the near totality of its trajectory in the hermeneutical space of the question of the truth (of being)." Once, however, the undecidability of truth and non-truth, and also of identity and otherness, property and non-property, is taken into account, Heidegger's exegesis is bound to be disoriented. "On such a track," he notes, "we might perhaps flush out again Heidegger's reading of 'Nietzsche', and abscond with it outside the hermeneutical circle and everything it reflects, towards a field of enormous dimensions, a field immeasurable except perhaps by the steps of a dove." According to Derrida, the impossibility of finding a single, comprehensive meaning in Nietzsche is not due to a shortcoming of Heidegger or any other interpreter: not even Nietzsche may have possessed the key to his opus. "Could Nietzsche," he asks, referring to a particular fragment, "have disposed of some more or less secret code which, for him or some unknown accomplice of his, would have made sense of this statement? We shall never know; at least it is possible that we will never know and that possibility (of ignorance) must somehow be taken into acount." This inability is "imprinted on the remains of this nonfragment as a trace, withdrawing it from any assured horizon of a hermeneutical query." The fragment in question—a scribbled note say-

ing "I have forgotten my umbrella"—thus assumes a prototypical status for exegesis: "If Nietzsche had indeed meant to say or express
something, might it not be just that limit of the will to mean—which,
as effect of a necessarily differential will to power, is forever divided,
folded, and multiplied? To whatever lengths one might carry a con-
scientious interpretation, the hypothesis that the totality of Nietzsche's text, in some monstrous way, might well be of the type 'I have
forgotten my umbrella' cannot be excluded."[25]

III

In light of the preceding amplifications, the broader parameters
of the discussed exchange should have emerged into sharper relief.
What surely has surfaced is the multidimensionality of the issues at
stake. On a first level—perhaps the most prominent one—the exchange
revolves around a conflict of interpretations or conceptions of interpretation, conjuring up a powerful array of dichotomies or oppositions:
understanding versus non-understanding, immanence versus otherness, continuity versus rupture, truth versus non-truth. On another
level—not sharply segregated from the first—the issues have to do with
modes of inquiry and categories of human behavior, giving rise to another set of antinomies: intentional activity versus non-intentional
playfulness, ethics versus art, practical hermeneutics versus aesthetics. Behind these levels, as I shall argue, yet another cluster of questions lies in wait: one dealing with the status of political interaction
and communication in our time. Viewed in a gross and overly sim-
plified manner, the two spokesmen might each be assigned to one
side of the polar oppositions: with Gadamer representing understanding, immanence, continuity, and truth, and Derrida non-understanding, rupture, and artistry. However, both thinkers are too adroit and
subtle to fit neatly into these rubrics—although a certain overall tendency can hardly be denied, namely, the tendency in one case to return to traditional metaphysics and, in the other, to leap briskly beyond it. My ambition here is not to award a palm to the winning side
of the debate (if there were such a winning side); more modestly, I
seek to cut a path through the thicket of arguments which defies easy
solution. Fortunately, my venture is facilitated by the life-work of the
thinker to whom both spokesmen, from diverse angles, pay tribute.

    Focusing first on Gadamer's comments, one can hardly fail to
appreciate the intensity of his hermeneutical élan and commitment
to transpersonal understanding—a commitment, I believe, embody-

ing the best features of the great tradition of humanistic learning and education. Equally attractive, to me, is his close association of hermeneutics and dialogue—with dialogue signifying not a sequence of soliloquies but an existential encounter involving mutual testing and risk-taking. Despite these and many similar virtues, however, I am troubled by Gadamer's persistent oscillation or by a certain half-heartedness of his "ontological turn"—an oscillation which has been noted repeatedly above and which only needs to be recalled here briefly. A central ambivalence concerns the relation between the "universality" or "universal claim" of hermeneutics and the notion of hermeneutical "limits"—two views Gadamer seems to endorse simultaneously (but without clarifying their compatibility). Can one plausibly argue that "the universal claim of hermeneutics is undeniable" and that the hermeneutical circle in particular enjoys "true universality," and yet add almost instantly: "For my part I was always careful not to forget the limits implicit in the hermeneutical experience of meaning. When I wrote that 'intelligible being is language' I meant to say that being can never be completely understood"? A related quandary has to do with the status of traditional philosophical (or metaphysical) discourse, a quandary highlighted by the issue of "logocentrism." Is it possible to criticize the "logocentrism of Greek ontology" from the vantage point of biblical and theological sources, and yet extol the merits of Plato's *eumeneis elenchoi* and affirm that, on the model of Platonic dialogues, "the exchange of speech and counterspeech, question and answer, can produce genuine consensus"? A more specific issue in the same context is the status of German idealism and particularly of Hegelian dialectics—a dialectics which, on the one hand, is closely assimilated to hermeneutical interaction and, on the other, castigated for skirting the domain of otherness ("the boundary which he did not transgress").[26]

Both in the Paris exchange and in *Truth and Method*, a crucial ambivalence concerns the role of "rupture" or transformative change, and the relation between continuity and discontinuity. In formulating an "ontological" conception of art, *Truth and Method*—as indicated—places heavy stress on the rupturing or transformative quality of art-works, a quality radically different from merely incremental, continuous change. In contrast to a "gradual transition" leading from one point to the next, the transformation occurring in art-works is said to imply "that something turns suddenly and as a whole into something else." Relying on Heideggerian teachings, Gadamer also refers to the rupturing "push" (*Stoss*) involved in the experience of art-works, a push which disrupts or disorients "complacent meaning expectations." With regard to subjective agents (artists and interpreters alike), the rupturing effect is claimed to be such that "the identity of the players remains for no one the same." As also noted, however, comments of this kind do not prevent Gadamer in the end from reaffirming the ineluctable primacy of understanding or "hermeneutical consciousness": even what transcends or outstrips our immediate grasp belongs, in his view, to "the continuity of self-understanding in which human existence moves" or that "hermeneutic continuity which constitutes our being." What remains unresolved at this point—or unevenly resolved by fiat—is a question Gadamer articulates in *Text und Interpretation:* namely, the question "how the unity of meaning established in dialogue and the impenetrability of otherness can be reconciled or mediated—that is, what language (*Sprachlichkeit*) ultimately signifies: bridge or barrier?"

The question clearly affects the status and range of hermeneutics. Perhaps Heidegger was not ill-advised when, following *Being and Time,* he became apprehensive of, and even turned his back on, hermeneutics since—as Gadamer states—"he realized its inability to help him break through the parameters of transcendental reflection" or through the "sphere of phenomenological immanence." Needless to say, hermeneutics cannot simply be vindicated hermeneutically; nor can the scope and possible limits of hermeneutics be assessed through a recourse to self-understanding. In *Truth and Method* Gadamer asserts that we do not have a "standpoint" which would "allow us to see" what limits or conditions us. However, in portraying the rupturing effect of art and the dislocation of identity, does he not himself implicitly invoke such a standpoint—which, I would add, is nothing but the standpoint of philosophy or, better still, the vantage point of that post-philosophical (or post-metaphysical) reflection which Heidegger calls "poetic" or "recollective" thinking (*Andenken*). The dimension of such thinking is actually not alien to *Truth and Method.* "The question of philosophy," the study observes at one point, "asks what is the 'being' of self-understanding? With this question it transcends in principle the horizon of this self-understanding." The question, Gadamer adds, is raised with particular intensity in Heideggerian philosophy: "In uncovering time as its own hidden ground, this philosophy does not preach blind commitment out of nihilistic despair; rather, it opens itself to a hitherto concealed experience transgressing subjectivity or subjective reflection, an experience that Heidegger calls 'being'."[27]

In comparison with Gadamer's opus, Derrida is much more resolute in seeking to transgress phenomenological "immanence" and the boundaries of transcendental reflection. Aiming his critique beyond Gadamer at the legacy of Cartesian metaphysics, his writings confront subjectivity or subjective complacency at every step with the challenge of non-understanding, rupture, and non-identity. Following Heidegger's lead but attempting to outdistance him, "deconstruction" pinpoints the limits of an intentional or existential hermeneutics —limits not externally imposed but endemic to the endeavor of understanding itself. While admiring the intellectual and stylistic zest of Derrida's work, however, I am troubled by a certain aloofness or nonengagement characterizing his thought (at least over long stretches) —more pointedly put: by a potential indifference or apathy resulting from the celebration of "difference." In part, this concern is prompted by the occasional exuberance of his deconstructive zeal: his tendency not so much to engage traditional philosophy or divergent views as to circumvent and elude them. On this score, it would be easy to quote Derrida against Derrida. As he stated in one of his earlier writings: "The step 'beyond or outside philosophy' is much more difficult to conceive than is commonly imagined by those who pretend to have made it long ago with cavalier ease, and who in general remain tied to metaphysics together with the entire body of discourse they claim to have severed from it." Echoes of these sentiments can still be found, intermittently, in *Spurs*. "Heidegger," we read there, "warns us against an aestheticizing confusionism which, as blind to art as it is to philosophy, would—in its precipitate interpretation of Nietzsche's propositions regarding the beginning era of the philosopher-artist—have us conclude that conceptual rigor is now less intractable and that it will henceforth be admissible to say anything in militating for the cause of irrelevance."[28]

Taking one's cues from these statements, one cannot help feeling uneasy about some of Derrida's recent arguments—especially his treatment of key metaphysical categories like truth, being, or totality. In this respect, incidentally, he seems often less than generous in acknowledging Heideggerian motifs; for, is it really necessary to instruct the latter about the complexity or ambivalence of these categories? Was it not Heidegger who (in "The Essence of Truth" and elsewhere) first enlightened us about the correlation of truth and non-truth, being and non-being, concealment and unconcealment—a correlation which did not lead him to abandon these terms but to reformulate them (as in the case of "truth")? In portraying both "woman" and Nietzsche's position, Derrida sometimes pretends to be entirely beyond such categories. "There is no such thing as a woman or a truth in itself about woman in itself," we read in *Spurs*. "For the same reason there is also no such thing as the truth of Nietzsche or of Nietzsche's text."

Commenting on Nietzsche's phrase "these are only—*my* truths" he adds: "The very fact that '*my* truths' is so underlined, that they are multiple, variegated, contradictory even, can only imply that these are not *truths*. There is then no such thing as a truth in itself, but only a surfeit of it; even about myself, truth is plural." However, to say that truth is plural is clearly not the same as to claim that there are no truths or no such thing as truth—because even a multiple, variegated truth still invokes the category of truth. Moreover, does not Derrida himself aim to disclose the truth about woman and about Nietzsche—to be sure, the truth in all its complexity and multiplicity? Equally difficult as the surrender of truth seems to me the escape from "being." Juxtaposing Heidegger's notion of "propriation" (*Ereignis*) and the category of being, Derrida affirms: "Because it is finally undecidable, propriation is more powerful than the question *ti esti*, more powerful than the veil of truth or the meaning of being." And he instantly continues: "Propriation is all the more powerful since it is its process that organizes both the totality of language's operation and symbolic exchange in general." But the phrase "propriation is" already enlists in its service the entire question of "*ti esti*" and thus the problematic of (the meaning of) being.[29]

A central target in both *Spurs* and the Paris exchange is the category of "unity" or "totality" as applied to Nietzsche's thought. Countering Heidegger's interpretation, Derrida insists on the variegated and refracted character of Nietzsche's writings, a character which cannot be assembled into a unified or holistic synthesis of meaning. As a first reaction one probably might want to question the holistic compactness of Heidegger's approach. As is well known, his exegesis originated in a series of lectures held, and essays written, during an extremely turbulent decade in German history (1936–1946) and in explicit response to this turbulence—a fact Derrida acknowledges when he notes that "these dates are of utmost importance if one wishes to relate this exegesis, in whole or in part, to its historical-political context." On closer inspection, the different parts of Heidegger's analysis actually reveal distinct shifts in focus and emphasis (shifts particularly evident between the first and second volumes of the German edition).[30] At the same time, Derrida's own reading is not free of unifying or holistic elements. In presenting woman's (and Nietzsche's) relations to truth, *Spurs* assembles these relations into a threefold matrix or "finite number of typical and matrical propositions" (woman as truth, as non-truth, and as artist)—an arrangement which may be less than a code but still forms an intelligible combination. More important here is the status of unity or totality itself. In shunning unitary meaning, Derrida asserts, Nietzsche's work also "unhinges what governs the thought or simple anticipation of wholeness: namely, the species-genus relationship. What prevails, rather, is a singular inclusion of 'whole' in the 'part', and this without any totalization." As a critical stratagem this point is elusive. For, did Heidegger not expressly exempt "being" from the species-genus nexus? Moreover, does the postulated inclusion of the "whole" in the "part" not presuppose a notion, however inchoate, of the whole?[31]

Regarding Derrida's own reading of Nietzsche, I would add, the source of the claimed multiplicity deserves further investigation. In some passages this source seems to be the thinker himself. To repeat a previous citation: "Who has decided that one carries only one name? Surely not Nietzsche ... Next to Kierkegaard, was Nietzsche not one of the few who multiplied his names and played with signatures, identities, and masks—who named himself several times and with different names?" In this passage, Nietzsche appears as the master-artist who playfully toyed with identities and ingeniously concealed himself behind a multitude of masks and disguises. But where, in this case, is the supposed exit from metaphysics? Far from evading its stranglehold, Nietzsche on this reading seems firmly entrenched in Cartesian-Kantian subjectivity or, in Gadamer's terms, in "aesthetic consciousness." The impression is reinforced by the stress on non-dialogue and non-communication—which seems to ensconce the thinker even more safely in the bulwark of self-identity (if not solipsism). Derrida, to be sure, is not satisfied with this reading and strenuously seeks to avoid its consequences. "Not that we need to side passively with heterogeneity or parody," he writes in *Spurs*. "Nor should one conclude from all this that the unavailability of a unique and ungraftable master-meaning is actually due to Nietzsche's infinite mastery, to his impregnable power, his impeccable manipulation of some trap, or to a sort of infinite calculus like that of Leibniz' God— only this time to a calculus of the undecidable so as to foil the grasp of hermeneutics. In seeking to elude the latter absolutely, one would just as surely fall back into its trap, by turning parody or simulacrum into an instrument of mastery."[32]

As a result, the source of multiplicity must be found elsewhere. In this respect, I find instructive and inspiring Gadamer's comments on aesthetics and especially on the transformative quality of art and play. As previously noted, play in his portrayal involves not merely a sequence of intentional activities but rather a kind of reversal of intentionality or counter-intentionality: in his words, "all playing is a being-played." Equally attractive in my view is his stress on the experiential dimension of play and genuine dialogue: the aspect of exposure, vulnerability, and risk. "Being played" in his assessment denotes not merely a passive endurance or external happening but rather a human "pathos": the labor or travail undergone in the process of transformation. Such labor, moreover, is rarely smooth and painless; for, how could we really be dislodged or "decentered" from our customary identity or way of life without discomfort or pain? On this score, Gadamer's position bears some affinity with Nietzsche's Zarathustra who at one point proclaimed himself the teacher or advocate "of life, of suffering, and of the circle." Derrida is not entirely a stranger to this perspective. "The festival of Nietzsche," he says in the Paris exchange, "implies the risk for the thinker to be torn to pieces and to be dispersed into his masks." But how can such a dispersal happen on the level of "styles" alone—the level of a formal-literary "spurring-operation" divorced from "any content, any thesis, any meaning"? How can we be torn away from our moorings through "mere" words or an infinite "play of signifiers"—a play which does not penetrate to and transform us in our substance or "being"?[33]

At this point, the normative or ethical dimension of play and dialogue also comes into view—the relevance of what Gadamer calls "good will." In denying a master-key to Nietzsche's self-understanding, Derrida states in *Spurs*: "No, somewhere parody always presupposes a naiveté, backed up by the unconscious, a vertiginous non-mastery, a loss of consciousness. An absolutely calculated parody would be either a confession or a table of law." But how is such naiveté, such a loss of mastery possible without a curtailment of self-centeredness, that is, without an overcoming of all those selfish impulses and desires that block the road to innocence? In participating in play or dialogue, do agents not have to curb or put aside their private vendettas and animosities? And is this overcoming or curbing not the gist of ethics seen as striving for "goodness"? In alerting to the role of "good will" Gadamer (I think) is again not far from the spirit of Nietzsche and his notion of "overcoming." On the other hand, in stressing only "styles" and artistry Derrida tends to slight or disregard Nietzsche's ethical fervor, his search for ever new "values"—although this search aimed at nobility above and beyond conventional "goodness." "The noble man wants to create something new or a new virtue, while the good want the old and its preservation," Zarathustra affirms, adding: "But this is not the danger of the noble man that he might become one of the good, but that he might turn into a churl, a mocker, a destroyer." The same fervor also pervades the "three metamorphoses" or the ascending sequence of camel, lion, and child—although

Nietzsche himself tended to prefer mostly the roaring of the lion, a roar calling for the coming of the child. To quote Zarathustra again: "Why must the preying lion still become a child? The child is innocence and forgetting, a new beginning, a game (*Spiel*), a self-propelled wheel, a first movement, a sacred 'Yes'."[34]

The neglect (if not disparagement) of the ethical dimension is particularly evident in Derrida's stress on non-judgment or "undecidability." In seeking to evade metaphysics, *Spurs* presents all traditional categories as basically exchangeable or undecidable—including truth and non-truth, meaning and non-meaning, being and nothingness (and, by implication, good and evil). The question of woman at one point is said to "abstract truth from itself," suspending it "in indecision, in the *epoché*"; according to a later passage, the same question is claimed to "suspend the decidable opposition of true and non-true, inaugurating the epochal regime of quotation marks." Still later, *Spurs* speaks of the "undecidable oscillation" in women between "giving oneself" and "giving oneself for," and also of the "undecidable equivalence" of "gift-poison" (or gift-*Gift*). Turning to Heidegger's notion of "propriation," Derrida discovers a more profound, quasi-ontological undecidability. Although propriation, he writes, "is as if magnetized by a valuation or ineradicable preference for the proper or property, it all the more surely leads to property's abyssal structure," a structure where "property is literally sunk" by "passing into otherness." This abyssal structure is finally presented as the vortex in which being and non-being become interchangeable and where all distinctions or decidable issues vanish into nothingness: "Once the question of production or the question of the *event* (which is one meaning of *Ereignis*) has been uprooted from ontology," we read, "property or propriation is named exactly as that which is proper to nothing and no one; it (propriation) no longer decides of the appropriation of the truth of being, but rather casts into its bottomless abyss truth as well as non-truth, concealment and unconcealment, enlightenment and dissimulation. The history of being becomes a history in which no being, nothing, happens (except *Ereignis'* unfathomable process)."[35]

It is (at the latest) at this juncture that Derrida's key notion of "difference" shades over into a celebration of indifference, non-engagement, and indecision. Coupled with the emphasis on discontinuity and fragmentation, this indifference begins to approximate closely Gadamer's "aesthetic consciousness" (if not the "aestheticizing confusionism" castigated by Derrida elsewhere). In Gadamer's words: "Absolute discontinuity, that is, the disintegration of the unity of the aesthetic object into a multiplicity of experiences, is the necessary consequence of

an aesthetics of feeling." Gadamer at this point invokes Kierkegaard's
decisionism—the Danish thinker's powerful "Either-Or"—as an antidote to aesthetic indifference. "As it seems to me," he writes, "Kierkegaard has demonstrated the untenability of this position, by recognizing the destructive consequences of subjectivism and by describing
—prior to anyone else—the self-destruction of aesthetic immediacy.
His theory of the aesthetic stage of existence is developed from the
standpoint of the moralist, one who has realized the desperate and
untenable state of an existence lived in pure immediacy and discontinuity. Hence, his critique of aesthetic consciousness is of fundamental importance because he shows the inner contradictions of aesthetic existence, contradictions which force it to go beyond itself."
What emerges behind Kierkegaard's "Either-Or" is the question of the
relation betwen ethics and aesthetics—including an aesthetics reformulated along Gadamerian or Heideggerian lines. As it seems to me,
aesthetics—especially a non-subjectivist aesthetics—can by no means
be divorced from ethics, to the extent that the latter signifies the overcoming of subjective self-centeredness. Not that aesthetics can in any
way be derived from ethics: as non-intentionality, play or art cannot
be deliberately produced or fabricated. Rather, the two appear mutually (but non-causally) implicated: to guard its naiveté, art presupposes
ethics; but the latter, in turn, can only arise through "recollection"
of playful innocence.[36]

This leads me finally to the practical-political connotations of
the reviewed exchange. In this domain, Gadamer is known for his long-
standing insistence on the linkage between hermeneutics and "praxis"
(although, in his treatment, the latter term shares some of the ambivalence of hermeneutical inquiry). His Paris comments presented
the "capacity for understanding" as a "basic human endowment which
sustains social life," while the possibility of consensus was described
as prerequisite of "all human solidarity and the viability of society."
Seen from this perspective, social and political interaction clearly requires ethical engagement or the reciprocal display of "good will"—
though an engagement which, in its more intense or accomplished
modes, makes room for non-intentional playfulness. This combination or sequence seems to me to be the gist of "*Bildung*" or of public
education and culture. Again, Gadamer deserves praise for having
rescued this notion from its contemporary oblivion or effacement.
"Viewed as elevation to a universal or common vista," he writes in
Truth and Method, "*Bildung* constitutes a general human task. The
task requires sacrifice of (mere) particularity for the sake of something
common or universal—where sacrifice of particularity means, in nega-

tive terms, the curbing of desire and hence freedom from the object of desire and freedom for its objectivity."[37] Construed as educational process or the formation of public "character," I should add, *Bildung* need not be confused with the imposition of an abstract-universal scheme or an external pedagogical system; rather, like Gadamerian dialogue, it involves mutual exposure and risk-taking—and above all, participation in the labor or travail of individual and communal transformation. Needless to say, such participation is a far cry from the non-engagement and neutral indifference prevalent in liberal societies (a stance present at least as a tendency in Derrida's occasional aestheticism).

Projected onto a broader scale, the hermeneutics-deconstruction theme has repercussions for cross cultural political relations, that is, for the emergence of the "global city." On this level, the central issue concerns the appropriate character of political communication and interaction. Rooted in the venerable tradition of humanistic learning and *Geisteswissenschaften*, Gadamer's hermeneutics encourages us to venture forth and seek to comprehend alien cultures and life-worlds; however, the question remains whether, in this venture, cultural differences are not simply assimilated or absorbed into the understanding mind (which is basically a Western mind). On the other hand, by stressing rupture and radical otherness Derrida seeks to uproot and dislodge the inquirer's comfortable self-identity; yet (probably against his preferences), his insistence on incommensurability may encourage reciprocal cultural disengagement and hence non-learning. In *Truth and Method* Gadamer at one point expresses the central maxim of philosophical hermeneutics: "To recognize oneself (or one's own) in the other and find a home abroad—this is the basic movement of spirit whose being consists in this return to itself from otherness." But clearly this maxim engenders, and needs to be complemented by, another maxim: namely, the challenge to recognize otherness or the alien in oneself (or one's own). Much, perhaps everything, will depend on our ability to find a mode of interaction balancing hermeneutics and counter-hermeneutics, cumulative self-understanding and self-abandonment, identity and transformation. As it seems to me, some incipient steps along this road have been made by Heidegger in his "Dialogue on Language" (subtitled, dialogue "between a Japanese and an Inquirer"). Referring to the "hermeneutical circle" as a relation of calling and being called, message and addressee, the inquirer states: "The messenger must come from the message; but he must also already have moved toward it." Whereupon the Japanese: "Did you not say earlier that this circle is inevitable and that, instead of trying to avoid it as an alleged logical contradiction, we must follow it?" And the reply: "Yes. But this necessary acceptance of the hermeneutical circle does not mean that the hermeneutic relation is properly experienced through a conceptual formulation of the accepted circle."[38]

6

Tale of Two Cities:
Ricoeur's Political and Social Essays

THE OPINION IS OFTEN voiced that phenomenology is completely unrelated to, and irrelevant for, social and political theory. To the extent
that the writings of Sartre and Merleau-Ponty are not sufficient coun-
terevidence, Ricoeur's *Political and Social Essays* should lay this view
definitely to rest. In these essays, which were first published in French
between 1956 and 1973, Ricoeur emerges as a subtle and penetrating
thinker deeply concerned about contemporary social and political
problems.[1] The essays, one should note, are by no means private "after-
hours" ruminations but are intimately connected with Ricoeur's life-
work as a professional philosopher. This linkage accounts in large part
for the fascination of the essays. Broadly speaking, Ricoeur's philosophical position appears to be located somewhere between Husserl
and Heidegger—or else between Jaspers and Lévi-Strauss; and it can
plausibly be argued, I believe, that some of the most crucial issues
for social and political thought today arise precisely in this field of
coordinates.

As is evident in all of his publications, Ricoeur's thinking prefers to move in broad arenas and resists premature synthesis; typically, his endeavor is to delineate the boundaries of a theme in antithetical fashion before embarking on the task of coordination or
reconciliation. The procedure is amply illustrated in *Political and
Social Essays*. Repeatedly the collection speaks of "balanced tensions"
or mediated conflicts and "oppositions." A striking example of the
procedure occurs in the discourse on *freedom* where, steering a course
between categorical principles and dialectics, the author appeals simultaneously to Kant and to Hegel: the former for securing "the conditions of possibility of freedom" and the latter for establishing "the
conditions for its actualization."[2] The reader may recall in this context other "balanced tensions" which characterize Ricoeur's philosophical opus. Although profoundly indebted to transcendental phenomenology (a debt manifest in his study on Husserl and in his translation

159

into French of the first volume of *Ideas*) and to the entire legacy of the philosophy of consciousness, Ricoeur early in his intellectual career shifted his focus from cognition to questions of human will and action and, in doing so, built a bridge to existentialism. His *Philosophie de la volonté* in particular juxtaposed the analysis of transcendental freedom and autonomy to the experiences of guilt, finitude, and fallibility endemic to man's status as a being-in-the-world.[3] Somewhat later, when the problem of language and the interpretation of symbols moved to the center of his thought, he contrasted and correlated two major types of hermeneutics (in *Freud and Philosophy*): one directed to the recovery and recollection of latent intentional meaning, and another concerned with the decoding and removal of systematic distortions of meaning. Almost simultaneously, responding to the challenge issuing from contemporary linguistics and anthropology, Ricoeur endeavored to establish a *modus vivendi* between hermeneutics and structuralism (especially in *The Conflict of Interpretations*).[4]

In *Political and Social Essays,* tensions and their mediations are discussed on the level of ideas and methodologies, but are also seen to be operative in all facets of practical life. Building on the earlier study on human will, the opening essay explores the correlation or dialectic of *nature* and *freedom* and presents two complementary interpretations of human history: in terms of an "ascending genesis of *libido*" and a "descending genesis of freedom."[5] A subsequent essay probes further the conflict between freedom and social-cultural institutions, in the context of a critique of Skinner's behaviorism. In a modified form, the same conflict emerges in an essay on "Violence and Language" which examines the tension between organized power and normative meaning in diverse settings, including politics, poetry, and philosophy. Politics in particular is said to be lodged at the crossroads of two conflicting imperatives: an "ethic of conviction" stressing internal perfection and autonomy and an "ethic of responsibility" concerned with concrete options and outcomes in a given situation. Among political institutions, the volume pays special attention to the modern state and its "adventures," stressing the Janusfaced character of its role and impact: while meant to function as a pacemaker of enlightenment, rationalization, and large-scale planning in the public interest, it also has served as a tool of tyranny and oppression. In Ricoeur's words: "The State is, among us, the unresolved contradiction of rationality and power."[6]

A similar ambiguity is said to be at work in the entire modern process of secularization and urbanization: although they engender

anonymity, rootlessness, and bureaucratic domination, these trends
are also perceived as possible harbingers of human autonomy and social renewal. According to Ricoeur, incidentally, social and political
renewal today cannot be restricted to the reform of established institutions (typically anchored in the state) but must foster the growth
of global structures embracing mankind as a whole—although such
structures should not simply replace or dismantle inherited frameworks. The dialectic of freedom and institutions at this point gives
rise to another dialectic of innovation and social change: while important as a corrective to the arrogance of nation-states, "planetary
consciousness" can also entail global uniformity and anonymity—an
insight which renders desirable the maintenance of the tension between "mondialization" and local or national particularism. The same
dialectic pervades the discussion of the respective merits of hermeneutics or historical understanding and the critique of ideology (as
exemplified in the works of Gadamer and Habermas). Ricoeur at this
point counsels a balance between "participation" in tradition and critical "distantiation" or emancipation. The concluding essay identifies
the chief task of the political educator as the mediation between past
and future, between the temporalities of "creation" and "memory." The
preservation of culture, we are told, is possible "only to the extent
that we entirely assume our past, its values and its symbols, and are
capable of reinterpreting it totally."[7]

Although significant in their domains, the sketched tensions are
overshadowed by a more deep-seated antagonism: the drama of the
interplay between the Augustinian "two cities." As a Christian thinker,
Ricoeur views politics not simply as the clash of competing ideolo-
gies, but as the meeting ground of secular arrangements and eschatological hopes. His conception of the relation between the two cities,
one should note, is by no means a replica of the medieval juxtaposition of temporal and spiritual powers. Ricoeur is firmly opposed to
a direct political role of the Church or to any institutionalized Christian politics. In his words: "The new type of witnessing which will
appear must be completely dissociated from any institutional aspect."
Far from vouchsafing political abstinence, the rejection of clericalism
is meant to allow the Christian to become an "efficacious" participant
in the "earthly city." Christians are reminded of the biblical injunction to be the "salt of the earth"—an injunction which is bypassed by
a retreat to a holy mountain or an exclusive preoccupation with personal salvation. According to Ricoeur, there is perhaps tension but
not a stark opposition between personal piety and "commitment in
the world." With regard to the modern state—a structure "simultane-

ously instituted and fallen"—Christians are exhorted to assist both in strengthening its rational operation and in curbing its proclivity to abuse of power. The leavening role of Christians, however, extends beyond the state to all aspects of modern life. The process of secularization in this context emerges less as a threat to organized religion than as an opportunity for Christian involvement in the world. The essay "Urbanization and Secularization" speaks of a theology of the "secular city" and of social change, indicating how the modern "disenchantment of nature" and "desacralization of politics" can encourage an endeavor to sanctify and redeem the profane. Ultimately, believers viewed as "God's avant-garde" are assigned three services or ministries in the midst of the world: the services of "proclamation" (*kerygma*), of "healing by reconciliation" (*diakonia*), and of "eschatological communion" (*koinonia*). Performance of these services keeps the "salt" of faith intact: "The non-parish will save the parish. We shall have to learn to see the face of the Church wherever the ministries of announcement, of diakonia, and of concrete community confront the city as a whole, such as the modern world has made it: that is, the secular city."[8]

The goal of communion, in Ricoeur's view, requires not only spiritual pleas but also efforts to establish social preconditions for community life. Regarding economic wealth he writes that "the cards will have to be reshuffled" and that "it is one of the basic tasks of the Christian Church to show the 'haves' that they must give to the 'have-nots' on a world-wide scale." Statements to this effect are not incidental. In terms of political outlook, the entire volume is an argument in favor of Christian socialism or of a socialism tempered by religiously motivated liberal principles. Concerning economic and social policy, Ricoeur even is a friendly critic or critical friend of Marxism—provided the latter is seen as a "humanist realism" rather than as a "crude materialist" doctrine. The essay "Socialism Today" defines socialism as a comprehensive movement operative in the domains of economics, politics, and culture. On the economic level, socialism denotes "the transition from a market economy to a planned economy that is responsive to human needs" and that is characterized by "collective or public" ownership of the means of production; on the political and social level, the movement advocates "the participation of the greatest number of individuals in economic decisions," that is, the establishment of "industrial democracy" or a "democracy of labor," while culturally it implies a struggle against alienation and for "solidarity with the most underprivileged fraction of humanity." As Ricoeur recognizes, however, large-scale planning and public ownership may also entail new forms of exploitation and manipulation. From this danger arises the need for a "revindication of true liberalism, that is, the revindication of an area recognized and guaranteed by the State for critical and creative activity of the man of culture." Precisely at a time when socialist planning is required for the removal of social injustice, Ricoeur notes, liberal safeguards have to be jealously maintained: "In the period in which we must extend the role of the State in economic and social matters and advance along the path of the *socialist State*, we must also continue the task of *liberal politics*, which has always consisted of two things: to divide power among powers, to control executive power by popular representation."[9]

Written two decades ago, these lines still have a timely ring. Ricoeur's pleas for a liberal socialism or socialist liberalism are bound to strike responsive chords in a generation (in France and elsewhere) numbed by bloc politics and weary both of capitalist exploitation and Stalinist or post-Stalinist tyranny. On a more strictly theoretical level, the volume contains numerous observations which are prone to captivate readers familiar with contemporary philosophical trends. Given the prominence of language philosophy today, Ricoeur's comments on the topic—especially on the twin pitfalls of cultural relativism and universalism—deserve careful attention. The "partial possibility of translating certifies that humanity, in its depth, is one," he writes, adding: "Whereas on the technical level men can become identical with one another, on the deeper level of historical creation, diverse civilizations can only communicate with each other according to the model of the translation of one language into another." In the discussion of hermeneutics and critical theory, the reader is likely to be struck by the comparison of Habermas's notion of "interest" both with the Heideggerian category of "care" and the Marxist concept of "praxis." In the same intellectual context, one may wish to ponder the relationship between Habermas's three types of interests and the three dimensions of civilization—"industries, institutions, and values"—delineated by Ricoeur in his comments on political education. His views on "disengaged" thought and literature, incidentally, bring back to memory the earlier Frankfurt school, in particular Adorno's defense of artistic freedom against propagandistic manipulation.[10]

Despite its considerable merits, the volume frequently tends to leave the reader perplexed. The predilection for tensions and antinomies often impales arguments on the proverbial horns of dilemmas, while mediations acquire overtones of weak compromise. Although not obliged to offer solutions, the author might at times have probed more thoroughly the challenges opened up by philosophical quandaries. Thus, concerning the dialectic of nature and freedom, it is hardly sufficient to be told that a clue for tackling the antinomy can be found in the Leibnizian notion of "appetition" and the Spinozistic concept of "effort" (conatus)—especially if one learns shortly afterwards that one must reject "the wholly positive ontology of Spinoza." Cryptic is also the description of the dialectic (in terms borrowed from Nabert) as "the *appropriation* by the ego of a certainty of existing which constitutes the ego, but of which it is in many ways dispossessed."[11] More generally, the role of the ego or of man in relation to nature, culture, or the universe is never fully clarified in the volume. The essay "Humanism" acknowledges that "man determines and chooses himself," while insisting simultaneously on a "philosophy of limits" which treats man as "only human." The latter qualification does not prevent Ricoeur from arguing at another point that "God, in creating man, creates his creators" and that "through the passion for the limit beyond all vanity, man unfolds the *magisterium* which was entrusted to him at the beginning." The ambivalence of man's status carries over into ethics and especially into the question of the origin of values. The essay on hermeneutics affirms that "ethical life is a perpetual transaction between the project of freedom and its ethical situation outlined by the given world of institutions"—leaving the origin of the ethical situation in doubt. Another passage states more ambitiously, but no less elusively, that man "invents concrete values, but within a realm of value which determines his will on primordial grounds."[12] Political theorists and students of philosophy must be grateful to Ricoeur for having broached issues whose further elaboration and development will demand their best efforts.

7

Pragmatism and Hermeneutics:
Bernstein

As MANY OBSERVERS HAVE noted, ours is a time of crisis or deep ferment —not only politically but also intellectually: older school doctrines and entrenched philosophical positions are crumbling or being swept aside and replaced by more flexible and unconventional vistas. In the Anglo-American context, the sway of logical positivism—focused on scientific epistemology—has largely come to an end, making room for "post-empiricist" experimentation and the resurgence of pragmatist (or neo-pragmatist) modes of discourse; simultaneously, these changes are buttressed and intensified by the influx of Continental European perspectives stressing the interpretive and concrete-existential underpinnings of cognitive pursuits. Among American philosophers today, no one has kept his finger more attentively and probingly on the pulse of these developments than Richard Bernstein. In a string of publications Bernstein has made accessible to American audiences diverse European orientations (including phenomenology, existentialism, and critical theory), while at the same time remaining a keen diagnostician of trends in analytical philosophy. Most importantly, his writings provide a kind of logbook of the contemporary shift from epistemology to pragmatics, a shift inaugurating a potential rejuvenation of social and political thought. As he writes in the "Preface" to his recent book, *Beyond Objectivism and Relativism,* multiple philosophical strands today point in the direction of "an underlying common vision": one "that illuminates the dialogical character of our human existence and our communicative transactions," and which discloses "not just a perplexing theoretical quandary but a practical task that can orient and give direction to our collective *praxis.*"[1]

Seen from Bernstein's perspective, present-day intellectual changes signal a move beyond traditional philosophy, especially beyond the confines of Cartesianism or (what he calls) the "Cartesian Anxiety"; but they do not herald an "end" or demise of philosophical argument as such. More specifically, the abandonment of posi-

tivist epistemology inaugurates a greater tolerance of conflicting approaches, but not a reign of cognitive anarchy and personal whim. As
the title of the new study indicates, the basic sense of contemporary
transformations resides in the transcendence of both "objectivism"
and "relativism"—where "objectivism" designates a cognitive essential-
ism wedded to the quest for apodictic truth, while "relativism" means
the denial of this quest and of the possibility of any shared conception of truth. Phrased in this manner, of course, the title merely provides a negative demarcation, that is, a designation of intellectual
hazards or pitfalls to be avoided. The more positive or constructive
ambitions of the author emerge already in the subtitle which pro-
grammatically lists three prominent road markers toward philosophical renewal: namely, "science" (as construed by post-empiricists), hermeneutics, and *praxis*. Viewed together or cumulatively, the three
markers point to a strengthening of the classical legacy of "practical
philosophy"—suitably adapted to modern needs—with its emphasis
on practical deliberation and judgment. Gadamer's hermeneutical insights in particular—singled out for their fruitfulness for both the
natural and social sciences—are said to stand in "the tradition of practical philosophy that has its sources in Aristotle's *Nicomachean Ethics* and *Politics*" where understanding takes the "form of *phronesis*."[2]

I

Beyond Objectivism and Relativism guides the reader through
a complex and multifaceted panorama spanning the regions of post-
empiricist philosophy, Gadamerian hermeneutics, and practical-
political theory. The opening chapter provides a rapid overview of
these regions and of the central themes or theses discussed in the
study. Starting from the proposition that "a new conversation is now
emerging among philosophers," Bernstein contrasts this conversational
stance both with positivist orthodoxy and with "fashionable varieties"
of skepticism which "frequently lead to cynicism and a growing sense
of impotence." The contrast is restated in greater detail as the opposition between objectivism and relativism, with the first term being
defined as an apodictic outlook "closely related to foundationalism
and the search for an Archimedean point," and the second as the claim
that all presumed foundations are "relative to a specific conceptual
scheme, theoretical framework, paradigm, form of life, society, or culture." In Bernstein's vocabulary, the option between the two terms—
or the assumption that these are the only alternatives—is called the

"Cartesian Anxiety" or the grand Cartesian "Either/Or": "*Either* there is some support for our being, a fixed foundation for our knowledge, *or* we cannot escape the forces of darkness that envelop us with madness, with intellectual and moral chaos." As he tries to show, efforts to "exorcise" the Cartesian dilemma have for some time been under way in both the Anglo-American and European contexts. Pointing to the aftermath of Thomas Kuhn's initiatives, Bernstein notes the progressive shift from immediate sense certainty to an appreciation of "the role of tradition in science as mediated through research programs or research traditions"—a shift evident in both the natural and the social sciences and ultimately testifying to the ongoing "recovery of the hermeneutical dimension" in all these disciplines. The implications of the latter recovery have been spelled out with particular eloquence by Gadamer whose work, we are told, is marked by a pervasive "critique of the Cartesian persuasion" and who, in his own manner, has sought "to exorcise the Cartesian Anxiety and to elaborate a way of thinking that moves beyond objectivism and relativism"—thereby opening a new path for practical-political discourse.[3]

Post-empiricist developments in the philosophy of science occupy center-stage in the second chapter. Focusing on the issue of "paradigms" and of paradigm (or theory) choices, Bernstein defends Kuhn against the charge of irrationalism, approximating his arguments closely to the tradition of practical deliberation and judgment: "Many of the features of the type of rationality that is exhibited in such disputes (about paradigms) show an affinity with the characteristics of *phronesis* (practical reasoning) that Aristotle describes," that is, a type of reasoning "in which there is a mediation between general principles and a concrete particular situation that requires choice and decision" and where "there are no determinate technical rules by which a particular can simply be subsumed under that which is general and universal." Actually, according to Bernstein, Kuhn's entire "revolution" in scientific thinking can be construed as an assault on the Cartesian legacy and the objectivism-relativism doublet: His "persistent attacks on the idea of an algorithm for theory-choice, his criticism of the idea of a permanent, neutral observation language, and his undermining of the notion of a determinate set of scientific criteria that can serve as rules or necessary and sufficient conditions for resolving scientific disputes can all be interpreted as calling into question the Cartesian Anxiety. . . . The fierceness of the attacks on Kuhn is indicative of the grip of the Cartesian Either/Or." Notwithstanding these attacks, the chapter finds some "common ground" between Kuhn and his critics, namely, in their common attachment to practical judgment. Thus,

despite the extravagance of his claims, Feyerabend's writings are said
to revolve around a "proper understanding of man's 'reason and humanity' which stresses its practical character"; similarly, when Rorty
asserts "that the very notion of what it is to be scientific and rational
was being 'hammered out'," he is making essentially the Kuhnian
point "that we can give a correct narrative account of why certain reasons and modes of argumentation prevailed and others did not." The
chapter closes with a detailed discussion of the issue of "incommensurability," a discussion sharply distinguishing between incompatible, incommensurable, and incomparable perspectives and stressing
that incommensurability does not exclude comparison and thus does
not coincide with a relativistic closure of frameworks.[4]

Having traced the practical-interpretive turn in contemporary
philosophy of science, the next chapter shifts attention to the hermeneutical tradition, and especially to Gadamer's "philosophical" brand
of hermeneutics where understanding and exegesis acquire existential-
ontological status. "Implicit in Heidegger, and explicit in Gadamer,"
we read, "are two interrelated fundamental claims: the claim for the
ontological significance of hermeneutics, and the claim for its *universality*. Hermeneutics is no longer conceived of as a subdiscipline of
humanistic studies or even as the characteristic Method of the *Geisteswissenschaften*, but rather as pertaining to questions concerning what
human beings are." Due to its ontological thrust, Gadamer's work is
portrayed as antithetical to the "Cartesian legacy" which is said to contain "the seeds for the typical Enlightenment contrasts between reason and tradition, reason and authority, reason and superstition." The
bulk of the chapter provides a competent tour through Gadamer's
Truth and Method—ranging from his ontological treatment of works
of art (as distinguished from a Kantian "aesthetic consciousness"), over
his discussion of exegesis (involving an interchange between texts or
events and interpreter), to his vindication of "authority" and "prejudice" in the process of understanding, and finally to his conceptions
of "effective-historical consciousness" and the "hermeneutical circle."
The latter notion, in particular, is shown to have ontological meaning in Gadamer's study: "The most important consequence of Gadamer's understanding of the hermeneutical circle is that it clarifies
the relation between the interpreter and what he or she seeks to understand. . . . When Gadamer says that works of art, texts, or tradition
'speak to us', he is not referring to a loose, metaphorical way of 'speaking' that we ourselves 'project' onto the texts; rather, he is expressing
what he takes to be the most fundamental ontological character of

our being-in-the-world." The overview is rounded out by an exploration of the concept of "application" and thus of the linkage between hermeneutics and *praxis:* "Gadamer tells us that recognizing the intrinsic role of application in all understanding represents 'the rediscovery of the fundamental hermeneutical problem'. . . . It is here that we discover the fusion of hermeneutics and *praxis,* which becomes the most central theme in Gadamer's analysis of philosophical hermeneutics."[5]

The concluding chapter pursues the linkage between hermeneutical and practical judgment into the domain of contemporary practical-political discourse, with an emphasis on four leading practitioners of such discourse: Gadamer, Habermas, Rorty, and Arendt. As in the case of post-Kuhnian debates, Bernstein finds a "common ground" between these thinkers, manifest in their vindication of a practical-dialogical mode of reasoning: "I want to show how they can be read as different voices in a coherent conversation." In an effort to narrow the gulf between hermeneutics and critical theory, the chapter portrays Habermas as speaking precariously "with two voices, which might be called the 'transcendental' and the 'pragmatic'"—or else the idioms of "strict dialectics" and "interpretative or hermeneutical dialectics"—with the second idiom being in Bernstein's view by far the more plausible or persuasive: "The reading of Habermas that I want to bring out and endorse is the one that underscores this aspect of his thinking—that sees his work not as another failed attempt of strict dialectics or transcendental argument, or even as proposing a 'new' scientific research program. Rather, it is a perspective that sees his project as really one of interpretative or hermeneutical dialectics which seeks to command our assent by the overall plausibility of the interpretation that it gives." Despite his "deconstructive" leanings, Rorty likewise emerges on the whole as a practical hermeneuticist, mainly because of his "rhetorical apologia for pragmatism" and his "defense of the Socratic virtues": the "willingness to talk, to listen to other people, to weigh the consequences of our actions upon other people." Although relying more on Kant than on Aristotelian *phronesis,* Arendt too is said to share the bent toward practical hermeneutics: "Like Gadamer, she seeks to show the importance of taste as a communal civic sense, a *sensus communis* that is basic for aesthetics, understanding, and politics. Her analysis of judgment as an intrinsically political mode of thinking is also motivated by the desire to show how this mode of thinking escapes the dichotomy of objectivism and relativism."[6]

II

Having traversed the terrain of the successive chapters, the reader is prone to feel exhilarated by the broad sweep of the surveyed panorama and the new vistas opened up by Bernstein's study. There is hardly another American philosopher alive who, with equal competence, could narrate and assess the complex developments in post-empiricist philosophy of science, social-science methodology, Continental hermeneutics, and practical-political thought. Also, given the dark thunderclouds on our historical and political horizon, the reader is liable to appreciate the eloquence of Bernstein's plea: "At a time when the threat of total annihilation no longer seems to be an abstract possibility but the most imminent and real potentiality, it becomes all the more imperative to try again and again to foster and nurture those forms of communal life in which dialogue, conversation, *phronesis*, practical discourse and judgment are concretely embodied in our everyday practices." The study, I should add, impresses not only by its breadth of vision, but also by the craftsmanship displayed in details. Thus, the discussion of post-Kuhnian and post-Winchian debates manifests both a thorough familiarity with relevant literature and a striking ability to elucidate central issues in a new and concise fashion; the review of Gadamer's *Truth and Method* is probably the most illuminating succinct treatment available in the English language. However, I want to alert here to an even smaller detail: the vignettes of Hegel contained in the study. With reference to paradigm changes Bernstein comments: "This point, so vital for Kuhn's new image of science, which stresses the element of conflict, incompatibility, and destruction of earlier paradigms, bears a very strong resemblance to one aspect of Hegel's understanding of dialectic, his concept of *Aufhebung*." And later on we read: "Few thinkers have had a more profound sense of the meaning of communal life—what he called *Sittlichkeit*—than Hegel. . . . More trenchantly than many subsequent thinkers, (he) is constantly showing us the obstacles, conflicts, and contradictions that stand in the way of a new, mediated form of *Sittlichkeit*."[7]

Given the many virtues of the study, my critical comments are bound to be relatively subdued and nonpolemical. One comparatively minor point has to do with the title of the study. As Bernstein himself acknowledges, his choice of the title is somewhat idiosyncratic: the more normal opposition would have been between "objectivism" and "subjectivism" or between "absolutism" and "relativism," respectively; also his usage does not entirely conform to standard definitions. Thus, the term "objectivism" is employed in a way "that is far more inclusive than some of its standard uses. 'Objectivism' has frequently been used to designate metaphysical realism — the claim that there is a world of objective reality that exists independently of us and that has a determinate nature or essence that we can know." In Bernstein's treatment, however, this type of objectivism is only "one variety of the species." One consequence of this approach is that thinkers like Kant and Husserl appear as "objectivists"— despite Kant's rigorous detachment of mind from reified "things-in-themselves" and despite Husserl's life-long struggle against the tentacles of naturalism or objectivism (and historicism). "Husserl," we read, "fails to stress the dialectical similarity between the objectivism that he attacks and the transcendentalism that he defends. *Au fond*, both share the aspiration to discover the real, permanent foundation of philosophy and knowledge." The reason Bernstein dismisses competing terms is that "absolutism" in his view is "no longer a live option," while "subjectivism" has been "extensively and devastatingly criticized." Yet, I doubt that even Descartes or Kant would have considered their apodictic claims to be "immune from criticism"; and relativism has hardly been less extensively challenged than subjectivism. The latter point is evident in subsequent passages where "subjectivist" and "relativist" are frequently used interchangeably.[8] Moreover, one may wonder whether the turn to discursive practice does not itself harbor a form of (collective) subjectivism (I shall return to this aspect later).

One of the most valuable features of the book is the discussion of individual contemporary thinkers from Kuhn over Winch to Gadamer and Arendt; due to their closer proximity to social-political thought, I intend to focus mainly on Continental writers. Notwithstanding its subtlety and sensitivity, the review of Gadamer's work elicits a number of queries and possible reservations. Exploring Gadamer's linkage of hermeneutics and *praxis*, Bernstein discovers "not just an innocent omission but a glaring substantive deficiency." Gadamer tells us, he writes, "that the contemporary understanding of practical reason as 'technical control' has degraded the concept of *praxis*. But if this is true . . . then one wants to know what it is about modern societies that has *caused* this to happen." Pursuing the issue into the domain of research strategies, Bernstein at this point invokes the traditional understanding-explanation dichotomy as well as the distinction (articulated among others by Habermas) between causal-empirical and hermeneutical dimensions of social inquiry: "There is a fundamental unresolved ambiguity in Gadamer's philosophy concerning the social sciences. However much one recognizes the importance of the hermeneutical dimension of the social sciences, one must also forthrightly confront those aspects of these disciplines that seek to develop *theoretical* and *causal explanations* of social phenomena," especially explanations of the "structure and dynamics of modern technological society." Irrespective of the prominence of structural or "systemic" components, however, the criticism squares uneasily with the remainder of Bernstein's arguments, in particular his comments on the post-empiricist "turn." If post-empiricism, as he claims, has indeed engendered a "recovery of the hermeneutical dimension" even within the confines of empirical or natural-scientific research, then the customary bifurcation of explanation and understanding appears to be in jeopardy or at least in need of serious reconsideration. (In an appended letter, incidentally, Gadamer politely declines any imputed sociological ambitions.)[9]

The issue has repercussions on the overall classification of Gadamer's opus. In an effort to buttress the fairness of his criticism, Bernstein notes that "Gadamer *does* claim to illuminate the essential character of the *Geisteswissenschaften*" and thus presumably to shed light on essential social features. At an earlier juncture, however, the study had already stressed the broader horizons of Gadamer's work: namely, "the *ontological* significance of hermeneutics" and its aspiration to "*universality*"; accordingly, hermeneutics is "no longer conceived of as a subdiscipline of humanistic studies or even as the characteristic Method of the *Geisteswissenschaften*, but rather as pertaining to questions concerning what human beings are." In a more forceful and pointed manner, a subsequent passage affirms: "The understanding of the hermeneutical circle primarily as the Method of the *Geisteswissenschaften*, and as a rival and alternative to the Method of the *Naturwissenschaften*, still is wedded to a Cartesian framework, with its acceptance of the categorial distinction between what is objective and what is subjective. But Heidegger transformed the meaning, scope, and significance of the hermeneutical circle." Still later, this anti-Cartesian thrust is turned against the opposition between "truth and method" itself: "Given the strong claims that Gadamer makes about the universality of hermeneutics, there is something misleading about this contrast. For if understanding underlies all human inquiry and knowledge, then what Gadamer labels Method must itself be hermeneutical." I do not wish to maintain that Gadamer fully clarified the "ontological" status of hermeneutics (especially in view of his linkage of existential ontology with intentional exegesis). However, Bernstein's study—at several points—seems not so much to resolve as to intensify or deepen Gadamer's quandaries. Thus, when elaborating on the ties of hermeneutics with both social inquiry and human *praxis*, his review readily slips into a Diltheyan frame of reference. The "stress on the moment of appropriation in hermeneutical understanding," we read, "enables us to see why Gadamer believes that the *Geisteswissenschaften*, when truly practiced, are practical-moral disciplines."[10]

The preceding passages also elicit comments on the truth-method correlation in Gadamer's work. Repeatedly, Bernstein voices concern especially about the first term in this correlation. "Although the concept of truth is basic to Gadamer's entire project of philosophic hermeneutics," he writes, "it turns out to be one of the most elusive concepts in his work," one which "he never fully makes explicit." The situation is all the more grievous since the appeal to truth "is absolutely essential in order to distinguish philosophic hermeneutics from a historicist form of relativism." As Bernstein observes, Gadamer's concept of truth is a "blending" of Hegelian and Heideggerian motifs; but, he adds, Gadamer "also distances himself from both Hegel and Heidegger"—by rejecting Hegel's "absolute knowledge" and by drawing back from Heidegger's "radical thinking." Again, I do not mean to suggest that Gadamer fully elucidates the status and meaning of truth; however, somewhat more detailed attention might have been given at this point to his writings on the topic (including the essay "What is Truth?" in *Kleine Schriften*). Some mention might also have been made of the fact that Gadamer cannot "distance" himself too neatly from Hegel and Heidegger—provided the ontological status of his hermeneutics is to be preserved or vindicated. From Heidegger's perspective, traditional notions of truth—including the correspondence model and the Cartesian stress on apodictic evidence—presuppose or are predicated on a prior ontological context of disclosure which sustains both the appearance of "objects" and the self-assertion of the *cogito*. A similar context or space, however, seems to be presupposed in the "pragmatist" version of truth which Bernstein proposes as solution to Gadamer's approach. "He emphasizes *our* thinking, understanding, and argumentation," he writes. "But then this casts the entire question of truth in a very different light. When it comes to the validation of claims to truth, then the essential issue concerns the reasons and arguments that we can give to support such claims. . . . In effect, I am suggesting that Gadamer is appealing to a concept of truth that (pragmatically speaking) amounts to what can be argumentatively validated by the community of interpreters who open themselves to what tradition 'says to us.'"[11]

In Bernstein's view, reliance on argumentation supplies critical standards of judgment and thus infuses hermeneutics with a certain rigor or methodical quality. Instead of submerging "method" in the event of interpretation, his analysis tends to bestow on understanding and the quest for truth a structured (if not properly methodological) character. Gadamer, he states, "is at his weakest in clarifying the role of argumentation in the validation of all claims to truth and in elucidating the nature of criticism in hermeneutical interpretation. His contrast between Method and Truth is overdrawn." Argumentation as critical method is the central ingredient in Bernstein's proposed remedy. To be sure, he is far from ignoring the difficulty of establishing critical yardsticks: "All criticism appeals to some principles, standards, or criteria. Gadamer is extremely incisive in exposing the fallacy of thinking that such principles, standards, or criteria can be removed from our own historicity and in showing that there is an essential openness and indeterminacy about them." This admission, however, does not mitigate his strictures against hermeneutics: "One can be sympathetic with Gadamer's critique of objectivism, foundationalism, the search for some Archimedean point that somehow stands outside of our historical situation. But if we press the theme of application and appropriation to our historical situation, then we must still address the question, What is the basis for our critical judgments? . . . What is required is a form of argumentation that seeks to warrant what is valid in this tradition." What seems neglected at this point is that argumentation itself can scarcely be postulated outside "our own historicity" or "our historical situation." Clearly, the kind of argumentative subjects involved in critical discourse—as well as the kind of arguments persuasive to them—can hardly be taken as invariant a priori principles but require themselves genetic or genealogical elucidation (that is, inquiry into their ontological status).[12]

What holds for argumentation can be extended to the pragmatic or pragmatist framework. In a sense, pragmatism—as presented at least in some of Bernstein's formulations—can be seen as a version or phase of modern philosophy which, while skeptical about its own premises, still asserts the primacy of cognitive subjects. This accent is evident in the passage (previously cited) which appeals to "*our* thinking, understanding, and argumentation" and to the community of interpreters "who open themselves to what tradition 'says to us.'" The accent is precariously related to, or in tension with, other passages restricting the role of subjectivity. Thus, commenting on the ontological dimension of hermeneutics, Bernstein observes that "understanding is not one type of activity, to be contrasted with other human activities" and is actually "misconceived when it is thought of as an activity of a *subject*; it is a 'happening', an 'event', a *pathos*." Somewhat later the same point is reiterated in the statement that "it is misleading to characterize understanding as an 'activity of a subject'. It is true, of course, that understanding requires effort and care, imagination and perceptiveness, but this is directed to the *pathos* of opening ourselves to what we seek to understand"; interpretation from this perspective means participation in a "play" that "fulfills its purpose only if the player loses himself" in it. Given this distantiation from subjective intentions or purposes, the reader is somewhat surprised to find dialogue and freedom portrayed elsewhere as intentional goals or as the implicit *telos* of Gadamer's work. "If the quintessence of what we are is to be dialogical," we are told, ". . . then whatever the limitations of the practical realization of this ideal, it nevertheless can and should give practical orientation to our lives." Notwithstanding a certain traditionalism (or Aristotelianism) in Gadamer's work, "there is an implicit *telos* here, not in the sense of what will work itself out in the course of history, but rather in the sense of what ought to be concretely realized."[13]

Beyond Objectivism and Relativism repeatedly profiles Gadamer's work through comparison with Habermas's position. The comparison is particularly important in light of the relativism-objectivism dilemma. In its opening pages, the third chapter tends to exempt Gadamer from relativist leanings. Although "frequently and persistently" advanced, Bernstein affirms, the charge of relativism misunderstands "what he is doing and saying." At the close of the same chapter, however, the tone of the argument changes almost into the opposite: "I have tried to show that many of the problems that Gadamer leaves unsolved are related to the ambiguities he allows concerning the meaning of truth, and especially concerning the validation of the 'claims to truth' that tradition makes upon us. And here one must frankly admit that there is a danger of lapsing into relativism." This is chiefly the point where Habermas's position is invoked as an antidote or corrective. "The theme of our historicity," we read, is "no less fundamental for Habermas than it is for Gadamer. But for Habermas the primary problem becomes one of how we can reconcile this 'performative participation' with the type of intersubjective understanding that makes the claim of objectivity." According to Habermas—at least in one of his prominent "voices" or idioms—individuals acting communicatively "must, in the performing of a speech action, raise universal validity claims and suppose that they can be vindicated or redeemed"; against Weber and "all forms of emotivist and decisionist understanding of norms" he maintains "that there is a type of argumentation and rationality that is appropriate for the redemption of universal normative validity claims." This thesis is said to be particularly crucial for a renewal of *praxis:* "The primary problem today, if we are concerned with *praxis* in the contemporary world, is to gain some clarity about the critical standards for guiding *praxis* and about how such standards are to be rationally warranted." Pursuit of this goal, in turn, requires "developing a comprehensive theory of rationality. This is what Habermas means when he speaks of the *foundations* of a critical theory of society."[14]

Rigorously applied, the invoked standards would clearly curtail the range and variability of hermeneutical exegesis; yet, their impact is jeopardized or eroded by Bernstein's own reservations. Regarding the apodictic or "unavoidable" status of universal validity claims the study concedes that "Habermas has not established that such a commitment is built into the very nature of communicative action." Particularly in view of Habermas's scientific or quasi-scientific aspirations, the question appears legitimate: "What evidence or arguments would even be relevant to refute the counterfactual claim that despite all signs to the contrary every speaker who engages in communicative action is committed to the presupposition of the discursive redemption of universal normative validity claims?" Both in the domains of ethics and universal pragmatics, Habermas's writings are said to exhibit "the flavor of those transcendental arguments that are supposed to be over-come by reconstructive analysis"; to this extent, his work "still seems to be haunted by the dichtomy of objectivism and relativism" with its two stark alternatives: "*either* there is a communicative ethics grounded in the very structures of intersubjectivity and social repro-duction, *or* there is no escape from relativism, decisionism, and emo-tivism." Bernstein's reservations are deepened when correlated with MacIntyre's notion of different rational "genres" and Rorty's "meta-critique" of modern rationality. From Rorty's perspective, Habermas's appeal to rational consensus and universal validity claims actually "turns out to be retrogressive" by compressing all viewpoints into a "commensurable" mold. Moreover, retrogression has clear detrimen-tal effects: "To speak of the argumentative redemption of validity claims through an appropriate type of discourse is either potentially stifling or sheer bluff: It becomes either a glorification and reification of existing, normal, contingent social practices or a pious and vacu-ous generality. We do not have the slightest idea, before the fact, of what rules or procedures of argumentation (if any) will be applicable to new, abnormal forms of discourse."[15]

Bernstein's ambivalence regarding validity claims extends to the Habermasian methodology of reconstruction. As he notes, the method was initially adopted to counteract the "strong transcendental strain" evident in some early writings; with the passage of time, Habermas had come to see "more clearly that a theory of communicative action is not intended to be a transcendental, a priori theory, but an empirical, scientific theory." Precisely in an effort to bypass the Kantian legacy, Habermas "now prefers to speak about the logic of *reconstruction* or *reconstructive analysis* and to argue that within the domain of scientific theories we must distinguish empirical-analytical theories . . . from reconstructive theories." Although presumably expediting the move beyond objectivism and relativism, Bernstein finds reconstructive methodology flawed on several grounds, especially in terms of scientific cogency and validity. "There is still a crucial ambiguity," he writes, "concerning the theory of communicative action as a 'reconstructive' scientific theory," even if one accepts the distinction between types of scientific approaches. Regarding the issue of validity or validation, for example, contemporary literature contains "extensive discussions of whether empirical or experimental evidence does or does not support the hypotheses advanced by Chomsky, Piaget, and Kohlberg" (writers exemplifying the reconstructive method). Does Habermas wish to make his theory contingent on the outcome of these scientific discussions? If this is not the case—and the tenor of his arguments militates against the option—reconstructive analysis still seems to be infected with Kantian apriorism: "Despite his manifest break with the Kantian tradition of transcendental argument, he nevertheless leads us to think that a new reconstructive science of communicative action can establish what Kant and his philosophic successors failed to establish—a solid ground for a communicative ethics." (This criticism does not prevent Bernstein from endorsing the "moral-political intention" of Habermas's work, that is "the desire to show that there is a *telos* immanent in our communicative action that is oriented to mutual understanding.")[16]

Given these strictures against Habermasian premises and postulates, Bernstein's view of discourse and hermeneutics seems to return basically to a Gadamerian mold. This is also the impression given in the opening pages of the discussion devoted to Arendt. "Like Gadamer," we read, "Arendt sees that the essential feature of the type of reasoning appropriate to *praxis* is the ability to do justice to particular situations in their particularity." What attracted her to Kant's *Critique of Judgment* was the conception of "reflective judgment" seen as a mode of judging that "ascends from particular to universal": "What fascinated Arendt about Kant's insight . . . is that he was able to define the 'specific validity' of judgment, which is not to be identified with the 'universal validity' of cognition." In Kant's treatment, reflective judgment was based on taste—but taste, in turn, was predicated on common sense or "community sense," not merely on private preferences: "What Arendt is struggling to discriminate and isolate for us is a mode of thinking that is neither to be identified with the expression of private feelings nor to be confused with the type of universality characteristic of 'cognitive reason.'" In this commitment to judgment, Bernstein also discovers an initial similarity or affinity with Habermas: "What Arendt calls 'judgment' and Habermas 'practical discourse' must be understood within the context of communicative action that is oriented to mutual understanding. . . . For both, too, there is a sharp distinction to be made between 'subjective private feelings' and those 'generalized interests', or communal opinions, that are tested and purified through public debate."[17]

As in the case of Gadamer, however, the initial affinity quickly turns into a contrast—with Habermasian theory acting as a corrective to Arendt's less rigorous perspective. Focusing on her distinction between opinion and truth (or judgment and cognition), Bernstein criticizes Arendt for neglecting the validity basis of judgment: "In stressing the gap between opinion and truth she tends to underestimate the importance of a concept that is most essential for her own understanding of judgment—argumentation. Argumentation does not make any sense unless there is some common acceptance of what is to count in support of, or against, an opinion." By neglecting this feature of argumentation, her perspective is said to approximate a noncognitive stance and even to court the danger of relativism: "Arendt failed to realize that in exaggerating the differences between truth and opinion and between the validity tests for each of them, she was leading us down the slippery slope of 'noncognitivism'"; Habermas's rational-cognitive approach at this point furnishes a remedy by showing "that the implicit claim to validity is just as essential for practical discourse as it is for theoretical discourse." Again as in Gadamer's case, however, this indictment is quickly offset by the admission of Habermas's limitations. In vigorously combatting relativism and decisionism, Habermas—in Bernstein's view—"carries out his analysis at a level of abstraction that is intended to isolate the 'formal-pragmatic" universals of the norms of rational speech," universals overarching individual or temporal variations. While also rejecting relativism, Arendt on the other hand is claimed to be "much more wary of the invidious ways in which action and politics are threatened when we fail to acknowledge the irreducible plurality and variability of opinions that are to be tested." As a result, Bernstein concedes, to invoke in any

rigorous fashion "the dichotomy of the cognitive and the noncognitive to characterize the difference between Habermas and Arendt is
misleading."[18]

III

As the comparison of Gadamer, Habermas, and Arendt indicates,
a centerpiece of Bernstein's own perspective is the notion of practical
discourse seen as critical argumentation—a notion which itself deserves critical scrutiny. In discussing both post-empiricism and contemporary political thought, the study is emphatic in stressing the
importance of the notion   as for instance in this statement: "We never
escape from the obligation of seeking to validate claims to truth
through argumentation and opening ourselves to the criticism of others." With specific reference to post-empiricist philosophy of science
another passage asserts that "alternative paradigms, theories, and research programs can be warranted by communal rational argumentation. What is to count as evidence and reasons to support a proposed
theory can be rationally contested—even what is to count as proper
criticism." Assertions of this kind clearly run into the difficulty of
specifying appropriate criteria and the tolerable range of agreement
and disagreement. As post-Kuhnian discussions have made amply
clear, scientific debates require a shared or "communal" framework
and even (to some extent) a shared way of life. Despite the plausibility of the study's overall intent, the reader is bound to wonder whether
Bernstein confronted the question he at one point poses to Kuhn: "Are
the criteria or values accepted by scientific communities rational because these are the values *accepted* by scientific communities, *or* are
they accepted by scientific communities because they are *the criteria
of rationality?*" The reader's puzzlement is likely to be increased in
light of some sympathetic comments on MacIntyre and Rorty; in particular, the latter's metacritique cannot fail to give pause: "To speak
of the argumentative redemption of validity claims through an appropriate type of discourse is either potentially stifling or sheer bluff."[19]

My concern, however, is not so much with these issues—well-
rehearsed in post-Kuhnian literature—as rather with the underlying
premises of argumentation. Is discourse a sufficient warrant of truth—
or, to put it somewhat differently: can argumentation itself be validated argumentatively? In sketching the road beyond objectivism and
relativism, Bernstein tends to present argumentation as a series of
"speech acts," that is, a sequence of intentional claims and propositions

—a formulation which raises a host of questions. Can language be entirely reduced to speech, and is speech simply an instrument of argumentative subjects? Does speaking not also presuppose listening, and what sort of "claim" does the latter advance? More importantly, does reciprocal speech not require attentiveness to a common "subject matter" or topic, and how is such attentiveness motivated or nurtured? At this point, Gadamer's emphasis on the "non-subjective" character of hermeneutics becomes pertinent—his argument that understanding is "misconceived when it is thought of as an activity of a subject" (or subjects) and should rather be construed as participation in an ongoing "happening" or play-like event. Given the central place accorded in the study to Gadamer's work, the "ontological significance" of hermeneutics would seem to deserve more careful consideration—including the ontological dimensions of dialogue and argumentation. Like the postulates of correspondence and self-evidence, practical discourse appears predicated on an ontological space or mode of disclosure buttressing the status of speakers and their truth claims.

Similar observations apply to Bernstein's views of *praxis* and practical teleology. Paraphrasing (very loosely) one of Arendt's formulations, he defines *praxis*—or "what *praxis* really is"—as "the highest form of human activity, manifested in speech and deed"; simultaneously he adds—again in an Arendtian vein—that "in the modern age a fabricating or means-end mentality (*techne*) and a laboring mentality have distorted and corrupted *praxis*." However, the linkage between the two phrases—especially between intentional activity and fabrication—is never fully pondered or explored. Repeatedly, discourse or discursive solidarity is presented as a normative goal awaiting concrete-intentional implementation. Thus, as previously indicated, Gadamer's work is said to contain an implicit practical "*telos*" revealing "what ought to be concretely realized." In another passage, Bernstein refers to the "radical thrust" in Gadamer's thought which "points to the goal of nurturing the type of dialogical communities in which *phronesis* can be practiced," adding: "We must ask what it is that blocks and prevents such dialogue, and what is to be done . . . to make such genuine dialogue a reality." At other points, however, Bernstein seems wary of the project of implementation. What, he asks in the concluding pages, is "to be done" in a situation in which there is a breakdown of communities and "where the very conditions of social life have the consequence of furthering such a breakdown?" We know, he continues, what has been "a typical modern response to this situation: the idea that we can make, engineer, impose our collective will to form such communities. But this is precisely what cannot be done, and the. attempts to do so have been disastrous." More broadly phrased: "A community or a *polis* is not something that can be made or engineered by some form of *techne* or by the administration of society."[20]

Comments of this kind conjure up complex issues and dilemmas relevant to political thought: especially the issue of the relation between *phronesis* and intentional action (and more generally between ethics and ontology). Can *phronesis* be treated as a goal to be consciously produced or enacted? If not, is there not grounds to re-examine the status of *praxis*—along the lines not of purposive rationality but of participation in an ongoing happening? And does the latter focus not provide a warrant to the notion of a creative or "poetic" *praxis* (combining activity and passivity), such as it has been outlined in Heidegger's "The Origin of the Work of Art" (and elsewhere)? Lacking such a notion, Bernstein's study is constrained to oscillate between acceptance of traditional practices and intentional-revolutionary change. This dilemma is easily one of the most obscure and unresolved features of the study. Focusing on the implications of hermeneutics, Bernstein at one point criticizes the linkage of *phronesis* and tradition: "Gadamer realizes—but I do not think he squarely faces the issues that it raises—that we are living in a time when the very conditions required for the exercise of *phronesis* . . . are themselves threatened (or do not exist)." Although sensitive to contemporary deformations of *praxis*, Gadamer "stops short of facing the issues of what is to be done when the *polis* or community itself is corrupt." In keeping with the general line of exegesis, Habermas surfaces again as the keener analyst: "Whereas Gadamer's primary experience has been one of historical continuity, the primary formative experience for Habermas was that of discontinuity—the trauma of almost a total break in tradition." Notwithstanding the radical flavor of these statements, Bernstein in the end retreats to the haven of established conventions. For *phronesis* and dialogue to operate, he notes, "the shared understandings and experiences, intersubjective practices, sense of affinity, solidarity . . . must already exist." Underscoring this point, he stresses "the danger of the type of 'totalizing' critique that seduces us into thinking that the forces at work in contemporary society are so powerful and devious that there is no possibility of achieving a communal life based on undistorted communication, dialogue, communal judgment, and rational persuasion."[21]

As it seems to me, the move beyond objectivism and relativism needs to be expanded into a move beyond intentionality (or intentional hermeneutics) and receptivity—and perhaps also beyond rational discourse and compulsion. Such a move, I want to emphasize, is by no means synonymous with a simple surrender of commitment and autonomy. In this light, Heidegger's phrase "only a god can save us now" deserves perhaps a sympathetic hearing—provided it is not equated, as Bernstein suggests, with the temptation to "yield up one's identity" to "some mighty inhuman force." In our age of discontinuity and large-scale cultural and political dislocations, the fostering of *phronesis* and understanding may require more than rational persuasion and argumentation: namely, the "poetic" generation of a public space through common living experiences and shared agonies. Precisely because community is not so much a rational construct as a mode of life, *phronesis* cannot simply be reduced to argumentative discourse. With this proviso, however, Bernstein's vision for the future is surely entitled to serious attention and reflection. "What we desperately need today," he writes, in an eloquent passage which no sensible reader would wish to dispute, "is to learn to think and act more like the fox than the hedgehog—to seize upon those experiences and struggles in which there are still the glimmerings of solidarity and the promise of dialogical communities in which there can be genuine mutual participation and where reciprocal wooing and persuasion can prevail."[22]

8
Virtue and Tradition:
MacIntyre

Sicut cervus . . .

QUESTIONS OF ETHICAL conduct arc again emerging as legitimate topics of inquiry. Having long been banished from official discourse both in philosophy and the social sciences, ethics—seen as concern with the quality of human behavior—is beginning to return from its involuntary exile. Its eclipse was due mainly to prominent trends in our century which by now are acknowledged to be on the wane: the sway of epistemology or theory of knowledge in philosophy; the fact-value dichotomy imposed by positivism on the social sciences; and the premium placed on (technical) efficiency both in academia and popular culture. Jointly, these trends had the effect of reducing moral conduct to a matter of feeling or emotive preference and ethical yardsticks to the status of arbitrary fiat. Yet, positivism and "emotivism" were not solely responsible for the mentioned eclipse; they were buttressed by a long-standing proclivity in modern philosophical ethics itself: the tendency to subordinate practical conduct to abstract moral rules, ethical content to formal procedure, and issues of human "goodness" to considerations of "rightness" (the latter term construed as conformity with general principles). What remained unanswered in this pervasive shift—from modern natural law to Kant and beyond—was how conduct was to be motivated by theoretical rules, and principle to be translated into social practice. In the context of modern liberal regimes, the tendency surfaced in the bifurcation between public legal frameworks and private morality or ethics—again with little or no attention to the question of their mutual correlation. In the absence of public exemplars, individual conduct was liable to drift progressively into randomness, a drift encouraged further by the positivist climate of our age.

Seen against this background, Alasdair MacIntyre's *After Virtue* constitutes a radical summons to philosophical (as well as practical) reorientation—although its radicalism is far from a "deconstructive" pose.[1] In terms of intellectual affinities, the study in fact offers an intriguing blend of innovation and reminiscence, or else of "postmodern" and premodern perspectives. In its emphasis on "narratives" and historical contexts, MacIntyre's argument inserts itself squarely into the post-Wittgensteinian retreat from extralinguistic "foundations," whether these foundations were anchored in epistemology or (Cartesian) metaphysics. Applied to the ethical domain, this retreat encourages a reversal of Enlightenment priorities, with concrete (contextualized) content ascending again over abstract form. At the same time, however, MacIntyre is deeply imbued with the legacies of Continental and Western philosophy, ranging from Hegel over scholasticism to the classics. Using a summary label, one might describe his outlook as a contextual-hermeneutical neo-Aristotelianism—with the accent placed on the moral fabric of concrete social traditions or on the "*telos*" implicit in ongoing social and political practices. My concern in the following is going to be chiefly with the relation between concrete moral conduct and social context, or between "virtue" and tradition. After having given a brief overview of MacIntyre's central arguments, I intend to highlight some of the chief strengths or merits of his study in order to conclude finally with some critical queries and afterthoughts.

I

After Virtue presents itself in a sense as a storybook—a book about the rise and fall, or the changing fortunes and misfortunes, of ethical reasoning. However, contrary to customary conventions of the genre, MacIntyre's account is not simply a linear or straightforward story, but prefers at different points to move backward or forward in time, thus in effect interlacing and artfully combining a number of narrative episodes. The book opens with a startling and "disquieting suggestion": the suggestion or invitation to imagine a large-scale fiasco or social disaster as a result of which most of the ingredients of modern natural science—both empirical and theoretical—have been destroyed or wiped out. In the wake of such a disaster, the author speculates, people would be left only with isolated fragments or bits and pieces of the previous sciences, fragments which they can no longer assemble into a coherent and meaningful fabric. Having depicted this grim scenario, MacIntyre quickly shifts the focus from natural science to the humanities and especially to ethics—a shift which, in his view, involves a move from the imaginary plane to something close to historical reality. "The hypothesis I wish to advance," he writes, "is that in the actual world which we inhabit the language of morality is in the same state of grave disorder as the language of natural science in the imaginary world which I described. What we possess, if this view is true, are the fragments of a conceptual scheme, parts which now lack those contexts from which their significance derived." Although we still possess some "simulacra of morality" and "continue to use many of the key expressions," we actually "have—very largely, if not entirely—lost our comprehension, both theoretical and practical, of morality."[2]

In an effort to buttress the claimed decay and fragmentation, the study in its next two chapters concentrates on the character of contemporary "moral disagreement" and especially on the role and impact of "emotivism." In MacIntyre's portrayal, moral discourse in our time is marked by three chief features: the conceptual "incommensurability" of rival arguments and hence the "interminability" of moral debate; the heterogeneity of philosophical mentors or sources of inspiration; and finally the paradoxical and spurious appeal to allegedly "impersonal" yardsticks and criteria. With the exception of the last, these features are openly embraced and advocated by defenders of "emotivism"—the latter term denoting "the doctrine that all evaluative judgments and more specifically all moral judgments are *nothing but* expressions of preference, expressions of attitude or feeling," and this irrespective of changing historical or cultural settings. Assuming the narrator's stance, MacIntyre proceeds to tell the story of the doctrine's evolution—from G. E. Moore's intuitionism over C. L. Stevenson to latter-day emotivists among analytical philosophers (like Hare). Countering the self-understanding of its proponents, the story fleshes out the substantive premises as well as the concrete social context of contemporary emotivism. In substantive terms, MacIntyre finds the salient characteristic of the doctrine in the "obliteration of any genuine distinction between manipulative and non-manipulative social relations," that is, in the reduction of ethics either to the "expression of my own feelings or attitudes" or else to the manipulation of the "feelings and attitudes of others." This trait is said to be crystallized in certain stock characters of present-day (Western) civilization —where "characters" denote "moral representatives of their culture" or the "masks" worn by dominant moral philosophies. Prominent among these characters, according to the study, are the "aesthete" wedded to personal gratification; the "manager" devoted to efficient bureaucratic control (along Weberian lines); and the "therapist" engaged in the manipulation of others' lives. What is common to these stock figures is the divorce between a privatized, autonomous self and a social arena governed by heteronomous constraints. In MacIntyre's words, the "peculiarly modern self" or "emotivist self" belongs to a "distinctive type of social order, that which we in the so-called advanced countries presently inhabit": an order marked by the bifurcation between the "realm of the organizational" amenable to manipulation, and the "realm of the personal" ruled by arbitrary whim. Thus, contemporary society is one in which "bureaucracy and individualism" are peculiarly linked, and it is in this setting that "the emotivist self is naturally at home."[3]

To provide background for this state of affairs, the following chapters of the study trace the genealogy of our present malaise, adopting a reversed-time sequence for this part of the narrative. According to MacIntyre, the intellectual roots of our ills lie basically in the Enlightenment—termed our "predecessor culture"—and especially in the Enlightenment project of giving a non-classical account of ethics. The first stop on this genealogical journey is Kierkegaard's *Either/Or* —with attention being focused chiefly on its ethical conception and premises. Although ethical standards, in Kierkegaard's view, were to enjoy authoritative status, the adoption of the ethical way of life itself was attributed to arbitrary choice: "But how can that which we adopt for no reason have any authority over us? The contradiction in Kierkegaard's doctrine is plain." To grasp the sources of this incoherence we are asked to move further back in time to Kant whose teachings set the stage for Kierkegaard's position—particularly in segregating sense experience rigorously from morality—despite Kant's more resolute reliance on "reason" (in lieu of arbitrary will). In identifying reason with logical consistency Kantian ethics, we are told, ultimately lapsed in tautology devoid of substantive content—a failure which was merely radicalized in *Either/Or*. Kant's moral theory, in turn, was chiefly a "historical response" to the efforts of Diderot and Hume to ground ethics in desire and the human passions—efforts, MacIntyre notes, which were deeply flawed and bound to collapse, notwithstanding laborious distinctions between enlightened and unenlightened, or between long-term and short-term desires. The overall result of the genealogical journey is the indictment of the "predecessor culture" on the ethical plane; for, from Hume over Kant to Kierkegaard, "the vindication of each position was made to rest in crucial part upon the failure of the other two, and the sum total of the effective criticism of each position by the others turned out to be the failure of all." The underlying cause of this general bankruptcy is ascribed to the modern conception of reason as a pure instrument of calculation, and especially to the expulsion of natural "ends" from moral reasoning. With the removal of teleology, ethical argument was transformed into the correlation of abstract moral norms and factual human nature —a correlation which, apart from its intrinsic tension, was bound to run into the problem of the "naturalistic fallacy": the prohibition to derive "ought" from "is." Hence, Enlightenment philosophers "engaged in what was an inevitably unsuccessful project": the attempt "to find a rational basis for moral beliefs in a particular understanding of human nature" (empirically construed). As MacIntyre adds, however, the mentioned fallacy is itself a modern invention and predicated on the rejection of the classical legacy and its teleological functionalism: "For according to that tradition to be a man is to fill a set of roles each of which has its own point and purpose: member of a family, citizen, soldier, philosopher, servant of God. It is only when man is thought of as an individual prior to and apart from all roles that 'man' ceases to be a functional concept."[4]

Following this genealogical excursion, the narrative moves again into forward gear, reciting some of the "consequences" or aftereffects of the Enlightenment debacle. At this point the spotlight shifts to utilitarianism and some recent forms of neo-Kantianism, that is, to attempts to derive moral rules from self-interest or else from the nature of practical reason. In the case of Bentham, ethics was conflated with individual psychology and with a quantitative calculus of pleasures and pains—an approach MacIntyre attacks both for its intrinsic psychologism amd the (possible) discrepancy of individual and collective happiness. The subsequent story of utilitarianism, in his view, was one of progressive dissolution and self-cancellation—a trend evident in John Stuart Mill's turn to "higher" pleasures and qualitative standards, and in Sidgwick's dismissal of utility in favor of intuition. Regarding neo-Kantianism, the study focuses briefly on Alan Gewirth's *Reason and Morality* and its endeavor to derive moral yardsticks— specifically universal "rights" to freedom and well-being—directly from the definition of rational agency. According to MacIntyre's rebuttal, the needs and wants of human agents are not equivalent to rights-claims, especially since the latter presuppose the existence of a set of social rules—a context bracketed in Gewirth's definition. In light of the failure of both offshoots of the Enlightenment project, the narrative returns to its initial starting point: the present malaise of emotivism with its blending of arbitrary freedom and bureaucratic controls—a scenario populated, as mentioned, by the stock characters of the aesthete, the manager, and the therapist. In order to illustrate the spurious and deceptive role of these characters, MacIntyre turns to the issue of managerial effectiveness, that is, to the manager's claim to "expertise" in the enterprise of human and organizational manipulation. The conclusion to which he seeks to move in this analysis is "that such expertise does indeed turn out to be one more moral fiction, because the kind of knowledge which would be required to sustain it does not exist." Typically, he notes, managerial expertise is predicated on two cognitive assumptions: one concerns "the existence of a domain of morally neutral fact about which the manager is to be expert," while the other involves the presence of "law-like generalizations" permitting the overall manipulation of events. Both assumptions, MacIntyre holds, are completely untenable—an assertion which is fleshed out in two successive chapters dealing respectively with the status of "facts" (and their presumed neutrality) and the ascertainable range of social predictability and unpredictability.[5]

In terms of narrative structure, the pivotal or "hinge" section of the study is a chapter whose title—"Nietzsche or Aristotle?"—captures the author's deepest concerns. Recapitulating his initial "disquieting suggestion," MacIntyre seeks to enhance its plausibility through an analogy with various "taboo" rules in Polynesian island kingdoms. Although at one point these rules formed part of a meaningful cultural fabric, their status had become largely unintelligible by the time of Captain Cook's travels—a fact demonstrated by their easy abolition in 1819 by King Kamehameha II. Transferring this lesson to European moral discourse, MacIntyre finds a similar transition from coherence to incoherence, with Nietzsche simply drawing the final, logical conclusion. "Why should we not think of Nietzsche as the Kamehameha II of the European tradition?" he asks, adding: "For it was Nietzsche's historic achievement to understand more clearly than any other philosopher . . . not only that what purported to be appeals to objectivity were in fact expressions of subjective will, but also the nature of the problems that this posed for moral philosophy." The gist of Nietzsche's argument, according to the study, resided in the formula: "If there is nothing to morality but expressions of will, my morality can only be what my will creates." With his resolute turn to private will, Nietzsche became "*the* moral philosopher of the present age," a prophetic voice anticipating both its moral chaos and its proclivity to bureaucratic (or Weberian) modes of control. As the modernist thinker *par excellence*, Nietzsche is also the most prominent and extreme antipode of the premodern or classical tradition, and especially of the Aristotelian account of ethics; their opposition, in fact, pinpoints a crucial moral and metaphysical divide. For, MacIntyre explains, "it was because a moral tradition of which Aristotle's thought was the intellectual core was repudiated during the transitions of the fifteenth to seventeenth centuries that the Enlightenment project of discovering new rational secular foundations for morality had to be undertaken. And it was because that project failed, because the views advanced by its most intellectually powerful protagonists, and more especially by Kant, could not be sustained . . . that Nietzsche and all his existentialist and emotivist successors were able to mount their apparently successful critique of all previous morality." As a result of this double reversal, the original rejection of Aristotle is called into question—which yields this stark alternative: "*Either* one must follow through the aspirations and the collapse of the different versions of the Enlightenment project until there remains only the Nietzschean diagnosis and the Nietzschean problematic, *or* one must hold that the Enlightenment project was not only mistaken, but should never have been commenced in the first place. There is no third alternative."[6]

Congruent with his preference for the second option, MacIntyre at this point embarks on a new narrative episode, an episode recounting the story of "Aristotelianism" (broadly conceived) and of the "classical tradition" in the ethical domain. The story actually begins in preclassical times, with a chapter describing the "virtues in heroic societies" and particularly in the Homeric age. According to the study, Homeric society was elaborately structured along kinship and household lines, with a clearly defined role and status assigned to all members of the community. Actions performed in pursuance of roles were judged in terms of their "excellence" (*areté*) which was the basic ethical standard. Given the war-prone character of the age, the central and most valued excellence was courage—which was not merely an individual trait but a quality needed for the defense of household and community and for this reason closely related to friendship and fidelity. Moreover, courage was required not only in the face of enemies but also in the face of violent death and more generally of a fickle and inscrutable fate or destiny. The pervasive power of fate infused Homeric life with an epical or narrative aura, an aspect which in turn was captured and poetically highlighted in the epics or sagas of heroic times. "What we have to learn from heroic societies," MacIntyre comments, "is twofold: first that all morality is always to some degree tied to the socially local and particular and that the aspirations of the morality of modernity to a universality freed from all particularity is an illusion; and secondly that there is no way to possess the virtues except as part of a tradition in which we inherit them and our understanding of them from a series of predecessors, in which series heroic societies hold first place."[7] From Homeric times the study's narrative shifts to classical Greece, with a focus on the "virtues in Athens." Four chief Athenian teachings on virtue are differentiated: those of the sophists, the tragedians, Plato and Aristotle—views whose contrasts do not blot out their common moorings in the *polis*. While the sophists tended to reduce virtue to immediate self-interest and individual success (thus anticipating modern emotivism), both Plato and the tragedians sought to integrate moral conduct in a psychic and cosmic order—but with this crucial difference that Plato stressed the unity and compatibility, the tragedians the possible rivalry of competing (though equally binding) virtues and norms.

The story of Aristotelianism unfolds in two subsequent chapters devoted respectively to the *Nicomachean Ethics* and to its repercussions and modifications during the Middle Ages. From Aristotle's perspective, ethics was rooted in human nature, and specifically in the distinctive *telos* of human life which he termed *eudaimonia* and which—as MacIntyre notes—is difficult to translate: "blessedness, happiness, prosperity. It is the state of being well and doing well in being well, of man's being well-favored himself and in relation to the divine." The practice of virtue was required in the pursuit of this goal or *telos*—not as a mere means to an end, but in the sense of a constitutive nexus and reciprocal implication. "Practicing" virtue, in Aristotle's view, was a process of character formation and moral habituation —though not the performance of a thoughtless habit devoid of deliberation. To qualify as ethical, human action presupposed an element of deliberate choice—a choice, however, embedded in and nurtured by a concrete way of life which, in turn, was not individually or arbitrarily chosen. For Aristotle, MacIntyre comments, "choices demand judgment and the exercise of the virtues requires therefore a capacity to judge and to do the right thing in the right place at the right time in the right way. . . . Hence judgment has an indispensable role in the life of the virtuous man which it does not and could not have in, for example, the life of the merely law-abiding or rule-abiding man." Apart from discussing judgment (*phronesis*) and practical reasoning, the chapter also voices doubts or reservations about some key Aristotelian teachings, including the doctrine of the "unity" of the virtues— doubts to which I shall return at a later point. The subsequent development of Aristotelianism is ascribed mainly to the complex blending of diverse and often conflicting strands in medieval culture: strands which include Nordic heroic legacies, the accretion of newer Christian virtues (like charity and forgiveness), and a restored classical heritage (now often infused with a heavy dose of Stoicism). To illustrate the shifting accents of this culture, MacIntyre focuses on Abelard, with his strong Augustinian bent, and Alan of Lille, with his effort to synthesize classical and biblical teachings in the context of a new social and political narrative. In comparison with the *Nicomachean Ethics*, medieval Artistotelianism is said to be characterized by a more radical construal of evil or sin and by a more narrative-historical view of ethical life. Curiously, against this background, Thomas Aquinas emerges as an "unexpectedly marginal figure"—as an "uncharacteristic medieval thinker, even if the greatest of medieval theorists."[8]

The preceding account of the background and changing fortunes of Aristotelianism is meant as a stepping-stone to a coherent theory of ethics and the "nature of the virtues," at least as envisaged by MacIntyre. Despite the diversity of shifting accents, the study discovers in premodern (or pre-Enlightenment) thought a central or "core conception" of virtue, a feature which is said to provide the above narrative with its "conceptual unity." Actually, the core concept is not so much a uniform or unidimensional idea as a structure composed of at least three layers or strands: the first layer is the immediate context of ethical behavior termed a "practice"; the second aspect is the larger individual context called "narrative order of a single human life", while the third comprises the broader fabric labeled a "moral tradition." In MacIntyre's usage, "practice" means "any coherent and complex form of socially established cooperative human activity through which goods internal to that form of activity are realized in the course of trying to achieve those standards of excellence which are appropriate to, and partially definitive of, that form of activity." Given that participation in a practice involves acceptance of its internal yardsticks—particularly those of justice, courage, and truthfulness—the study arrives at this definition: "A virtue is an acquired human quality the possession and exercise of which tends to enable us to achieve those goods which are internal to practices and the lack of which effectively prevents us from achieving any such goods." This definition is claimed to be Aristotelian in a number of key respects—while abandoning at the same time some dubious aspects of this legacy (including the doctrine of the congruence of the virtues). Construed in terms of practices, however, ethics is found to be still too amorphous and fragmentary to give direction to human conduct. To remedy this defect, MacIntyre introduces the notion of an individual life-story or biographical narrative. "The unity of a virtue in someone's life," he writes, "is intelligible only as a characteristic of a unitary life, a life that can be conceived and evaluated as a whole." This notion concurs with another idea central to the entire study: the conception of man as "essentially a story-telling animal. He *is* not essentially, but becomes through his history, a teller of stories that aspire to truth." Personal biography or narrative selfhood, however, is not an isolated fragment but in turn integrated into a network of stories which together form a moral tradition: "The narrative of any one life is part of an interlocking set of narratives. . . . The individual's search for his or her good is generally and characteristically conducted within a context defined by those traditions of which the individual's life is a part, and this is true both of those goods which are internal to practices and of the goods of a single life."[9]

Compared with these theoretical formulations and initiatives the remainder of the study—with the exception of the conclusion—is relatively anticlimactic. The immediately following chapter returns to the earlier story of decay: the progressive disintegration of Aristotelianism into emotivism, a story now depicted as a long process "during which the dominant lists of the virtues have changed, the conception of individual virtues has changed and the concept of a virtue itself has become other than it was." Two initial manifestations of this decay are singled out: the reduction of virtues to natural passions—exemplified by Humean ethics—and their reconstruction in terms of universal rules and imperatives—an approach characteristic of modern Stoicism and especially of Kant's philosophy (the "preeminent modern heir of the Stoics"). Temporary efforts to halt the decay are found in eighteenth-century republicanism and in the writings of Jane Austen, portrayed as "the last great effective imaginative voice of the tradition of thought about, and practice of, the virtues which I have tried to identify." A further chapter delineates the specific changes undergone in modern and recent times by the concept of "justice," changes highlighted in the works of Rawls, Nozick, and Dworkin. The conclusion reaffirms the basic alternative of "Nietzsche *or* Aristotle," now supplementing the antithesis with the more positive (and startling) conjunction of "Trotsky *and* St. Benedict." Given his vindication of the Aristotelian tradition, MacIntyre asserts that the Nietzschean assault on this tradition, and on classical ethics in particular, has been "completely unsuccessful." In light of this outcome, what is needed is a radical ethical reorientation; for, while modernity has failed to produce "any coherent rationally defensible statement of a liberal individualist point of view," Aristotelianism can be recast "in a way that restores intelligibility and rationality to our moral and social attitudes and commitments." Reorientation of this kind, however, is bound to be arduous and difficult—akin to the perils encountered by early Christians in their withdrawal from a decaying Roman Empire and their attempt to create new communities devoted to the prac-

tice of virtue. "If my account of our moral condition is correct," Mac-
Intyre notes, "we ought also to conclude that for some time now we
too have reached that turning point. What matters at this stage is the
construction of local forms of community within which civility and
the intellectual and moral life can be sustained through the new dark
ages which are already upon us. . . . We are waiting not for a Godot,
but another—doubtless very different—St. Benedict."[10]

II

Among contemporary writings on ethics, *After Virtue* clearly
constitutes a high-water mark in terms of intellectual verve, scope
of concerns, and boldness of vision. Before turning to critical comments, I want to single out some features which appear to me particularly attractive and deserving of attention. Although frequently
quoted with shock or dismay, I find the concluding chapter largely
congenial and persuasive. Given our contemporary intellectual and
moral malaise, I have little quarrel with the stated need for a radical
reorientation, a reversal or turning-about (*Kehre*)—a reorientation
which in many ways may be akin to experiences and initiatives during late-Roman and hellenistic times. Contrary to the modern infatuation with universal rules or principles, I concur with the argument
that ethics presupposes a communal context—the construction and
maintenance of "local forms of community"—where the quality of
human life and individual actions *matters* in a concrete and persistent manner. In comparison with abstract theoretical speculation,
ethics (I believe) is a domain peculiarly and constitutively linked with
particularity, a domain in which general maxims are pointless unless
instantiated and exemplified in concrete actions or behavior patterns.
One may disagree with the specific exemplars or "role models" singled out in the concluding chapter (I shall return to this point); but
the importance of exemplars is for me beyond doubt. As MacIntyre
comments, rightly and eloquently in my view: "Without those moral
particularities to begin from, there would never be anywhere to begin;
but it is in moving forward from such particularity that the search
for the good, for the universal, consists. . . . The notion of escaping
from it [particularity] into a realm of entirely universal maxims which
belong to man as such, whether in its eighteenth-century Kantian form
or in the presentation of some modern analytical moral philosophies,
is an illusion and an illusion with painful consequences."[11]

Equally persuasive to me is the portrayal of the "core conception" of ethics and virtue, with its focus on concrete social and political practices which, in turn, are embedded in life histories and finally in historical traditions. With his emphasis on practices, MacIntyre joins the "contextualist" or "antifoundational" trend in contemporary Western philosophy, a trend extending from Wittgenstein (and Heidegger) to Rorty and Foucault; in a more immediate sense, the emphasis reflects the pervasive "pragmatic turn" in recent language philosophy and scientific theory—a change evident in the shift from epistemology to practical "conversation," from syntax to linguistic pragmatics, or from *langue* to *parole*. I shall later voice some reservations about the notion of "practice" as articulated in the study; but again these reservations are secondary to a more basic consensus. Regarding the focus on life histories and the tragic conflicts of human life, *After Virtue* echoes arguments and preoccupations of twentieth-century existentialism—although not the individualistic and emotivist variant of existentialism deprecated in the study (and associated chiefly with the work of the early Sartre). The stress on historical traditions as presuppositions of human self-understanding, in turn, carries overtones of Gadamer's hermeneutics, and more distantly of Hegelian dialectics —although references to Hegel are curiously furtive and sporadic in *After Virtue*. Again, MacIntyre's comments on the correlation of "core" layers of ethics strike me as cogent and insightful. "The virtues," he writes, "find their point and purpose not only in sustaining those relationships necessary if the variety of goods internal to practices are to be achieved and not only in sustaining the form of an individual life in which that individual may seek out his or her good as the good of his or her whole life, but also in sustaining those traditions which provide both practices and individual lives with their necessary historical context."[12]

My sympathy and general agreement extends even to that aspect of the study which, more than any other, has been the target of polemical rejoinders and attacks: the critique of liberalism and its ethical implications. As it seems to me, liberalism has indeed produced a bifurcation between universal principles and arbitrary particular preferences, between a public domain governed by (presumably) neutral legal rules and a private and societal domain controlled by self-interest and narrowly ideological commitments. In MacIntyre's terse language: "For liberal individualism a community is simply an arena in which individuals each pursue their own self-chosen conception of the good life, and political institutions exist to provide that degree of order which makes such self-determined activity possible. Government and law are, or ought to be, neutral between rival conceptions of the good life for man, and hence, although it is the task of government to promote law-abidingness, it is on the liberal view no part of the legitimate function of government to inculcate any moral outlook." In this situation, little or no room is left for politics conceived as a communal learning experience and as a central ingredient in individual character formation. To this extent, we inhabit in fact the kind of Weberian universe depicted in *After Virtue:* a universe divided uneasily between managerial bureaucrats and emotivists. There are "only two alternative modes of social life" open to us, MacIntyre notes in another instructive passage: "one in which the free and arbitrary choices of individuals are sovereign and one in which the bureaucracy is sovereign, precisely so that it may limit the free and arbitrary choices of individuals. Given this deep cultural agreement, it is unsurprising that the politics of modern societies oscillate between a freedom which is nothing but a lack of regulation of individual behavior and forms of collectivist control designed only to limit the anarchy of self-interest."[13]

Since, with MacIntyre, I cherish a notion of politics which is neither bureaucratic nor emotivist, I necessarily share his chagrin over our present Weberian condition. For the same reason, I appreciate thoroughly his comments on friendship seen as a basic bond and constitutive virtue of political life. Referring to the *Nichomachean Ethics,* he notes that justice, for Aristotle, is "the virtue of rewarding desert and of repairing failures in rewarding desert within an already constituted community; friendship is required for that initial constitution." In a larger political setting, to be sure, friendship cannot be equated with personal intimacy and not at all with an emotional attachment, but only with a complex network of relationships which together sustain the fabric of public life. "We are to think then of friendship," MacIntyre states, "as being the sharing of all in the common project of creating and sustaining the life of the city, a sharing incorporated in the immediacy of an individual's particular friendships." In modern times, this view of friendship as a public virtue has atrophied if not vanished altogether. In a liberal political context, the notion is restricted at best to the field of "schools, hospitals or philanthropic organizations"; but we have no longer any conception of "a form of community concerned, as Aristotle says the *polis* is concerned, with the whole of life—not with this or that good, but with man's good as such. It is no wonder that friendship has been relegated to private life and thereby weakened in comparison to what it once was." In Aristotelian terms, modern social relationships approximate at best "that inferior form of friendship which is founded on mutual advan-

tage." Judged by Aristotelian standards, however—MacIntyre adds—
the self-interested egotist prevalent in our age is "someone who has
made a fundamental mistake about where his own good lies and someone who has thus and to that extent excluded himself from human
relationships."[14]

According to *After Virtue*, the selfish individual did not always
occupy the center-stage he enjoys today; one of the most captivating
stories told in the study concerns the historical transformations of
selfhood and the rise or "invention" of the modern, emotivist self. As
MacIntyre observes (correctly in my view), the latter self was largely
unknown both in heroic and classical times. Particularly with regard
to the relation between individual and society, he in fact finds the
"sharpest of contrasts" between modernity and the heroic age: "The
self of the heroic age lacks precisely that characteristic which we have
already seen that some modern moral philosophers take to be an essential characteristic of human selfhood: the capacity to detach oneself from any particular standpoint or point of view, to step backwards,
as it were, and view and judge that standpoint or point of view from
the outside." In contrast with the coincidence of the heroic self and
his life-world, the "Sophoclean self" or the agent in Greek tragedies
was able to question and transcend his social roles, but without exit-
ing from the binding norms of his communal existence. The classical
city-state and the ensuing tradition of Aristotelianism witnessed the
emergence of a "narrative concept of selfhood": a perspective in which
each agent was expected to give a responsible account of his actions,
and demand a similar account from his partners, in the context of
a shared social story or history: "The narrative of any one life is part
of an interlocking set of narratives; moreover this asking for and giving of accounts itself plays an important part in constituting narratives." Narrative accountability, however, is shown to disintegrate and
finally come to a halt under the onslaught of modern emotivism. In
MacIntyre's words; the progressive "liquidation of the self into a set
of demarcated areas of role-playing allows no scope for the exercise
of dispositions which could genuinely be accounted virtues in any
sense remotely Aristotelian." The chief reason for the decay of classical virtues in modernity is the absence of any concrete context allow-
ing for character formation, that is, for a shared experience exceeding
the realm of privacy and private individual preferences: "The self thus
conceived, utterly distinct on the one hand from its social embodiments and lacking on the other any rational history of its own, may
seem to have a certain abstract and ghostly character. . . . The self is
now thought of as lacking any necessary social identity, because the

kind of social identity that it once enjoyed is no longer available; the self is now thought of as criterionless."[15]

The moral corollary of modern selfhood, as MacIntyre shows, is not only a rampant emotivism but also a pervasive legalism or attachment to legal frameworks seen as divorced from ethical life. In this respect, his comments on Stoicism seem to me particularly telling and instructive. In his portrayal, Stoicism signifies not merely "an episode in Greek and Roman culture"; rather it serves as label for a more general moral perspective: namely, for "all those later European moralities that invoke the notion of law as central in such a way as to displace conceptions of the virtues." Adherence to law becomes prevalent wherever social practices are fragile, fragmented, or decayed. In such instances, the only moral guidelines are found in abstract rules and general principles—but in the end even the moral relevance of rules is bound to be jeopardized. For, MacIntyre notes, with the disappearance of communal life—a disappearance as was involved, for example, in "the replacement of the city-state as the form of political life by first the Macedonian kingdom and later the Roman *imperium*"—any connection or "intelligible relationship between the virtues and law" would likewise disappear. The focus on rules necessarily curtails or undermines the moral significance of particularity, and thus the relevance of practical-prudential judgment. As a result, the complex fabric of classical virtues tends to be streamlined and collapsed into a uniform categorical yardstick: "Virtue is, indeed has to be, its own end, its own reward and its own motive. It is central to this Stoic tendency to believe that there is a single standard of virtue and that moral achievement lies simply in total compliance with it."[16]

Modern Stoicism—especially in its Kantian version—carries as a further implication the neglect or bracketing of human inclinations, including such communally cultivated inclinations as sociability or empathy. On this score I consider MacIntyre's arguments particularly fruitful and revealing: following in the footsteps of Aristotle, he is able to recapture the genuine sense of *"eudaimonia"*—as blessedness or well-being—without endorsing in any form the empiricist or utilitarian reduction of ethics to pleasure. In the Aristotelian tradition, to be *"eudaimon"* is not a goal which can be directly or frontally pursued, and which is only vitiated if so approached. Far from being a straightforward empirical or psychological propensity, well-being (one might say) is an ontological quality which supervenes indirectly on the practice of virtues. "Aristotle's characterization of enjoyment as supervening upon successful activity," MacIntyre writes, "enables us to understand *both* why it is plausible to treat enjoyment—or pleasure or

happiness—as the *telos* of human life *and* why nonetheless this would
be a mistake. The enjoyment which Aristotle identifies is that which
characteristically accompanies the achievement of excellence in activity." On a common-sense level, he adds, it may be tempting to con-
flate well-being and activity and simply to conclude "that we seek to
do that which will give us pleasure and so that enjoyment or pleasure
or happiness is the *telos* of our activity." Yet, however plausible this
formulation may be, it is crucial to resist the temptation to avoid the
pitfall of utilitarianism: the "very same" Aristotelian considerations
which emphasize *eudaimonia* "debar us from accepting any view
which treats enjoyment or pleasure or happiness as a criterion for guiding our actions." What MacIntyre's comments intimate here—without
sufficiently elaborating the point, it is true—is an ethics which is
neither "noumenal" nor simply "phenomenal," which coincides neither
with abstract duty nor with empirical impulses. The critique of empirical heteronomy, in any event, is unequivocal: "The standard of utility or pleasure is set by man *qua* animal, man prior to and without
any particular culture. But man without culture is a myth."[17]

III

Moving in the direction of a critical assessment I want to note
first of all a few minor points which, I think, adversely affect the even-
ness of the presentation. The book is written in an elegant and freely
flowing style—and entirely without footnotes. While this fact may
prevent pedantry, it also tempts the author occasionally into overly
sweeping statements which probably should be qualified. Thus, in
discussing the modern "moral scheme," MacIntyre treats as particularly flimsy the concepts of "rights," of "protest," and of "unmasking."
By "rights" he means those prerogatives "which are alleged to belong
to human beings as such" and "which were spoken of in the eighteenth
century as natural rights or as the rights of man." Reviewing this legacy he concludes caustically that "the truth is plain: there are no such
rights, and belief in them is one with belief in witches and in uni-
corns." Surely, this "truth" would have deserved further elaboration—
especially in view of the fact that it seems to aim itself at some sort
of "unmasking." Equally precarious, in my view, is the assertion that
the notion of bureaucratic or managerial "effectiveness" is simply "another moral fiction, and perhaps the most culturally powerful of them
all." Given that the "bureaucrat" or "manager" is identified as one of
the stock "characters" of our age, might one then conclude that emo-

tivism itself is only a fiction or popular myth? This leads me to the problematic status of stock characters in an emotivist era. As indicated, MacIntyre presents the emotivist self as "utterly distinct" from its social embodiments and historical settings. As he adds: "Of the self as presented by emotivism we must immediately note: that it cannot be simply or unconditionally identified with *any* particular moral attitude or point of view (including that of those *characters* which socially embody emotivism) just because of the fact that its judgments are in the end criterionless." At the same time, however, we are told that "emotivism is a theory embodied in *characters* who all share the emotivist view of the distinction between rational and non-rational discourse." And regarding these characters we read that they are objects "of regard by the members of the culture generally or by some significant segment of them. . . . Hence the demand is that, in this case, role and personality be fused. Social type and psychological type are required to coincide." Surely some further elucidation would have been in order to show the compatibility of these statements.[18]

More troublesome is a certain nonchalance pervading the portrayal of some key figures or key perspectives in the study's narrative. Thus, the notion of "sympathy" in Hume's ethics is described simply as an "invention" designed to bridge the gulf between general rules and particular passions. Hume-scholars are bound to be chagrined when being told, without much further argument, that "the gap of course is logically unbridgeable, and 'sympathy' as used by Hume and Smith is the name of a philosophical fiction." Similarly, Kant-scholars (and general readers of Kant as well) are unlikely to be swayed by a summary passage like the following: "It is not just that Kant's own arguments involve large mistakes. It is very easy to see that many immoral and trivial non-moral maxims are vindicated by Kant's test quite as convincingly—in some cases more convincingly—than the moral maxims which Kant aspires to uphold." In my view, it is not at all easy to see why "Always eat mussels on Mondays in March" would pass "Kant's test"—unless the concepts of universalizability and consistency are torn out of the complex fabric of Kant's metaphysics of morals. I shall comment later on the issue of Nietzsche. At this point I want to allude briefly to a perspective which is loosely linked with Nietzsche and virtually identified in the study with the emotivist paradigm: existentialism. Among recent philosophical trends, analytical philosophy is said to be prone to, and existentialism hopelessly infected with, the emotivist virus. Thus, the emotivist "separation" between the individual and his or her roles is claimed to be characteristic of "Sartre's existentialism"; throughout *After Virtue*, Sartre's work

appears in fact as key example of the emotivist theory of selfhood.
It seems fair to point out, however, both that Sartre's opus extends
beyond *La Nausée* and—more importantly—that existentialism exceeds the confines of Sartre's version. MacIntyre seems ready to concede the first limitation when he writes "I speak of Sartre/Roquentin
to distinguish him from such other well-known characters as Sartre/
Heidegger and Sartre/Marx"; but frequently his judgment is not circumscribed in this manner. Regarding the second point, the study
surely would have gained by occasional references to such non-emo-
tivist writers as Heidegger or Merleau-Ponty.[19]

Given the overall tenor of the study, a central figure of its narrative is clearly Aristotle, seen as founder of the Aristotelian or
classical tradition. MacIntyre himself anticipates objections on this
score, by noting in his concluding comments that his account "differs
in a variety of ways, some of them quite radical, from other appropria-
tions and interpretations of an Aristotelian moral stance." My concern is not with the unorthodox character of his account (which, on
the contrary, I find original and refreshing in many ways), but only
with its implications for a viable ethics in our time. MacIntyre's departure from orthodoxy—as he repeatedly emphasizes—involves at
least three central aspects of Aristotle's teachings: his metaphysical
biology; his lack of historical awareness; and his belief in the unity
of the virtues. Particularly with regard to ethics, he writes, the issue
must be confronted in which way "Aristotle's teleology presupposes
his metaphysical biology. If we reject the biology, as we must, is there
any way in which that teleology can be preserved?" Noting profound
philosophical disagreements regarding the meaning of *eudaimonia*
he adds that "any adequate teleological account must provide us with
some clear and defensible account of the *telos*; and any adequate generally Aristotelian account must supply a teleological account which
can replace Aristotle's metaphysical biology." The second issue arises
because of the close relationship of Aristotelian ethics to the Greek
polis. For, we are told, if his theory of the virtues depends in large
measure on "the now-long-vanished context of the social relationships
of the ancient city-state, how can Aristotelianism be formulated so
as to be a moral presence in a world in which there are no city-states?"
In MacIntyre's view, this problem points up a deeper deficiency in the
philosopher's outlook—his disregard of historical change: "Aristotle
writes as if barbarians and Greeks both had fixed natures and in so
viewing them he brings home to us once again the ahistorical character of his understanding of human nature. Individuals as members
of a species have a *telos*, but there is no history of the *polis* or of Greece

or of mankind moving towards a *telos*." The last issue concerns the
unity of the virtues, a doctrine deriving from "Aristotle's inheritance
of Plato's belief in the unity and harmony of both the individual soul
and the city-state" and their consequent "perception of conflict as
something to be avoided or managed." This legacy, we read, affects
not only Aristotle's ethics and politics, but his poetics and theory of
knowledge as well: "In all three the *agôn* has been displaced from its
Homeric centrality."[20]

There is room to doubt whether *After Virtue* fully succeeds in
answering the above queries or in offering a coherent reformulation
of the classical legacy. First a few words on teleology. MacIntyre is
adamant in rejecting Aristotle's metaphysical biology or biological
metaphysics, relying for this purpose on the rigorous distinction between nature and culture or nature and mind. "Our biological nature
certainly places constraints on all cultural possibility," he writes; "but
man who has nothing but a biological nature is a creature of whom
we know nothing. It is only man with practical intelligence . . . whom
we actively meet in history." One may wonder here whether modern
categories are not transferred somewhat blandly into antiquity (in a
manner violating the study's historical bent). More importantly, the
argument jeopardizes or obfuscates the radical contrast, running
through the study, between the communal order of ancient times and
the anarchy of our emotivist age. Regarding heroic societies, we are
told that "every individual has a given role and status within a well-
defined and highly determinate system of roles and statuses" revolving around kinship and household; while able to question communal
standards, "Athenian man" in turn is said to recognize that he "possesses his understanding of the virtues only because his membership
in the community provides him with such understanding." Repeatedly, MacIntyre in explaining this communal cohesion relies on functional terminology and a functionalist model of explanation—a model
(as is well known) anchored in and derived from biology. Modern ethics from the Enlightenment to emotivism, he writes at one point, "took
it for granted that *no* moral arguments involve functional concepts.
Yet moral arguments within the classical, Aristotelian tradition—
whether in its Greek or its medieval versions—involve at least one
central functional concept, the concept of *man* understood as having
an essential nature and an essential purpose or function." Given the
rejection of Aristotelian metaphysics, one surely can ask what man
is supposed to "function" for or to be a function of; and this question
is hardly resolved by the further comment that, traditionally, "to be
a man is to fill a set of roles each of which has its own point and pur-

pose: member of a family, citizen, soldier, philosopher, servant of God. It is only when man is thought of as an individual prior to and apart from all roles that 'man' ceases to be a functional concept."[21]

Partly with the help of functionalist teleology, MacIntyre tends to pit ancient ethical stability against modern individualist confusion. Thus, in discussing classical friendship, he notes that, from an Aristotelian point of view, modern liberal society "can appear only as a collection of citizens of nowhere who have banded together for their common protection" and who "have abandoned the moral unity of Aristotelianism, whether in its ancient or medieval forms." Apart from the quasi-biological overtones of functionalism, comments of this kind clearly raise the issue of ethical "unity," including that of the unity or harmony of the virtues. On this score, MacIntyre's position appears at best ambivalent. While criticizing Plato's and Aristotle's neglect of conflict, his own account is not free of holistic features. His treatment of "practices," for example, explicitly invokes a series of virtues whose joint cultivation is said to be crucial for the maintenance of such practices. "I take it then," he writes, "that from the standpoint of those types of relationships without which practices cannot be sustained truthfulness, justice and courage—and perhaps some others— are genuine excellences, are virtues in the light of which we have to characterize ourselves and others, whatever our private moral standpoint or our society's particular codes may be." In a similar direction point his comments on the "unity of an individual life"—where unity means the "narrative embodied in a single life" and where ethics responds to the question "how best I might live out that unity and bring it to completion." To be sure, narrative unity in this sense is by no means a placid story devoid of tension or inner drama. I previously alluded to the affinity between MacIntyre's "life-philosophy" and (non-Sartrean) existentialism; the stress on the "*agôn*" even carries distinct Nietzschean connotations. In terms of teleology, in any event, what this life-philosophy yields is hardly a compact structure rooted in functional roles and statuses, but at most a fragile and ongoing search or quest, that is, the notion of human life as a journey or as being *in via*. "A quest," we read, "is not at all that of a search for something already adequately characterized, as miners search for gold or geologists for oil. It is in the course of the quest and only through encountering and coping with the various particular harms, dangers, temptations and distractions which provide any quest with its episodes and incidents that the goal of the quest is finally to be understood."[22]

The notion of a narrative quest or life-journey brings into view the third, and probably most significant, departure from Aristotle's

teachings: the turn from an "ahistorical" to a frankly historical construal of ethics. By failing to grasp the "transience of the *polis*" and
the character of "historicity in general," MacIntyre asserts, Aristotle
necessarily neglected a whole range of issues pertaining to moral
development and character formation, including the issue of how "men
might pass from being slaves or barbarians to being citizens of a *polis*."
As indicated, the stress on narratives carries echoes of Gadamer's hermeneutics, the focus on moral "*Bildung*" even traces of Hegel's dialectics. Behind these affinities, however, a host of quandaries lie in wait.
Clearly, the turn to narratives conjures up the broad question of the
relationship between nature and history, and also the issue of the compatibility between a frankly historical and a pre-modern (or Aristotelian) teleology. In more concrete terms, what requires inquiry is the
distinctive character of MacIntyre's historical ethics, including the
meaning of key terms of his "core conception" like practice and narrative. While his discussion of the Greek *polis* frequently borders on
functionalist reification, his treatment of these key terms (I believe)
tends to be strongly indebted to modern, historicist arguments. This
is true of the notion of "practice" which, in *After Virtue*, is closely
patterned on certain "neo-teleological" trends in contemporary analytical philosophy. The term "neo-teleological," in this context, denotes
an approach concentrating on human intentionality, that is, on the
fact that human "actions"—in contrast to mechanical behavior—are
governed by freely chosen purposes or goals which render them intelligible. "We cannot," MacIntyre affirms, "characterize behavior independently of intentions, and we cannot characterize intentions independently of the settings which make those intentions intelligible
both to agents themselves and to others." In this formulation, intentionality clearly occupies a pivotal place in sorting out actions from
behavior. "We need to know," he adds, "which intention or intentions
were primary, that is to say, of which it is the case that, had the agent
intended otherwise, he would not have performed that action." Differently phrased: "We need to know both what certain of his beliefs
are and which of them are causally effective; and . . . we need to know
whether certain contrary-to-fact hypothetical statements are true or
false." In any event, there is "no such thing as 'behavior' to be identified prior to and independently of intentions, beliefs and settings."[23]
    In the preceding passages, "settings" seem to be factors decisively
conditioning or structuring human goals or purposes. At a closer look,
however, they appear to be at best external boundaries or horizons cir-
cumscribing actors' intentions (not too differently from the way "situations" serve to limit Sartrean "projects")—largely for the reason that

settings themselves are historically and intentionally construed. As MacIntyre observes, the word "setting" is used as a "relatively inclusive" term: "A social setting may be an institution, it may be what I have called a practice, or it may be a milieu of some other human kind." In every instance, however, the term is said to imply a history "within which the histories of individual agents not only are, but have to be, situated." The prominence of actors' intentions, at this point, derives from the centrality assigned to the concept of intelligibility. "The importance of the concept of intelligibility," we read, "is closely related to the fact that the most basic distinction of all embedded in our discourse and our practice in this area is that between human beings and other beings. Human beings can be held to account for that of which they are the authors; other beings cannot." Consequently, MacIntyre adds, "to identify an occurrence as an action is in the paradigmatic instances to identify it under a type of description which enables us to see that occurrence as flowing intelligibly from a human agent's intentions, motives, passions and purposes. It is therefore to understand an action as something for which someone is accountable, about which it is always appropriate to ask the agent for an intelligible account." Seen as initiating sources of actions and practices human agents, from MacIntyre's perspective, thus appear not only as actors but as "authors" of their life-stories—although, admittedly, they are rarely more than partial "co-authors" of these stories. Curiously, then, a study which decisively seeks to counteract or combat modern subjectivism on all fronts, at a crucial juncture invokes a subject-centered concept of agency, albeit in an attenuated and contextualized form.[24]

Similar considerations extend to other key concepts in *After Virtue*, especially the notions of narrative and tradition. In MacIntyre's portrayal, "tradition" suggests or implies a steadily unfolding process, whose continuity is provided by the intelligibility of the overall story. What is central to the concept of a "tradition," he writes, is "that the past is never something merely to be discarded, but rather that the present is intelligible only as a commentary upon and response to the past in which the past, if necessary and if possible, is corrected and transcended, yet corrected and transcended in a way that leaves the present open to being in turn corrected and transcended by some yet more adequate future point of view." Thus, tradition denotes a cumulative process of human self-understanding (and self-correction) in which each stage or phase functions "only as a member of an historical sequence." The medium in which this process is rendered coherent and intelligible is termed "narrative" or "narrative history"—with

narration being defined as the "essential genre for the characterization of human actions" and history as "an enacted dramatic narrative
in which the characters are also the authors." What emerges against
this background is—in MacIntyre's own words—a "central thesis" pervading his study: namely, that "man is in his actions and practices,
as well as in his fictions, essentially a story-telling animal. He *is* not
essentially, but becomes through his history, a teller of stories that
aspire to truth." The presentation of man as a "story-telling animal"
is a variation on, but by no means synonymous with, the notion of
homo loquens or man as a creature endowed with language. As in
the case of practices, the focus on agency and story-telling injects
subject-centered connotations into the concepts of narrative and historical tradition, obscuring their constitutive or generative power.
What recedes into the background or vanishes from view at this point
is the structuring role of language: the aspect that, far from being a
simple medium of speakers, language is a condition of speech—with
the result that story-telling always presupposes a communal story or
narrative engulfing speakers and listeners alike.[25]

The preceding comments are not meant to deprecate the importance of action and storytelling for social theory, but only to suggest
the need for a rethinking and reformulation of these notions. This
need concurs with MacIntyre's own critique of modernity and modernist selfhood. Some cues for such a rethinking might be derived
from the invoked Aristotelian legacy, particularly from *Nichomachean
Ethics.* Commenting on the issue of *eudaimonia,* MacIntyre detects
a rift and possible conflict between the goal of happiness (or blessedness)—the contemplation of the divine—and practical human agency
with its imperfections and tragic dilemmas. Since contemplation of
the divine, he writes, is "the ultimate human *telos,* the essential final
and completing ingredient in the life of the man who is *eudaimon,*
there is a certain tension between Aristotle's view of man as essentially political and his view of man as essentially metaphysical." The
tension is underscored by the suspicion that the divine "can itself take
no interest in the merely human, let alone in the dilemmatic," and
that in the case of some virtuous practices their subordination to contemplation "would seem oddly out of place." This suspicion, I believe,
is at odds with the Aristotelian assumption of the intrinsic goodness
of virtuous action: his notion that virtuous action or *praxis*—in contrast to instrumental or technical activity—carries its purpose or *telos*
within itself. On this assumption, action can no longer be construed
as a linear, subject-centered project (aimed at an ulterior goal), but
needs to be rethought as an endeavor structured by or submerged in

goodness itself (that is, in being or the divine). MacIntyre himself
provides an inkling of such a contemplative (or ontological) *praxis*
in his comments on friendship. "The good man's final achieved self-
sufficiency in his contemplation of timeless reason," he observes, "does
not entail that the good man does not need friends, just as it does
not entail that he does not need a certain level of material prosperity.
Correspondingly a city founded on justice and friendship can only be
the best kind of city if it enables its citizens to enjoy the life of metaphysical contemplation."[26]

From action and practices the need for reformulation carries over
into other key ingredients of *After Virtue*—foremost among them the
notion of "virtue" and its relation to freedom. Running through the
entire study is a pervasive polemical bias or slant: a slant pitting modern emotivist license against "Aristotelian unity" and the ethical order
of the ancient world. However, for most modern philosophers including Hume and Kant, arbitrary license was by no means synonymous
with genuine freedom or autonomy. MacIntyre seems ready, at one
point, to acknowledge the ambivalence (or dialectic) of the Enlightenment legacy when he comments on its possible gains. "What I have
described in terms of a loss of traditional structure and content," he
states, "was seen by the most articulate of their philosophical spokesmen as the achievement by the self of its proper autonomy. The self
had been liberated from all those outmoded forms of social organization which had imprisoned it simultaneously within a belief in a the-
istic and theological world order and within those hierarchical structures which attempted to legitimate themselves as part of such a world
order." Whatever its drawbacks, this achievement was by no means
marginal or negligible, and it cannot simply be dismissed without
destructive effects on virtue itself. In my view, contrary to MacIntyre's
slant, freedom cannot simply be abandoned in favor of order—for the
decisive reason that virtue cannot be grounded on "heteronomy" nor
ethics be construed as an external fiat imposed on man in violation
of freedom. Liberalism's strength (I believe) resides precisely in its persistent commitment to autonomy—notwithstanding its many defects
ably and eloquently portrayed in the study. What seems required
against this background is not so much a rejection of freedom as rather
a critique of its subject-centered and ultimately emotivist construal
—perhaps in the direction of the Heideggerian notion of the "essence
of being" as freedom.[27]

Given such a reassessment of freedom and its relation to ethics,
however, the basic narrative structure of *After Virtue* is liable to be
affected: I mean the pivotal bifurcation between "Nietzsche or Aris-

totle." Occasionally, MacIntyre's own account casts doubt on the radicalness of this contrast. "Suppose," he writes at one point, "that in articulating the problems of morality the ordering of evaluative concepts has been misconceived by the spokesmen of modernity and more particularly of liberalism; suppose that we need to attend to *virtues* in the first place in order to understand the function and authority of rules. . . . On this interestingly Nietzsche and Aristotle agree." In light of the centrality assigned to virtue and its possible recovery, this "agreement" between the two thinkers surely would deserve more attention. Unhappily, such attention is blocked by a one-sided and stereotypical portrayal of Nietzsche: as a radical individualist and even solipsist. The image is repeated in nearly doctrinaire fashion. Thus, in the discussion of Homer, we hear about Nietzsche's "own nineteenth-century individualism" which he projected back on the archaic past. Later on, the language becomes more acerbic. "Nietzschean man, the *Übermensch*, the man who transcends," we read, "finds his good nowhere in the social world to date, but only in that in himself which dictates his own new law and his own new table of the virtues." Yet, "to cut oneself off from shared activity in which one has initially to learn obediently as an apprentice learns, to isolate oneself from the communities which find their point and purpose in such activities, will be to debar oneself from finding any good outside of oneself. It will be to condemn oneself to that moral solipsism which constitutes Nietzschean greatness." In the end, the Nietzschean stance "turns out not to be a mode of escape from or an alternative to the conceptual scheme of liberal individualist modernity, but rather one more representative moment in its internal unfolding." What these passages neglect is the rich multi-dimensionality of Nietzsche's work, including his attempt to transcend (in his own way) modernity and modern individualism—an aspect rightly underscored in recent times by Derrida and others. Once this internal diversity is taken into account, the rigid dichotomy of Nietzsche versus Aristotle emerges as extremely fragile if not entirely untenable.[28]

No doubt, the formula "Nietzsche and Aristotle" involves a more generous and open-ended program than the proposed restoration of Aristotelianism. As it seems to me, however, this openness is precisely required by MacIntyre's departure from liberalism and his plea for the construction of new communities. The liberal bifurcation of abstract frameworks and particular preferences cannot really be overcome by a simple cultivation of self-enclosed, local particularities. Rather, the contemporary task is more complicated and more challenging: namely, to foster life-forms open to the global dimensions of our present age, that is, communities whose particularism (in a Hegelian sense) really reflects the "universal" or "infinite" aspirations of mankind. In a sense, MacIntyre comes close to this openness in his concluding pages when he invokes as guideposts "Trotsky and St. Benedict." Trotsky's name appears in this context because of his pessimism about the project of planned social progress—a disenchantment for which Benjamin and Adorno would have been, in my view, more representative and instructive figures. But I believe the list of guides could and should radically be expanded in our time: to include not only MacIntyre's unlikely pair, but mentors as diverse as Gandhi and Martin Luther King, Rosa Luxemburg and Mother Teresa. Inspired by such guides, communities would nurture generosity and care not only toward immediate members but toward strangers as well—approximating that "perfect" mode of friendship to which Aristotle assigned a meditative or contemplative cast. In ethical terms, such life-forms would seek to practice virtue not so much through appeal to abstract principles as through example and exemplary actions, actions steeped in concern for the "good life." Regarding the latter prospect, mankind presently is indeed in a state of attendance or waiting—which, as MacIntyre rightly remarks, is a waiting not merely "for a Godot."

9
Dialogue and Otherness:
Theunissen

THE PROBLEM OF "OTHERNESS"—of the relation between the thinking and acting subject and the surrounding world—looms large in contemporary thought and experience. To the extent that the Cartesian *cogito* served as central metaphysical pillar of the modern era, twentieth-century philosophy has seen vigorous strides, in diverse contexts, to move in a "postmodern" or post-Cartesian direction. Whereas the "picture theory" of the early Wittgenstein reduced the *cogito* to a boundary or extreme limit of the intelligible world, his later conception of "language games" submerged the subject entirely in ongoing linguistic and cultural practices. On the Continent, the phenomenological movement heralded both a radicalization of the Cartesian legacy and progressively resolute steps toward its transgression. Husserl's transcendental phenomenology was predicated on the cognitive potency of a refined, transempirical "subjectivity" or consciousness; but his life-long ambition was always to grasp the genesis of an "objective" or intersubjectively shared world and thus to elucidate the link between ego and *alter ego*, between subject and fellow-subjects. Recasting the Husserlian perspective, Heidegger during the interbellum period redefined the subject as a situated mode of being (*Dasein*) enmeshed in a setting made up of human and non-human components. Roughly at the same time, spokesmen of "dialogical" existentialism —foremost among them Martin Buber—portrayed the subject not so much as a fixed premise, but as a derived category emerging through interpersonal encounter. The phenomenological-existentialist concern with intersubjectivity was continued, in the postwar era, by a host of French thinkers, notably by Sartre and Merleau-Ponty. More recently, the reversal of Cartesianism has assumed dramatic, new forms. Launching a broad-scale attack on the traditional outlook, structuralist and post-structuralist writers have advocated a complete "decentering" or dislocation of the subject in favor of systemic correlations or the transpersonal interplay of "differences." Simultaneously, champions of "critical theory" (or a post-Kantian critical philosophy) insist on the need to replace the *cogito* by the notion of communicative intersubjectivity as the foundation of reflective thought.[1]

The sketched trends, one might add, are not purely speculative ventures. In large measure, the post-Cartesian turn to "otherness" is paralleled and nourished by the broader mutations and dislocations of our age: dislocations manifest in the confrontation between Western and revitalized non-Western cultures on a global scale, and also in the clash between competing social classes and experiential lifeworlds. Particularly with regard to the latter types of contests, the impact of otherness has frequently been thematized under such labels as "reification" and "alienation." Whereas Marxists have tended to associate reification or loss of autonomy with expropriation and the prevailing mode of production, existentialist writers have preferred to construe alienation more ontologically as involving an estrangement between man and universe or, more narrowly, between human experience and the imperatives of a technological civilization. Despite a certain common-sense plausibility, however, arguments of this kind lack theoretical cogency as long as the boundary between "I" and "Other"—between the indigenous and the alien—is not elucidated or simply taken for granted. Contrary to the assumption of a fixed or easily defined boundary, there is a strong tradition in Western thought —stretching back to Hegel, Schelling and beyond—according to which the linkage between I and Other is not a relation of exclusivity, but one of mutual dependence. In light of this background, it seems desirable to differentiate between an alienation which is simply synonymous with oppression or repression, and a more nuanced estrangement seen as a road to self-discovery. The second alternative has been powerfully reasserted by many post-Cartesian authors. Thus, from the vantage point of dialogical existentialism, self-discovery presupposes the passage through otherness, specifically interaction with a different, nonobjectifiable "Thou." A similar insight is voiced in Adorno's later work. The theory of alienation, he notes in *Negative Dialectics*, confounds the legitimate yearning to comprehend the "heteronomous world" with the "barbaric" unwillingness or incapacity to respect and "cherish what is alien or different." Alienation, he adds, "would mostly cease if strangeness were no longer vilified."[2]

I

The recent translation of Michael Theunissen's *Der Andere* renders available to English-speaking readers a milestone in the literature on otherness and intersubjectivity. First published in 1965 and re-edited in 1977, Theunissen's work is easily the most comprehensive and detailed study devoted to diverse treatments of the theme in our century.[3] As the author rightly states in his "Introductory Remarks," otherness "has never penetrated as deeply as today into the foundations of philosophical thought"—to the point that it qualifies as a "theme of *prima philosophia.*" The chief aim of the study is to unearth the basic metaphysical underpinnings of approaches to intersubjectivity; accordingly, its investigations proceed (in the words of the subtitle) on the level of "social ontology" rather than that of concrete social or sociological theory. In its broad outline, the presentation juxtaposes or opposes two major theoretical frameworks or conceptions: transcendental phenomenology, abbreviated as "transcendentalism," and the "philosophy of dialogue" or "dialogism." While, starting from the premise of the ego, the first position seeks access to intersubjectivity by construing the Other basically as an "other I" or *alter ego,* the second position derives ego or self in some manner from an original encounter with a "Thou." These contrasting vantage points give rise to additional, more specific divergences. As articulated by Buber and other representatives, dialogism insists on the immediacy and reciprocity of interpersonal relations and on the simultaneous genesis of both partners through encounter (defined as an "in-between" realm)—features which stand in marked opposition to the egological outlook of Husserlian transcendentalism and its stress on the relatively "mediated" and dependent status of the *alter ego.* In the discussion of both frameworks, close attention is given to the respective role and significance of estrangement or "alteration" (*Veranderung*), in its varying meanings of reification, alienation, and self-discovery.

The study is remarkable not only for its broad scope but also for its philosophical subtlety and rigor. The author brings to his task a solid background in the rich tradition of Continental thought, extending from contemporary phenomenology and existentialism backward over German idealism to classical Greek philosophy. Presently a professor in Berlin, Theunissen received his training in philosophy, theology, and German philology at the universities of Bonn and Freiburg. His early writings established his reputation as a perceptive analyst of existential philosophy and its historical antecedents. His first publication in 1958—a revised version of his doctoral dissertation—dealt with a central notion in early formulations of existentialism: the category of "seriousness" in Kierkegaard's teachings. During the same year Theunissen wrote a long essay on the "Kierkegaard image" as "reflected in recent research and exegesis." Subsequent publications probed such topics as the linkage between Husserl and Heidegger, the relationship between Kierkegaard, Schelling, and Hegel, and the significance of Buber's "negative ontology of the In-Between."[4] The present study was originally submitted as second dissertation or *Habilitation* at the Free University of Berlin, the place where Theunissen began his academic career (and to which he eventually returned after interludes in Bern and Heidelberg).

As an examination of intersubjectivity in twentieth-century thought *Der Andere* (*The Other*) is too wide-ranging and complex to permit easy summary. At this point I merely intend to highlight some particularly outstanding features and arguments. According to its basic design, the study places primary emphasis, in the discussion of each of the two contrasted frameworks, on one leading thinker or spokesman: that is, on Husserl in the field of transcendentalism, and on Buber in the domain of dialogism; subsequently, attention is given to amplifications or modifications of a given framework by less prominent or else less typically representative authors. Under the rubric of transcendental phenomenology, the opening section offers a detailed and instructive account — hardly matched elsewhere in the literature — of Husserl's persistent attempts to formulate a coherent theory of intersubjectivity on transcendental-egological premises. The account begins with an outline of the philosophical or metaphysical "foundations" of transcendentalism, and moves on to a steadily more focused analysis of Husserl's conception of the "I-Other" relationship. Among foundations Theunissen mentions the reliance on an "extramundane" subjectivity or transcendental "facticity," the role of "phenomenological reduction" as gateway leading from the "natural attitude" to eidetic intuition and transcendental reflection, and the stress on the "constitutive" or meaning-generating function of consciousness. With regard to the theory of intersubjectivity, the presentation concentrates chiefly on Husserl's *Cartesian Meditations*, especially on the famous fifth meditation, without neglecting prior or subsequent treatments of the same topic (in such works as *Logical Investigations*, the three volumes of *Ideas, Formal and Transcendental Logic,* and *Crisis*). After tracing the basic "course" or path of Husserl's theoretical effort, Theunissen himself offers a convenient brief synopsis of the five basic steps involved in the move from ego to *alter ego*. The starting point for Husserl, he notes,

> was my primordial world as the pure thing-world transformed into a phenomenon, the transcendentally reduced 'mere nature',

in whose midst I had constituted myself as primordially personal, psycho-physical ego, as the moving agent of my animated body from which I am nevertheless distantiated. The first step toward the Other—initially toward the 'Other in general'—is the perception of the (alien) physical body as an animated body on the basis of the analogy with my own body (which, in part, is constituted also as a physical body). The second step is psychologically the experience of the Other's psychic life and, on a transcendental level, the experience of the pure *alter ego*. While the vehicle of the first step is a quasi-analogical perception, the second relies on a purified process of analogy in the form of empathy. . . . This leads us to the third step: the constitution of the objective world through identification of the primordial worlds. In the objective world I perceive—this is the fourth step—the Other as a unified, self-contained object situated in time and space. In this manner the Other loses the sense 'Other in general' and becomes another human being. In the fifth and last step, finally, I transfer the objective unit 'human being' back to myself by representing to myself via empathy how and as what the Other perceives me.[5]

Apart from outlining the various steps on the road to intersubjectivity, Theunissen accentuates a number of distinctive traits of transcendentalism as manifest in Husserl's perspective. A central trait is the "mediacy" or mediated character of the I-Other relationship, a character deriving both from the focus on the Other's worldly or bodily appearance and from the constitutive role ascribed to egological empathy. "Very generally," the study notes, "it is the interest in *world* or mundane phenomena—a trademark of transcendentalism—which prompts Husserl to thematize the 'Other'; and thus it is also the world which stipulates the apriori boundaries within which the Other can be approached in a transcendental-phenomenological sense." Due to the constitutive functions of "my" body and "my" subjectivity on the levels of analogical perception and empathy, however, mediation through the world ultimately coincides with mediation through the ego. Husserl's departure, in the fifth Cartesian mediation, from the ego's "primordial sphere" entails a number of further implications or distinctive aspects—among which Theunissen mentions mainly these: the encounter of the Other as a bodily phenomenon, situated in a "spatial world" and experienced chiefly through visual "perception," a perception transforming the Other into an object and, at best, into a nondescript fellow-being among a multitude of similar beings. In the broader context of the study, the last two aspects are particularly

significant. For Husserl, we read, the Other "never enters my awareness in the sense that I exist *for him:* never does he figure as primordial subject and I originally as his object." Moreover, the Other as
thematized from a transcendental vantage point is "from the beginning only one among many others who inhabit my world; he is not
the unique individual related to me in singular fashion. The distinction between the intimate Thou and the world of strangers has no
place in the sphere of primordial-transcendental constitution."[6]

Theunissen's comments on phenomenological intersubjectivity,
it goes without saying, are based on his broader assessment of transcendentalism and of Husserl's enterprise as a whole. Students of Husserl are liable to find startling or controversial several of the theses
advanced in the study; but they are bound to respect the author's schol-
arship and his painstaking effort to substantiate arguments through
reference to primary and secondary literature. One of the more startling or striking theses is the assertion that, far from forming a radical antithesis, Husserl's conception of the "natural attitude" is itself
overshadowed by transcendental reflection or by a "transcendental-
theoretical pre-judgment"—in the sense that, by treating the partner
in a natural everyday encounter as an object in the world, "Husserl's
notion of the experience of the Other is itself shaped by a transcendental interest oriented toward the constitution of the world." Coupled with this "pre-judgment," in Theunissen's view, is a pervasive
parallelism and even "surprising identity of content" between the
transcendental-theoretical perspective and the "naturalistic attitude"
as practiced in the natural sciences. Equally startling and perhaps even
provocative is his thesis regarding the derivative status of the *alter
ego* and the final coincidence of the Other with "my" ego (in particular with "my past ego"). Transcendental empathy, he writes, "*posits*
or constitutes the *alter ego* rather than *presupposing* it." Just as, in
mediating the Other's concrete existence, "my body plays the 'role of
the primary body' (*Urleib*), so in mediating the Other's subjectivity
my ego has the significance of a 'basic norm' (*Urnorm*). In this manner the *alter ego* becomes an 'analogue' of my own ego. . . . Husserl
even advances beyond analogy and mirror reflection in the direction
of *identity:* the Other's ego is experientially my own." These considerations undergird the author's views on solipsism. In rejecting the
"equal primordiality" of the Other, he notes, Husserl reveals the "undeniable limits" of his attempt "to overcome in his theory of intersubjectivity the 'transcendental solipsism' of pure egology."[7]

The analysis of Husserl's perspective is followed in the study by
a discussion of two thinkers in whose writings transcendentalism was

"further elaborated and transformed": Heidegger and Sartre. In Theunissen's presentation, Heidegger's fundamental ontology—as outlined in *Being and Time*—appears essentially as a "modified repetition" of the transcendental-phenomenological approach, particularly in the domain of intersubjectivity or "social ontology." Among modifications or "seminal innovations" the study acknowledges chiefly the following: the treatment of co-being or "being-with" as a structural characteristic of existence or *Dasein*; the ontological rather than merely ontic-factual status of the I-Other relation; and finally, the rejection of the visual-perceptual paradigm. "Husserl," we read, "stands in the long and great tradition of those for whom truth is tied to perception and the vision of theoretical cognition; by contrast, Heidegger exchanges perception for the disclosure of mundane phenomena through practical involvement." None of these deviations, however, affects Heidegger's moorings in transcendentalism. According to Theunissen, the linkage is most clearly evident in the stress on the indirect or mediated character of interpersonal contact. "Among all commonalities," he writes, "the most important is this: that neither (Husserl's) theory of intersubjectivity nor the analysis of co-being make room for the *immediacy* of encounter because I and Other are uniformly connected through the *medium of the world*." Radiating into other facets of the two versions of transcendentalism, the congruence is said to surface in the affinity between phenomenological "constitution" and the Heideggerian notion of "project," in the parallel between natural attitude and "inauthenticity," and also in the respective transcendence of everyday life through recourse to absolute subjectivity or "authentic" existence.[8]

Somewhat more autonomous or unconventional arguments are found in Sartre's *Being and Nothingness*. The chief innovation in Sartre's approach, according to *Der Andere*, resides in his partial endorsement of intersubjective immediacy, in the sense of a direct impact of the Other on "my" experience. As delineated in the "dialectic of the Look," the Other originally approaches me as an alien reality or an "extra-mundane existence," completely immune from the grasp of phenomenological reduction. In contrast to Husserl's constitutive egology, Theunissen notes, "the Other's initial appearance in Sartre's view reveals 'a *real* being beyond this world', that is, a being which gains its reality for me not through reference to a (constituted) world" and which thus imposes itself as an "*immediate* presence." To the extent that mediation plays a role, it operates in a reverse manner from Husserl's model: instead of being a medium of "my" world, the Other in the end "mediates *me with myself*." A similar reversal affects other facets of intersubjectivity. Thus, in opposition to transcendental phenomenology, the "passivity" of encounter or "my" alienation by the Other takes precedence over active-constitutive appropriation; as a corollary, far from being simply a derivative of the ego, the *alter ego* places its imprint on "my" subjectivity. While Husserl, we read, seeks transcendence in the confines of an immanent constitution, "Sartre probes absolute immanence in search of absolute transcendence; figuratively speaking: he tries to pierce the shell of immanence in the direction of a hidden transcendence." As in Heidegger's case, however, Sartre's novel departures are insufficient to rupture the transcendentalist mold. Despite the mentioned differences, transcendentalism triumphs at last in the identification of "being-for-itself" with consciousness, in the stress on the "internality" of consciousness, and in the construal of intersubjectivity as an "internal negation." Thus, the reversal of Husserl's scheme remains on the level of a "destructive repetition": "What the reversal leaves intact is the transcendental-philosophical dualism, the bipolar unity of constituted and phenomenal world, of apriori constitution and facticity, of horizon and inner-horizontal phenomena."[9]

The second part of the study is devoted to "dialogism," chiefly as exemplified in Buber's writings. In a slight deviation from the book's guiding methodology—the initial focus on one leading spokesman of each framework—the discussion of Buber's work is interspersed from the beginning with references to a host of other authors active during the interbellum period. As spelled out in the "Introductory Remarks," the reasons for the deviation have to do with the character of dialogism as a "trend of the time" and also with the comparatively subordinate philosophical stature of all its spokesmen, a circumstance which entails that dialogism is "less well represented so-to-speak" in Buber's arguments than is transcendentalism in Husserl's opus. In line with these considerations the opening chapter offers, together with a brief synopsis of Buber's teachings, a delineation of the historical background and of the central thrust of dialogism or the "ontology of the in-between" as a broad intellectual movement. English-speaking readers will appreciate especially the careful portrayal of "historical contexts" and of the respective role of such authors as Franz Rosenzweig, Hans Ehrenberg, Gabriel Marcel, Ferdinand Ebner, and Eugen Rosenstock-Huessey. Regarding its overall thrust, dialogism is presented as a counterpoint to transcendentalism, and particularly as an antidote to the notions of an abstract-general consciousness and of the constitutive function of subjectivity. Challenging these notions, Buber and other dialogical writers insist on the need to differentiate cognitive subject-object or "I-It" relations from genuine interpersonal contacts where "I" and "Thou" meet in an "in-between" sphere underived from egological intentions. While "I-It" connections are typically relations of domination and subordination rooted in the designs of subjectivity, interpersonal encounter yields an "immediate"—that is, egologically not mediated—human bond predicated on the complete "reciprocity" of engagement and the "equal primordiality" of partners.

Descending from the level of a broad overview, Theunissen subsequently examines the distinctive traits of dialogism and the concrete steps involved in its attempted "destruction" of the transcendentalist model. Of central significance for the entire endeavor is the linguistic construal of the "in-between" fabric of encounter. In contrast to the Husserlian and Sartrean focus on perception, he notes, the proper "home of the Thou is *language*"—a medium which, by its nature, "undercuts the 'sphere of subjectivity' presupposed by the model of intentionality." In light of its linguistic character, the structure of encounter is most poignantly displayed in reciprocal speech or dialogue, in the interplay of address and response (an exchange which makes room for meaningful silence). In dialogue, the partners face each other in full temporal "presence"—as opposed to the past tense prevalent in "I-It" relations. Based on the linguistic medium of encounter, dialogism's departure from the transcendentalist framework occurs in two basic, interrelated steps: namely, through the removal of the "Thou" from the field of intentional objects, and through the segregation of "I-Thou" contacts from the range of intentional-noetic acts. In sharply differentiating between "It" and "Thou," Buber's approach phrased the contrast between the two modes of experience in terms of a stark being-nothingness antithesis; in his own words: "Where 'Thou' is spoken, there is no Something or It . . . Who utters Thou, faces no Something, but nothing." While the objects of the "It-world" are firmly lodged in time and space, the members of the "Thou-world" are temporally and spatially discontinuous—a feature deriving from the Thou's "exclusiveness" and lack of "fixity." With the transgression of the object-domain the I's engagement with the Thou loses the quality of an intentional act; more precisely: the engagement eludes the distinction between active constitution and passive reaction (to objects). In Theunissen's words: "The relation to the Thou recedes into a region located beyond the difference of action and passivity"—a region where action simultaneously acquires a new meaning. Differently put: through encounter "my" activity comes into its own "by abandoning itself as intention and by turning into an action which is simultaneously non-action by being the Other's deed." The move be-

yond action and passivity can also be viewed as the coincidence of
freedom and destiny—to the extent that the latter is genuine destiny
"only as freedom," just as the former is freedom "only as destiny."[10]

The German original includes a number of additional chapters
which have been omitted from the English translation, partly because
of their more theological than philosophical bent and partly because
of the relative distance of their content from contemporary concerns,
especially in the Anglo-American context. The omitted portions include a chapter dealing with Buber's "theology of the in-between," a
theology culminating in the notion of an "eternal Thou" completely
irreducible to worldly objects. Also omitted are detailed discussions
of such dialogical thinkers of the interbellum period as Rosenstock-
Huessey, Marcel, and Grisebach, and also chapters reviewing various
types of rapprochement between transcendentalism and dialogism developed by writers initially influenced by Husserl's and Heidegger's
arguments (Adolf Reinach, Karl Loewith, and Ludwig Binswanger).
Mainly because of their relevance to ongoing philosophical and sociological debates, the translation does include two appendices or "ex-
curses" dealing with particularly prominent versions of the mentioned
rapprochement: the "social ontology" of Alfred Schutz and the communications theory of Karl Jaspers. In both cases the author underscores the precariousness of the effected symbiosis—a precariousness
due chiefly to the pervasive impact of the transcendentalist legacy.
The reader may also wish to note a third appendix contained in the
present translation (and attached to the chapter on Sartre), in which
the main themes of *Critique of Dialectical Reason* are compared with
the "dialectic of the Look" as outlined in *Being and Nothingness.*

II

Since its first publication *Der Andere* has attracted a fair amount
of attention on the Continent. Several aspects of the study have been
taken up and further explored by authors from various disciplines, including philosophers, social theorists, and literary critics. Owing to
its innovative insights, primary attention has tended to be given to
the discussion of dialogism in the second part, particularly to the
analysis of Buber's "ontology of the in-between."[11] Among the more
general concepts employed throughout the work, the category of "alteration" (in the sense sketched above) has found favorable reception,
for its assistance in clarifying the issues surrounding alienation and
reification.[12] Despite its profuse virtues, the study is not, and has

not been, immune from criticism. Given its broad-ranging review of twentieth-century thought, some readers may miss a detailed treatment of such prominent phenomenological thinkers as Scheler and Merleau-Ponty. Doubts may also be raised regarding the book's general stucture: the somewhat rigid bifurcation between the two frameworks of transcendentalism and dialogism. Rejecting the dichotomy as such, some authors and reviewers have in effect defended a closer interpenetration of transcendentalist and dialogical perspectives, citing as evidence the works of leading phenomenologists.[13] Even if one accepts (as I do) the general plausibility of the bifurcation as an ideal-typical tool, one may still question some aspects of the concrete implementation of the adopted classification scheme. Questions of this kind pertain primarily to the opposition between Buber's dialogism and Heidegger's fundamental ontology. Regarding the latter, despite remnants of transcendentalism, one can hardly overlook the persistent critique leveled in *Being and Time* at intentional constitution and the foundational role of subjectivity. If this aspect is taken into account and if on the other hand—as Theunissen himself asserts—Buber's position remains tied in important ways to the transcendentalist model, the respective classification of the two thinkers becomes elusive or at best a matter of emphasis.

Notwithstanding a sympathetic treatment of his aims, reservations regarding Buber's approach—and regarding dialogism in general—are repeatedly voiced in *Der Andere*. Thus, commenting on the distinction between "I-It" and "I-Thou" relations, the study notes that both modes can be construed as ego-based "attitudes"—in the Husserlian sense of that term—in which "I orient myself intentionally toward something. All their differences rest on the basis of this commonality." More pointedly phrased: "I—this human being with such and such attitudes—am the one who constitutes something as Thou or It." Thus, intentionality "forces the Thou into a perspectival alignment with the ego as world center." At another point the study detects the effects of transcendentalism precisely in its presumed negation or reversal. "It will become apparent," we read, "that, in its implementation, the ontology of the in-between remains in large measure a merely *negative* ontology—which means basically that Buber comprehends the 'in-between sphere' only in contrasting reference to the 'sphere of subjectivity'. . . . Accordingly, he construes both the I-It and the I-Thou relation in terms of a model whose ontological basis is able to support only the I-It, not the I-Thou relation." However, quite independently of the "I-It" model, the conception of encounter as an "I-Thou" relation is not free from doubt. In particular,

one may wonder whether the stress on the world-transcending immediacy of encounter and the treatment of the "Thou" as nothingness
do not necessarily entail idealist and transcendentalist implications.
This issue is acknowledged by Theunissen himself when he queries
at one point "whether the construal of the 'I-Thou' relation as transcendence of the 'It' does not ultimately derive from a transcendentalist metaphysics and from the framework of intentionality." The
same concern, one might add, has been voiced by Heidegger in his
Letter on Humanism, where he questions the feasibility of grasping
existence (*Dasein*) in either "It" or "personhood" categories. Only a
properly ontological perspective, attentive to the "openness of being,"
he states, brings into view "the clearing of the 'in-between'" in which
subject-object (and subject-subject) relations can occur.[14]

The "Postscript," written after completion of the study (and included in the English translation), contains several afterthoughts relevant to the status of dialogism and the respective merits of competing
frameworks. Despite a continued attachment to Buber's goals, the Postscript reiterates and reinforces the mentioned reservations regarding
implementation. Particularly striking is the author's self-distantiation
from a certain existentialist "mood" prevalent at the time which was
in danger of reducing dialogical tenets to slogans or "popular currency."
On a more substantive level, apprehensions are expressed regarding
the strict philosophical viability of dialogism when measured against
transcendentalist standards. In light of the gulf between aspiration and
implementation, one passage even speaks of "the impotence of dialogical thought vis-à-vis the power of the transcendental-philosophical
enterprise." As Theunissen recognizes, these apprehensions stand in
contrast to the confident outlook adopted in *Der Andere* where, on
the whole, transcendentalism is criticized from the vantage point of
the "philosophy of dialogue." "In its basic approach," he writes, "the
present study is animated by the conviction that philosophy *is* able
completely to overcome the negativity of existing dialogism. In the
meantime, this conviction has not been entirely abandoned, but been
replaced and relativized by a partial skepsis." The main outgrowth of
the noted skepsis is the suspicion that the limitations or shortcomings of dialogism coincide ultimately with the boundaries of philosophy itself: "After long hesitation I have come to the conclusion that
the inability of dialogism to explicate the genesis of the 'I' purely
through encounter with a 'Thou' discloses a basic limit of philosophical thought. Philosophy, it seems, falters in the radical conception of
the primordiality of the in-between."[15]

While expressing reservations regarding the dialogism of the interbellum period, the Postscript hints at a new and more favorable assessment of Heidegger's approach (an assessment which may not mesh with the assumption of fixed limits of philosophy—especially if these limits are set by transcendentalism). As Theunissen observes, Heidegger's treatment in the study was prompted in large measure by the adopted scheme of interpretation: the confrontation of two ideal-typical frameworks. This confrontation, he admits, dictated a general "deemphasis of all those aspects which, already in *Being and Time,* concur with dialogical thought." Apart from these procedural considerations, the Postscript attributes the same deemphasis also to the circumstance "that the positive relations between fundamental ontology and dialogism are situated not on the level of the analysis of 'being-with', but on the higher level of the question of being. The latter topic—dominant and all-pervasive in *Being and Time*—had in turn to be deemphasized, however, in order not to stretch endlessly an inquiry which only wishes to offer a circumscribed exegesis." One may question here the segregation of "being-with" or of interhuman relations from the broader fabric of *Being and Time* and especially from its "all-pervasive" ontological theme.[16] Yet, given his methodological premises, one cannot doubt the fairness of Theunissen's comments regarding a certain "perspectival foreshortening" in his study: "While I examined Husserl's phenomenology chiefly with respect to its seminal aspects for the future, I probed Heidegger's fundamental ontology with reference to its past (so to speak). . . . It is clear that, in this manner, *Being and Time* could not fully come into view." The Postscript, one should add, also draws attention to the more intimate affinity between dialogism and Heidegger's later opus. The "substantive proximity" between the two modes of thought, we are told, resides chiefly in the fact that in both instances thinking is focused on language.[17]

The skeptical afterthoughts on dialogism, outlined in the Postscript, are meant to foster not an uncritical acceptance of transcendentalism, but rather a tentative reconciliation of frameworks: "In rejecting first the absolute claims of the transcendentalist version of social ontology, and in showing next the untenability of such claims in the case of dialogism, the present study ultimately aims at *mediation.*" In Theunissen's view, the most promising avenue in this direction resides in a genetic or developmental treatment of the I-Other relationship, a conception starting from a transcendentally construed ego and leading through various steps to a genuine I-Thou encounter. The adopted starting point, we are told, is justified primarily by the ego's prevalence in a civilized setting: especially in light of the loss of (pre-reflective or pre-historical) "origins," one must "concede that there is for us initially no alternative to the transcendentally construed reality." Once this premise is granted, a genetic approach renders possible an adjudication between the competing frameworks in the sense that "transcendentalism is accorded primacy at the point of departure and dialogism primacy on the level of the goal or final destination: the beginning on this account is my individual ego, the goal my selfhood or individuality resulting from encounter (with a Thou)." For purposes of illustration and corroboration Theunissen refers both to some of Marcel's writings and also to Hegelian teachings. "In the ontological history of man which Marcel sketches in broad strokes," he notes, "the transcendental construction of the world is the first, the mundane alienation of the constituting subject the second, and the process of dialogical individuation the third and final epoch." In the context of Hegelian thought, the same genesis appears as the "history of a 'spirit' which, transgressing its being-for-itself in the direction of otherness, finally overcomes alienation by recapturing itself through mediation with the Other. . . . On the first level the I is nothing but ego; on the second it embraces otherness to the point of becoming Other itself; and on the third, being-with-the-Other coincides with self-being."[18]

Theunissen's afterthoughts are not restricted to the pages of the Postscript; his Preface (not included in the translation) to the second edition of the study in 1977 articulates a number of additional caveats and qualifications. The chief caveat has to do with a certain abstract-idealistic bent inherent in both transcendentalism and dialogism, and with the neglect of the concrete-social underpinnings of intersubjectivity. According to the Preface, the mentioned bent derives from the "elimination of a social (or sociological) theory from whose vantage point both anonymous modes of interaction and interpersonal contacts could have been perceived as historically situated." The drawbacks of this elimination surface primarily in the study's failure "to weigh the preconceptions implicit in the competing frameworks regarding the distinctness of the ego in its confrontation with the Other," and also in the "bracketing of distorted or pathological forms of dialogical life." Such preconceptions or preconditions, Theunissen argues, occupy a status which antedates both the thesis of a subjective-transcendental constitution and the dialogical notion of an I-Thou encounter. Prior to an assessment of these doctrines, he notes, "one would have to examine to which extent we are still capable of being an I for a Thou, and to which degree the objective requisites of subjectivity can presently be found." In the same vein, a proper grasp of the distortions and breakdowns of dialogical life demands "scrutiny of the process through which an I-Thou relationship genuinely comes into being by extricating itself from the constraints of socially prescribed patterns of behavior." As the Preface adds, the separation of dialogue and reality, and especially the notion "that personal togetherness is not affected by social conditions," reveal "a naiveté which is not only sentimental but dangerous in its effects."[19]

III

Theunissen's more recent writings, published since the first appearance of *Der Andere*, elaborate further on intersubjectivity and related themes, in a manner sensitive to the sketched afterthoughts and reservations. A prominent common thread linking these writings is a steadily intensified preoccupation with Hegelian thought, a move designed to remedy both the philosophical weaknesses of dialogism and its neglect of "temporality" or the historical dimension of human interaction. A study of 1969, devoted to an examination of the Frankfurt School and especially of Habermas's work, presented a Hegelian (or quasi-Hegelian) critique of the transcendentalist ingredients in "critical theory"—while simultaneously acknowledging affinities between "ideal speech" and dialogical encounter.[20] Theunissen's Hegelian sympathies, one should note, embrace not only the *Phenomenology of Spirit* but extend to Hegel's later opus, including his *Science of Logic*. However, while—in recent literature—Hegel's mature thought is frequently invoked as an antidote to "existentialist" leanings of the *Phenomenology*, Theunissen's approach never segregates conceptual "dialectics" too rigidly from dialogue and reciprocal struggle for recognition. Thus, a study of 1970 portrayed Hegel's theory of the "absolute spirit" as a "theological-political" doctrine, closely akin (in central aspects) to Buber's "theology of the in-between" and his notion of an absolute encounter.[21] Subsequent writings probed in greater detail the intersubjective elements in Hegel's philosophical outlook, in an effort to reveal "the unity which overarches the contrast between dialogical immediacy and dialectical mediation" and to show that "dialogism thematizes what is tacitly presupposed in dialectics."[22]

Both in terms of volume and depth, the high point among Theunissen's recent writings is a book published in 1978 whose title in English translation reads: *Being and Appearance, The Critical Function of Hegel's Logic*. Devoted to a detailed exegesis of the *Science of Logic*, the book presents Hegel's work not only as the culmination of Western metaphysics, but also in central portions as a critique of metaphysics, more specifically: of the metaphysics of "substances" as well as the metaphysics of (reflectively constituted) "essences"— perspectives marked respectively by the "indifference" or unrelatedness of elements and by their subordination to dominant categories. In contrast to both indifference and domination, Theunissen postulates as "normative standard" of Hegel's logic the idea of "communicative freedom" or of a "complete unity of self-relation and other-relation." "Communicative freedom," he writes, "signifies that one part experiences the other not as boundary or limit, but as the condition of possibility of its own self-realization." Under ideal circumstances, that is, in a "reality which would have found its substantive 'truth' and thus become fully real," he adds, "everything would be *relatio* to such an extent that the *relata* would not retain their separateness. True reality in this sense is characterized by the specific New-Testament coincidence of love and freedom."[23]

Although superbly developed in the *Science of Logic*, the idea of communicative freedom is probably not an exclusively Hegelian insight. As it seems to me, the integration of *relata* into a comprehensive *relatio* can also be found—though without the arsenal of conceptual dialectics—in Heidegger's later thought, especially in his notion of *Ereignis* signifying a "gathering" or "appropriation" which allows elements to come into their own without fusion or indifference. Heidegger's later thought—especially his view of the relation between thinking and "holiness"—also seems relevant to the concluding passage of the Postscript where Theunissen writes: "Considered as 'theology' the philosophy of dialogue . . . can only be a philosophy of the kingdom of God. But this kingdom is not God; rather, in it human thinking, transcending its narrow limits, anticipates God's splendor or the 'holy' as revealed in the Thou—although this revelation can never transform philosophy fully into theology, that is, into discourse about God."[24]

10

Structuration and Agency:
Giddens

THE STATUS OF THE individual or of the accountable human agent today hangs in thc balance: not only in the political arena (in the face
of technocratic and totalitarian dangers), but also in the context of
social and sociological theory. Several factors have contributed to this
precarious condition. At least since the turn of the century, strong
positivist trends in sociology have tended to deemphasize if not efface the individual in favor of larger collectivities or of quasi-organic,
functional imperatives. During subsequent decades, philosophically
more ambitious efforts — predicated on nonpositivist premises — were
undertaken seeking to explore the ontological underpinnings and historical genesis of individual consciousness and autonomy. The labels
attached to these efforts range from "language games" to contextualism and deconstruction.

No doubt, efforts of this kind provided a valuable antidote to the
modern infatuation with "subjectivity" and ego-centrism, an infatuation permeating in large measure both rationalist and empiricist perspectives in recent centuries. Nevertheless, if rashly or thoughtlessly
pursued, the endeavor to "decenter the subject" and to dislodge modern "egological" metaphysics is prone to entail detrimental or noxious
effccts: practically-politically by lending implicit support to collectivist designs, and theoretically by obfuscating important themes of
social analysis. For clearly, as long as the modern aspiration of human autonomy is still alive, "social action"—no matter how closely
interwoven with non-intentional forces—is bound to remain a crucial sociological topic. Contemporary social theory offers few if any
guideposts for tackling the topic in a manner congruent with its intrinsic complexity. Against this background, Anthony Giddens' work
must be seen as a rare exception and indeed as a major contribution
to the task of formulating a post-metaphysical theory of human agency.
A prolific writer, Giddens has authored a long string of publications
dealing with a great number of sociological themes—all of which,

225

however, are connected directly or obliquely with the issue of agency. For present purposes I intend to focus chiefly on a relatively concise and compact statement of his theoretical position, titled *Central Problems in Social Theory,* while also shedding occasional glances at his more extensive *magnum opus, The Constitution of Society.*[1]

I

Giddens takes his departure squarely from the malaise or "state of disarray" characterizing the social sciences today—the disarray resulting from the disintegration of the "orthodox consensus" which prevailed in English-speaking countries during the postwar period and which was marked by the widespread endorsement of the "theory of industrial society" (a society devoid of class conflicts and ideological fervor) and by the intellectual commitment to various brands of positivism, especially "functionalism" (associated with "the idea that biology provides the proximate model for sociology") and "naturalism" (understood to refer to "the thesis that the logical frameworks of natural and social science are in essential respects the same"). Surveying the "Babel of theoretical voices" that "clamour for attention" following the collapse of this consensus, Giddens distinguishes three prevalent reactions to the "seemingly disoriented situation of social theory": namely, first, a "reaction of despair or disillusionment" insisting on the irrelevance or impotence of theoretical inquiries; secondly, a "reversion to dogmatism" prompted by a "search for security at any cost"; and thirdly, a reaction of exuberance or "rejoicing" which welcomes intellectual anarchy as "testimony to the inherent fruitfulness of social theory." Deviating from these three alternatives, *Central Problems* opts instead for a renewed systematic theoretical effort or a "systematic reconstruction" of social theory, "not in the anticipation of substituting a new orthodoxy for an old one, but in the hope of providing a more satisfactory ground for the discussion of central issues in social theory than that provided by the erstwhile consensus, or permitted by the hermetic isolation in which the diversity of current theoretical standpoints tend to exist."[2]

The chief aim of the proposed "systematic reconstruction" is to assemble building blocks and develop a coherent framework for a "theory of structuration," a theory involving an intimate meshing of structure and agency. In Giddens' words, the task of developing such a theory proceeds first of all "from an absence: the lack of a theory of action in the social sciences." As he notes, there exists "a large philosophical literature to do with purposes, reasons and motives of action"—a literature partly inspired by Anglo-American analytical philosophy and partly by Continental hermeneutics (as reflected in "interpretative sociology"). However, this literature has "to date made little impact upon the social sciences," mainly because it "has not paid much attention to issues that are central to social science: issues of institutional analysis, power and social change." On the other hand, perspectives which have focused on these problems, especially "functionalism and orthodox Marxism," have tended to do so "from a point of view of social determinism," thus ignoring "just those phenomena that action philosophy makes central to human conduct." Instead of simply patching up the "opposition between voluntarism and determinism," Giddens advocates a thoroughgoing reformulation of action theory: "An adequate account of human agency must, first, be connected to a theory of the acting subject; and second, must situate action in *time and space* as a continuous flow of conduct, rather than treating purposes, reasons, etc. as somehow aggregated together." As with respect to agency, the notion of structuration presupposes a reinterpretation of "structure" diverging from the way the term is used both by functionalist and structuralist writers. While "in both bodies of thought the notions of structure and system are often used more or less interchangeably," Giddens claims that "not only is it important to distinguish between structure and system, but that each should be understood in a rather different way from how they are ordinarily taken." According to the proposed theory, the differentiation can be effected by treating "social systems as situated in time-space" while "regarding structure as non-temporal and non-spatial, as *a virtual order of differences* produced and reproduced in social interaction as its medium and outcome."[3]

In light of Giddens' overarching objective, the first two chapters of *Central Problems*—entitled respectively "Structuralism and the Theory of the Subject" and "Agency, Structure"—are clearly of crucial importance. The former offers a lucid and penetrating discussion of the main issues involved in contemporary debates surrounding "anti-humanism" and the "end of subjectivity," debates which have been carried on with particular poignancy in the context of French structuralism and post-structuralism. In probing and disentangling its complex theme, the chapter highlights a quality which is evident throughout Giddens' works: the author's impressive intellectual versatility, especially his ability to combine a solid training in Anglo-American sociological theory and philosophy with a perceptive grasp of leading trends in Continental thought. Defining structuralism for social-theoretical purposes as "the application of linguistic models influenced by structural linguistics to the explication of social and cultural phenomena," Giddens gives attention to a number of particularly influential formulations: to Saussure's linguistic theory, characterized by the distinction of *langue* and *parole*, the separation of "synchrony" and "diachrony," and the juxtaposition of "signifier" and "signified"; to Lévi-Strauss's structural anthropology and especially his analysis of the logic of myth; and to the development of semiotics and the efforts of some recent thinkers — above all, Derrida and Kristeva — to articulate something like a "theory of structuration" by means of a "critique of the sign." After presenting both a descriptive account and a critical evaluation of each position, the author concludes the chapter by drawing up a balance sheet of the major strengths and weaknesses of structuralist thought, as they appear from the vantage point of "the typical preoccupations of Anglo-Saxon sociology." Prominent items on this balance sheet are the following: First, structuralism points to an underlying "code" and thus to *the significance of spacing through difference* in the constitution of both language and society"; but it has neglected to link "difference" with the domains of real *"physical space"* and of social practices. Secondly, the structuralist movement has encouraged attempts *"to incorporate a temporal dimension into the very center of its analyses"* through the notion of structuration overarching the synchronic-diachronic distinction; but it has not produced "explanatory accounts of social change." Furthermore, the movement makes possible *"a more satisfactory understanding of the social totality than that offered by its leading rival, functionalism"*; but implementation of this possibility requires a careful differentiation of "structure" and social "system." Finally, structuralism envisages a departure "of major significance for social theory: *an attempt to transcend the subject/object dualism"*; yet, this dualism — together with the related dichotomies of individual and society and of conscious and unconscious modes of behavior — cannot be successfully repudiated unless "we acknowledge that this is not a dualism but a *duality"* operative within the *"duality of structure"* (where structure is seen as "both medium and outcome of the reproduction of practices").[4]

For present purposes the overall assessment of structuralism is less significant than its implications for the "theory of the subject." In this respect the opening chapter in *Central Problems* contains a number of suggestive and valuable formulations. The critique of "humanism" and the theme of the *"decentring of the subject,"* Giddens observes, are "of essential importance to social theory," because they offer "an escape from those philosophical standpoints which have taken consciousness as either a given, or transparent to itself." Recognition of this merit, however, should not lead "to the disappearance of the reflexive components of human conduct, or to their treatment as some sort of epiphenomena of deeper structures." Commenting on semiotics and recent critics of the "sign," he insists that "we must actually repudiate the *cogito* in a more thoroughgoing way than Kristeva does" and acknowledge "the vital importance of the theme that being precedes the subject-object relation in consciousness," an acknowledgement which requires attentiveness to the connection of *"being and action."* Yet, simultaneously it is crucial to resist the *"genetic sociological fallacy"* which consists in the assumption "that, because the subject, and self-consciousness, are constituted through a process of development . . . they are merely epiphenomena of hidden structures. The de-centring of the subject is quite as noxious as the philosophies of consciousness which are attacked if it merely substitutes a structural determination for subjectivity." According to Giddens, the endeavor to avoid the twin pitfalls of idealism and the genetic fallacy points up the need to develop an adequate theory of human agency or a "theory of the acting subject": "The pressing task facing social theory today is not to further the conceptual elimination of the subject, but on the contrary to promote *a recovery of the subject* without lapsing into subjectivism. Such a recovery, I wish to argue, involves a grasp of 'what cannot be said' (or thought) as *practice*," a grasp which, in turn, "depends upon stressing the importance of the 'reflexive monitoring of conduct' as a chronic feature of the enactment of social life."[5]

Regarding the linkage of action and structuration, the chapter on "Agency, Structure" deserves close attention. The argument of the chapter starts from the proposition "that, in social theory, the notions of action and structure *presuppose one another*, but that recognition of this dependence, which is a dialectical relation, necessitates a reworking both of a series of concepts linked to each of these terms, and of these terms themselves." Commenting on Anglo-American philosophy of action, Giddens finds it insufficiently attentive to the concrete situatedness of human conduct: a deficiency which is manifest in its disregard of social institutions and also in its neglect of the dimensions of "temporality" and of "power." Social activity, he notes, "is always constituted in three intersecting moments of difference: temporally, paradigmatically (invoking structure which is present only in its instantiation) and spatially. All social practices are *situated* activities in each of these senses." Elaborating on the situated character of practices, the chapter outlines a "stratification model" of human

agency, a model which connects intentionality or the "reflexive monitoring of conduct" with broader motivational factors and the latter
with the "unacknowledged conditions" and the "unintended consequences" of action. In Giddens' view, the distinctive feature about the
"reflexive monitoring of conduct" resides in "what Garfinkel calls the
accountability of human action," where accountability means that
"the accounts that actors are able to offer of their conduct draw upon
the same stocks of knowledge as are drawn upon in the very production and reproduction of their action." The distinction between the
"giving of accounts" and the available "stocks of knowledge" corresponds to the distinction between *discursive* and *practical consciousness*," with the latter term designating "tacit knowledge that
is skilfully applied in the enactment of courses of conduct, but which
the actor is not able to formulate discursively." In contrast to "reflexive monitoring" the motivational components of actions are said to
refer to the "organization of an actor's wants" and to "straddle conscious and unconscious aspects of cognition and emotion." The role
of the "unconscious" is presented as "essential to social theory"—
although one has to guard against a "reductive" approach treating "the
reflexive features of action only as a pale cast of unconscious processes." In addition to being pervaded by unconscious motives, typically operative as "unacknowledged conditions" of action, conduct also
has to be seen as bounded by "unintended consequences" which tend
to be systematically incorporated in the "reproduction of institutions."⁶
   The reproduction of situated practices in time and space lends
to social interaction a "systemic" quality or the quality of a "system"—
a term which, in Giddens' account, needs to be carefully differentiated from "structure." "'Structural analysis' in the social sciences," he
writes, "involves examining the structuration of social systems"; in
this context, "the connotation of 'visible pattern' which the term 'social
structure' ordinarily has, as employed in Anglo-American sociology,
is carried in my terminology by the notion of system: with the crucial proviso that social systems are patterned in time as well as space,
through continuities of social reproduction." Structures, by contrast,
do not exist in "time-space," but rather manifest "a 'virtual order' of
differences"; they "exist paradigmatically, as an absent set of differences,
temporally 'present' only in their instantiation." In specifying more
clearly the character of "structure" seen as underlying social code, Giddens advances a succinct and elegant formulation focusing on the two
basic aspects of "rules" and "resources": "As I shall employ it, 'structure' refers to 'structural property' or more exactly, to 'structuring property,'" that is, to traits which provide "the 'binding' of time and space

in social systems" and which "can be understood as rules and resources, recursively implicated in the reproduction of social systems." The term "rules" is subsequently further differentiated into rules relating to signification or the "*constitution of meaning*" and its communication, and rules relating to norms and "*sanctions* involved in social conduct." Similarly, the notion of "resources" is subdivided into the two types of "authorization" and "allocation," the former designating "capabilities which generate command over *persons*" and the latter "capabilities which generate command over *objects*" (especially property). As a result, social "structure" is said to manifest itself in three or four major dimensions or modes: those of "signification," normative "legitimation," and "domination," with the latter comprising both political power and economic allocation. The theory of "structuration" as a whole links structural modes with recurrent practices, a linkage secured through the "duality of structure" which "*expresses the mutual dependence of structure and agency.*"[7]

The remaining portions of *Central Problems* in large measure elaborate upon, and draw additional implications from, the sketched theoretical framework; the briefest synopsis must suffice in the present context. The third chapter focuses on "problems of institutional analysis," where "institutions" are seen as deeply sedimented practices which "play a basic part in the time-space constitution of social systems." After discussing some of the interrelations of cultural-symbolic, political, economic, and normative-legal institutions, Giddens draws attention chiefly to the relevance of sedimented practices and non-intentional motivations for class analysis, role theory, and the theory of socialization—suggesting, in reference to the first topic, that "a theory of class can only be satisfactorily elucidated as involving the influence of an institutional order of 'class society' upon the formation of collectivities," and regarding the second, that "*social systems are not constituted of roles but of (reproduced) practices.*" Concerning socialization, the study urges a stronger reliance than is customary on Freudian teachings and especially on the insights of "Lacan's Freud." "Lacan," we are told, "reads *Wo es war soll Ich werden,* not as a therapeutic injunction of psychoanalytic practice (cf., by contrast, Habermas's model of psychoanalysis as critical theory), not as implying that 'the ego must dislodge the id,' but as a developmental formula: 'it' precedes 'I,' and the latter always remains bound to the Other." The emphasis on the unconscious and the "internally divided" character of the ego, however, must not be allowed to jeopardize the role of reflection and intentional action: "A 'stratified model' of personality, in which human wants are regarded as hierarchically connected, involving a basic security system largely inaccessible to the conscious subject, is not at all incompatible with an equivalent stress upon the significance of the reflexive monitoring of action, the latter becoming possible only following the 'positioning' of the actor in the Lacanian sense."[8]

Two subsequent chapters—titled respectively "Contradiction, Power, Historical Materialism" and "Ideology and Consciousness"—explore important aspects of the process of structuration, especially the structural interplay between "rules" and "resources." The former chapter advances a methodological yardstick which is "almost the obverse of functionalism; its guiding tenet is: don't look for the functions social practices fulfil, look for the contradictions they embody." In line with the agency-structure nexus, "contradiction" is defined as the "opposition or disjunction of structural principles" of system organization, in contradistinction to "conflict" seen as "struggle between actors or collectivities" on the level of social practices. Applying a structural perspective to the Marxist analysis of capitalism, Giddens— instead of embracing the "forces versus relations of production" scheme as universal formula—identifies as *"primary contradiction"* in capitalist society the "contradiction between *private appropriation* and *socialized production."* Proceeding to a consideration of the "materialist interpretation of history," the chapter proposes further modifications or amendments of Marxist teachings. Abandoning the emphasis on general economic determinism, Giddens argues that "Marx gave so much of his effort to studying capitalism that he underestimated its distinctiveness, as compared to other historical forms of society." Actually, from a historical vantage point, both economic factors and class struggles are overshadowed by a more basic structural contradiction: namely by man's *"contradictory relation to nature.* Human beings exist in a contradictory relation to nature because they are in and of nature, as corporeal beings existing in material environments; and yet at the same time they are set off against nature, as having a 'second nature' of their own, irreducible to physical objects or events." This contradiction, Giddens adds, is mediated in primitive cultures or "cold societies" (in Lévi-Strauss's terminology) through *"internal incorporation,"* in the sense that nature is integrated in "the categories of human thought and action"; only in later or "hot" societies does the same opposition give rise to class antagonism or "sectional group formation." Even at this point, however, the "forces/relations of production" scheme does not immediately go into effect; rather, it is important to differentiate between "class-divided societies" in which political *"authorization has primacy over allocation,"* and "class societies" (typified by capitalism) where economic allocation achieves supremacy.[9]

The chapter on ideology would presumably have presented an opportunity to investigate the interference of "resources" in the domain of "rules" seen as symbolic or "interpretative" orders; instead, the author offers mainly a historical overview of successive conceptions of ideology, ranging from Comte and Marx over Mannheim to Habermas and Althusser. The chief conclusion drawn from this overview is the need to differentiate between an epistemological and a practical-political sense of "ideology": the former treating it as a distortion of scientific knowledge, the latter viewing it as a camouflage of interests. In Giddens' view, the interest-ideology polarity has to be treated as *"basic to the theory of ideology, rather than the opposition of ideology and science,"* primarily because of its implication that *"the chief usefulness of the concept of ideology concerns the critique of domination."* A corollary of this conclusion is that ideology should not be regarded as a "type of symbol-system" contrasted to science; rather, all symbol-systems acquire "ideological aspects" or qualities when used as instruments of domination: "To analyse the ideological aspects of symbolic orders . . . is to examine *how structures of signification are mobilized to legitimate the sectional interests of hegemonic groups."* The concluding chapters of *Central Problems* return to, and reiterate, some basic ingredients of the author's outlook. In particular, the section dealing with "Time, Space, Social Change" stresses the need to overcome synchronic-diachronic and actor-environment dichotomies in favor of a more intimate integration of time and space in the conception of social action. Regarding social change, the author advocates abandonment of "unfolding models of change"—models which treat development as "the progressive emergence of traits that a particular type of society is presumed to have within itself from its inception"—and their replacement by a perspective attentive to "relations of autonomy and dependence among societies or nation states" and to the aspect of "uneven development of different sectors or regions of social systems."[10]

II

The broad range of theoretical issues touched upon in the preceding summary renders difficult a succinctly focused critical commentary. More importantly, the rich profusion of suggestive and innovative insights advanced by the author is prone to pale or dwarf possible shortcomings; the following comments are offered in full appreciation of this disproportion. The chief strength or theoretical contribution of *Central Problems* resides clearly in the reinterpretation and córrelation of "agency" and "structure." The structural perspective advocated by Giddens has in my view distinct advantages over competing functionalist frameworks—while simultaneously salvaging the main analytical insights of these frameworks. The accentuation of "rules" and "resources" as main structural properties strikes me as theoretically fruitful (and as admirable in its conceptual parsimony); the delineation of the four structural dimensions—signification, political authority, economic allocation, and legitimacy—captures the central features of the well-known functional "sub-systems" (social integration, polity, economy, and culture), while giving broader room to linguistic symbolization.

Apárt from its greater attentiveness to language, the basic advance of Giddens' outlook over functionalism consists in his professed rejection of the latter's "positivist" and "naturalist" (or quasi-organic) thrust. It is precisely on this point, however, that I find his presentation occasionally vacillating or inconsistent; differently phrased: the author sometimes seems bent on "domesticating" the full potential of the adopted perspective. As Giddens himself admits, his theory of structuration is indebted at least in part to Derrida's notion of the "structuring of structure"; the description of structure as a "virtual order" or an "absent set of differences" is likewise reminiscent of Derrida's conception of *"différance."* As employed by Derrida, however, the latter concept involves not only a factual differentiation of elements but a more basic ontological difference; as a corollary, structuration injects into social analysis a profoundly non-positive or (if one prefers) "transcendental" dimension. Against this background, Giddens' approach appears at points half-hearted. In some passages, the notion of a "virtual order" seems to imply no more than the contingent and essentially remediable constellation of "present" and "absent" factors (compare, for instance, the discussion of "physical presence/absence" in the chapter on social change). The same impression results from the attempt to treat structure as "compatible with a realist epistemology": to the extent that "structure" is claimed to precede the "subject-object" dichotomy, it is hard to see how it can simultaneously reflect a cognitive "realism" (which seems inevitably tied to the same dualism).[11]

The notion of "agency" as articulated by Giddens seems particularly attractive. In a formulation which can serve as yardstick for further inquiries in this area he notes that the concept "cannot be defined through that of intention, as is presumed in so much of the literature to do with the philosophy of action; the notion of agency, as I employ it, I take to be logically prior to a subject/object differentiation." Formulated in this manner, "agency" undercuts or transcends the customary bifurcation between subjectively intended conduct and externally stimulated reactive behavior—a bifurcation which in large measure permeates Weberian sociology (although the relation between "agency" and the Weberian categories of "traditional action" and "affective conduct" would deserve to be investigated). The connotations of agency, incidentally, spill over into many other conceptual domains, for example the domain of "power"—where we read that "the notion of power has no inherent connection with intention or 'will,' as it has in Weber's and many other formulations." From Giddens' perspective, "power" is placed between structure and social practices; it is said to intervene "conceptually between the broader notions of transformative capacity on the one side, and of domination on the other" and to operate "through the utilization of transformative capacity as generated by structures of domination." (One is then slightly surprised to be told shortly afterward that "power" will be used as "a sub-category of 'transformative capacity,' to refer to interaction where transformative capacity is *harnessed to actors' attempts to get others to comply with their wants.*")[12]

Despite its fruitfulness as a general guidepost, one may wonder how the notion of "agency" is implemented or translated into a theory of action. On this score, several comments seem in order. A relatively minor irritation, in my view, is the author's tendency to identify "intentional action" with "strategic conduct" (for example, in the statement that "the telling of lies necessarily applies to intentional action, and thus operates solely on the level of strategic conduct"); in this respect, Habermas's distinction between "instrumental" and "strategic" behavior, on the one hand, and "communicative action," on the other, appears preferable. More important is the relationship between agency and social action in general. As in the case of "structure," I find in Giddens' treatment of agency an occasional tendency of "domestication"—this time in the direction of tying the notion closely to everyday conduct understood as "activity" or "doing." This linkage is evident in the definition of "practical consciousness" as "tacit knowledge that is skilfully applied in the enactment of courses of conduct" and in the identification of tacit knowledge with "stocks of knowledge, in Schutz's terms." As is well known, the emphasis on "stocks of knowledge" in Schutzian phenomenology does not contravene but rather undergirds the methodological insistence on the interpretation of subjective intentions pursued in mundane practices. The same tendency is manifest in the persistent focus on the "reflexive monitoring of conduct" as a "chronic feature of the enactment of social life" and on "accountability" understood in Garfinkel's sense; as we are told at one point, social theory must "comprehend the meshing of rules and practices in day-to-day activities. This demands acknowledging the significance of 'ethno-methods' as the means whereby accountability is sustained." On a par with the invocation of ethnomethodology is the frequent reliance on ordinary language and speech-act theory. With specific reference to Searle, Giddens comments that "reasons and intentions are not definite 'presences' which work behind human social activity, but are routinely and chronically (in the *durée* of day-to-day existence) instantiated in that activity."[13]

Although valuable as a defense against naturalism and objectivism, the stress on mundane, everyday activity shortchanges important potential features of agency. A major aspect deemphasized by this focus is the nexus of action and non-action within agency itself. If the latter notion is really "logically prior to a subject-object differentiation" and actually adumbrates the "connection of *being and action*," then social theory has to make room for an "openness to being" and remain attentive not only to "doing" but also to human suffering or to what happens to man (not in the sense of merely reactive behavior). Against this background, language cannot simply be described as "intrinsically involved with *that which has to be done*"; nor can one completely assent to the assertion that social theory today needs "a grasp of 'what cannot be said' (or thought) as *practice*"—an outlook also reflected in the statement, referring to the teachings of the later Wittgenstein, that "what cannot be said is no longer a mysterious metaphysic, that cannot even be talked *about*. What cannot be said is, on the contrary, prosaic and mundane. It is what has to be *done*."[14] Another aspect which is likely to be obscured by the concentration on "doing" as everyday activity is the relationship between "practical" and "discursive consciousness," the latter seen as the arena in which norms and cognitive beliefs can be critically assessed. As Giddens himself admits at one point: "It is a notable feature of the 'rediscovery of ordinary language and common sense' that it has frequently eventuated in a sort of *paralysis of the critical will*." Pointing especially to Winch's discussion of Zande magic and to Garfinkel's principle of "ethnomethodological indifference" he adds: "Having come to see that ordinary language and the world of the natural attitude cannot merely be disregarded or corrected by the social analyst, some authors have been tempted to conclude that no kind of critical evaluation of beliefs or practices is possible where such beliefs and practices form part of an alien cultural system." Although insisting on the need to distinguish between *"respect for the authenticity of belief"* and the *"critical evaluation of the justification of belief,"* however, Giddens' own presentation does not clarify the basis of such evaluation. In another context he refers to a "normative irrationalism which I want to repudiate (although I shall not give the grounds for this here)."[15]

III

To some extent, the mentioned unevenness in the treatment of "structure" and "agency" can be traced to imbalances in the interpretation of leading intellectual figures of our age: especially Heidegger, Wittgenstein, Derrida, and Chomsky. While endorsing the "structuring of structure" as a general guidepost, the opening chapter sees crucial defects in Derrida's thought, defects which are claimed to be remediable only through a recourse to Wittgensteinian philosophy. Although acknowledging that "Derrida breaks in a radical way both with Saussure's distinctions between *langue* and *parole* and between synchrony and diachrony," Giddens charges the former's writings with "giving new impetus to Saussure's formalism," namely through an exclusive preoccupation with "signification" and a neglect of the content of signs and their embeddedness in a concrete social world: "Substance, or the 'concrete,' is repudiated both on the plane of the sign (rejection of the 'transcendental signified'), and on that of the referent (an objectively given world that can be 'captured' by the concept)." According to the author, Derrida's notion of "writing" implies "purified structuration, bereft of any possibility of the recovery of context or of the semantic"; his concept of *différance* is said to denote simply the temporal and spatial distinction of diverse elements of *langue* and thus "to indicate the constant process of mutation which all signification implies."

The philosophy of the later Wittgenstein is invoked by way of contrast, in order to correct the alleged weaknesses of Derrida's standpoint. In Giddens' view, *différance* is not an alien conception to Wittgensteinian philosophy since "for Wittgenstein meaning is created and sustained by the play of difference 'in use'"; as (presumably) in the case of Derrida, language to Wittgenstein is "a system of differences in the sense that the meanings of words are not constituted through the nature of utterances or marks as isolated items, but only through the ways in which they acquire an identity through their differentiation as elements of language-games." The crucial contrast resides in the focus on social practice and external reality. Wittgenstein's repudiation of metaphysics, we read, is "not so much an argument against the misuse of words, as an emphasis upon the inevitable interweaving of language and the practical conduct of social life." While Derrida's outlook "acknowledges only the spacing of the signifier," for Wittgenstein "language is a situated product involved in the temporal, material and social spacing of language-games — or so I want to interpret Wittgenstein here." Moreover, Derrida's concentration on the nexus between signifier and signified "replaces that between meaning and reference" which is claimed to be "prominent in Wittgenstein." Although admitting that "the later Wittgenstein, of course, also rejects any notion that the nature of linguistic terms can be explicated either in terms of 'corresponding' features of the object-world, or in terms of ostensive reference," Giddens affirms that the Wittgensteinian identification of that which cannot be said as "the *practical organization of social life*" entails that this rejection does not lead in the direction of "an attempted retreat *from the object to the idea*": "Whatever the obscurities that may be involved in the account of reference that is implied in the later Wittgenstein's philosophy, it is clear that, for Wittgenstein, to know a language is to have knowledge of an object-world as a relation of practice."[16]

Several doubts or queries can be raised with regard to these propositions. First of all, the interpretation of "*différance*" in the sense of a factual differentiation of elements carries overtones of a quasi-positivist conception of structuralism, a conception criticized by Derrida on several occasions (notably in *Writing and Difference*). Also, the claimed segregation of "writing" from context does not seem to square entirely with the thrust of Derrida's essay on "Signature Event Context" (an essay repeatedly cited by Giddens). More importantly, the invocation of Wittgenstein as an antidote to Derrida appears questionable on several counts. Clearly, the linkage of language games and external reality is complicated by Wittgenstein's rejection of "ostensive reference." Even assuming a Wittgensteinian doctrine of external reference, however, its status would be doubtful given his view that "meaning is created and sustained by the play of difference 'in use.'" The equation of meaning and use either encourages a mundane subjectivism which jeopardizes the desired connection with "reality"; or else it promotes an empiricist pragmatism or a pragmatic behaviorism (as it has among many Wittgensteinians) — an option which conjures up the peril of positivism and naturalism. The difficulty of a straightforward invocation of Wittgenstein, incidentally, is recognized by the author in several passages in which he distances himself from ordinary "post-Wittgensteinians." Despite "the great interest of Wittgenstein's later philosophy for the social sciences," he notes at one point, "we rapidly come up against its limitations in respect to the theoretization of institutions," and also in regard to issues dealing "with social change, with power relations, or with conflict in society." In another context he refers critically to "Wittgenstein's suspicions about the logical status of psychoanalysis."[17]

In a less pronounced manner, interpretative quandaries also beset the treatment of Chomsky and Heidegger. What is at issue in Chomsky's case is the status of "linguistic competence"—which appears lodged between naturalism and voluntarism. On the one hand, structuralism is chided for lacking *a theory of the competent speaker or language-user* such as has been developed by Chomsky "on the level of syntactics" with his notion of linguistic competence seen as "rule-governed creativity"; on the other hand, reference is made to Chomskyan linguistics as well as recent work in psychology suggesting "that there are 'serial orders' in learning processes that might have a definite biological base, a base of 'inbuilt' competencies rather than needs." A similar ambivalence prevails in Heidegger's case — although the tension here involves more the relationship between humanism and objectivism. The "Introduction" to *Central Problems* professes a close intellectual affiliation: "The point of view I advocate in these papers is strongly influenced by Heidegger's treatment of being and time: not so much as an ontology, but as a philosophical source for developing a conceptualization of the time-space constitution of social systems." Subsequent elaborations on this kinship reflect primarily a humanist or "anthropological" reading of *Being and Time.* "The temporality of the interweaving of nature and society is expressed, I want to say, in the finitude and contingency of the human being, of *Dasein,*" Giddens asserts, adding that "for Heidegger *seiend* is a verb form: every existent is a being that is temporal." The emphasis on mundane-human temporality leads him to detect a weakness or deficiency, namely, the absence of structural moorings: "What Heidegger appears to ignore — and it is this which makes strongly historicist readings of his work possible — is the necessary insertion of a paradigmatic dimension in time-space relations." At another point, however, the study perceives "certain overall similarities" between Heidegger and Lévi-Strauss's structuralism: "Lévi-Strauss's belief that the concept of 'man', as distinct from 'nature', is a creation of European culture subsequent to the Renaissance, and his distancing from notions of 'self' and 'consciousness', had some resemblance to Heidegger's attempt to break with traditional views of philosophy as anchored in the knowing subject."[18]

The preceding allusion to historicism invites a final comment. In his treatment of social change, Giddens stresses the linkage between history or historiography and the social sciences and advances the following strong claim: *"There simply are no logical or even methodological distinctions between the social sciences and history — appropriately conceived."* Unfortunately he does not fully spell out what such an appropriate conception would be like — beyond indicating that it would have to transcend the bifurcation between "interpretations of human actions in terms of agents' reasons, versus interpretations in terms of universal laws that have the same logical form as laws in the natural sciences." What is fairly clear is that "history" in Giddens' perspective has to be segregated from "historicism" which he denounces on several occasions (for example, when saying somewhat obscurely that, in Derrida's case, structuralism "eventuates in a form of historicism that denies the possibility of history in its own name"). However broadly construed, the stress on "historiography" seems to conjure up inevitably the opposition between history and nature and also the contrast between modern and premodern attitudes to temporality — a contrast acknowledged in the statement that "the development of writing underlies the first emergence of the 'linear time consciousness' which later, in the West, became the basis of historicity as a feature of social life."[19]

The linkage between history and social science — or its significance — is particularly puzzling in view of Giddens' overall endeavor to move beyond customary demarcations of disciplines. "There can be no reversion," the concluding pages of *Central Problems* affirm, "to the opposition of *verstehen* and *erklären* which, in the hermeneutic tradition, served to differentiate the tasks of the social sciences from those of the natural sciences." The main reason given for this stand is the contemporary state of flux in which both humanities and natural sciences are caught: "We are involved in rotating two axes simultaneously: that of our understanding of the character of human social activity, and that of the logical form of natural science. *These are not entirely separate endeavours, but feed from a pool of common problems.* For just as it has become apparent that hermeneutic questions are integral to a philosophical understanding of natural science, so the limitations of conceptions of the social sciences that exclude causal analysis have become equally evident."[20] Despite the mentioned quandaries, one certainly has to agree that Giddens' work makes important strides toward overcoming these "limitations" and to laying the groundwork for a more "integral" conception of social inquiry.

11
System, State and Polis:
Luhmann

THAT MODERN AND CONTEMPORARY society is no longer fashioned "*à la taille de l'homme*" has often been remarked, sometimes gleefully, sometimes as a complaint. Among sociological perspectives readily endorsing, or at least uncomplainingly accepting, this state of affairs the foremost and most influential has for some time been functionalist "systems theory." An outgrowth of the positivist "unified science" program, systems theory was first developed into a comprehensive sociological framework by Talcott Parsons—probably the dominant social thinker in mid-century America. From sociology the approach quickly radiated into other human and social sciences, including psychology, economics, and political science, sometimes acquiring near-paradigmatic status. In recent decades, under the impact of the "second industrial" (or informational) revolution, the approach has been further amplified and refined through the incorporation of cybernetic categories and electronic technology. This change or revision is particularly evident in the work of the German sociologist Niklas Luhmann —whose relative obscurity in the American context stands in sharp contrast with his imposing stature as a theorist and prolific writer. To some extent his obscurity is due to the dearth of translations—a situation which is fast being remedied; several of his books have recently appeared in English and further translations are in progress.[1] In no small measure his writings account for the fact that—following a period of pronounced disenchantment—systems theory is now experiencing a comeback in social and political analysis.

Luhmann's theoretical perspective is complex, sophisticated, and not simply synonymous with positivist reductionism or Parsonian functionalism. It is not my ambition here to offer a general introduction to his thought—a task I can all the more readily forego given the availability of a perceptive English synopsis (by Peter Beyer).[2] A few brief pointers must suffice here. Basically, in Luhmann's usage, "system" means a network of elements standing in interaction—with in-

teraction being construed chiefly in terms of processes of communication. Systems always are seen as standing in relation to various kinds
of environments whose challenges provide the occasion for a system's
reactions and initiatives. In contradistinction to inorganic and biological systems, "social" systems are presented as networks or patterns
of semantic "meaning"—a focus reflecting the impact of Husserlian
phenomenology on Luhmann's outlook. The same impact can also
be detected in the emphasis on systemic "self-referentiality"—the aspect that systems structure their responses to environments in terms
of their internal patterns of meaning.[3] In dealing with environmental
challenges, the basic task of social systems is said to reside in the
"reduction of complexity," that is, in the transformation of diverse
stimuli into manageable alternatives or discrete behavioral strategies.
In the course of social evolution, this input management takes different forms. Departing from traditional sociological bifurcations (such
as Toennies' *Gemeinschaft-Gesellschaft* dichotomy), Luhmann postulates three main evolutionary stages, namely, segmentary, stratified,
and functionally correlated societies—with the last type showing the
highest degree of internal differentiation and subsystem autonomy.
In modern, functionally organized societies—he argues—subsystems
are held together by their own specialized communications "media"
or interactive "codes"; among such media he emphasizes particularly
those of scientific "truth," money, and power, with the last one serv-
ing as primary currency in the political subsystem.

My comments in the following shall be restricted almost entirely
to the political subsystem or the organization of power. My special
focus will be on an essay entitled "The 'State' of the Political System"
(originally presented by Luhmann at a conference on "The State in
Contemporary European Thought," held at Ohio State University in
fall of 1984). Given the difficult accessibility of the paper, I shall initially recapitulate briefly Luhmann's main arguments as contained
in the essay. In order to flesh out and sharpen the contours of these
arguments I shall occasionally draw on other publications bearing on
the same theme. Subsequently I intend to alert to some quandaries
and possible reservations in order finally to comment on the issue
of the role and meaning of the "state" and of politics in general.

I

As is evident already from its title, Luhmann's essay inserts itself squarely into the ongoing reconsideration and revival of the con-

cept of the "state"—albeit with a peculiar twist. For several decades, the concept seemed to have been almost completely exorcised from the vocabulary of the social sciences. I am referring to the period of the dominance of functionalism in sociology and of behavioralism in political science, that is, the decades following World War II. In the writings of Parsons, David Easton, and others, the "state" was absorbed—virtually without a trace—in the conceptual framework of systems theory; in Easton's political analysis, in particular, the "political system" appeared as the sole legitimate heir of "state" theories (despite allusions to a mysterious "black box" in the system).[4] More recently, especially in the post-Vietnam era, the "state" concept resurfaced emphatically and dramatically, notably in Marxist and neo-Marxist literature: namely, as a tool or instrument of class domination, a tool not digestible by the neutral categories of systems theory. The effects of this theoretical insurgence soon spread through empirical analyses in the social sciences in general.[5] In his essay, Luhmann likewise seeks to revive the "state" concept in and for contemporary social theory—but without any Marxist leanings. What is intriguing in his approach is the attempt to salvage the "state" not in opposition to, but as an ingredient of, the system-theoretical paradigm.

As a backdrop to his own perspective, Luhmann initially refers to the conflict of vocabularies presently operative in social and political analysis. "Today," he writes, "the theory of the state and the theory of political systems belong to different realms of scientific discourse." On the one hand, "if we speak of the political system our object is a subsystem of the society on the same level as the economic system, the system of science, the educational system etc." On the other hand, the vocabulary of the state is "based upon a distinction of state and society which suggests that the state exists outside of the society"—in the sense that the state is seen as "a legal person or as a collective actor being different from the network of private needs and private interests" constitutive of the social domain. From the vantage point of empirical social scientists, the latter concept appears at best as a legal fiction; stripped of fictional attributes the state is viewed as synonymous with "the public bureaucracy, including parliaments and eventually courts, schools and public services." In the lawyers' eyes, by contrast, the exclusive use of system terminology tends to denude governments of autonomous agency and legal responsibility. Weighing these conflicting views Luhmann opts for a third alternative: "I want to crosscut the two ways of speaking about politics, the two languages, the two discourses because I see no reason to keep them separate." The proposed alternative presents the state as a modality or mode of operation of the political system itself, a modality required for the latter's efficient management: "Starting with the concept of the political system we can see the formula 'state' as a *self-description of the political system.*" In view of the growing complexity of systemic environments, the state is said to be the means for the simplification of heterogeneity (or reduction of complexity) and for the maintenance of self-referential identity: "All self-awareness and all communication about the system within the system needs *self-simplifying devices,* i.e., identities. For the political system this function is fulfilled by the state."[6]

On the basis of this definition Luhmann launches into an inquiry of the genealogy or semantic history of the state. In his portrayal the state as territorial political unit emerged first in the late Middle Ages from the decay of feudal vassalage and patrimonial households (organized along clan or kinship lines). Beginning with the age of Enlightenment, the state was increasingly associated with the political system (functionally construed) and segregated from economic, cultural, and other systems, that is, from "society" in the broad sense. This development marked the ascendancy of the "modern state" with its distinctive functional and organizational qualities. From this time forward, Luhmann notes, "the state was no longer thought of as the 'political society' itself, but was defined by a distinction between state and society, roughly equal with the distinction of force and property." In light of functional differentiation, the state was perceived as hedged in by various internal and external boundaries — a feature captured initially under the rubric of the "constitutional state" (*Verfassungsstaat*), an arrangement seeking to perform the "miracle of self-limitation of sovereign power" chiefly through legalistic means. The further development of the modern state, in Luhmann's account, was marked by progressive "democratization" and finally, in our time, by the establishment of the "welfare state," that is, a state assuming "increasing social engagements and activities" and thus steadily transgressing or obviating the lines of functional differentiation. In systemic terms, the welfare state appears decidedly as a "state in crisis" and even as "a state that wills its own crisis." In Luhmann's words: "Whereas the constitutional state could rely to a large extent on the mechanisms of negative feedback, eliminating deviations from the law or eventually adapting the law by a slow process of juridical change, the welfare state has to cope with positive feedback, with increasing deviation as the very structure of its own policies. There is a close similarity to the flight of locusts: It can be stopped only by exhaustion."

In its concluding pages, Luhmann's essay returns to the relationship between state and the political system, or state and politics in general. Under systemic auspices, he states, the function of politics can be defined as "providing for the continuing possibility of collectively binding decision-making"—a possibility which also includes the alternative of "avoiding situations" in which final or irreversible decisions need to be made. In political theory, a problem has traditionally been how to circumscribe the potential arbitrariness of decisions. In Luhmann's view, this problem cannot be resolved ethically or even legally, but only through increased functional differentiation and societal complexity: "No fixed point, no *Sittengesetz*, no principle of justice can be assumed as given and as framing the arbitrary will of the sovereign power. And even if this were possible it would, as thinkers of the 18th century knew well, impose not enough constraint on the sovereign. Only complexity *as such* can help." By treating the state as "self-description" of the political system and the latter as distinguished from society or the social environment, systems theory is able to grasp both the decisional autonomy and the limitations of political power. "Seen from this viewpoint," Luhmann concludes, "the state is the important and, until today, irreplaceable evolutionary universal which makes it possible to control relatively high complexity and to articulate the conditions which restrict the process of defeating and re-establishing, dissolving and re-introducing bindingness."

II

Before critically assessing the reviewed essay, I want to mention first some of the obvious strengths or virtues of Luhmann's arguments. As I see it, a major virtue of the essay resides in the historical treatment of the state and related concepts like politics and (civil) society. It is commonplace to say that we live in an age of linguistic-semantic analysis and self-conscious hermeneutical erudition; yet, the lessons of contemporary semantics have not sufficiently penetrated, I believe, into the ongoing practice of social and political inquiry. Inadequate attention, I think, is given to the fact that key political or sociological terms are not universal integers but rather ingredients in a complex linguistic web operative at a given time and place. In this sense, we do not yet have detailed historical studies of such concepts as "state" or "civil society"—although recent German literature offers important guideposts in this direction. I am referring, for example, to Weihnacht's work on the semantic genealogy of the state or to the multi-volume study on "Basic Historical Concepts" (*Geschichtliche Grundbegriffe*), subtitled "Historical Lexicon of the Political-Social Language in Germany"—both invoked and utilized in Luhmann's essay.[7] In my estimate, his presentation accords with and makes a contribution to this literature, while distinguishing itself at the same time by its more pronounced theoretical ambitions.

While appreciating and applauding Luhmann's historical semantics, I must note right away certain limitations—mainly a certain paleness or detachment—of his overall historical narrative. This paleness, I believe, has much to do with his reliance on the system-theoretical paradigm. Thus, the emergence of the modern state from the web of feudal households is presented simply as the differentiation of one subsystem within a larger social system; little or no attention is given to the intensive political and religious struggles surrounding this emergence and to the implications of political and economic class division—implications stressed, for example, by Habermas in his discussion of the modern state.[8] The treatment of the "constitutional state" focuses almost entirely on the solution of a systemic paradox—the "self-limitation of sovereign power" conjoining "in one legal document the unlimited and the limited"—while bypassing the pathos and animating spirit of liberal constitutionalism. The entire process of "democratization" is subsumed somewhat blandly under the system-theoretical category of "re-entry," referring to the internalization of an inside/outside or system/environment distinction: "What kind of internal structure of this self-description (i.e., the state) generated the complex framework of constitutional provisions, including basic human rights, division of powers, legitimate opposition and public elections? The answer to this question can be given by using the logical concept of re-entry." The discussion of the welfare state slights "superficial" political accounts in favor of "deep-structure," that is, system-theoretical analysis concentrating on the operation of positive feedback mechanisms.

However, my reservations are not limited to the lack of drama in Luhmann's account, to a certain sovereign neglect of the self-understanding of historical agents. Differently put: my point is not simply or solely a plea for the reintegration of observer perspective and participant perspective—a plea which has been eloquently formulated by Habermas in several of his writings, including his recent *Theory of Communicative Action* where "system" and "life-world" are correlated in an ongoing process of "coupling" and "uncoupling."[9] Although sympathetic to the objective of reintegration, I find it stops short (and Habermas stops short) of raising more general issues. Somewhat baldly stated, one of my general concerns can be pinpointed with the label of "positivism." As practiced by Luhmann, systems theory surely is a far cry from a simple fact-gathering empiricism, and even some distance removed from the logical positivism of a Carnap or Schlick. However, despite this distance, his approach still constitutes, I think, a version of positivism — albeit a very sophisticated or "cybernetic" version. In this version, social systems are seen not simply as mute empirical objects, but as objects endowed with the capacity of self-reference, self-description, self-regulation, and internal communication. To American students of political science, this cybernetic version is familiar to some extent from the work of Karl Deutsch who defined social evolution as a "learning process" and systemic self-maintenance as dependent on increasingly streamlined modes of self-regulation and self-steering.[10]

Although sensitive to the sophistication of cybernetics, I want to indicate briefly some convergences with positivism or positivist epistemology. One such convergence resides in the treatment of "subsystems"—like politics, economics, or law—as distinct "object domains" integrated in a larger objective structure. As Luhmann writes in his mentioned comments on contemporary terminology: "If we speak of the political system, our object is a subsystem of the society on the same level as the economic system, the system of science, the educational system etc." In this juxtaposition politics is subordinated to sociology, and the political system to "society" seen as a comprehensive empirical category. Another way the positivist legacy surfaces is in the emphasis on empirical description and observation, and generally in the accent on an external observer perspective. As indicated, Luhmann defines the state as the "self-description of the political system"; he also speaks of "superficial" or "first-level" description, of "deep-structure" or systemic description, and of the "normal self-observation of the political system." The preference for the observer perspective is perhaps not fully evident in "The 'State' of the Political System"; however, Luhmann has repeatedly voiced this preference on other occasions, for example, in an essay of 1983 entitled "The Welfare State Between Evolution and Rationality." Arguing against a Habermasian concern with "life-world" experience, he wrote there: "The theory of politics thus faces today the dilemma of having to concede to all practical operations and especially to the praxis of political communication limited horizons, reduced complexity, and intelligible language, while simultaneously realizing that the problems of the welfare state are not even stable in these terms."[11]

A further trace of the same legacy is manifest in evolutionary theory. In Luhmann's account, evolution signifies basically a process of differentiation and growing complexity, accompanied by parallel efforts of reintegration and complexity-reduction. Despite important modifications, this account clearly bears the imprint of Spencer's evolutionary scheme as well as Parsons' theory of "evolutionary universals." The empiricist bent is limited not only to the evolutionary domain, but affects Luhmann's general concept of "theory"—which basically coincides with "positive" or "empirical" theory. As he stated in the essay of 1983: "Theory could turn out to be more important than ever before, namely, as the capacity of a system for comparative self-observation. The concept of observation functions here in a very formal sense: it means the operational utilization of a difference for purposes of gathering information."[12] A final indication of positivism consists in the general endorsement of the "fact-value" dichotomy, that is, in the deemphasis of normative considerations in favor of positive "information" about the course of the world. From Luhmann's systemic perspective, terms like the "common good" or the "good life" are largely old-fashioned if not obsolete phrases devoid of scientific payoff. As he noted in a paper of 1984 entitled "The State and Politics" ("Staat und Politik"): "The progressive differentiation and autonomy of a political subsystem of society put adaptive pressure on the semantics of the 'good life' which hitherto had governed the understanding of political (or civil) society."[13]

If or to the extent that systems theory is linked with positivism, it shares the latter's dilemmas. One such dilemma is unreflectiveness or a truncated reflectiveness regarding its own premises. At least since Husserl it is a popular adage that empiricism cannot be justified empirically or scientism by means of scientific method. Likewise, unable to account for itself system-theoretically, systems theory relies on a reservoir of metaphysical premises—premises which are bracketed or concealed in favor of the rhetoric of scientific progress or empirical payoff. Although largely unacknowledged, these assumptions infiltrate the systemic paradigm at numerous junctures or levels, bestowing on the paradigm itself a metaphysical cast. A prominent manifestation of this imprint is the indebtedness to traditional dualisms or antinomies. Clearly, systems or subsystems can be treated as "object domains" only from the perspective of a predicating consciousness—a correlation faithful to the subject-object polarity familiar from Cartesian metaphysics. Closely associated with this polarity are a number of other dualisms of which I shall mention only a few: the dualisms of form and content, inside and outside, freedom and necessity. Luhmann's paper squarely presents systems theory as a mode of formal analysis. As he writes with regard to "re-entry": "A distinction made to indicate a form, different from something else, re-enters the form." The distinction quickly shades over into the opposition of inside and outside: "The outside as the side from which the distinction is supposed to be seen becomes a premise of internal operations. A system, using re-entry, can observe and describe itself. It can process information by taking the distinction of itself and the environment as its guideline." The dualism of freedom and necessity (or obligation) pervades primarily the discussion of the "constitutional state," focused on the "miracle of the self-limitation of sovereign power." In another context, the essay of 1983, Luhmann himself provided a list of system-theoretical dualisms and polarities. "Interdisciplinary developments during the last few decades," he wrote, "are primarily characterized by the fact that the older typology of differences (i.e., status/contract, community/society) has begun to be replaced by a 'new generation' which is more abstract but also more scientifically useful. I mean the distinctions of system/environment, substance/relation, variation/selection, order/disorder, event/structure, identity/difference."[14]

Despite the startling character of such pairs as event/structure or identity/difference, what all the mentioned dualisms have in common —at least in Luhmann's treatment—is the "positivity" of the opposing terms, that is, the aspect that their juxtaposition yields or is meant to yield positive information. What the enumeration neglects is the correlation of positivity and negativity or (more appropriately) of presence and absence—what Derrida has labeled "différance." As Derrida observed at one point, différance may be called "the play of the trace," a play which juxtaposes and exceeds "the alternative of presence and absence" and which itself "has no meaning and is not; which does not belong."[15] Seen as a virtual or nonpositive matrix, différance transgresses the confines of traditional metaphysics and also (and in principle) the confines of systems theory since the juxtaposition of terms here does not, and is not meant to, generate positive information. One may also recall in this context Derrida's critique of a positivist or reified structuralism in favor of a looser theory of "structuration" focused on the interplay of presence and absence—an outlook which has recently been applied to sociological inquiry by Anthony Giddens.[16]

Indebtedness to metaphysics is also evident in Luhmann's strong reliance on traditional logic. Together with logical empiricism, systems theory tends to treat politics and the state under the auspices of "pure" or theoretical reason—to use Kantian vocabulary—rather than those of "practical" reason (not to speak of aesthetic judgment). It is

only against the standard of pure logic that politics and the state appear embroiled in unresolvable "paradoxes" or antinomies. As the essay states: "Since paradox is the logical equivalent of self-reference,
we have to expect that social evolution can never avoid the paradoxical constitution of systems, but can only transform and update the
ways in which a system tackles its own paradoxical identity." A different assessment would have been reached—and has been reached
by thinkers like Camus and Merleau-Ponty—when politics is seen as
a practical enterprise guided not by logic but by practical judgment,
a judgment inevitably pervaded by "ambiguity." Such ambiguity is
bound to be heightened where political engagement is defined as
"praxis" and praxis itself as instantiation of the ontological interplay
of presence and absence. Luhmann himself seems to lean in this direction when he says that "evolution did not take the time to produce
a world according to logical and mathematical order." However, his
conclusion that, from this perspective, "the loss of the paradise was
no accident" seems to involve a confusion of terms—since paradise has
never been equated with "mathematical order" (except by logicians).[17]

III

By way of conclusion let me turn to the implications of the preceding discussion for the central theme of these pages: the role and
meaning of the "state." From the vantage point of systems theory, the
state has a purely formal and, in a sense, technical significance. To
some extent, the state plays the role of a sophisticated cybernetic
"regulator," a kind of thermostat of the political system which, in turn,
fulfills the function of "goal-achievement" for the total society. In Luhmann's words, the state denotes the "self-description" of the political
system where self-description operates as a "self-simplifying device"
within the system. As he elaborates in the paper on "State and Politics," the term "self-description" modifies the usual cybernetic notion
of a "regulator" by placing regulation *inside* the regulated context,
thus making it a means of systemic self-maintenance. Seen as a means
of self-maintenance, the state clearly carries functional-instrumental
overtones. Although opposed (for various reasons) to technological social planning, and although clearly deviating from the Marxist stress
on instrumental class domination, Luhmann's own approach pays tribute to the legacy of "instrumental reason" or to the equation of reason
with calculation or calculating control. This is evident in "The 'State'
of the Political System" when we read that, through self-description,

the political system "not only knows the difference between itself and the environment (this every living system is supposed to do) but can *control* this difference as well by using the identity of the difference as a distinction within the system." The convergence of self-regulation with management or managerial control is even more obvious in the statement that self-observation has to occur on at least two levels: "on the level of the total (managed) system, and on the level of the managing part-system."

In siding with management and instrumental control, Luhmann takes a stand against a very different tradition of the "state": one which sees the state as embodiment of "substantive reason" or of the "common good." This opposition is repeatedly voiced, always in sharply polemical terms. Thus, after spelling out the system-theoretical concept of "self-description," Luhmann continues: "The Continental, and particularly the German doctrine of the state, has prevented this kind of analysis by mystifying the paradox, imitating, of course, theology. The state was described as a real actor, as a collective individual, as a spiritual unity demanding moral participation and obedience." The essay of 1983 is even more biting on this score: "Only those who view the state as a collective individual, as a spiritual quality or as historical *Gestalt* of a people are likely to agree with Carl Schmitt's judgment that the epoch of the 'state' is coming to an end. If, by contrast, we take our departure not from an identity described as 'objective spirit' or in similar terms, but rather from the difference between system and its own self-description, the state shrinks from the inflated ideals of the past into a mode of reduced complexity or self-simplification; by the same token, however, the state can be functionally grasped and for the first time be justified in its contingent-historical necessity." The paper on "State and Politics" adds to this that, with the advances of systems theory, it becomes "superfluous to burden the concept of the state with metaphysical, ethical or community-related connotations. It [the concept] can now be grasped functionally: namely, with reference to the function of an asymmetrical management of politics" (i.e., a hierarchical ordering of decisions).[18]

The references to "objective spirit" or "spiritual unity" are veiled, or not so veiled, allusions to German idealism, especially to Hegel (perhaps also to Rousseau). Curiously, most of Luhmann's polemical forays are addressed at Carl Schmitt—who was only a very distant and by no means very faithful heir of Hegelian teachings. The confrontation is even more curious in view of the fact that Luhmann seems to concur at least in part with Schmitt's "decisionistic" outlook —for example, by defining the function of politics as "providing for the continuing possibility of collectively binding decision-making."[19] However, rather than lingering on the aspect of decisionism I want to return to the broader issue of substantive reason. On this score (Luhmann's) systems theory is only the terminal point in the long process of the dissolution of Hegel's philosophical system, a system which defined the state as the arena of "*Sittlichkeit*" and as embodiment of the public or common good. As is well known, already Marx—in his "Critique of Hegel's *Philosophy of Right*"—had attacked this concept as an idealist mystification, but not without trying to find a concrete substitute for the concept in the notion of a classless society or a "general class." Later Marxists (for the most part) abandoned this circumspection. Leninists and post-Leninists briskly defined the state as an instrument of class domination, without worrying in the least about the possibility or prospect of substantive reason in a postrevolutionary setting. A similar disintegration occurred outside the Marxist framework. Unencumbered by any notion of dialectics, Max Weber saw the state as final instrument of territorial control—although an instrument still circumscribed by considerations of legitimacy or legitimate authority. Positivist followers of Weber tended to relinquish these considerations, restricting themselves to issues of legality and effective control. From here the road to systems theory is not very far.

My point here is not a full-fledged defense or vindication of Hegel's philosophical perspective, especially not of (what has been called) his metaphysics of "subjectivity" or mind. Yet, I believe some of his core teachings have been prematurely dismissed—if they were understood at all—by his detractors. Hegel's "objective spirit" was not a mysterious entity hovering somewhere above the heads of social agents; rather, it was the common spirit or rational "common sense" of those agents themselves—that is, a synonym for the mutual recognition and interpenetration of individual rationalities embodied in common institutions and practices. Differently phrased: it was the common space presupposed in public discourse and in discursive strategies of any kind.[20] Luhmann's approach is far removed from notions of this sort. His essay of 1983 polemicizes sharply against the traditions both of substantive reason ("*Vernunft*") and of practical wisdom (or "*phronesis*"). "No one," he asserts blandly (forgetting Oakeshott and Gadamer, among others), "would even dream today of postulating 'wisdom' (*sagesse*) for politics. . . . The semantics of rationality has retreated to basic concepts, confined islands of reality and partial calculations, and articulates from there its difference from the world. . . . Rationality is grasped not as an essential continuum in the world, but as an element of discontinuity whose unity can no longer be formulated or assessed. Rationality operates only as critique; with this (development) one loses the right to speak of wisdom." In the confines of systems theory, rationality is reduced to the capacity of self-observation and systemic control. In Luhmann's words: "The rationality of a system would depend on the extent to which it is able . . . to reflect systemically on its capactiy to utilize the difference between system and environment for purposes of gathering information. Translated into causal categories this means that a system would have to be able to control its effects on its environment in terms of feedback repercussions on itself."[21]

From a Hegelian (or perhaps a linguistically revised Hegelian) perspective, a counterargument could readily be advanced: namely, that systems theory presupposes or is itself parasitical on the broader notion of rationality it repudiates. For, how could Luhmann's discursive strategy even be intelligible to others without reliance on the rational common sense which Hegel called, perhaps grandly, "objective spirit"? But I do not wish to simplify matters unduly. The trouble is that Luhmann's theory is on one level quite intelligible to us. What I want to suggest, in a nutshell, is that his account is largely correct as a diagnosis, but wrong as a therapy. It is indeed hardly deniable that the "state" in our time has been largely denuded of common meaning or substantive reason (in fact, the very "meaning" of meaning and reason is shifting under our feet); as a result, the state can no longer function as the public space or arena in which discursive and intersubjective recognition can properly occur. For all intents and purposes, the state has been transformed—or is in process of being transformed, both in the East and the West—into a formal-analytical structure operating in accordance with technical-cybernetic imperatives; as a corollary, individual or group rationalities are progressively marginalized, fragmented, or particularized.[22] This development, however, is not simply a neutral process or routine event, because the diagnosis reveals a problem or agony: the lack of a common space creates havoc not only in public life, but also in the intelligible conduct of private life. We live, I believe, in an age of transition where an older public space (the state) is vanishing and a new one has not yet been found. Such transitional ages—one can think of the transition from the Roman Empire to feudalism, or from feudalism to the modern state—are high-risk periods: periods prone to major social dislocations, large-scale warfare, and other political calamities. In the face of such risks, a mere celebration of elegant system-theoretical formulas will hardly suffice.[23]

Yet, I do not wish to end on this grim note. I have said that the

previous public space has eroded or atrophied, and that our thinking
is presently *en route*. But perhaps we are not entirely without com-
pass or guideposts. Tradition—including the Hegelian tradition—can
serve as a beacon or marker, provided it is not pressed into the service
of a simple repetition. Perhaps we can also find some contemporary
or near-contemporary markers or clues. Recently I read the text of a
lecture course which Martin Heidegger offered in 1942 in Freiburg,
a text published for the first time in early 1984. In this lecture course
—which deals centrally with Hölderlin's hymn "Der Ister" ("The Dan-
ube")—I discovered to my surprise some fascinating comments on the
notion of *polis* seen as an ontological human space. As Heidegger indicates, *polis* cannot simply be equated with an object domain among
other object domains, accessible to a predicating consciousness; least
of all can it be identified with a fixed historical structure like the "state."
"We are already going astray," he writes, "if—translating *polis* as state
—we consciously or unthinkingly take our bearings from the structure of modern states." In Heidegger's account, *polis* denotes neither
the "state" nor the "city," but is more basically a name for "place" or
"space" (*"die Statt"*): namely, "the place of the historical dwelling of
man in the midst of being." As such a dwelling place, *polis* is not a
stable habitat but rather the site of ceaseless inquiry or questioning:
the site of the perennial human quest for understanding and self-
understanding. In Heidegger's words: "Perhaps *polis* is the place and
space around which everything that is questionable and undomesticated revolves in a preeminent sense. *Polis* then is *polos*, that is, the
pole or vortex in which and around which everything turns."[24]

Notes

INTRODUCTION

    1. The latter phrase is the French rendition of *Holzwege*. Compare Martin Heidegger, *Holzwege* (4th ed., Frankfurt: Klostermann, 1963); also Gabriel Marcel, *Homo viator*, trans. Emma Craufurd (New York: Harper & Row, 1962).

    2. Compare Dallmayr, *Twilight of Subjectivity: Contributions to a Post-Individualist Theory of Politics* (Amherst, MA: University of Massachusetts Press, 1981); *Polis and Praxis: Exercises in Contemporary Political Theory* (Cambridge, MA: MIT Press, 1984). Regarding the linguistic implications of post-individualism see my *Language and Politics: Why Does Language Matter to Political Philosophy?* (Notre Dame: University of Notre Dame Press, 1984).

    3. See John G. Gunnell, *Between Philosophy and Politics: The Alienation of Political Theory* (Amherst, MA: University of Massachusetts Press, 1986), pp. 142–46. The segregation between politics and philosophy is also couched in terms of the distinction between "theory" and "metatheory," between "theory *in* politics" and "theory *about* politics," and between "functional or practical" epistemology and "professional or disciplinary" epistemology (pp. 145–52).

    4. Gunnell, *Between Philosophy and Politics*, pp. 34, 193–94. Regarding Habermas's work, the study finds in it even "the reductio ad absurdum of academic political theory" (p. 194). Although Gunnell presents his argument as a move toward the resumption of "significant dialogue" in political theory (p. 42), the charge of alienation—as voiced in the above citations— seems to me to function essentially as a conversation-stopper.

    5. On all these issues, my quarrel is not so much with Heidegger as with Heideggerians—especially with a tendency among the latter to treat his thought as "edifying" in a precious-aesthetic sense. Needless to say, I do not accept the label of "edifying philosopher" affixed to Heidegger by Rorty and others; see Richard Rorty, *Philosophy and the Mirror of Nature* (Princeton: Princeton University Press, 1979), pp. 357–68.

    6. Commenting on Adorno's notion of "mimetic" thought, Habermas observes that the later Adorno "comes shockingly close to [Heidegger's] recollection of being"; see Jürgen Habermas, *The Theory of Communicative Action*, vol. 1: *Reason and the Rationalization of Society*, trans. Thomas Mc-

255

Carthy (Boston: Beacon Press, 1984), p. 385. But this convergence is "shocking" only from the perspective of an unreconstructed philosophy of identity.

7. The proximity to Habermas's position is still evident in my *Beyond Dogma and Despair: Toward a Critical Phenomenology of Politics* (Notre Dame: University of Notre Dame Press, 1981).

8. In the above, I speak of an occasional tendency and by no means of a systematic doctrine. The charge of nihilism has been eloquently rebutted by Derrida himself in an interview with Richard Kearney: "I totally refuse the label of nihilism which has been ascribed to me and my American colleagues. Deconstruction is not an enclosure in nothingness, but an openness towards the other." See Richard Kearney, *Dialogues with Contemporary Continental Thinkers* (Manchester: Manchester University Press, 1984), p. 124.

9. I find traces of such anti-intellectualism in Allan Megill's attack on Nietzsche, Heidegger, and Foucault, whom he labels "quintessentially thinkers of crisis" articulating a "metapolitics of crisis": "I write of 'metapolitics' because theories like Heidegger's are radically out of touch with political reality. They are 'beyond' that reality, and this is their true danger. For Nietzsche, son of a pastor, and Heidegger, the son of a sexton, the 'death of God' was a profoundly disturbing event. So too was the collapse of the 'two-worlds' theory of morality for philosophers within 'the tradition'. But for most people, and particulary for us, these events are nothing." See Allan Megill, "Martin Heidegger and the Metapolitics of Crisis," in John S. Nelson, ed., *What Should Political Theory Be Now?* (Albany: SUNY Press, 1983), pp. 293, 303.

10. Given my emphasis on interplay or engagement, I am hesitant to embrace Foucault's notion of an "aesthetics of experience," to the extent that it involves a basically solitary activity of aesthetic self-formation; see Michel Foucault, "On the Genealogy of Ethics," in Paul Robinow, ed., *The Foucault Reader* (New York: Pantheon Books, 1984), pp. 340–72. Curiously, there seems to be a convergence of views between Foucault and Habermas on the issue of aesthetic subjectivity. For a critique of a subject-centered aesthetics of "aesthetic consciousness" (a critique which could be further radicalized) see Hans-Georg Gadamer, *Truth and Method* (New York: Seabury, 1975), pp. 39–119.

11. Michael Theunissen, "Vorrede zur zweiten Auflage," in *Der Andere* (2nd ed.; Berlin: W. de Gruyter, 1977), pp. ix–x.

12. Martin Heidegger, "Hölderlin's Hymne 'Der Ister,'" ed. Walter Biemel (*Gesamtausgabe*, vol. 53; Frankfurt: Klostermann, 1984), pp. 100–101. For more detailed comments on "structuration" and an attempt to apply the concept to politics see my "Political Inquiry: Beyond Empiricism and Hermeneutics," in Terence Ball, ed., *Idioms of Inquiry* (Albany: SUNY Press, 1987), pp. 169–86. For discussions of various approaches in contemporary political inquiry see my essays: "Between Theory and Practice," *Human Studies*, vol. 3 (1980), pp. 175–84 (on Thomas McCarthy's interpretation of Habermas); "Life-World and Politics," *Research in Phenomenology*, vol. 11 (1981), pp. 256–63 (on Hwa Yol Jung's phenomenological approach); "Language and Praxis," *Human Studies*, vol. 5 (1982), pp. 249–59 (on Michael Shapiro's *Language and Political Under-*

standing); "Between Kant and Aristotle: Beiner's *Political Judgment*," *New Vico Studies* (forthcoming).

1. FAREWELL TO METAPHYSICS: NIETZSCHE

1. The difference between the earlier courses and the war-time lectures and writings has been emphasized by Hannah Arendt, *The Life of the Mind*, vol. 2: *Willing* (New York: Harcourt Brace Jovanovich, 1978), pp. 172–73. For a slightly more nuanced discussion of the same difference see David F. Krell, "Analysis," in Martin Heidegger, *Nietzsche*, vol. 4: *Nihilism*, ed. Krell, trans. Frank A. Capuzzi (New York: Harper & Row, 1982), pp. 272–76; also J. L. Mehta, *The Philosophy of Martin Heidegger* (New York: Harper & Row, 1971), pp. 110–11.

2. Heidegger, "European Nihilism," in *Nihilism*, p. 22. (In these and subsequent citations the translation has been slightly altered for the sake of clarity.) Regarding "classical nihilism" compare the earlier statement (p. 5): "'Nihilism' is the increasingly dominant truth that all prior aims of being have become untenable. But with this transformation of the erstwhile relation to ruling values, nihilism has also perfected itself for the free and genuine task of a *new* valuation. Such nihilism—perfected in itself and decisive for the future—may be described as 'classical nihilism.'"

3. *Nihilism*, pp. 70, 80–82.

4. Emphasizing Nietzsche's place in the history of metaphysics Heidegger notes: "The sole reason for the inadequate portrayals of the Nietzschean doctrine of the overman lies in the fact that, until now, one has not managed to take the will to power seriously as a metaphysics and to grasp the doctrines of nihilism, overman, and (above all) the *eternal recurrence of the same* as necessary constituents of such a metaphysics. . . . Contrary to what Nietzsche has told us about the history of metaphysics, it is necessary to take a *more original* look into this history. Such an intent requires first of all an endeavor to elucidate more clearly Nietzsche's description and conception of metaphysics. It is a 'moral' conception—where 'moral' means a system of valuations." See *Nihilism*, pp. 82–83.

5. Ibid., pp. 83–84, 89.

6. Ibid., pp. 86, 90, 93–94.

7. Ibid., pp. 96–98, 100. As Heidegger adds (p. 99): "The securing of supreme and unimpeded self-development of all human capacities for absolute dominion over the entire earth is the secret goal that prods modern man again and again to new initiatives and that forces him into commitments securing for him the surety of his actions and the certainty of his aims."

8. Ibid., pp. 105–06, 108, 114.

9. Ibid., pp. 28, 121. Compare also Heidegger's comments (pp. 86, 103): In Cartesianism "the reality of the real means representedness *through* and *for* the representing subject. Nietzsche's doctrine which makes everything that is into the 'property and product of man', merely carries out the final

development of Descartes' teaching to the effect that truth is grounded in the self-certainty of the human subject. . . . We do not believe that Nietzsche teaches a doctrine identical to that of Descartes; rather, we affirm something far móre essential, to wit, that he thinks the 'same' in its historical culmination. What begins metaphysically with Descartes reaches in Nietzsche's metaphysics the historical phase of its completion."

10. Ibid., pp. 127–29.

11. Ibid., pp. 129–31, 133. Heidegger is vehement in denouncing the equation of truth with a "kind of error." As he writes (pp. 132–33): The traditional "concept of truth is the presupposition and yardstick for the interpretation of truth as semblance and error. But then, does not Nietzsche's own construal of truth as semblance become semblance? It becomes even less than semblance: by appealing to the essence of truth as agreement with the real, Nietzsche's interpretation of 'truth' as error leads to the reversal of his own thinking and thus to its dissolution. . . . The entanglements from which Nietzsche can ño longer extricate himself are at first covered over by the basic notion that everything is sustained, necessitated, and therefore justified by the will to power. This is made explicit in the fact that Nietzsche can simultaneously say that 'truth' is semblance and error, but that as semblance it is still a 'value'. Thinking in values veils the collapse of the essence of being and truth."

12. Ibid., pp. 147–49.

13. See, e.g., François Laruelle, *Nietzsche Contre Heidegger* (Paris: Payot, 1977); compare also Pierre Klossowski, *Nietzsche et le cercle vicieux* (Paris: Mercure de France, 1969); Maurice Blanchot, *L'Entretien Infini* (Paris: Gallimard, 1969); Gilles Deleuze, *Nietzsche et la Philosophie* (Paris: Presses Universitaires de France, 1962); also David B. Allison, *The New Nietzsche: Contemporary Styles of Interpretation* (New York: Dell Publishing Co., 1977). One should recall that the Nietzsche-resurgence in France was in part fueled by the publication of Heidegger's *Nietzsche*, 2 Vols. (Pfullingen: Nerke, 1961), in which the lectures of 1940 became first available to the public.

14. Jacques Derrida, *Of Grammatology*, trans. Gayatri C. Spivak (Baltimore: Johns Hopkins University Press, 1976), p. 19.

15. Derrida, "The Ends of Man" (1968), in *Margins of Philosophy*, trans. Alan Bass (Chicago: University of Chicago Press, 1982), pp. 135–36.

16. Derrida, *Spurs: Nietzsche's Styles*, trans. Barbara Harlow (Chicago: University of Chicago Press, 1979), pp. 73–75 (in these and subsequent citations the translation has been slightly altered for purposes of clarity). The monograph relies in part on an earlier essay (of 1973) which, under the title "The Question of Style" (trans. Ruben Berezdivin), appears in Allison, *The New Nietzsche*, pp. 176–89.

17. *Spurs*, pp. 75, 79–83. For Nietzsche's fable see Walter Kaufmann, ed., *The Portable Nietzsche* (New York: Viking Press, 1968), pp. 485–86.

18. *Spurs*, pp. 107, 111–13. As Derrida admits, however (p. 113): "It would be precipitate to conclude that, in general or more specifically in a reading of Nietzsche, the critical resources of the ontological problematic could sim-

ply be dispensed with. Equally naive would be the inference that, since it is no longer derivable from the question of being, the issue of the proper (propriation) is thus available to direct inspection — as if one even *knew what is* property, propriation etc."

19. Ibid., pp. 115–19.

20. Derrida, "Guter Wille zur Macht (II): Die Unterschriften interpretieren (Nietzsche/Heidegger)," in Philippe Forget, ed., *Text und Interpretation* (Munich: Fink Verlag, 1984), pp. 63, 66–67. Derrida had explored the biographical dimension of Nietzsche's thought also in an earlier essay entitled "Nietzsches Otobiographie oder Politik des Eigennamens; Die Lehre Nietzsches," in *Fugen: Deutsch-Französisches Jahrbuch für Text-Analytik,* vol. 1 (Freiburg: Walter Verlag, 1980), pp. 64–98; now published in French: *Otobiographies: L'enseignement de Nietzsche et la politique du nom propre* (Paris: Editions galilée, 1984).

21. *Text und Interpretation,* pp. 69–70, 72. As Derrida adds (p. 73): "Since Aristotle and at least until Bergson (Western metaphysics) has persistently repeated and assumed that thinking and speaking means to think and to say 'something' which would be *one* thing and a *thing* (or topic). . . . It is the saying (*legein*) of this *logos* and the gathering of this entire logic which the 'Nietzsches' (in plural) call into question. This plural begins to resemble the family name of tricksters and mountebanks."

22. Ibid., pp. 75–76.

23. Ibid., p. 70.

24. "Nietzsches Otobiographie," *Fugen,* p. 91. As Derrida adds: "However, if — in the still open contours of our epoch — the only so-called Nietzschean politics has been a Nazi politics, this is necessarily significant and must be interrogated in its full weight." Regarding "political" statements in Heidegger's text I merely want to alert to a passage which (in 1940) virtually predicts German defeat and which starts: "In these days we are ourselves witnessing a mysterious law of history, namely, that a people at some point is no longer equal to the metaphysics it has historically produced. . . ." See *Nihilism,* p. 116.

25. *Nihilism,* pp. 25–26, 48. Compare also Friedrich Nietzsche, *The Will to Power,* ed. Walter Kaufmann, trans. Kaufmann and R. J. Hollingsdale (New York: Vintage Books), pp. 12–13.

26. *Nihilism,* pp. 130–33. My comment on French phenomenology refers, of course, mainly to the work of Gabriel Marcel and Maurice Merleau-Ponty. Regarding Heidegger's notion of power and empowerment see Hermann Mörchen, *Macht und Herrschaft im Denken von Heidegger und Adorno* (Stuttgart: Klett-Cotta, 1980).

27. *Text und Interpretation,* p. 75; *Spurs,* p. 79.

28. *Text und Interpretation,* pp. 71, 74; *Fugen,* p. 71. "The relation of a philosopher to his 'great name', that is, to the margin of the signature of his system," Derrida adds (*Fugen,* p. 76), "belongs to psychology — but to such a new type of psychology that it can no longer be grasped *within* the system

of philosophy as one of its parts nor within psychology seen as region of a philosophical encyclopedia."

29. Derrida, "Violence and Metaphysics," in *Writing and Difference*, trans. Alan Bass (Chicago: University of Chicago Press, 1978), esp. p. 146; *Spurs*, pp. 51, 103. On numerous occasions, it is true, Derrida retreats from a simple leap beyond metaphysics; e.g., when he says (*Spurs*, p. 85): "It is not the contrary (which once again would only amount to the very same thing) of what Heidegger is doing that we ourselves are about to do."

30. *Spurs*, pp. 81, 159; Heidegger, "Time and Being" (1961), in *On Time and Being*, trans. Joan Stambaugh (New York: Harper & Row, 1972), pp. 21–22. As the attached seminar synopsis states (p. 54): "The discussion of propriation is indeed the site of the farewell from Being and Time, but Being and Time remain, so to speak, as the gift of propriation."

31. *Text und Interpretation*, pp. 68, 72; *Fugen*, p. 75. The lingering subjectivism, it is true, if offset by passages pointing in the opposite direction; e.g., this statement (*Fugen*, p. 77): "Because the 'I' is constituted by the eternal recurrence, it does not exist nor sign prior to the narrative seen as eternal recurrence. Up to that point, *until now*, I as a living being am perhaps only a prejudice; it is the eternal recurrence which signs or seals. Thus, you cannot think or hear the name(s) of Friedrich Nietzsche prior to . . . the ring or bond of the eternal recurrence."

32. Nietzsche, *Ecce Homo*, trans. R. J. Hollingdale (New York: Penguin Books, 1979), pp. 33, 126; also *The Will to Power*, pp. 85, 196. From this perspective Nietzsche's love-hate relationship with Wagner appears less puzzling.

33. *The Portable Nietzsche*, pp. 50–51, 56, 171, 186–87; *The Will to Power*, p. 267. Compare also these lines, from the first part of *Thus Spoke Zarathustra* (*The Portable Nietzsche*, p. 146): "'I,' you say, and are proud of the word. But greater is that in which you do not wish to have faith—your body and its great reason: that does not say 'I,' but does 'I.'"

34. *Ecce Homo*, p. 38; *The Portable Nietzsche*, pp. 196–97.

35. *The Portable Nietzsche*, p. 233.

2. PHENOMENOLOGY AND CRITIQUE: ADORNO

1. Richard M. Zaner, *The Way of Phenomenology: Criticism as a Philosophical Discipline* (New York: Pegasus, 1970), p. xii.

2. Thus, Zaner (ibid., p. 207) elaborated on his own notion of criticism in these terms: "Critical philosophy is the rigorous science of presuppositions: of beginnings, origins, of foundations."

3. As Martin Jay comments (with some overstatement): "The Institute's zealous preservation of its outsider status was rooted in the recognition that such a position was in some way a precondition for the maintenance of a truly critical posture in its theoretical work. This meant, however, autonomy not only from normal politics, academic establishments, and mass culture, but also from any social forces claiming to embody negation. . . .

Despite their scorn for Mannheim's ideas about free-floating intellectuals, the Frankfurt School's members came increasingly to resemble his model." See *The Dialectical Imagination: A History of the Frankfurt School and the Institute of Social Research 1923–1950* (Boston: Little, Brown and Co., 1973), p. 292.

˝ 4. As the résumé of the dissertation (first published in 1924) stated, Husserl's thought was marked by "a basic contradiction: on the one hand, Husserl demands the constitution of all things or objects through a return to immediate evidence; on the other hand, objects are for him 'absolutely transcendent entities' which epistemologically may only be ascertainable through reference to consciousness but whose existence is in principle independent of consciousness." See Theodor W. Adorno, *Philosophische Frühschriften* (Gesammelte Schriften, Vol. 1), ed. by Rolf Tiedemann (Frankfurt-Main: Suhrkamp, 1973), p. 375 (abbreviated in the following as *PF*).

5. *PF*, pp. 13–17. For the English version of Husserl's statements see Edmund Husserl, *Ideas: General Introduction to Pure Phenomenology*, translated by W. R. Boyce Gibson (London: George Allen & Unwin, 1931), esp. Sections 42 and 49, pp. 133–35, 150–53.

6. Adorno, *PF*, pp. 34, 53–54, 71, 74–75, 377.

7. Ibid., esp. pp. 201–02, 218–23, 313–14.

8. Ibid., pp. 81, 320.

9. Ibid., pp. 318–19.

10. His second *Habilitationsschrift*, written at the close of the decade (and submitted to Paul Tillich in 1931), was indicative of a dramatic metamorphosis: devoted to an analysis of Kierkegaard's theory of aesthetics, the study launched a sustained and forceful attack on bourgeois subjectivism and spiritual "inwardness." See *Kierkegaard: Konstruktion des Ästhetischen* (Tübingen, 1933; rev. ed. Frankfurt-Main: Suhrkamp, 1966). According to Jay, the study was published on the very day Hitler took power in 1933; compare Jay, *The Dialectical Imagination*, pp. 66–68.

11. "Die Aktualität der Philosophie," *PF*, pp. 325–26.

12. *PF*, pp. 327–30. Adorno in this context refers to Heidegger's "so far available publications," presumably chiefly to *Sein und Zeit* (of 1927). As it seems to me, his comments capture a certain "anthropological" bias in Heidegger's early work; however, he neglects that *Dasein*, as presented in *Sein und Zeit*, cannot simply be equated with the traditional notion of "subjectivity" or subjective experience.

13. As Adorno worte, paraphrasing Benjamin: "The task of philosophy is not to search for manifest or latent intentions of reality, but rather to decipher non-intentional reality by means of the construction of designs and patterns of isolated elements which are able to dissolve those questions whose precise (empirical) formulation is the province of science." *PF*, p. 335.

14. Ibid., pp. 336–38.

15. The instrumentalist thrust was evident in many passages. In contrast to archetypes and mythical symbols, Adorno noted at one point, inter-

pretive designs are "man-made constructs": they are "handy and usable, instruments of human reason even in those cases when, like magnetic forces, they are able to focus objective reality in their direction." *PF,* p. 341.

16. In Adorno's words: "The neo-ontological conception of the structure of historicity provides only an apparent reconciliation of nature and history; despite the acknowledgment of history, access to the historical phenomenon or the ontological elucidation of this phenomenon is prevented by its immediate transsubstantiation into ontology." See "Die Idee der Naturgeschichte," *PF,* p. 351. The relationship of history and ontology was the topic of the so-called "Frankfurt Debate" during 1931 and 1932, a controversy in which Horkheimer and his friends attacked ontology as an ideological camouflage, while followers of Scheler and (to some extent) Heidegger insisted on the ontological foundation of history. Adorno's paper was meant as a contribution to this controversy.

17. *PF,* pp. 355–60. Adorno referred in this context chiefly to Benjamin's *Ursprung des deutschen Trauerspiels* (Berlin: de Gruyter, 1928). The notion of "natural history," incidentally, was not meant to denote a ready-made synthesis. As Adorno insisted, the student of natural history had first of all to accept the general discontinuity or dispersal of elements, including the discontinuity between "nature" (viewed as archaic-ontological substance) and "history" (viewed as innovative process). Instead of producing an indiscriminate amalgam or total vision, the task was to proceed from this discontinuity by exploring the "historical" implications of archaic (quasi-natural) myths and the archaic fiber of historical development; *PF,* pp. 361–65.

18. See "Thesen über die Sprache der Philosophen," *PF,* pp. 366–71, at p. 370. The notion of "configuration" was foreshadowed in the term "constellation" employed in the essay on natural history. The term referred to a procedural requirement in the study of natural history: the requirement to bring together a correlated assembly or structure of diverse concepts or categories, instead of a reliance on one-dimensional or unilinear exegesis. For a discussion of Adorno's literary and aesthetic views compare Fredric Jameson, *Marxism and Form: Twentieth-Century Dialectical Theories of Literature* (Princeton: Princeton University Press, 1971), pp. 3–59.

19. Max Horkheimer and Theodor W. Adorno, *Dialektik der Aufklärung: Philosophische Fragmente* (first published in Amsterdam, 1947; republished Frankfurt-Main: Fischer Verlag, 1969), p. 6. Compare also these statements (p. 46): "Enlightenment is more than enlightenment: namely, nature which becomes accessible in its alienation. . . . Enslavement to nature results from the very domination of nature without which reason cannot exist. The claim to domination can subside or dissolve only in a self-limiting move in which reason recognizes itself as mastery and thus as an element of nature." For comments on the study see Jay, *The Dialectical Imagination,* pp. 260–66; also his *Adorno* (Cambridge, MA: Harvard University Press, 1984), pp. 36–40.

20. Adorno, "Husserl and the Problem of Idealism," *The Journal of Phi-*

losophy 37 (January 1940), p. 6. Compare also the comment (p. 17): "Roughly his (i.e., Husserl's) problem may be stated as follows: he rebels against idealist thinking while attempting to break through the walls of idealism with purely idealist means, namely, by an exclusive analysis of the structure of thought and of consciousness."

21. In Adorno's words: Husserl's "struggle against psychologism does not mean the reintroduction of dogmatic prejudices, but the freeing of critical reason from the prejudices contained in the naive and uncritical religion of 'facts' which he challenged in its psychological form. It is this element of Husserl's philosophy in which I see even today its 'truth.'" "Husserl and the Problem of Idealism," p. 9. Somewhat later he added (p. 12): "If there were alive in Husserl some authoritarian drives, the desire to vindicate for truth a superhuman objectivity which must merely be recognized, there was also the contrary alive in him, a very critical attitude with an almost exaggerated fear in committing himself to any truth which could not be regarded as eternal and absolutely certain."

22. "Husserl and the Problem of Idealism," p. 18. Compare also the statement (p. 16): "The synthesis of judging is no categorial intuition because, according to Husserl, judgment in the sense of spontaneous thinking just requires its fulfillment by some sort of intuition. Reflection, however, being the necessary condition of that evidence which according to Husserl is guaranteed by categorial intuition, is as little intuitive as it is immediate."

23. Adorno, *Zur Metakritik der Erkenntnistheorie: Studien über Husserl und die phänomenologischen Antinomien* (1956, republished Frankfurt-Main: Suhrkamp, 1972), pp. 12–14; trans. by Willis Domingo under the title *Against Epistemology: A Metacritique* (Cambridge, MA: MIT Press, 1983), pp. 3–6. In the above and subsequent citations I have partially changed the translation for purposes of clarity.

24. *Against Epistemology*, pp. 6–8, 10, 12.

25. Ibid., pp. 13, 21–23.

26. Ibid., pp. 23–24, 193–94. Compare also the comment (p. 194): "While the phenomenologist insists on the subjective 'constitution' of objects, he actually treats these objects as completely alien and congealed entities to the point of contemplating and describing them as a 'second nature'—neglecting their subjective constituents."

27. Ibid., pp. 17–18, 190–91, 194–98, 210–12. Compare also the statement (p. 230): "'My' ego is actually an abstraction and by no means the primary experience claimed by Husserl. The possessive relationship is mediated in complex ways: 'intersubjectivity' is asserted simultaneously with the pronoun—not merely as a pure condition of possibility, but as a real premise of subjectivity without which the restrictive focus on 'my' ego is incomprehensible. By defining the ego as a category belonging to itself, Husserl's logic reveals precisely that it does not belong to itself. The impossibility, however, to grasp 'essences' from the perspective of an absolute monad is indicative of the position of the individual in monadological society."

28. Ibid., pp. 24–28, 38–40, 233–34. For further comments on the study compare Jay, *The Dialectical Imagination*, pp. 68–70; *Adorno*, pp. 32–33.

29. *Against Epistemology*, pp. 19–20, 22, 187–88. According to Adorno, the political dangers of an objectivist ontology were evident in fascism with its simultaneous stress on "blood and soil" and the "will to power": "Fascism tried to implement *prima philosophia*. The most archaic and most enduring was supposed to rule immediately and in a literal sense. In this manner the linkage of first beginnings and usurpation was placed into stark relief" (pp. 20–21).

30. Adorno, *The Jargon of Authenticity*, trans. Knut Tarnowski and Frederick Will (Evanston: Northwestern University Press, 1973), pp. 10–12. In the above and subsequent citations I have partially changed the translation for purposes of clarity.

31. Ibid., pp. 113–14, 116–18.

32. Ibid., pp. 124, 126–27. As Adorno added at another point (pp. 114–15): "Until further notice, authenticity and inauthenticity have as their criterion the decision of the individual subject choosing himself as his own possession. . . . Unable to rely any longer on other types of property, the individual clings to himself in his extreme abstractness as the last and supposedly inalienable possession." See also Jay, *Adorno*, p. 52.

33. *Jargon*, pp. 120–21. Compare also Trent Schroyer's comments ("Foreword," p. xvi): "Adorno's reconstruction of Heidegger's philosophy attempts to show that it becomes an ontology that retreats behind, rather than overcomes, the tradition of transcendental philosophy. In the universalization of transcendental subjectivity into *Dasein*, the empirical is totally lost and, as Adorno claims, an essence-mythology of Being emerges. This is exemplified in the claim that the primacy of *Dasein* is a realm beyond fact and essence and yet one which maintains itself as an identity."

34. Adorno, *Negative Dialectics*, trans. E. B. Ashon (New York: Seabury Press, 1973), p. xx. In the above and subsequent citations I have partially changed the translation for purposes of clarity.

35. Ibid., pp. 5, 10, 12, 22–23, 27. Compare also the statement (p. 5): "Dialectics is the consistent awareness of non-identity; it does not adopt an apriori standpoint. Thought is driven toward dialectics by virtue of its inevitable insufficiency, by its guilt toward its subject matter." As Adorno added, negative dialectics involved not so much the construction of a new philosophical system as the arrangement of conceptual configurations or "constellations" sensitive to the non-systematic and idiosyncratic character of reality (p. 53): "The inadequacy of every concept necessitates the reliance on other concepts; thus arise those constellations which alone preserve some of the virtues of individual names. The language of philosophy approximates names through their negation." Regarding "constellations" (and their relationship to "ideal types") see also p. 164.

36. Ibid., pp. 61, 68, 70, 80–81, 95.

37. Ibid., pp. 84, 105, 127–28.

38. Ibid., pp. 85, 106, 174–175. On the issue of "totality" compart Martin Jay, *Marxism and Totality* (Berkeley: University of California Press, 1984), esp. pp. 241–275.

39. *Negative Dialectics*, pp. 78, 114–15. Compare also the comment (p. 76): "Elevated above facticity and idea, being is exempt from criticism; whatever target the critic may choose, is dismissed as misunderstanding. From facticity the concept borrows the air of solid concreteness, of not being subjectively constituted, of a thing-in-itself; conversely, ontic reality derives from synthesizing reflection the aura of the supraempirical: the sanctity of transcendence."

40. Ibid., pp. 104, 115–17.

41. Ibid., pp. 82–83, 136, 207. Regarding the relationship between Heidegger and Marx, Adorno noted (p. 200): "Despite some affinity, the term 'being' means something entirely different to Marx and to Heidegger. the ontological doctrine of the primacy (or transcendence) of being over thought contains a distant echo of materialism. The doctrine of being turns into ideology when it spiritualizes the materialist element by transposing it to a level of pure essence beyond ontic reality—thus discarding the critique of false consciousness inherent in the materialist notion of being. The notion which was meant to mobilize truth against ideology degenerates into complete falsehood: the denial of idealism into the proclamation of an ideal sphere."

42. For somewhat similar arguments, formulated on the level of language philosophy, see Jacques Derrida, *Speech and Phenomena, And Other Essays on Husserl's Theory of Signs*, trans. David B. Allison (Evanston: Northwestern University Press, 1973).

43. Compare, e.g., Heidegger, *Die Technik und die Kehre* (Pfullingen: Neske, 1962).

44. *Negative Dialectics*, p. 54.

45. Compare the statement: "The suspicion may arise that the attempted experience of the essence of a 'thing' is predicated on arbitrary etymological construction. . . . In reality, however, what is involved here and in other instances is not that our thinking is parasitical on etymology but that etymology depends on the contemplation of essential traits which are implicitly intimated in words." See Heidegger, "Das Ding," in *Vorträge und Aufsätze* (3rd ed., Pfullingen: Neske, 1967), Part II, pp. 46–47. One can also not ignore in this context the peculiarity of Adorno's own style.

46. Heidegger, *On Time and Being*, trans. by Joan Stambaugh (New York: Harper & Row, 1972), p. 71.

47. Heidegger, "Das Ding," pp. 46, 50, 52–53. Regarding "appropriation" (*Ereignis*) see also Otto Pöggeler, "Being as Appropriation," *Philosophy Today* 19 (1975), pp. 152–78.

48. Heidegger, ". . . Dichterisch wohnet der Mensch . . . ," *Vorträge und Aufsätze*, Part II, p. 67.

49. See Heidegger, *Identität und Differenz* (Pfullingen: Neske, 1957),

pp. 14–15, 20, 25–28, 36–37, 50, 53–54; also "Überwindung der Metaphysik," *Vorträge und Aufsätze*, Part I, pp. 69–70, and "Moira," ibid., Part III, p. 36.

50. Compare in this context Jürgen Habermas, "Mit Heidegger gegen Heidegger denken: zur Veröffentlichung von Vorlesungen aus dem Jahre 1935," *Frankfurter Allgemeine Zeitung*, July 25, 1953; reprinted in *Philosophisch-politische Profile* (Frankfurt-Main: Suhrkamp, 1971), pp. 67–75.

51. Concerning passages alleged to betray a "rustic" ideology see Adorno, *The Jargon of Authenticity*, pp. 52–58. Compare also Habermas, "Urbanisierung der Heideggerschen Provinz: Laudatio auf Hans-Georg Gadamer," in Gadamer and Habermas, *Das Erbe Hegels* (Frankfurt-Main: Suhrkamp, 1979), pp. 11–31, trans. by Frederick G. Lawrence under the title "Hans-Georg Gadamer: Urbanizing the Heideggerian Province" in Habermas, *Philosophical-Political Profiles* (Cambridge, MA: MIT Press, 1983), pp. 189–97; and Robert Sokolowski, *Husserlian Meditations* (Evanston: Northwestern University Press, 1974), pp. 212, 213, n. 7.

52. Adorno, *Negative Dialectics*, p. 365; Heidegger, *Discourse on Thinking*, trans. John M. Anderson and E. Hans Freud (New York: Harper & Row, 1969), pp. 48–49, 53–54.

3. LIFE-WORLD AND COMMUNICATIVE ACTION: HABERMAS

1. Jürgen Habermas, *Theorie des kommunikativen Handelns*, 2 vols. (Frankfurt-Main: Suhrkamp, 1981); hereafter cited as *Theorie*. In the meantime the English translation of the first volume has appeared under the title *The Theory of Communicative Action*, vol. 1: *Reason and the Rationalization of Society*, trans. Thomas McCarthy (Boston: Beacon Press, 1984), hereafter cited as *Reason*. I have compared my translation with McCarthy's, but have not always adapted mine to his. In the text I shall refer to the entire study as *Theory of Communicative Action*, to approximate more closely the German title.

2. *Theorie*, vol. 1, pp. 367–452, vol. 2, pp. 171–293. In his translation McCarthy renders *Zwischenbetrachtungen* as "intermediate reflections"; see *Reason*, p. 273.

3. Habermas, *Knowledge and Human Interests*, trans. Jeremy J. Shapiro (Boston: Beacon Press, 1971), p. 137 (translation slightly altered).

4. Habermas, "Nachwort (1973)" to *Erkenntnis und Interesse* (Frankfurt-Main: Suhrkamp, 1973), p. 397; for an English version see "A Postscript to *Knowledge and Human Interests*," *Philosophy of the Social Sciences* 3 (1975), p. 181. Compare also the sections on "knowledge and interest" and "action and discourse" in the "Introduction" (1971) to *Theory and Practice*, trans. John Viertel (Boston: Beacon Press, 1973), pp. 7–10, 16–19. The distinction between life-praxis and discourses (or between the "apriori of experience" and the "apriori of argumentation") was further fleshed out in Habermas, "Wahrheitstheorien," in Helmut Fahrenbach, ed., *Wirklichkeit und Reflexion: Walter Schulz zum 60.Geburstag* (Pfullingen: Newke, 1973), pp. 211–65.

5. Compare, e.g., Habermas, "Towards a Theory of Communicative Competence," *Inquiry* 13 (1970), pp. 360–75; also the essays "What is Universal Pragmatics?" and "Moral Development and Ego Identity," in Habermas, *Communication and the Evolution of Society*, trans. Thomas McCarthy (Boston: Beacon Press, 1979), pp. 1–68, 69–94.

6. *Theorie*, vol. 1, pp. 28, 30; *Reason*, pp. 10–11. I prefer to translate *Verständigung* as "consensus" (or consensual interaction) rather than "understanding" since the latter can be unilateral whereas *Verständigung* is always reciprocal.

7. *Theorie*, vol. 1, pp. 37, 44; *Reason*, pp. 17, 22. As a fourth arena of communication amenable to discursive validation (by means of "explicative discourse") the study mentions linguistic "comprehensibility" or the correctness of symbolic expressions. Reformulating the same basic perspective a later passage states (*Theorie*, vol. 1, p. 114; *Reason*, p. 75): "The concept of communicative rationality refers, on the one hand, to different forms of the discursive redemption of validity claims (in this sense Wellmer speaks of 'discursive rationality'); on the other hand, it points to different 'world' relations into which communicative agents enter by raising validity claims for their utterances."

8. *Theorie*, vol. 1, pp. 126–27, 129–30; *Reason*, pp. 85, 87–88.

9. *Theorie*, vol. 1, pp. 127–28, 132, 137, 140; *Reason*, pp. 85–86, 88–91, 93. The "dramaturgical" approach has been articulated chiefly by Goffman and some spokesmen of phenomenological interactionism.

10. *Theorie*, vol. 1, pp. 128, 141–43, 147–48; *Reason*, pp. 86, 94–96, 98–99.

11. *Theorie*, vol. 1, pp. 385–87, 389–90, 396; *Reason*, pp. 285–87, 289–90, 295. The distinction is further elaborated in these terms (*Theorie*, vol. 1, p. 394; *Reason*, p. 293): "Perlocutionary effects, like the results of teleological actions in general, can be described as mundane states of affairs produced by intervention in the world. By contrast, illocutionary effects are reached on the level of interpersonal relations in which participants achieve a consensus about something in the world; these effects are thus not '*innerworldly*' but extra-mundane."

12. *Theorie*, vol. 1, pp. 398–401, 406, 410, 412–14; *Reason*, pp. 296–98, 305, 307–09. Habermas rounds out his scheme of speech acts (*Theorie*, vol. 1, p. 436; *Reason*, p. 326) by adding "communicative acts" (dealing with the organization of discourse) and "operative acts" (reflecting the internal logic or syntax of speech). Introducing the new category of "conversation," he also links speech acts with corresponding action types (*Theorie*, vol. 1, pp. 437–39; *Reason*, pp. 327–29): namely, constatives with conversation, regulatives with norm-regulated action, expressives with dramaturgical action, and perlocutionary acts with teleological-strategic action.

13. *Theorie*, vol. 1, pp. 449, 451; *Reason*, pp. 335–36. Habermas also depicts the life-world as "a continent that remains hidden so long as the theorist analyses speech acts from the perspective of the speaker who, in his ut-

terance, places himself in relation to something in the objective, social and subjective worlds" (*Theorie*, vol. 1, p. 452; *Reason*, p. 337).

14. Habermas, *Legitimation Crisis*, trans. Thomas McCarthy (Boston: Beacon Press, 1975), pp. 4–5.

15. *Theorie*, vol. 1, pp. 32, 106–08; *Reason*, pp. 13, 69–71. For the distinction between "world" and "life-world" compare also pp. 123–24 (*Reason*, p. 82) where Habermas places the accent on the different attitude — nonreflective vs. reflective — which members assume toward the cultural tradition: "In the *one* case the shared cultural tradition of a community is constitutive for the life-world which members encounter as a pre-interpreted context; the shared life-world forms here the background for communicative action. . . . In the *other* case particular ingredients of the cultural tradition are specifically thematized; now members must adopt a reflective attitude toward cultural meaning patterns which otherwise render possible their efforts of interpretation."

16. *Theorie*, vol. 2, pp. 179, 187–89, 192.

17. Ibid., vol. 2, pp. 208–09, 218. In this context (pp. 210–12) Habermas chides Schutz, Durkheim, and Mead for a one-sided focus on *one* component of the life-world: Schutz on culture, Durkheim on society, and Mead on socialization.

18. *Theorie*, vol. 2, pp. 226–28, 273, 293.

19. *Knowledge and Human Interests*, pp. 137, 167; "Technology and Science as 'Ideology'," in Habermas, *Toward a Rational Society*, trans. Jeremy J. Shapiro (Boston: Beacon Press, 1970), p. 91.

20. *Theorie*, vol. 1, pp. 28, 32, 386–87; vol. 2, pp. 193–94; *Reason*, pp. 10, 13, 287. Compare also the comment (*Theorie*, vol. 1, p. 410; *Reason*, p. 305): "As communicative action we describe all those interactions in which participants coordinate their individual action plans without reservations on the basis of a communicatively achieved consensus. . . . Communicative action embraces only those speech acts with which a speaker raises reviewable validity claims." What these and similar statements leave open is whether achieved consensus yields a common or joint action plan or only the pursuit of divergent goals on the basis of a reciprocal acknowledgment of differences.

21. *Theorie*, vol. 1, pp. 141, 143, 148, 370; vol. 2, pp. 190–92; *Reason*, pp. 94, 99, 274. Even when presenting language as precondition of interaction Habermas oscillates between an "ontological" and a "transcendental" construal (where the latter specifies a foundational or apriori "condition of possibility"). Thus, after noting the "non-surpassable" character of language and the life-world, he adds (*Theorie*, vol. 2, p. 192): "The structures of the life-world determine the forms of possible intersubjective consensus. . . . The life-world is, so to speak, the transcendental plane on which speaker and hearer encounter each other."

22. Anthony Giddens, "Labour and Interaction," in his *Profiles and Critiques in Social Theory* (London: Macmillan, 1982), p. 108.

23. *Theorie*, vol. 1, pp. 371, 390, 394, 396; *Reason*, pp. 274, 290, 293, 295.

24. *Theorie,* vol. 1, pp. 150–51; vol. 2, pp. 193–94; *Reason,* p. 101.

25. *Knowledge and Human Interests,* pp. 167–68, 172; "Nachwort (1973)" to *Erkenntnis und Interesse,* pp. 386, 397. Habermas acknowledged only an indirect linkage between discourses and life-praxis: argumentation or the praxis of inquiry could proceed only within the boundaries of a given experiential domain. Compare also *Theory and Practice,* p. 18.

26. Agnes Heller, "Habermas and Marxism," in John B. Thompson and David Held, eds., *Habermas: Critical Debates* (Cambridge, Mass.: MIT Press, 1982), pp. 25, 29; *Theorie,* vol. 1, pp. 400–01; *Reason,* pp. 297–98. For an argument that Habermas's general framework tends to resolve the theory-practice issue in favor of theory see my "Between Theory and Practice," *Human Studies* 3 (1980), pp. 175–84.

27. Karl-Otto Apel, *Transformation der Philosophie* (Frankfurt-Main: Suhrkamp, 1973), vol. 1, pp. 38–39; Habermas, *Legitimation Crisis,* pp. 4–5; *Theorie,* vol. 2, pp. 179, 187–88, 200. In a more critical fashion Alexandre Métraux pointed to a certain half-heartedness in the phenomenological approach: "Although taking as its point of departure quite correctly the 'world of the natural attitude', Husserl's account continues to be permeated by a dualist conception of the relationship between subject and world which finds no warrant in everyday experience." See his preface to Aron Gurwitsch, *Die mitmenschlichen Begegnungen in der Milieuwelt* (Berlin and New York: de Gruyter, 1977), p. xx. For a defense of the "strong view" of the life-world, against Habermas's own half-heartedness, see Ulf Matthiesen, *Das Dickicht der Lebenswelt und die Theorie des kommunikativen Handelns* (Munich: Fink, 1983); also Dieter Misgeld, "Communication and Societal Rationalization: A Review Essay of Jürgen Habermas's *Theorie des kommunikativen Handelns,*" *Canadian Journal of Sociology* 8 (1983), pp. 433–53, esp. pp. 438–39.

28. *Theorie,* vol. 2, pp. 192, 210–12, 223, 229, 561, 589.

29. For a general critique of Habermas's view of social development see my *Twilight of Subjectivity: Contributions to a Post-Individualist Theory of Politics* (Amherst: University of Massachusetts Press, 1981), pp. 179–207; also Michael Schmid, "Habermas's Theory of Social Evolution," in *Habermas: Critical Debates,* pp. 162–80.

30. *Theorie,* vol. 2, pp. 233–34, 237–38, 244. The dilemma carries over into sociological and anthropological methodology. Though admitting the problem Habermas fails to draw broader theoretical conclusions from it. Due to the coincidence of archaic society with the "socio-cultural life-world," he claims (pp. 245–46), anthropology has tended to be a "hermeneutical science *par excellence.*" Simultaneously he recognizes, however, that the overlapping of systemic and social integration renders social processes at that stage "not only transparent but also in many ways opaque." The latter aspect, in his view, accounts for the incursion of depth psychology and linguistic structuralism into anthropology.

31. *Theorie,* vol. 1, pp. 104, 112; vol. 2, pp. 588–89; *Reason,* pp. 68, 72. Habermas's oscillation in these matters recurs also in his discussion of "worldviews" and of the meaning-context issue. "Through their holistic character,"

he writes (*Theorie*, vol. 1, pp. 92–93; *Reason*, p. 58), "world-views, it is true, are removed from the domain in which truth criteria can meaningfully be applied; even the choice of criteria determining the truth status of utterances may depend on the fundamental context of a world-view. This does not mean, however, that the idea of truth itself should be construed in a particularist sense: whichever language system we choose, we always rely intuitively on the premise that truth is a universal validity claim." Appealing to Searle's speech-act theory, Habermas notes at another point (*Theorie*, vol. 1, p. 450; *Reason*, pp. 335–36): "Once we begin to alter relatively deep-seated and trivial background conditions, we notice that apparently context-invariant validity conditions change their meaning and thus are by no means absolute." To which he adds: "Actually, the knowledge of the validity conditions of a speech act must not depend *completely* on contingent background assumptions— for otherwise formal pragmatics would lose its subject matter." To use Giddens' phrase, these instances are good examples of "wanting to have one's cake and eat it too." See *Profiles and Critiques in Social Theory*, p. 108.

32. *Theorie*, vol. 2, pp. 165, 178–79, 488, 536, 541. As in the case of other key issues, Habermas is profoundly ambivalent regarding the formalization and "juridification" of ethics. In modern societies, he notes (vol. 2, p. 166), traditional life-forms "have lost their totalizing and exclusive sway, having been subordinated to the universalism of law and ethics; but as concrete life-forms they obey a standard other than universalization." Concerning juridification the study (vol. 2, pp. 541–42) finds the central ailment of contemporary welfare society in the use of the law as a functional "medium" rather than an "institution" adapted to life-world processes (a diagnosis of disarming simplicity).

33. *Theorie*, vol. 1, pp. 106–07; vol. 2, pp. 15–30, 65–68, 147–63 (on Mead), 192, 197–98; *Reason*, pp. 69–70. Compare Habermas's somewhat bland observation (*Theorie*, vol. 2, p. 279): "After the paradigm change brought about by the theory of communication the formal properties of possible intersubjective consensus can take the place of the (Kantian) conditions of possibility of objective experience." The restatement of Mead's approach is problematical not only because of implicit idealist or quasi-idealist premises but because, in Habermas's own account, the process of rationalization is liable to render increasingly tenuous the self-society correlation (or the mediation between personal identity and social solidarity). In his Introduction McCarthy is more sanguine on this issue (*Reason*, pp. xx–xxi)—an assessment I cannot fully share. For a detailed discussion of intersubjectivity, especially in the context of phenomenological literature, see my *Twilight of Subjectivity*, pp. 38–115; also Michael Theunissen, *The Other: Studies in the Social Ontology of Husserl, Heidegger, Sartre, and Buber* (Cambridge, Mass.: MIT Press, 1984).

34. *Theorie*, vol. 1, pp. 75, 80–81, 83, 100, 376, 386, 415; *Reason*, pp. 45, 49, 51, 64, 278, 286, 309. Indebtedness to the "philosophy of consciousness" is equally clear in the portrayal of art as subjective "expression"—a portrayal which ignores both Heidegger's and Gadamer's arguments to the con-

trary; see Hans-Georg Gadamer, *Truth and Method* (New York: Seabury Press, 1975), pp. 39–90, and Heidegger, "The Origin of the Work of Art," in *Poetry, Language, Thought,* trans. Albert Hofstadter (New York: Harper & Row, 1971), pp. 17–87.

35. A pioneering venture, of course, was Heidegger's notion of "being-in-the-world" as developed in *Being and Time* (of 1927), trans. John Macquarrie and Edward Robinson (London: SCM Press, 1962). Compare also Heidegger, "The Age of the World View," trans. Marjoric Grene, in W. V. Spanos, ed., *Martin Heidegger and the Question of Literature* (Bloomington: Indiana University Press, 1979), pp. 1–15; and Jacques Derrida, "Signature Event Context," *Glyph* 1 (Baltimore: Johns Hopkins University Press, 1977), pp. 182–97. *The-ory of Communicative Action* repeatedly singles out Heidegger and poststruc-turalist writers as "bêtes noirs" for their critique of rationalization; e.g., vol. 2, pp. 165, 222.

36. As Habermas asserts in the opening section (*Theorie,* vol. 1, pp. 18, 20; *Reason,* pp. 3, 5): Among the social sciences, and especially in contrast with political science and political economy, "it is sociology which in its conceptual structure is closest to the problematic of rationality. . . . Alone among social-scientific disciplines sociology has maintained attention to the questions of society as a whole." Compare also *Theory and Practice,* pp. 47–48.

37. *Theorie,* vol. 2, pp. 219, 221. In this and other passages Habermas uncritically accepts the positivist thesis of enlightenment leading from theology over metaphysics to positive science—an endorsement warranting the charge of the incipient positivism of his framework. See, e.g., Giddens, *Profiles and Critiques in Social Theory,* p. 97.

38. Heller, "Habermas and Marxism," in *Habermas: Critical Debates,* pp. 27, 31. Compare also her comments (pp. 23, 36): "Marx's theory had one advantage, as well as a certain grandeur which disappears in Habermas's in-terpretation: Marx grasped human progress as suffering. He conceives of the fate of the individual human being together with the development of produc-tion and of institutions. . . . Even in a world of organized discourse, our main needs will be those we once attributed to God: creation and love."

39. Martin Heidegger, "Hölderlins Hymne 'Andenken,'" (*Gesamtaus-gabe,* vol. 52), ed. Curd Ochwadt (Frankfurt-Main: Klostermann, 1982), pp. 157, 161, 165. For a detailed elaboration of the concept "world" in its various mean-ings see Heidegger, "Die Grundbegriffe der Metaphysik: Welt-Endlichkeit-Einsamkeit," (*Gesamtausgabe,* vol. 29/30), ed. F.-W. von Herrmann (Frankfurt-Main: Klostermann, 1983).

4. APEL'S TRANSFORMATION OF PHILOSOPHY

1. See Karl-Otto Apel, *Transformation der Philosophie,* 2 vols. (Frankfurt-Main: Suhrkamp, 1973); trans. by Glyn Adey and David Frisby under the title *Towards a Transformation of Philosophy* (London: Routledge & Kegan

Paul, 1980). Since the English translation does not contain all the essays assembled in the original two volumes, I shall in the following rely on both the German and English versions.

2. *Towards a Transformation*, p. ix; *Transformation der Philosophie*, vol. 1, pp. 9–12.

3. *Transformation der Philosophie*, vol. 1, p. 7.

4. Ibid., vol. 1, pp. 80, 87–89, 94–96, 98–100.

5. Ibid., vol. 1, pp. 142–46, 149–51, 154–56, 163–66. The constitutive conception of language is further explored in "Language and Order: Linguistic Analysis versus Linguistic Hermeneutics," pp. 167–96.

6. *Transformation der Philosophie*, vol. 1, pp. 225–29, 238–42, 246–50, 262–64, 268–72.

7. Ibid., vol. 1, pp. 280–86, 290–94, 330–34.

8. Ibid., vol. 1, pp. 344–48, 356–57, 364–71, 374–75; *Towards a Transformation*, pp. 8–12, 20–21, 27–32, 35–36.

9. *Transformation der Philosophie*, vol. 1, pp. 137 (note 36), 166 (note 41), 273–75, 377. The reference in the two footnotes is to Ernst Tugendhat, *Der Wahrheitsbegriff bei Husserl und Heidegger* (Berlin: Walter de Gruyter, 1967).

10. *Transformation der Philosophie*, vol. 2, pp. 9–10, 12–14, 18–20.

11. Ibid., vol. 2, pp. 96–100, 102–04, 111–14, 122–27, 153; *Towards a Transformation*, pp. 46–49, 51–53, 58–60, 67–72. The last citation is taken from the essay "Science as Emancipation?" ("Wissenschaft als Emanzipation?") In that essay Apel distanced himself explicitly from Habermas's parallel effort to formulate a tripartite epistemology closely linking interest and knowledge in *Knowledge and Human Interests*. Partly under the impact of that critique Habermas subsequently restated his position; see esp. Jürgen Habermas, *Theory and Practice*, pp. 1–40, and "A Postscript to *Knowledge and Human Interests*," *Philosophy of the Social Sciences* 3 (1975), pp. 157–89. For a more detailed discussion see "Critical Epistemology Criticized" in my *Beyond Dogma and Despair* (Notre Dame: University of Notre Dame Press, 1981), pp. 246–69.

12. *Transformation der Philosophie*, vol. 2, pp. 157–60, 163–64, 170–76; *Towards a Transformation*, pp. 77–80, 84–88. Compare also Apel, *Der Denkweg von Charles S. Pierce* (Frankfurt-Main: Suhrkamp, 1975).

13. *Transformation der Philosophie*, vol. 2, pp. 178–88, 199–201, 214–16; *Towards a Transformation*, pp. 93–102, 110–12, 122–24.

14. *Transformation der Philosophie*, vol. 2, pp. 220–25, 250–54; *Towards a Transformation*, pp. 136–40, 161–64. Compare also my "Hermeneutics and Historicism: Reflections on Winch, Apel, and Vico" in *Beyond Dogma and Despair*, pp. 139–55.

15. *Transformation der Philosophie*, vol. 2, pp. 311–12, 326, 329, 332–33, 354–55, 359–435; *Towards a Transformation*, pp. 225–85. Compare also my "Toward a Critical Reconstruction of Ethics and Politics," in *Beyond Dogma and Despair*, pp. 270–93; and my "Ordinary Language and Ideal Speech" in

Twilight of Subjectivity: Contributions to a Post-Individualist Theory of Politics, pp. 220–54.

16. *Transformation der Philosophie*, vol. 2, pp. 119–21; *Towards a Transformation*, pp. 64–66.

17. *Transformation der Philosophie*, vol. 2, p. 119; *Towards a Transformation*, p. 65. The issue of identity-formation in the context of universal normative principles is discussed by Habermas in "Können komplexe Gesellschaften eine vernünftige Identitat ausbilden?" in his *Zur Rekonstruktion des historischen Materialismus* (Frankfurt-Main: Suhrkamp, 1976), pp. 92–126.

18. *Transformation der Philosophie*, vol. 1, pp. 11–12, 38–39.

19. Ibid., vol. 1, pp. 117, 122.

20. Ibid., vol. 1, pp. 25–26, 39–40.

21. The difficulty of confining Heidegger's thought in the parameters of this framework is occasionally conceded by Apel himself: e.g., in pointing to the former's effort to escape the dualism or "abstract disjunction" of apriorism and empiricism. A similar concession is implicit in the notion of a post-idealist phenomenology. In the words of the Introduction: "A dialectical construed phenomenology can and should start dialectically, that is, at the point of the mediation of the 'equally primary' moments of spirit and matter; in doing so it would correspond to the 'pre-structure of understanding' discovered by Heidegger." *Transformation der Philosophie*, vol. 1, p. 52.

22. *Transformation der Philosophie*, vol. 1, pp. 35, 41, 43; see also Martin Heidegger, *Zur Sache des Denkens* (Tübingen: Niemeyer, 1969), pp. 76–77.

23. *Transformation der Philosophie*, vol. 1, pp. 41, 75.

24. *Transformation der Philosophie*, vol. 1, pp. 46, 54; vol. 2, pp. 18, 117; *Towards a Transformation*, p. 63.

25. *Transformation der Philosophie*, vol. 2, p. 15. For a critique of the notion of a neutral spectator or "transcendental subject" see especially Richard Rorty, *Philosophy and the Mirror of Nature*.

26. *Transformation der Philosophie*, vol. 1, pp. 46–47, 49.

27. Ibid., vol. 1, p. 51. Gadamer's objection to critique of ideology derives chiefly from the reluctance of critic or analyst to recognize and take seriously the "otherness" of the patient or fellow-citizen (afflicted with "false consciousness"). Although conceding the "scandalous" character of the objectification of patients, Apel considers the approach justified by virtue of a possible cognitive progress (vol. 1, p. 56).

28. Ibid., vol. 1, pp. 59–60; vol. 2, p. 354.

29. Ibid., vol. 1, pp. 61–62; vol. 2, p. 333.

30. Ibid., vol. 2, pp. 40, 186; *Towards a Transformation*, p. 100.

31. *Transformation der Philosophie*, vol. 1, pp. 376–77; vol. 2, pp. 87–89, 186; *Towards a Transformation*, p. 99. Compare also the essay on "The Community of Communication as Transcendental Premise of the Social Sciences" (*Transformation der Philosophie*, vol. 2, pp. 248–249; *Towards a Transformation*, pp. 159–60) where Apel discusses the dilemmas encountered both

by a transcendental and an empirical-behavioral interpretation of the theory of language games.

32. *Transformation der Philosophie*, vol. 1, pp. 132, 194, 247–49, 274.

33. Ibid., vol. 1, pp. 76, 369, note 44; vol. 2, pp. 99, 113; *Towards a Transformation*, pp. 48, 60.

34. *Transformation der Philosophie*, vol. 1, pp. 192–93, vol. 2, p. 23.

35. Apel, "Zur Idee einer transzendentalen Sprach-Pragmatik," in Josef Simon, ed., *Aspekte und Probleme der Sprachphilosophie* (Freiburg: Karl Alber, 1974), p. 297. Compare also "Das Problem der philosophischen Letztbegründung im Lichte einer transzendentalen Sprachpragmatik," in Bernulf Kanitscheider, ed., *Sprache und Erkenntnis* (Innsbrucker Beiträge zur Kulturwissenschaft, vol. 19, 1976), pp. 62–63; "Sprechakttheorie und transzendentale Sprachpragmatik zur Frage ethischer Normen," in Apel, ed., *Sprachpragmatik und Philosophie* (Frankfurt-Main: Suhrkamp, 1976), pp. 19–21.

36. *Transformation der Philosophie*, vol. 1, pp. 274–75, 377; *Towards a Transformation*, p. 38.

5. HERMENEUTICS AND DECONSTRUCTION: GADAMER AND DERRIDA IN DIALOGUE

1. Giambattista Vico, *The New Science*, trans. and ed. Thomas G. Bergin and Max H. Fisch (New York: Anchor Books, 1961), p. 88 (section 405).

2. Compare on this score especially the debate between Gadamer and Habermas in *Hermeneutik und Ideologiekritik* (Frankfurt-Main: Suhrkamp, 1971); see also Dieter Misgeld, "Critical Theory and Hermeneutics: The Debate between Habermas and Gadamer," in John O'Neill, ed., *On Critical Theory* (New York: Seabury Press, 1976), pp. 164–83, and Thomas McCarthy, "Rationality and Relativism: Habermas's 'Overcoming' of Hermeneutics," in John B. Thompson and David Held, eds., *Habermas: Critical Debates* (Cambridge, MA: MIT Press, 1982), pp. 57–78.

3. Philippe Forget, ed., *Text und Interpretation* (Munich: Fink Verlag, 1984).

4. Hans-Georg Gadamer, "Text und Interpretation," in Forget, *Text und Interpretation*, pp. 24–25. Gadamer's statement was originally presented as a lecture on April 25, 1981 in Paris.

5. *Text und Interpretation*, pp. 26–29.

6. Ibid., pp. 26–27, 29. At this point Gadamer endorsed a kind of "existentialist" reading of Hegel, a reading identifying Hegel's philosophy with what Charles Taylor has called "interpretive or hermeneutical dialectics"; see Taylor, *Hegel and Modern Society* (Cambridge: Cambridge University Press, 1979), p. 64.

7. *Text und Interpretation*, pp. 28–30. The last sentences seem to be directed chiefly against Habermas's discursive or consensual model of communication.

8. Ibid., pp. 30–31. For the Socratic model of dialogue see also Gadamer, *Truth and Method* (New York: Seabury Press, 1975), pp. 325–33.

9. *Text und Interpretation*, pp. 27–28.

10. Ibid., pp. 35–38, 43–46. Compare also Paul Ricoeur, *Freud and Philosophy: An Essay on Interpretation*, trans. Dennis Savage (New Haven: Yale University Press, 1970), pp. 32–36; also Gadamer, "The Hermeneutics of Suspicion," in Gary Shapiro and Alan Sica, eds., *Hermeneutics: Questions and Prospects* (Amherst, MA: University of Massachusetts Press, 1984), pp. 54–65. Gadamer's statement attributed a somewhat greater autonomy to the category of "literary texts"—where autonomy means relative independence both from the intended meaning of authors (and previous interpreters) and from any "reference" to real contexts. Even here, however, the hermeneutical yardstick was not suspended (p. 51): "Language and written text always imply an (ideal) reference: they *are* not, but they *mean* something, and this is true even if the intended meaning resides nowhere but in the text itself. Poetic language exists only in the performance of speaking or reading—which means: it does not exist without being understood."

11. Derrida, "Guter Wille zur Macht (I)," in *Text und Interpretation*, pp. 56–58. As the editor of the volume, Philippe Forget, rightly remarks in his Introduction, some points of Derrida's intervention seem to derive from "simple" misunderstanding: for example, the affiliation of "good will" with Kantian ethics tends to neglect Gadamer's Platonic-Aristotelian leanings, while the alleged hermeneutical absorption of psychoanalysis seems applicable more to Ricoeur than to Gadamer; see Forget, "Leitfäden einer unwahrscheinlichen Debatte," *Text und Interpretation*, pp. 8–9, 15.

12. Gadamer, "Und dennoch: Macht des guten Willens," *Text und Interpretation*, pp. 59–60. As he added (pp. 60–61), by shunning the hermeneutical yardstick Derrida was no longer "in agreement with himself. That he appeals to Nietzsche on this point makes sense—but only because both are in conflict with themselves: both speak and write in order to be understood."

13. Ibid., pp. 60–61.

14. Derrida, "Guter Wille zur Macht (II)," *Text und Interpretation*, pp. 62–63, 66, 69–70.

15. *Text und Interpretation*, p. 72. The term "cause" stands here as translation for "Sache," "Streitfall" or "Auseinandersetzung" which appear in the opening sentences of the Preface to Heidegger's Nietzsche-interpretation. As Derrida adds (p. 73): "Here is perhaps the point at issue between 'the Nietzsches' and Martin Heidegger, between the Nietzsches and the mentioned Western metaphysics. Since Aristotle and at least until Bergson, 'this' metaphysics has constantly reiterated and assumed that thinking and saying means to think and say 'something' which would be *one* thing and one *thing*. . . . It is the *legein* of this *logos*, and the whole unity of this logic, which is called into question by the Nietzsches. This plural begins to resemble the family names of tricksters and mountebanks." Compare also Martin Heidegger, *Nietzsche*, vol. I (2nd ed.; Pfullingen: Neske, 1961), p. 9.

16. *Text und Interpretation*, pp. 75–76.

17. Gadamer, *Truth and Method*, pp. 40, 76, 85 (translation slightly altered).

18. *Truth and Method*, pp. 91–92 (translation slightly altered). See also Heidegger, "The Origin of the Work of Art," in David F. Krell, ed., *Martin Heidegger: Basic Writings* (New York: Harper and Row, 1977), pp. 143–187.

19. *Truth and Method*, pp. 92–93, 95–96. These comments did not prevent Gadamer from stressing *also* the transitive character of playing and the intentional activity of players (p. 96): "Apart from these general determining features, it seems to me characteristic of human play that it plays *something*. This means that the structure of movement to which it submits has a definite quality which the player 'chooses'. . . . That all play is a playing of something is true here where the ordered to-and-fro movement of the game is determined as a behavior marked off from other modes of behavior."

20. *Truth and Method*, pp. 99–101 (translation slightly altered). In Gadamer's portrayal, transformative rupture is particularly pronounced in the case of literature or written texts (p. 145): "Literature has a unique and incomparable mode of being; it presents a specific problem to understanding. There is nothing so strange or alien and at the same time so demanding as the written text. Not even the encounter with speakers of a foreign tongue can be compared with this strangeness. . . . Writing and what partakes of it, literature, is the intelligibility of mind transferred to the most alien medium. Nothing is so purely mental trace as writing, but also nothing so dependent on the understanding mind."

21. *Truth and Method*, pp. 86, 146 (translation slightly altered). The last statement clearly illustrates Gadamer's ambivalence: his oscillation between an ontological "event or happening" (in Heidegger's sense) and the stress on intelligible "meaning" or significance. Gadamer, it is true, tends to construe this oscillation in a Hegelian (dialectical) vein—which is further evidence of his idealist moorings. Revealingly, both his critique of "aesthetic consciousness" and his defense of the "ontology" of art-works terminate in a discussion of Hegel; see pp. 87–89, 147–50.

22. Jacques Derrida, *Spurs: Nietzsche's Styles*, pp. 49–51, 57 (translation slightly altered). Compare also Derrida, "The Question of Style," in David B. Allison, ed., *The New Nietzsche: Contemporary Styles of Interpretation* (New York: Dell Publishing Co., 1977), pp. 178–80.

23. *Spurs*, pp. 39, 51, 61, 67, 97 (translation slightly altered). The treatment of Nietzsche as philosopher-artist finds support, of course, in the fragments assembled under the title "The Will to Power as Art," especially fragments 794 and 811: "Our religion, morality, and philosophy are decadence forms of man. *The countermovement: art*. . . . In all philosophy hitherto the artist has been lacking." See Friedrich Nietzsche, *The Will to Power*, pp. 419, 429. The latter fragment, among others, is cited by Derrida (*Spurs*, p. 77) who adds: "Before art, the dogmatic philosopher, a maladroit courtesan, remains —like a second-rate scholar—impotent, a sort of old maid."

24. *Spurs*, pp. 99, 107 (translation slightly altered). See also Derrida, "The Question of Style," pp. 186, 188.

25. *Spurs*, pp. 115, 123, 127, 133 (translation slightly altered).

26. Compare on this point also Gadamer, *Hegel's Dialectic: Five Hermeneutical Studies,* trans. P. Christopher Smith (New Haven: Yale University Press, 1976); and his *Dialogue and Dialectic: Eight Hermeneutical Studies on Plato,* trans. P. Christopher Smith (New Haven: Yale University Press, 1980).

27. *Truth and Method,* p. 89 (translation slightly altered).

28. *Spurs,* pp. 73–75; see also Derrida, *Writing and Difference,* p. 284.

29. *Spurs,* pp. 101–03, 111. Regarding the issue of "truth" compare especially Robert D. Cumming, "The Odd Couple: Heidegger and Derrida," *Review of Metaphysics* 34 (1981), pp. 487–522. See also Charles A. Pressler, "Redoubled: The Bridging of Derrida and Heidegger," *Human Studies* 7 (1984), pp. 325–42.

30. *Text und Interpretation,* p. 63. The shift of emphasis between the two volumes is particularly underscored by Hannah Arendt, *The Life of the Mind,* vol. II: *Willing,* pp. 172–73.

31. *Text und Interpretation,* p. 76; *Spurs,* p. 95. In the latter study, the possibility of a matrical arrangement or "congruence" is even advanced as "the thesis of the present communication" (p. 57).

32. *Spurs,* p. 99 (translation slightly altered); see also "The Question of Style," p. 186.

33. See *Text und Interpretation,* pp. 73–74; also Nietzsche, "Thus Spoke Zarathustra," in Walter Kaufmann, ed., *The Portable Nietzsche,* p. 328. On suffering compare also this passage (p. 199): "Creation—that is the great redemption from suffering and life's growing light. But that the creator may be, suffering is needed and much change. Indeed, there must be much bitter dying in your life, you creators." By resolutely bypassing this domain, Derrida sometimes seems more like the jester than the tightrope walker described at the beginning of *Zarathustra.* Note also Zarathustra's comments (p. 311): "There are many ways of overcoming: see to that *yourself.* But only a jester thinks: 'Man can also be *skipped over'.*"

34. See *Spurs,* p. 101; also Kaufmann, *The Portable Nietzsche,* pp. 139, 156. Derrida expressly chides Nietzsche for his emphasis on sublimation or "spiritualization of passion" (*Spurs,* p. 91).

35. *Spurs,* pp. 59, 107, 117–21. In my view, a closer reading of Heidegger shows that, far from constituting an undecidable vortex of being and nothingness, *Ereignis* is the "giving" or affirmative potency which sustains being (with its attendant non-being) in being; see Heidegger, *On Time and Being,* especially pp. 16–22. For an explicit effort to distinguish ontology from undecidability or indifference compare Heidegger, *Schellings Abhandlung Über das Wesen der menschlichen Freiheit (1809),* ed. Hildegard Feick (Tübingen: Niemeyer, 1971), pp. 123, 184–90.

36. *Truth and Method,* p. 85. For a brief sketch of the contours of a "recollective ethics" see my *Twilight of Subjectivity: Contributions to a Post-Individualist Theory of Politics,* pp. 250–54.

37. *Truth and Method,* p. 13. The Gadamerian linkage of hermeneutics and *praxis* is stressed by Richard J. Bernstein, *Beyond Objectivism and*

Relativism: Science, Hermeneutics, and Praxis (Philadelphia: University of Pennsylvania Press, 1983), pp. 109–69.

38. *Truth and Method*, p. 15; also Heidegger, *On the Way to Language*, trans. Peter D. Hertz (New York: Harper and Row, 1971), p. 51. Compare Hubert Dreyfus, "Beyond Hermeneutics: Interpretation in Late Heidegger and Foucault," in Shapiro and Sica, *Hermeneutics*, pp. 66–83.

6. TALE OF TWO CITIES:
RICOEUR'S POLITICAL AND SOCIAL ESSAYS

1. Paul Ricoeur, *Political and Social Essays*, ed. David Steward and Joseph Bien (Athens, Ohio: Ohio University Press, 1974).

2. *Political and Social Essays*, pp. 39, 65, 72.

3. See Ricoeur, *Husserl: An Analysis of His Phenomenology*, trans. Edward G. Ballard and Lester E. Embree (Evanston: Northwestern University Press, 1967); *Freedom and Nature: The Voluntary and the Involuntary*, trans. Erazim V. Kohák (Evanston: Northwestern University Press, 1966); *Fallible Man*, trans. Charles Kelbley (Chicago: Regnery, 1965); *The Symbolism of Evil*, trans. Emerson Buchanan (New York: Harper & Row, 1967).

4. Ricoeur, *Freud and Philosophy: An Essay on Interpretation; The Conflict of Interpretations: Essays in Hermeneutics*, ed. Don Ihde (Evanston: Northwestern University Press, 1974). Compare also Ricoeur, *Interpretation Theory: Discourse and the Surplus of Meaning* (Fort Worth: Texas Christian University Press, 1976); and *The Rule of Metaphor*, trans. Robert Czerny (Toronto: University of Toronto Press, 1977). For more detailed comments on *The Conflict of Interpretations* and *The Rule of Metaphor* see my *Language and Politics: Why Does Language Matter to Political Philosophy?* (Notre Dame: University of Notre Dame Press, 1984), pp. 120–23, 158–66, 179–82.

5. *Political and Social Essays*, p. 43. For more detailed comments on "Nature and Freedom" see my *Twilight of Subjectivity: Contributions to a Post-Individualist Theory of Politics*, 148–53.

6. *Political and Social Essays*, p. 208.

7. Ibid., pp. 135, 292.

8. Ibid., pp. 124, 149, 185, 197, 203.

9. Ibid., pp. 83, 117, 213, 230, 234, 237, 241.

10. Ibid., pp. 84, 261, 272, 282. Compare Theodor W. Adorno, *Aesthetic Theory*, trans. C. Lenhardt (London: Routledge & Kegan Paul, 1984).

11. Ibid., pp. 32–34.

12. Ibid., pp. 75, 87, 129, 131, 133, 269.

7. PRAGMATISM AND HERMENEUTICS: BERNSTEIN

1. Richard J. Bernstein, *Beyond Objectivism and Relativism: Science, Hermeneutics, and Praxis* (Philadelphia: University of Pennsylvania Press, 1983), p. xv. See also Bernstein, *Praxis and Action* (Philadelphia: University of Pennsylvania Press, 1971); *The Restructuring of Social and Political The-*

ory (New York: Harcourt Brace Jovanovich, 1976); and *Philosophical Profiles: Essays in a Pragmatic Mode* (Philadelphia: University of Pennsylvania Press, 1986).

2. *Beyond Objectivism and Relativism*, pp. xiv–xv.

3. Ibid., pp. 2, 4, 8, 18, 25, 30, 36–37.

4. Ibid., pp. 54, 60, 63, 67.

5. Ibid., pp. 113, 117, 137, 141.

6. Ibid., pp. 181, 184, 195, 219.

7. Ibid., pp. 84, 226–27, 229.

8. Ibid., pp. 10–12, 15, 22.

9. Ibid., pp. 159–60, 265. In Gadamer's words (p. 265): "Admittedly, to make me into a sociologist is something no one will succeed in doing, not even myself."

10. Ibid., pp. 113, 136, 150, 160, 168.

11. Ibid., pp. 151–54. Compare also Hans-Georg Gadamer, "Was ist Wahrheit?" in *Kleine Schriften I: Philosophie, Hermeneutik* (Tübingen: Mohr, 1967), pp. 46–58; also Martin Heidegger, "On the Essence of Truth," in David F. Krell, ed., *Martin Heidegger: Basic Writings* (New York: Harper & Row, 1977), pp. 117–41.

12. *Beyond Objectivism and Relativism*, pp. 155, 174.

13. Ibid., pp. 113, 121, 137, 163, 165. This switch from ontology to "ought" reminds me of the blurb a German publisher put on the cover of Hegel's *Philosophy of Right:* "What is real is rational. This means in the uncensored, decoded text: What is real ought to be rational."

14. *Beyond Objectivism and Relativism*, pp. 124, 168, 183, 186–87, 190.

15. Ibid., pp. 102, 193–94, 198.

16. Ibid., pp. 185, 192, 194–95.

17. Ibid., pp. 217, 219–20. Compare in this context Hannah Arendt, *Lectures on Kant's Political Philosophy* (Chicago: University of Chicago Press, 1982), and Ronald Beiner, *Political Judgment* (Chicago: University of Chicago Press, 1983), pp. 12–21. On the whole, Beiner distinguishes more neatly between the positions of Arendt, Gadamer, and Habermas than is done in Bernstein's study.

18. *Beyond Objectivism and Relativism*, pp. 221–22.

19. Ibid., pp. 58, 168, 172, 198. The fact that the "reasons" advanced in argumentation are only as good or cogent as the contextual consensus animating the argumentation is acknowledged by Albrecht Wellmer, *Ethik und Dialog* (Frankfurt-Main: Suhrkamp, 1986), esp. pp. 69–72.

20. *Beyond Objectivism and Relativism*, pp. 44, 163, 175, 226.

21. Ibid., pp. 157–58, 177, 226–28.

22. Ibid., pp. 206, 228.

8. VIRTUE AND TRADITION: MacINTYRE

1. Alasdair MacIntyre, *After Virtue: A Study in Moral Theory* (2nd ed.; Notre Dame: University of Notre Dame Press, 1984).

2. Ibid., p. 2.

3. Ibid., pp. 11–12, 23–24, 28, 34–35.

4. Ibid., pp. 42, 49–50, 55, 59.

5. Ibid., pp. 66, 75, 79. Regarding Gewirth compare also my critique in *Twilight of Subjectivity*, pp. 233–42.

6. *After Virtue*, pp. 113–14, 117–18.

7. Ibid., pp. 126–27.

8. Ibid., pp. 148, 150, 154, 178, 180.

9. Ibid., pp. 187, 191, 205, 216, 218, 222.

10. Ibid., pp. 226, 236, 240, 257, 259, 263.

11. Ibid., p. 221.

12. Ibid., p. 223.

13. Ibid., pp. 35, 195. Another passage (p. 119) refers to Ronald Dworkin's argument that "the central doctrine of modern liberalism is the thesis that questions about the *good life for man* or the ends of human life are to be regarded from the public standpoint as systematically unsettlable. . . . The rules of morality and law hence are not to be derived from or justified in terms of some more fundamental conception of the good for man. In arguing thus Dworkin has, I believe, identified a stance characteristic not just of liberalism, but of modernity." Compare also Michael Sandel, *Liberalism and the Limits of Justice* (Cambridge: Cambridge University Press, 1982).

14. *After Virtue*, pp. 156, 229.

15. Ibid., pp. 33, 126, 145, 205.

16. Ibid., pp. 169–70, 233–34.

17. Ibid., pp. 160–61.

18. Ibid., pp. 29–31, 68–69, 76. In a sense, MacIntyre wants to have it both ways: by assuming (p. 76) "that an emotivist account is both true of, and embodied in, a very great deal of our moral utterance and practice *and* that much of that utterance and practice is a trading in moral fictions (such as those of *utility* and of *rights*)."

19. Ibid., pp. 45, 46, 49, 204, 214. Regarding Kant, there is curiously no reference to the third critique or *Critique of Judgment*—a work which recently has inspired non-formalist (and quasi-Aristotelian) construals of ethical and political life; compare, e.g., Hannah Arendt, *Lectures on Kant's Political Philosophy*; Ronald Beiner, *Political Judgment*; Ernst Vollrath, *Die Rekonstruktion der politischen Urteilskraft* (Stuttgart: Klett, 1977).

20. *After Virtue*, pp. 157, 159, 162–63, 260.

21. Ibid., pp. 58–59, 133, 144, 161.

22. Ibid., pp. 156, 192, 218–19. "We have then arrived at a provisional conclusion about the good life for man," MacIntyre adds (p. 219): "the good life for man is the life spent in seeking for the good life for man, and the virtues necessary for the seeking are those which will enable us to understand what more and what else the good life for man is." As he admits (p. 175), this notion of a moral quest differs from Aristotelian teleology at least in two crucial respects: first, the *telos* for Aristotle is "not something to be achieved

at some future point, but in the way our whole life is constructed"; and secondly, the notion implies "a conception of evil of which there are at most only intimations in Aristotle's writings." Regarding the "unity" of the virtues, MacIntyre steers a middle course between complete harmony and emotivist pluralism—a course which seems to me precarious and in need of further clarification. "It has often been suggested," he writes (pp. 223–24), "that *either* we can admit the existence of rival and contingently incompatible goods which make incompatible claims to our practical allegiance *or* we can believe in some determinate conception of *the* good life for man, but that these are mutually exclusive alternatives. . . . What this contention is blind to is that there may be better or worse ways for individuals to live through the tragic confrontation of good with good. And that to know what the good life for man is may require knowing what are the better and what are the worse ways of living through such situations. . . . One way in which the choice between rival goods in a tragic situation differs from the modern choice between incommensurable moral premises is that *both* of the alternative courses of action which confront the individual have to be recognized as leading to some authentic and substantial good." What one might object here is that the notion of the jointly binding character of standards in different domains is precisely the meaning (or one of the meanings) of the "unity" of the virtues.

23. Ibid., pp. 159–60, 206–08. For a discussion of "neo-teleological" theories of action see Richard Bernstein, *Praxis and Action*, pp. 260–80.

24. *After Virtue*, pp. 206, 209, 213. For a different concept of "practice," in which the subject is much more radically decentered, compare Michel Foucault, *The Archaeology of Knowledge* (New York: Pantheon Books, 1972), esp. pp. 208–10.

25. *After Virtue*, pp. 146, 208, 215–16. MacIntyre, it is true, seeks to attenuate his actor-focus by pointing to the "stock of stories which constitute its (society's) initial dramatic resources. Mythology, in its original sense, is at the heart of things. Vico was right and so was Joyce" (p. 216). One might also note that the emphasis on historical continuity jeopardizes the "disquieting suggestion" offered at the beginning of the study. For, assuming the suggested moral catastrophe, history as a continuing tradition would seem to have come to an end.

26. Ibid., p. 158. For an attempt to develop an ontological conception of action or *praxis* see my "Praxis and Experience," in *Polis and Praxis: Exercises in Contemporary Political Theory* (Amherst, MA: MIT Press, 1984), pp. 47–76.

27. *After Virtue*, p. 60. For comments on the Heideggerian (ontological) notion of freedom see my "Ontology of Freedom: Heidegger and Political Philosophy," in *Polis and Praxis*, pp. 104–32.

28. *After Virtue*, pp. 119, 129, 257–59. MacIntyre's radical dismissal of Nietzsche is curiously at odds with his own conception of tradition as involving a necessary interplay of preservation and innovation. "We are apt to be misled here," we are told (pp. 221–23), "by the ideological uses to which

the concept of a tradition has been put by conservative political theorists. Characteristically such theorists have followed Burke in contrasting tradition with reason and the stability of tradition with conflict. Both contrasts obfuscate. . . . I am not praising those who choose the conventional conservative role of *laudator temporis acti*. It is rather the case that an adequate sense of tradition manifests itself in a grasp of those future possibilities which the past has made available to the present."

9. DIALOGUE AND OTHERNESS: THEUNISSEN

1. See, e.g., Karl-Otto Apel, *Towards a Transformation of Philosophy*; Jacques Derrida, *Writing and Difference*.

2. Theodor W. Adorno, *Negative Dialektik*, p. 172.

3. Michael Theunissen, *The Other: Studies in the Social Ontology of Husserl, Heidegger, Sartre, and Buber*, trans. Christopher Macann (Cambridge, MA: MIT Press, 1984). In subsequent citations I have slightly altered the translation for the sake of clarity.

4. See especially Theunissen, *Der Begriff Ernst bei Søren Kierkegaard* (Freiburg: K. Alber, 1958); "Das Kierkegaardbild in der neueren Forschung und Deutung," in *Deutsche Vierteljahresschrift für Literaturwissenschaft und Geistesgeschichte* 32 (1958), pp. 576–612; "Intentionaler Gegenstand und ontologische Differenz; Ansätze zur Fragestellung Heideggers in der Phänomenologie Husserls," in *Philosophisches Jahrbuch* 70 (1963), pp. 344–62; "Bubers negative Ontologie des Zwischen," in *Philosophisches Jahrbuch* 71 (1964), pp. 319–30.

5. Theunissen, *The Other*, p. 81.

6. Ibid., pp. 110, 116–17.

7. Ibid., pp. 130, 148–49, 162.

8. Ibid., pp. 176, 182, 185, 189.

9. Ibid., pp. 201, 218, 221, 236, 239.

10. Ibid., pp. 7–8, 295, 315, 332, 336, 342–43.

11. See especially Jochanan Bloch, *Die Aporie des Du: Probleme der Dialogik Martin Bubers* (Heidelberg: Lambert Schneider, 1977); Hans Duesberg, *Person und Gemeinschaft* (Bonn: Bouvier, 1970); Gerhard Bauer, *Zur Poetik des Dialogs* (Darmstadt: Wissenschaftliche Buchgesellschaft, 1969). In part this literature is influenced also by another study which appeared almost simultaneously with *Der Andere*: Bernhard Casper, *Das dialogische Denken* (Freiburg: Herder, 1967).

12. See, e.g., Jochen Hörisch, *Die fröhliche Wissenschaft der Poesie* (Frankfurt-Main: Suhrkamp, 1976).

13. See, e.g., Bernhard Waldenfels, *Das Zwischenreich des Dialogs* (The Hague: Martinus Nijhoff, 1971); Ernst Tugendhat, *Der Wahrheitsbegriff bei Husserl und Heidegger* (Berlin: W. de Gruyter, 1967).

14. Martin Heidegger, *Über den Humanismus* (Frankfurt-Main: Klostermann, 1949), pp. 16, 36; Theunissen, *The Other*, pp. 289–91, 293–94, 322.

15. These comments are qualified by recognition of the greater intellectual courage of dialogism in comparison with traditional philosophy: "If philosophizing means to venture into the terrain of the as yet unthought even at the risk of shipwreck, then the impotence of dialogism is actually more genuinely philosophical than the power of transcendentalism which yields less problematic conclusions only by taking fewer risks." Ibid., pp. 361, 363, 374, 377.

16. I have tried to present an interpretation of "being-with" or co-being, differing from Theunissen's, in my *Twilight of Subjectivity: Contributions to a Post-Individualist Theory of Politics*, pp. 56–71.

17. Theunissen, *The Other*, p. 413, note 5.

18. Ibid., pp. 364, 367, 369, 380.

19. Theunissen, "Vorrede zur zweiten Auflage," in *Der Andere* (2nd ed., Berlin: W. de Gruyter, 1977), pp. ix–x. "The conception suggested by Buber in any case," the Preface continues, "that—compared with the untruth of I-It relations—the I-Thou encounter represents always the truth and nothing but the truth, irresponsibly conceals the real fabric in which dialogical life is enmeshed under present conditions."

20. Theunissen, *Gesellschaft und Geschichte: Zur Kritik der kritischen Theorie* (Berlin: W. de Gruyter, 1969).

21. *Hegels Lehre vom absoluten Geist als theologisch-politischer Traktat* (Berlin: W. de Gruyter, 1970).

22. "Vorrede zur zweiten Auflage," p. ix; compare, e.g., "Begriff und Realität," in *Denken im Schatten des Nihilismus* (Darmstadt: Wissenschaftliche Buchgesellschaft, 1975), pp. 164–95.

23. *Sein und Schein: Die kritische Funktion der Hegelschen Logik* (Frankfurt-Main: Suhrkamp, 1978), pp. 45–46, 49.

24. Compare Heidegger's comments: "Only the truth of being renders possible thought about the nature of the holy. Only the nature of the holy renders possible thought about the nature of divinity. Only the nature of divinity renders it possible to think and articulate what the term 'God' might mean." *Über den Humanismus*, pp. 36–37. Theunissen's Postscript specifically refers to the notion of *Ereignis* as the gathering of earth and heaven, mortals and immortals; *The Other*, pp. 384, 413, note 9.

10. STRUCTURATION AND AGENCY: GIDDENS

1. Anthony Giddens, *Central Problems in Social Theory: Action, Structure and Contradiction in Social Analysis* (Berkeley and Los Angeles: University of California Press, 1979); and *The Constitution of Society: Outline of the Theory of Structuration* (Berkeley and Los Angeles: University of California Press, 1984). Compare also his *A Contemporary Critique of Historical Materialism*, vol. 1 (Berkeley & Los Angeles: University of California Press, 1981); *Studies in Social and Political Theory* (London: Hutchinson/New York: Basic Books, 1977); *New Rules of Sociological Method* (London: Hutchinson/

New York: Basic Books, 1976); *The Class Structure of the Advanced Societies* (London: Hutchinson, 1973); and *Capitalism and Modern Social Theory* (Cambridge: Cambridge University Press, 1971).

2. *Central Problems*, pp. 234–40. In *The Constitution of Society* (pp. 1–2) systematic reconstruction is presented as an alternative to the Scylla of "objectivism" (typified by functionalism and structuralism) and the Charybdis of "subjectivism" (typified by subjective-intentional hermeneutics and "interpretative sociology").

3. *Central Problems*, pp. 1–3. For a more detailed elaboration of "agency," "structure" and "structuration" see *The Constitution of Society*, pp. 5–25.

4. *Central Problems*, pp. 5, 9, 45–48. On the "duality of structure" compare also *The Constitution of Society*, pp. 25–28, 297–304.

5. *Central Problems*, pp. 39–40, 44, 47.

6. Ibid., pp. 53–54, 56–59. The themes of "reflexivity" and of "discursive" and "practical consciousness" are further elaborated in *The Constitution of Society*, pp. 41–45.

7. *Central Problems*, pp. 64–65, 69, 82, 93, 100.

8. Ibid., pp. 96, 109, 117, 120, 123. On institutions and role theory ("positioning") see also *The Constitution of Society*, pp. 28–34, 83–86.

9. *Central Problems*, pp. 131, 136, 141, 154, 161–62. On the notion of "contradiction" see also *The Constitution of Society*, pp. 193–99, 310–19; man's relation to nature is labelled there "existential contradiction" in contradistinction to "structural contradiction" (involving a clash of structural principles of society). The critique of Marxism is fleshed out in *A Contemporary Critique of Historical Materialism*. The distinction between political and economic class division is similar to Habermas's differentiation between traditional and capitalist societies in *Legitimation Crisis*, esp. pp. 18–24.

10. *Central Problems*, pp. 186–88, 223–26. The themes of time and space and their relation to social change receive much more detailed treatment in *The Constitution of Society*, esp. pp. 110–16, 227–62.

11. *Central Problems*, pp. 63, 206–09. On these issues, one has to admit, Giddens' views still seem to be in a process of fertile evolution and emendation. *The Constitution of Society* contains a fascinating "critical note" on structuration, and especially on "timing and spacing," in Foucault's writings; pp. 145–58.

12. *Central Problems*, pp. 92–93. On the theme of "power" see also *The Constitution of Society*, pp. 14–16, 256–62. In an aside, directed mainly against Habermas, Giddens notes there (p. 32) that "power is not an inherently noxious phenomenon, not just the capacity to 'say no'; nor can domination be 'transcended' in some kind of putative society of the future, as has been the characteristic aspiration of at least some strands of socialist thought."

13. *Central Problems*, pp. 39–40, 42–43, 57–58, 98. In *The Constitution of Society*, Garfinkel and ethnomethodology tend to be eclipsed by a detailed treatment of Goffman, pp. 64–83.

14. *Central Problems*, pp. 4, 34, 44. In *The Constitution of Society*, Giddens advances the claim (p. 32) that "the semantic has priority over the semiotic," a claim which can be vindicated in his view "through a comparison of structuralist and post-structuralist conceptions of meaning on the one hand, and that which can be derived from the later Wittgenstein on the other." As he explains: "The 'retreat into the code'—whence it is difficult or impossible to reemerge into the world of activity and event—is a characteristic tactic adopted by structuralist and post-structuralist authors. Such a retreat, however, is not necessary at all if we understand the relational character of the codes that generate meaning to be located in the ordering of social practices, in the very capacity to 'go on' in the multiplicity of contexts of social activity. This is a discovery which Wittgenstein himself surely made, albeit against a very different philosophical backdrop."

15. *Central Problems*, pp. 68, 250–51.

16. Ibid., pp. 30–31, 33–36.

17. Ibid., pp. 49–50, 59. Compare also Jacques Derrida, "Structure, Sign and Play in the Discourse of the Human Sciences," in *Writing and Difference*, pp. 278–93; also his "Signature Event Context," *Glyph* 1, pp. 182–97.

18. *Central Problems*, pp. 3, 17, 29, 54, 123. Compare also Martin Heidegger, *History of the Concept of Time: Prolegomena*, trans. Theodore Kisiel (Bloomington: Indiana University Press, 1985).

19. *Central Problems*, pp. 46, 201, 230–31. *The Constitution of Society* contains a more detailed and nuanced discussion of the status of history and historiography, esp. pp. 199–206, 236–43, 355–68. Nevertheless, the above strong claim is maintained (p. 358): "If there are divisions between social science and history, they are substantive divisions of labour; there is no logical or methodological schism. Historians who specialize in particular types of textual materials, languages or 'periods' are not freed from involvement with the concepts of, and the dilemmas inherent in, social theory. But, equally, social scientists whose concerns are the most abstract and general theories about social life, are not freed from the hermeneutic demands of the interpretation of texts and other cultural objects. Historical research is social research and vice versa."

20. *Central Problems*, pp. 258–59.

11. SYSTEM, STATE AND POLIS: LUHMANN

1. See Niklas Luhmann, *Trust and Power*, trans. with introd. Gianfranco Poggi (New York: Wiley & Sons, 1979); *The Differentiation of Society*, trans. Stephen Holmes and Charles Larmore (New York: Columbia University Press, 1982); *Religious Dogmatics and the Evolution of Societies*, trans. with introd. Peter Beyer (New York & Toronto: Edwin Mellen Press, 1984); *A Sociological Theory of Law*, trans. Elizabeth King and Martin Albrow (London: Routledge & Kegan Paul, 1985).

2. See Beyer's "Introduction" to *Religious Dogmatics and the Evolution of Societies*, pp. v–xlvii.

3. Although drawing some inspiration from Husserl, Luhmann shifts the process of meaning-constitution entirely from the human subject to systemic networks. In Beyer's words (*Religious Dogmatics*, p. viii), Luhmann "hopes to avoid what he sees as Husserl's problems with intersubjectivity while at the same time gaining a clear analysis of the constitution of meaning and, thereby, of social structures and processes in general. What is important here is that Luhmann seeks to avoid certain theoretical problems by rejecting the unifying and axiomatic starting point of the transcendental subject. For him, the transcendental subject is a semantic correlate of structural transformations in early modern society. At the time, it served to help that society through certain critical transitional phases and had its truth in that context. Today, it only masks the new socio-structural situation and therefore stands in the way of a more adequate theory of society."

4. See David Easton, *A Systems Analysis of Political Life* (New York: Wiley & Sons, 1965), and *A Framework for Political Analysis* (Englewood Cliffs, NJ: Prentice-Hall, 1965). The "state" was listed in the index of neither of these two works.

5. Compare, e.g., Gianfranco Poggi, *The Development of the Modern State: A Sociological Introduction* (Stanford: Stanford University Press, 1978); Theda Skocpol, *States and Revolution* (New York: Cambridge University Press, 1979); Martin Carnoy, *The State and Political Theory* (Princeton: Princeton University Press, 1984); Peter B. Evans, Dietrich Rueschemeyer and Theda Skocpol, eds., *Bringing the State Back In* (Cambridge: Cambridge University Press, 1985); Karl-Heinz Röder, ed., "The Future of the State," *International Political Science Review* 6, No. 1 (1985).

6. Luhmann, "The 'State' of the Political System" (unpublished manuscript).

7. See Paul-Ludwig Weihnacht, *Staat: Studien zur Bedeutungsgeschichte* (Berlin: Duncker & Humblot, 1968); and *Geschichtliche Grundbegriffe: Historisches Lexikon zur politisch-sozialen Sprache in Deutschland*, 3 vols. (Stuttgart: Klett-Cotta, 1970–1982).

8. Compare, e.g., Jürgen Habermas, *Legitimation Crisis*, pp. 18–31.

9. Habermas, *The Theory of Communicative Action*, vol. I: *Reason and the Rationalization of Society*. The contrast between observer and participant perspective has also been at the heart of Habermas's dispute with Luhmann; see Habermas and Luhmann, *Theorie der Gesellschaft oder Sozialtechnologie—Was leistet die Systemforschung?* (Frankfurt: Suhrkamp, 1971).

10. Karl W. Deutsch, *The Nerves of Government: Models of Political Communication and Control* (New York: Free Press, 1963). Compare also Norbert Wiener, *The Human Use of Human Beings: Cybernetics and Society* (Garden City, NY: Anchor Books, 1954).

11. Niklas Luhmann, "Der Wohlfahrtsstaat zwischen Evolution und Rationalität," in Peter Koslowski et al., eds., *Chancen und Grenzen des Sozialstaates* (Tübingen: Mohr, 1983), p. 38.

12. "Der Wohlfahrtsstaat zwischen Evolution und Rationalität," p. 33.

13. Luhmann, "Staat und Politik: Zur Semantik der Selbstbeschreibung politischer Systeme," *Politische Vierteljahresschrift* 25, Special Issue No. 15 (1984), p. 105.

14. "Der Wohlfahrtsstaat zwischen Evolution und Rationalität," p. 34.

15. Jacques Derrida, "Différance," in *Margins of Philosophy*, pp. 20, 22.

16. See Derrida, "Structure, Sign and Play in the Discourse of the Human Sciences," in *Writing and Difference*, pp. 278–93; Anthony Giddens, *The Constitution of Society: Outline of the Theory of Structuration*; also my "Political Inquiry: Beyond Empiricism and Hermeneutics" in Terence Ball, ed., *Idioms of Inquiry* (New York: SUNY Press, 1987).

17. From the vantage point of praxis, incidentally, the previous account of indebtedness to metaphysics could be reformulated in terms of an indebtedness to practical-political premises. Systems theory, on this score, could be seen—with Foucault—as a "discursive practice" or "discursive strategy" whose political assumptions are largely bracketed. The subordination of politics to sociology would at this point be revoked.

18. "Der Wohlfahrtsstaat zwischen Evolution und Rationalität," p. 35; "Staat und Politik," p. 109. The reference is to Carl Schmitt, *Der Begriff des Politischen* (new ed.; Berlin: Duncker & Humblot, 1963).

19. The similarity between Schmitt and Luhmann is noted by Habermas, *Legitimation Crisis*, p. 98.

20. For an interpretation of Hegel pointing in this direction see Michael Theunissen, *Sein und Schein: Die kritische Funktion der Hegelschen Logik* (Frankfurt: Suhrkamp, 1978).

21. "Der Wohlfahrtsstaat zwischen Evolution und Rationalität," pp. 36–37. For perspectives stressing *phronesis* see, e.g., Michael Oakeshott, *Rationalism in Politics, And Other Essays* (New York: Basic Books, 1962), and Hans-Georg Gadamer, *Reason in the Age of Science*, trans. Frederick G. Lawrence (Cambridge, MA: MIT Press, 1981).

22. Compare, e.g., David E. Apter and Nagayo Sawa, *Against the State: Politics and Social Protest in Japan* (Cambridge, MA: Harvard University Press, 1984).

23. Following Charles Péguy, Merleau-Ponty distinguished between normal historical "periods" and abnormal "epochs": "When one is living in what Péguy called an historical *period*, in which political man is content to administer a regime or an established law, one can hope for a history without violence. When one has the misfortune or the luck to live in an *epoch*, or one of those moments where the traditional ground of a nation or society crumbles and where, for better or worse, man himself must reconstruct human relations, then the liberty of each man is a mortal threat to the others and violence reappears." See Maurice Merleau-Ponty, *Humanism and Terror*, trans. John O'Neill (Boston: Beacon Press, 1969), p. xvii.

24. Martin Heidegger, "Hölderlins Hymne 'Der Ister,'" ed. Walter Biemel (*Gesamtausgabe*, vol. 53; Frankfurt: Klostermann, 1984), pp. 100–01.

Index